Lecture Notes in Computer Science 14794

The series Lecture Notes in Computer Science (LNCS), including its subseries Lecture Notes in Artificial Intelligence (LNAI) and Lecture Notes in Bioinformatics (LNBI), has established itself as a medium for the publication of new developments in computer science and information technology research, teaching, and education.

LNCS enjoys close cooperation with the computer science R & D community, the series counts many renowned academics among its volume editors and paper authors, and collaborates with prestigious societies. Its mission is to serve this international community by providing an invaluable service, mainly focused on the publication of conference and workshop proceedings and postproceedings. LNCS commenced publication in 1973.

Jin Song Dong · Masoumeh Izadi · Zhe Hou
Editors

Sports Analytics

First International Conference, ISACE 2024
Paris, France, July 12–13, 2024
Proceedings

Springer

Editors
Jin Song Dong
National University of Singapore
Singapore, Singapore

Masoumeh Izadi
Television Content Analytics Pte. Ltd.
Singapore, Singapore

Zhe Hou
Griffith University
Nathan, QLD, Australia

ISSN 0302-9743 ISSN 1611-3349 (electronic)
Lecture Notes in Computer Science
ISBN 978-3-031-69072-3 ISBN 978-3-031-69073-0 (eBook)
https://doi.org/10.1007/978-3-031-69073-0

This Springer imprint is published by the registered company Springer Nature Switzerland AG
The registered company address is: Gewerbestrasse 11, 6330 Cham, Switzerland

Preface

Sports analytics is the application of AI, data science, psychology, and smart devices to improve sports performance, strategy, and decision-making. It involves collecting, processing, and interpreting data from various sources such as video footage, performance metrics, and scouting reports, and using this information to gain insights into player and team performance, prevent injury, and help coaches and team managers to make more informed decisions and optimize their resources to achieve better results.

The vision of this new International Sports Analytics Conference and Exhibition (ISACE) series is to bring leading academics, researchers, coaches, psychologists, managers and technologists together to advance the state of the art of sports analytics.

ISACE 2024 — the 1st edition of ISACE — was hosted in Paris, France, on 12–13 July 2024, immediately before the Paris Summer Olympics. ISACE 2024 received 66 submissions covering theory and applications in sports analytics. Each paper was reviewed in a single-blind process by at least three reviewers, and the programme committee accepted 19 Regular papers, 7 Practical Experience papers, and 1 Short paper, leading to a competitive and attractive scientific programme.

This edition of ISACE was honoured to have two prestigious keynote speakers: Campbell Jamieson, General Manager at the International Cricket Council, spoke about the workforce of sport technology and the need for training talents. Kerrie Mengersen, an ARC Laureate Fellow, discussed how Bayesian analytics is applied in sports and introduced the AusiSTAR Hub, which aimed at improving Australia's sports profile in preparation for the Brisbane Olympics. The two keynotes covered trendy research and practical topics and revealed many promising new directions.

We also had a successful company exhibition with numerous interesting talks on the technologies, applications, and products in the sports industry.

ISACE 2024's success was due to the contribution and involvement of the Local Organisers at Institut Mines-Télécom and the Programme Committee members around the globe who contributed to the organisation and review process and the selection of the best contributions. This event would not have existed if the authors and contributors had not submitted their works. We address our thanks to every person, reviewer, author, programme committee member, and organizing committee member involved in the success of ISACE 2024.

The EasyChair system was set up for the management of ISACE 2024, supporting submission, review and volume preparation processes. It, again, proved to be a powerful tool.

Springer kindly accepted our proposal to publish the paper proceedings in their prestigious LNCS series. We hope to have a fruitful and long-term collaboration with them in future editions of ISACE. The other sponsors, Dependable Intelligence, Institut Mines-Télécom (IMT), IMT Transfert, Yonsei University, ENSIIE, National University of Singapore, and Griffith University, all contributed in different ways to help the conference run smoothly. Many thanks to all the organisers and sponsors.

Looking into the future, ISACE 2025 is planned to be hosted in Shanghai in September 2025, one week before the 2025 Rolex Shanghai Masters tennis. ISACE 2026 will be in Vancouver in May 2026, before the 2026 soccer World Cup. We hope to see everybody at the future events.

July 2024

Jin Song Dong
Masoumeh Izadi
Zhé Hóu

Organization

General Chair

Jin Song Dong	National University of Singapore, Singapore

Program Co-chairs

Masoumeh Izadi	Television Content Analytics, Singapore
Zhe Hou	Griffith University, Australia

Advisory Committee

Elia Hill	Queensland Government, Australia

Organising Committee

Bimlesh Wadhwa	National University of Singapore, Singapore
Jun Sun	Singapore Management University, Singapore
Yang Liu	Nanyang Technological University, Singapore
Mounir Mokhtari	Institut Mines-Télécom, France
Yamine Ait Ameur	National Polytechnic Institute of Toulouse, France
Zhiyong Huang	National University of Singapore, Singapore
Teck Khim Ng	National University of Singapore, Singapore
Chunyang Chen	Technical University of Munich, Germany
Bessam Abdulrazak	Université de Sherbrooke, Canada

Local Organising Committee

Mounir Mokhtari	Institut Mines-Télécom, France
Yamine Ait Ameur	INP Toulouse, France
Hamdi Aloulou	Institut Mines-Télécom, France
Nassim Khider	ENSIIE, France
Imrane Mokhtari	ESCP, France
Stéphane Renouard	Institut Mines-Télécom, France
Bessam Abdulrazak	Université de Sherbrooke, Canada

Jongbae Kim	Yonsei University, South Korea
Jean-Marie Bonnin	IMT Atlantique, France
Tayeb Lemlouma	Université de Rennes, France

Program Committee

Oliver Schulte	Simon Fraser University, Canada
Luke Wildman	RGB Assurance, Australia
Yamine Ait Ameur	National Polytechnic Institute of Toulouse, France
Bimlesh Wadhwa	National University of Singapore, Singapore
Zhiyong Huang	National University of Singapore, Singapore
Yun Lin	Shanghai Jiao Tong University, China
Michael Kan Jiang	National University of Singapore, Singapore
Wei-Yao Wang	National Yang Ming Chiao Tung University, Taiwan
Zhaoyu Liu	National University of Singapore, Singapore
Hadrien Bride	Dependable Intelligence, Australia
David Saxby	Griffith University, Australia
Chunyang Chen	Monash University, Australia
Lijun Guo	Ningbo University, China
Sebastian Binnewies	Griffith University, Australia
John Komar	National Institute of Education, Singapore
Elizabeth Bradshaw	Deakin University, Australia
Seungbok Lee	Yonsei University, South Korea
Xiaofei Xie	Singapore Management University, Singapore
Mehul S. Raval	Ahmedabad University, India
Srikrishnan Divakaran	Krea University, India
Tolga Kaya	Sacred Heart University, USA
Daniel Bolarinwa	Accenture, UK
Rajdeep Singh Hundal	National University of Singapore, Singapore
Tao Lin	Ethiqly, USA
Dileepa Fernando	Singapore University of Technology and Design, Singapore
Isuru Supasan	SLTC Research University, Sri Lanka
Karan Gupta	SunPower, USA
Raveendran Paramesran	Monash University, Malaysia
Bessam Abdulrazak	Université de Sherbrooke, Canada
Steven Lin	Azra Games, USA
Robert Moskovitch	Ben-Gurion University of the Negev, Israel
David Clausi	University of Waterloo, Canada
Ruchir Pandya	ex-Disruptive, ex-Meta, ex-NBA, USA

Contents

Time-Series Analysis of Ball Carrier Open-Space in Association Football

Ishara Bandara[1,2](✉), Sergiy Shelyag[1,3], Sutharshan Rajasegarar[1], Daniel B. Dwyer[4], Eun-jin Kim[2], and Maia Angelova[1,5]

[1] School of IT, Deakin University, Geelong 3220, VIC, Australia
isharabnd@gmail.com
[2] Research Centre for Fluid and Complex Systems, Coventry University, Coventry CV1 5FB, UK
[3] College of Science and Engineering, Flinders University, Tonsley 5042, SA, Australia
[4] School of Exercise and Nutrition Sciences, Deakin University, Geelong 3220, VIC, Australia
[5] Aston Digital Futures Institute, Aston University, Birmingham B4 7ET, UK

Abstract. Assessing team performances in association football (commonly known as football or soccer) is challenging due to its low-scoring and unpredictable nature. While space control and generating open spaces on the field have been used to evaluate strategies for team performance, the temporal nature of space available for the ball carrier has not been explored. This work proposes the temporal nature of space available for the ball carrier in the attacking third as a novel time-series performance evaluation metric to assess team performance. Furthermore, it suggests a novel approach to quantify the relatively open space available for the ball carrier in the attacking third using player information retrieved from television video footage. The machine learning model trained with the features extracted with the proposed time-series metric achieved 80% accuracy in classifying match-winning performances, indicating its importance as a performance evaluation metric. Correlation coefficients between temporal features and match results suggest that first-half performance is more crucial to the match result than second-half performance. Additionally, this work evaluates individual performances in the FIFA World Cup 2022 under two aspects: active open space creation and passive open space creation, assessing contributions to ball carrier open space creation through on-ball and off-ball actions, respectively.

Keywords: Football · Performance Evaluation · Time-Series Analysis · Space · On/Off Ball Player Actions · Soccer

1 Introduction

In association football, generating open spaces is a crucial strategy that contributes to creating goal-scoring opportunities by unsettling the defense. Xavier

J. S. Dong et al. (Eds.): ISACE 2024, LNCS 14794, pp. 1–17, 2024.
https://doi.org/10.1007/978-3-031-69073-0_1

Hernandez, former Barcelona player and current Barcelona manager, stated that, "I understand football as a time-space, and it is the use of space" [1]. Receiving the ball from an open space provides the ball recipient with ample time to assess the situation and execute effective attacking moves with reduced pressure and enhanced creativity. For the creation of open spaces for the ball carrier, either one or both ball carrier actions (such as: forward passes, through balls, or dribbling runs) and off-ball runs to open spaces are required. These open spaces can unsettle the defense structure by dragging them towards the open space. Pep Guardiola, current Manchester City manager, and the only manager to win the continental treble twice once stated that, "It is not about passing for the sake of it. The secret is to pass the ball with a clear intention to drag defenders to one side and create space on the opposite side. Then, move the ball to the created open space for attack." [24]. However, the open space created for the ball carrier and its time-series nature for team and individual player performance evaluation is relatively less explored in the existing literature.

Characterized as an invasion sport [13,14], association football often results in low scores and is considered to be heavily influenced by chance [20]. Consequently, assessing team or individual performance and predicting match outcomes proves extremely challenging. To address this issue, previous research has focused on evaluating the probability of scoring from shots using expected goals (xG) models [4,6,16], as well as analyzing the likelihood of scoring from particular event locations with non-shot expected goals models [22]. Nevertheless, these xG models do not value the opportunities created and the contributions of players who provide critical passes or moves, as these models solely focus on features associated with shot events. In response to this limitation, Karun Singh proposed Expected Threat (xT), which has become popular in evaluating individual and team performance [21].

The xT model prioritizes the assessment of individual or team actions performed on advancing the ball into high expected goals (xG) areas and threatening positions, irrespective of the eventual outcome of the possession [21]. To achieve this, the football field has been segmented into 192 equal-sized named regions (organized into 12 rows and 16 columns), where the probabilities of passing the ball and shooting are evaluated for each region. Movements have been assigned with values based on movement probability and with a movement transition matrix, which accounts for the likelihood of transitioning to each named region. Shots have been assessed using shot probabilities and their corresponding xG values. However, these xT models do not consider defender positions directly in their evaluations and disregard the importance of open space created for the ball carrier.

Fernandez and Bornn presented an approach to quantify spatial value occupation and generation in open-play scenarios [7]. Here, space occupation represents the creation of an open space for oneself, while space generation evaluates creating chances for teammates in open spaces while disrupting opponents' positioning. This study involves constructing a pitch control model that takes into account player movement data, the ball's relative location, and player positions.

By considering the pitch control areas of all players on the field, the authors introduce a potential pitch control map for any given moment of the game. Additionally, they developed a model to assign a relative value to any position on the field based on the ball's position, using feed-forward neural networks. This approach has been further developed by Martens et al. by introducing a data-driven movement model to quantify space and control [15]. Nevertheless, these works do not evaluate the time-series nature of the open spaces generation for the ball carrier and its relationship with match-winning performances.

Performance evaluation metrics like possession and territory are commonly used for assessing team performance. However, the existing literature presents conflicting findings regarding the relationship between these metrics and match-winning performances where some provide evidence that higher possession teams often end up winning [8,19], while some works suggested there is no significant relationship with them [3,12]. Due to the evolving tactics in football, teams vary in their strategic approaches. Some teams prioritize possession-based strategies, aiming to maintain control of the ball to create scoring opportunities. Conversely, others adopt defensive and counter-attacking tactics. Jose Mourinho, renowned as one of the most successful football managers, stated, "Many people believe that the team with more possession is the team that is more dominant. But that depends on the way you look at it; a team without the ball can still be in control of the game" [11]. Similarly, teams employing defensive and counter-attacking tactics may dominate without maintaining high possession percentages. Research by Tenga et al. indicates that the success rate of scoring from counterattacks (13.4%) surpasses that of general scoring attempts (8.8%) [25]. In counterattacks, teams typically regain possession in the defensive third and swiftly transition to the attacking third [25]. These scenarios often result in more open spaces in the attacking third, suggesting that evaluating open spaces created for the ball carrier could offer insights into the effectiveness of such tactics.

This work addresses the absence of investigation into the open space available to the ball carrier, as well as the lack of temporal analysis or time-series performance evaluation metrics in this context. It evaluates the temporal nature of team performances, and introduces a novel time-series performance evaluation metric based on the open spaces available for the ball carrier in the attacking third using information retrieved from televised video data.

2 Methodology

This work performs a temporal analysis of the significance of open space available for the ball carrier in the attacking third. It presents a novel approach for quantifying open space available for the ball carrier relative to the opposition, player locations, and viewable area from data obtained from televised videos of the game. The significance of extracted temporal features on match-winning performances was evaluated by developing a match-winning performance classification machine learning model. Having identified the importance of the proposed time-series performance evaluation metric, this work further evaluates individual player performances on open space available for the ball carrier under two aspects: Active Open-Space creation and Passive Open-Space creation. Figure 1 shows the summary of the proposed approach.

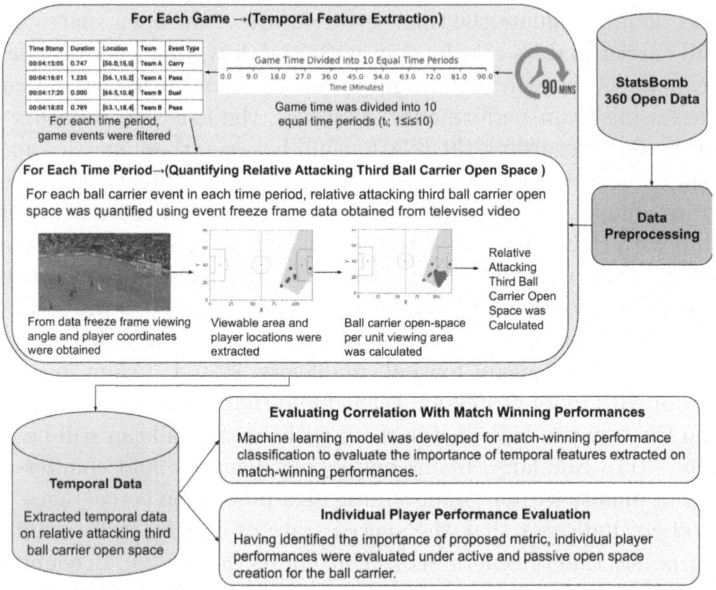

Fig. 1. Summary of the proposed approach which includes temporal feature extraction, machine learning model development and evaluation

Within this research, the term "event" denotes a specific game-related occurrence involving a player's action or the subsequent outcomes, which are capable of being documented. "Open space available for the ball carrier" ("ball carrier open space") refers to an unoccupied area of the field surrounding the player in possession of the ball, providing ample room for him/her to maneuver without any interference from opposition. For this, immediate surrounding open space available to the ball carrier upon receiving the ball following another event and all possible movements of surrounding opposition players towards immediate open space are considered. This preceding event could be executed by the same ball carrier or by a different player. For instance, when a pass is made, the preceding event is executed by a different player, whereas when the ball carrier dribbles past an opponent and shoots at the goal, the preceding event (dribbling past the opposition player while carrying the ball) is executed by the same player.

2.1 Data

For this work, "Statsbomb 360" data from the "Statsbomb open-data" dataset [23] was used. This dataset contains event-log data in top-tier international and club competitions in Europe along with player coordinates of players from both teams retrieved from televised video. Additionally dataset coordinates of the area of the field covered by the televised angle of a particular event. Further, considering tactical and physical differences identified between Men's and Women's games [17], the dataset was segmented under gender. However, due to a lack of data, this analysis was conducted on the men's dataset only. Men's dataset consisted of data from televised games from FIFA World Cup 2022, EUFA Euro Cup 2018, and Spanish La Liga 2020/2021.

Two teams in each game were represented by a home team (referred to as "Team A") and an away team (referred to as "Team B") for identification purposes in the original dataset. The event locations, viewing angles, and player locations within the games were mapped using coordinates on a grid measuring 120 × 80, with the direction of attack progressing from left to right across the grid. Additionally, each event contains additional information on events such as event type (e.g. pass, carry), and player information (e.g. player name).

For the purpose of temporal analysis and training the match winner prediction model, games that ended within regular time and those with a match winner were considered. This choice was made as the main focus was to evaluate the correlation between the proposed metric and match-winning performances, and including games that proceeded to extra time could significantly alter the game duration, thus affecting the consistency of the dataset. The final pre-processed dataset considered for model development consisted of 71 games. In the pre-processed dataset, 39 games have been won by Team A (54.9%) and 32 games (45.1%) have been won by Team B.

2.2 Attacking Third Ball Carrier Open-Space Calculation

Existing literature has separated football field into three regions based on the direction of the attack; Defensive third (first third), Central Third (second third), and attacking third (final third) [10,18] (Fig. 2). Given the recognized significance of performance in the attacking third according to existing literature [10], ball carrier open space in the attacking third and its temporal nature is evaluated for team performance evaluation. First, an approach to quantify the open space available for the ball carrier was evaluated.

In televised football games, the camera typically focuses on the ball carrier and their immediate surroundings. As a result, the visible portion of the pitch changes over time. The "Statsbomb 360" data provides coordinates of this visible area and the players within it, including the ball carrier, depicted on a 120 × 80 grid. The extent of the visible area was determined as a relative measure by the number of grid cells (grid pixels) it covers within the 120 × 80 grid, providing a standardized relative measure for analysis across different events. Similarly, the open space accessible to the ball carrier was determined relative

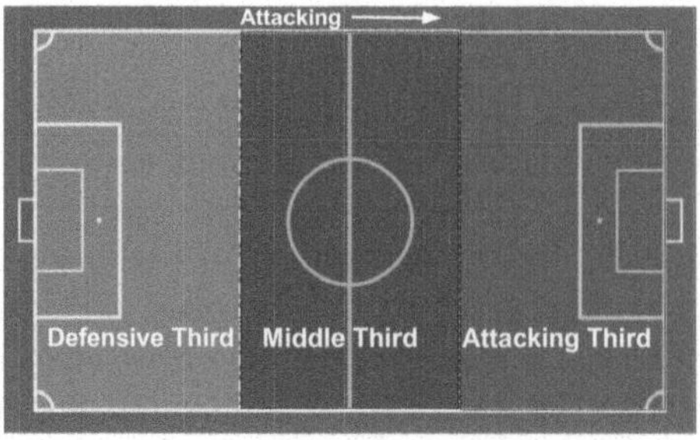

Fig. 2. Defensive, Middle (Central) and Attacking third on a football field

to the number of grid cells it occupies within the 120×80 grid. To generate this measure, the coordinates of the ball carrier and opposition players within the visible area and their all possible movements were taken into account. For this calculation, it was assumed that all the players could move at an equal velocity in any direction. The analysis did not consider the actual velocities of players due to data constraints. The velocities of individual players cannot be tracked from the data as all the players are not visible within the visible area for every event. Figure 3 illustrates the steps of ball carrier open space calculation from retrieving freeze frame coordinates to open space and visible area calculation and the pseudo-code presented in algorithm 1 outlines the process of calculating the relative visible area, the relative open space area for the ball carrier, and highlights the open space for the ball carrier on a 120×80 grid.

However, visible area (VA; $VA > 0$) varies with time. Therefore, in order to normalize and compare with other events, the open-space area for the ball carrier measure (OS) was divided by the visible area for that particular event. This results in an open space area for the ball carrier per unit area measure.

$$OS_{\text{per unit area}} = \frac{OS}{VA} \tag{1}$$

2.3 Temporal Feature Extraction

To conduct a time-series analysis on open space available for the ball carrier in the attacking third, features were extracted in a temporal manner. Each football game was segmented into ten equal time intervals (t; $1 \leq t \leq 10$), and the total open space area available for the ball carrier by each team in their attacking third during these intervals was computed. Only actions directly involving the ball carrier, such as passing, attempting a shot on goal, and carrying (running or dribbling while retaining control and possession of the ball), were taken into account when calculating the total open space area available for the ball carrier. Open space available during off-the-ball events was not considered, as the focus was on the space created around the ball carrier. Assuming n ball carrier events occurred with team A is in possession during time period t,

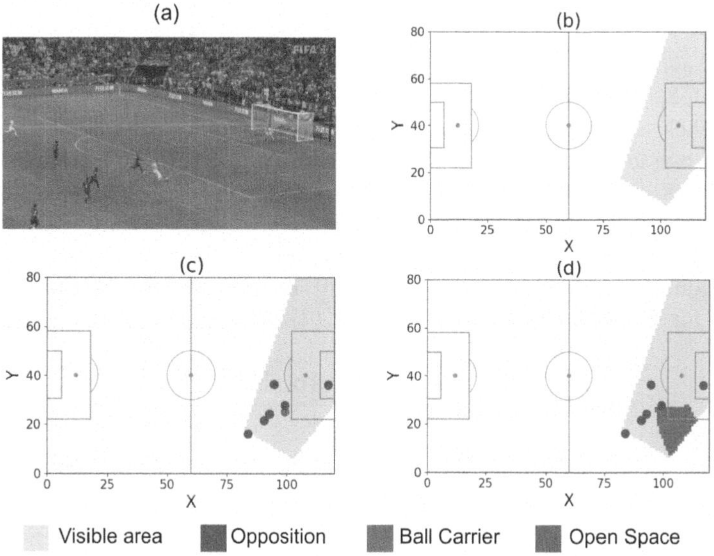

Fig. 3. Attacking third ball carrier open space calculation steps: (a) freeze frame, (b) visible area identification on a 120 × 80 grid, (c) ball carrier and opposition locations identification on the 120 × 80 grid, (d) ball carrier open space identification on the 120 × 80 grid.

Algorithm 1. Pseudo code for ball carrier open space calculation

Require: *ball_carrier_location*, *opposition_player_locations*, *max_velocity*, *visible_area*

Initialize a 2D array *open_space_grid* with all elements initialized to 0
Set *open_space_cells*, *visible_area_cells* to 0
for each cell (i, j) in the grid **do**
    if cell (i, j) is within the visible area **then**
        Increment *visible_area_cells* by 1
        distance_to_ball_carrier = Euclidean distance from (i, j) to the *ball_carrier_location*
        for each *opposition_player_location* in *opposition_player_locations* **do**
            distance_to_opposition_player = Euclidean distance from (i, j) to the *opposition_player_location*
            if *distance_to_opposition_player* < *distance_to_ball_carrier* **then**
                Exit the loop
            end if
        end for
        if the loop was not exited **then**
            Set *open_space_grid*$[j, i]$ to 1
            Increment *open_space_cells* by 1
        end if
    end if
end for
return *open_space_grid*, *open_space_cells*, *visible_area_cells*

$$\text{Total}\, OS^{A}_{\text{per unit area}}(t) = \sum_{j=1}^{n} \frac{OS^{A}_{j}}{VA_{j}} \tag{2}$$

for $\forall j \in \{1, 2, \ldots, n\}, \quad VA_j > 0$.

Nevertheless, with injury time in games, regular playing time of games may vary from one game to another. Therefore, to compare the temporal measures across games, attacking third open space area per unit area per unit time ($\text{Total}\, OS^{A}_{\text{per unit area/time}}(t)$) was calculated for each time period by dividing the attacking third open space area by the duration of the time period. Assuming the duration of time period t is Δt ($\Delta t > 0$), open space area per unit area per unit time for Team A during time period t ($\text{Total}\, OS^{A}_{\text{per unit area/time}}(t)$) is:

$$\text{Total}\, OS^{A}_{\text{per unit area/time}}(t) = \frac{\text{Total}\, OS^{A}_{\text{per unit area}}(t)}{\Delta t} \tag{3}$$

This results in ten temporal features for each team on total attacking third open-space area for the ball carrier per unit area per unit time.

2.4 Total Attacking Third Ball Carrier Open-Space Analysis

To visualize and explore potential relationships between total attacking third open space area per unit area per unit time in ten time periods, goals scored, and match outcomes, these temporal features were extracted from four FIFA World Cup 2022 second-round games. Specifically, these games were selected based on their close competitiveness, either ending in draws or with the winning team prevailing by just one goal. Figure 4 illustrates the temporal features plotted against time (in minutes) for the chosen FIFA World Cup 2022 quarter-final matches.

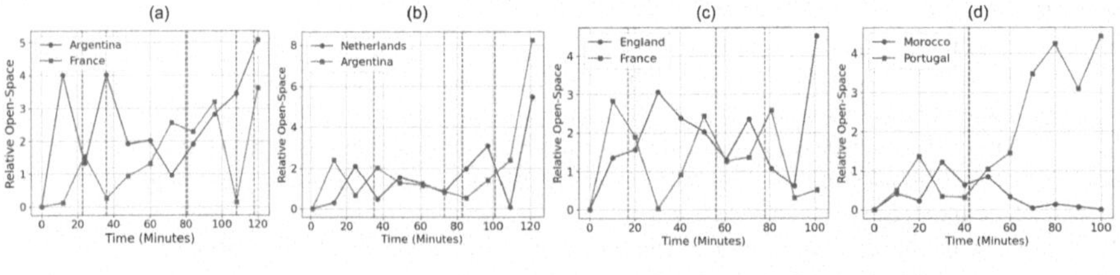

Fig. 4. Initial temporal feature analysis of FIFA world cup 2022 games; (a) Argentina (3) vs France (3) (final), (b) Netherlands (2) vs Argentina (2) (Quarter-Final), (c) England (1) vs France (2) (Quarter-Final), (d) Morocco (1) vs Portugal (0) (Quarter-Final). Dotted lines represent instances of goal scoring, with the color of each dotted line corresponding to the respective team.

In Fig. 4 games (a) and (b) end up with equal scores before deciding the game-winner with penalty shootouts. Games (c) and (d) were won by France and

Morocco with a single-goal advantage. In all these four games, it was observed with the majority of the goals that the goal-scoring teams have maintained higher total attacking third open space for the ball carrier than the opponent prior to the goal scoring. However, it was also observed that leading teams (Fig. 4 (c) and (d)) were not maintaining higher total open space for the ball carrier in the attacking third towards the end of the game compared to the opponent. This can be due to defensive approaches followed by leading teams towards the end of the game by employing tactics like parking the bus [9]. Nevertheless, in equal score games (Fig. 4 (a) and (b)) both teams have maintained higher total open space for the ball carrier in the attacking third toward the end of the game.

2.5 Relative Attacking Third Open-Space Calculation

To reduce the number of temporal features for machine learning model development, the difference between the attacking third open space area per unit time of two teams at a specific time period (t_i) was utilized as a relative measure of the open-space area available for the ball carrier ($\Delta OS_{\text{per unit area/time}}(t)$). This involved subtracting Team B's total attacking third open space created per unit area per unit time ($\text{Total}, OS^{B}_{\text{per unit area/time}}(t)$) from Team A's total attacking third open space area per unit area per unit time ($\text{Total}, OS^{A}_{\text{per unit area/time}}(t)$) for each time period.

$$\Delta OS_{\text{per unit area/time}}(t) = \text{Total}\, OS^{A}_{\text{per unit area/time}}(t) - \text{Total}\, OS^{B}_{\text{per unit area/time}}(t) \quad (4)$$

This resulted in ten temporal features of relative attacking third open space available for the ball carrier per unit of time for each game.

2.6 Machine Learning Model Development

To evaluate the relationship between extracted temporal features and match-winning performances, developing a match-winner prediction model was considered. Ten temporal features extracted were considered as the input features and the target contained a binary value on whether the match was won by Team A (1) or Team B (0).

The relationship between temporal features derived from the relative open space available for the ball carrier in the attacking third per unit of time and the performance of match-winning teams was assessed through a classification analysis using a Generalized Linear Model (GLM). GLM is a simple and relatively computationally inexpensive interpretable machine learning algorithm that offers a flexible statistical framework that extends beyond traditional linear regression models to accommodate various data types and structures.

To comprehensively evaluate the results from the GLM model, a five-fold cross-validation approach was employed. This involved conducting one hundred rounds of five-fold cross-validation, totaling five hundred evaluations. From these evaluations, the average classification accuracy, Mathews Correlation Coefficient (MCC), Area Under the Receiver Operating Characteristic Curve (ROC-AUC), F1-score, precision, and recall were calculated.

3 Results

3.1 Match Winning Performance Classification Model Results

The proposed match-winning performance classification model trained using temporal features extracted on attacking third open space for the ball carrier achieved 79.73% average accuracy in classifying match-winner performances with hundred rounds of five-fold cross-validation. Table 1 presents a summary of results with considered evaluation metrics for this work.

Table 1. Results with match winning performance classification

Evaluation Metric	Average Performance
Accuracy	0.79733
F1-Score	0.80202
Precision	0.82495
Recall	0.80839
ROC-AUC	0.87922
MCC	0.60154

3.2 Individual Temporal Feature Correlation

The correlation between individual temporal features of ten time periods and match-winning performances was evaluated to identify hidden insights and to identify time periods that contribute to the match result most. Correlation coefficients of each time period against the result of the game (Team A win or Team B win) were calculated with both Pearson and Spearman correlation (Table 2).

Table 2. Correlation coefficients of each time period against the result of the game

Metric	t_1	t_2	t_3	t_4	t_5	t_6	t_7	t_8	t_9	t_{10}
Pearson	0.36	0.36	0.39	0.28	0.20	0.10	0.08	−40.1	0.01	−0.31
Spearman	0.35	0.37	0.43	0.29	0.18	0.12	0.04	−0.05	0.00	−0.32

The correlation coefficients indicated a stronger positive correlation between match-winning performances and the open space available for the ball carrier in the attacking third during the first four time periods (approximately 0-40 min). These findings imply the importance of first-half performance over second-half performance. Additionally, it is noticeable that the magnitude of correlation coefficients gradually decreases from t_5 to t_9, indicating a diminishing contribution to the match result. However, for t_{10}, a notably higher negative correlation coefficient is observed. This could be attributed to cautious defensive tactics such as "parking the bus" adopted by leading teams towards the end of the game to safeguard their lead [9].

3.3 Comparison with Existing Literature

In this study, a novel approach is introduced for classifying match-winning performances based on temporal features extracted from the attacking third open space for the ball carrier. To the best of the author's knowledge, there has been no previous research examining team performance using similar temporal features or incorporating them into match-winner prediction models. However, this study presents a match-winner prediction model developed solely on the proposed temporal feature data. The aim was to assess the importance of these temporal features on match-winning performances, uncovering potential insights. Due to differences in datasets, direct comparison between this model and those in existing literature is not appropriate. Nevertheless, the developed classification model showcases superior accuracy compared to models trained on historical data or utilizing multiple performance metrics. This offers a preliminary understanding of the significance of the temporal features considered for determining match-winning performances. Table 3 provides a comparison between match-winner prediction models from recent literature and the approach presented in this study.

Table 3. Comparison with other match winner prediction models

Literature	Data	Approach	features	Model	Acc.	F1-Score	Perf. Eval. Aspect
Danisik et al. (2018) [5]	Top tier club leagues in Europe	Player attributes and results from last five games are considered	139 features	LSTM	70.21%	–	To analyze the best players' combinations among the squad
Al Mulla et al. (2023) [2]	Qatar Stars League	Player performance evaluated temporally	396 features	GRU	**80.77%**	80.93%	NA
This work (2024)	Statsbomb 360 data from top-tier men's international and club leagues	Attacking third Open-Space available for the ball carrier	10 temporal features (single metric is used)	GLM	79.73%	**87.92%**	Time-series team performance evaluation

While Al Mulla et al. (2024) employed a temporal feature extraction method from game data, they utilized 22 player evaluation metrics, resulting in 396 data points for prediction. Their primary focus was on developing an accurate match-winner prediction model using a computationally intensive deep learning technique known as Gated Recurrent Unit (GRU). However, due to GRU's black-box nature, it lacks the ability to provide insights into temporal features. In contrast, this study emphasizes the development of a time-series performance evaluation metric aimed at capturing and assessing team performance. Furthermore, a trained match-winner prediction model, using only the proposed time-series metric data, achieved a similar model performance using a computationally inexpensive, simpler GLM model. Both this work and the work by Al Mulla et al. (2024) involve the extraction of temporal features, allowing for the development of match-winner prediction models capable of predicting winners at different timestamps. This could be explored in future work.

The GLM model, trained with temporal features extracted on total open space available for the ball carrier at several time stamps of the game demonstrates an impressive average accuracy and ROC-AUC compared to models trained with multiple features [2] in classifying match-winning performances underscores the significance of open space available for the ball carrier for events in the attacking third as a determining factor in achieving victories in matches.

3.4 Individual Player Performance Evaluation

Having identified the importance of open space available for the ball carrier in attacking third events for match-winning team performances, it was considered for evaluating individual player performance at the FIFA World Cup 2022.

Ball carrier open spaces can be contributed by preceding ball carrier events in creating ball carrier open spaces through direct passes, through balls, and carries. In addition, this is also contributed by off-ball runs and placements by the ball-receiving player which utilizes the ball carrier's open space. Therefore, both actions in preceding ball carrier events and off-ball actions are required for successful ball carrier open space creation. Considering this, this work evaluated individual performance in two aspects:

1. Active Ball Carrier Open Space Creation: Actions by ball carriers to create open space for him/herself or teammates in immediate subsequent events. Actions include passes, through balls, carries with dribbles.
2. Passive Ball Carrier Open Space Creation: Actions by players to create open space when receiving the ball from preceding event. Actions include off ball runs, placements.

Active ball carrier open space creation was calculated by assigning the ball carrier open space available to the player who performed a ball carrier action (e.g. pass, through ball, run) in the preceding event. Passive ball carrier open space creation was calculated by assigning the open space available for the ball carrier amount to the same ball carrier.

Sixty-four (64) games played at FIFA World Cup 2022 were evaluated for individual performance analysis based on two aspects discussed above. Tables 4 and 5 present the top 10 players who have contributed with the most active and passive attacking third ball carrier open space creation per minute of game time. Figure 5 presents top 10 players who contributed most with both active and passive attacking third open space created per min. In the selection of top-performing players, only those who have accumulated more than 350 min of game time (for filtering out players who played for a considerable amount of time; at least four games) were taken into account, with the assumption that each player has participated in at least four games.

Table 4. Top 10* players who created ball carrier open-spaces in the attacking third

	Player	Team	Position	Minutes Played	Active open space created	Active open space created per min
1	Lionel Andrés Messi Cuccittini	Argentina	FW	690	26.432	0.038
2	Rodrigo Javier De Paul	Argentina	MF	599	21.873	0.037
3	Bernardo Silva	Portugal	MF	356	12.672	0.036
4	Ousmane Dembélé	France	FW	433	13.992	0.032
5	Pedro González López	Spain	MF	356	11.291	0.032
6	Kylian Mbappé Lottin	France	FW	598	18.671	0.031
7	Moon-Hwan Kim	S. Korea	DF	360	11.064	0.031
8	Bruno Fernandes	Portugal	FW, MF	356	10.409	0.029
9	Luka Modrić	Croatia	MF	653	18.112	0.028
10	Alexis Mac Allister	Argentina	MF	550	14.186	0.026

FW: Forwards, MF: Mid fielders, DF: Defenders, S. Korea: South Korea

Observations from Tables 4 and 5 revealed that a significant number of players are from Argentina and France, indicating their notable success at the FIFA World Cup 2022 (Finalists). Additionally, the metrics proposed herein identified Lionel Messi (Lionel Andrés Messi Cuccittini), recipient of the Golden Ball award (Player of the Tournament award), as the most outstanding player in active open space creation and ranked fourth in passive open space creation. Furthermore, it was observed that both Tables 4 and 5 include players from all three divisions (Forwards, Midfielders, and Defenders), underscoring the proposed metrics' effectiveness in evaluating offensive contributions despite of the player positions.

4 Discussion

This work evaluated the importance of open space available for the ball carrier in attacking third for match-winning team performances and proposes it as a novel

Table 5. Top 10* players who utilized ball carrier open-spaces in the attacking third

	Player	Team	Position	Minutes Played	Passive open space Utilized	Passive open space created per min
1	Pedro González López	Spain	MF	356	18.398	0.052
2	Kylian Mbappé Lottin	France	FW	598	29.675	0.050
3	Ousmane Dembélé	France	FW	433	19.036	0.044
4	Lionel Andrés Messi Cuccittini	Argentina	FW	690	29.210	0.042
5	Rodrigo Javier De Paul	Argentina	MF	599	24.203	0.040
6	Heung-Min Son	S. Korea	FW, MF	360	13.537	0.038
7	Luke Shaw	England	DF	424	15.843	0.037
8	Moon-Hwan Kim	S. Korea	DF	360	13.083	0.036
9	Ivan Perišić	Croatia	FW	669	19.521	0.029
10	Antoine Griezmann	France	FW	537	15.281	0.028

FW: Forwards, MF: Mid fielders, DF: Defenders, S. Korea: South Korea

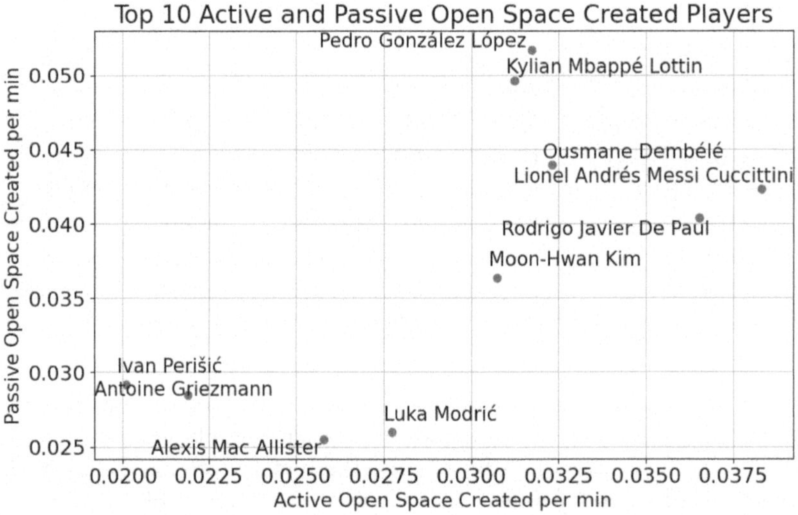

Fig. 5. Top 10 players who contributed most with both active and passive open space created per minute.

time-series performance evaluation metric. Machine learning model developed with temporal features extracted from open space available for the ball carrier in the attacking third achieved 80% accuracy in classifying the match-winning performances, highlighting the importance of the open space available for the ball carrier in the attacking third. This study further contributes by proposing a computationally inexpensive simpler approach for extracting temporal features on open space created for the ball carrier in association football. The developed approach uses player location information retrieved from television videos making it a simpler and computationally inexpensive approach that could be beneficial for television broadcasters and performance evaluators. The proposed approach requires no technologically advanced equipment to capture the player's performances. This work further evaluated individual player performances at the FIFA World Cup 2022 under active open space creation and passive open space creation evaluating significant passes/carries and off-ball movements/placements respectively. The majority of standout performers from France and Argentina demonstrate a correlation between the proposed metric and successful team performances. Notably, the recognition of Lionel Messi as the top performer in active open space creation aligns with expert opinions which nominated him as the tournament's most valuable player.

However, a relatively small dataset has been used in this work due to data availability and dataset limitations. Future work could explore a larger dataset with complex deep learning models that capture the temporal relationships (e.g., Long Short Term Memory network). Also, this work does not consider player velocities due to dataset deficiencies in capturing them. It can be expected that player velocities could add more value to the proposed work. Furthermore, this work values all the space created in attacking the third equally. However, in reality, space created in the attacking third closer to the goal could be more valuable than the space created in the flanks of the attacking third. This could be explored in future work.

5 Conclusion

In conclusion, this study presented a novel time-series team performance evaluation metric based on open space available to the ball carrier in the attacking third and a novel simpler approach for the calculation of the proposed metric based on information retrieved from televised video. The proposed machine learning model trained with features extracted only on the proposed metric achieving similar accuracy and higher ROC-AUC than the existing literature which has considered multiple features for match-winning performance classification highlighted the importance of open space available for the ball carrier in the attacking third. Furthermore, individual performances evaluated on active and passive open space creation correlating with team performances and expert opinions further highlight the importance of the proposed metric. Hence, it is reasonable to conclude that generating open spaces for ball carriers through both on and off-ball movements in the attacking third is a crucial factor contributing to winning performances.

References

1. Xavi - "I understand football as a time-space" INTERVIEW — youtube.com. https://www.youtube.com/watch?v=q61aaEnpYMg. Accessed 21 Nov 2023
2. AlMulla, J., Islam, M.T., Al-Absi, H.R.H., Alam, T.: SoccerNet: a gated recurrent unit-based model to predict soccer match winners. PLoS ONE **18**(8), 1–19 (2023). https://doi.org/10.1371/journal.pone.0288933
3. Aquino, R., et al.: Comparisons of ball possession, match running performance, player prominence and team network properties according to match outcome and playing formation during the 2018 FIFA world cup. Int. J. Perform. Anal. Sport **19**, 1026–1037 (2019). https://doi.org/10.1080/24748668.2019.1689753
4. Brechot, M., Flepp, R.: Dealing with randomness in match outcomes: How to rethink performance evaluation in European club football using expected goals. J. Sports Econ. **21**, 152700251989796 (2020). https://doi.org/10.1177/1527002519897962
5. Danisik, N., Lacko, P., Farkas, M.: Football match prediction using players attributes. In: 2018 World Symposium on Digital Intelligence for Systems and Machines (DISA), pp. 201–206 (2018). https://doi.org/10.1109/DISA.2018.8490613
6. Eggels, H., Pechenizkiy, M., Almeida, R., Van Elk, R., Agt, L.V.: Expected goals in soccer:explaining match results using predictive analytics (2016). https://research.tue.nl/en/studentTheses/expected-goals-in-soccer
7. Fernández, J., Bornn, L.: Wide open spaces: a statistical technique for measuring space creation in professional soccer. In: Sloan Sports Analytics Conference (2018)
8. Goral, K.: Passing success percentages and ball possession rates of successful teams in 2014 FIFA world cup. Int. J. Sci. Cult. Sport **3**, 86–95 (2015). https://doi.org/10.14486/IJSCS239 https://doi.org/10.14486/IJSCS239
9. Guan, T., Cao, J., Swartz, T.: Should you park the bus? (2021). https://www.sfu.ca/~tswartz/papers/bus.pdf
10. Guimarães, J.P., Rochael, M., Andrade, A., Glória, S., Praça, G.: How reaching the pitch's final third is related to scoring opportunities in soccer? Retos **43**, 171 (2021)
11. Hodson, T.: Play to win. the coaches' voice. https://www.coachesvoice.com/jose-mourinho-chelsea-inter-champions-league/. Accessed 27 Mar 2024
12. Kubayi, A., Toriola, A.: The influence of situational variables on ball possession in the South African premier soccer league. J. Hum. Kinet. **66**, 175–181 (2019). https://doi.org/10.2478/hukin-2018-0056
13. Lamas, L., Barrera, J., Otranto, G., Ugrinowitsch, C.: Invasion team sports: strategy and match modeling. Int. J. Perform. Anal. Sport **14**, 307–329 (2014). https://doi.org/10.1080/24748668.2014.11868723
14. Lemmink, K.A., Frencken, W.: Tactical performance analysis in invasion games: Perspectives from a dynamic systems approach with examples from soccer. Routledge Handbook of Sports Performance Analysis, pp. 89–100 (2013)
15. Martens, F., Dick, U., Brefeld, U.: Space and control in soccer. Front. Sports Active Living **3**, 676179 (2021). https://doi.org/10.3389/fspor.2021.676179
16. Mead, J., O'Hare, A., McMenemy, P.: Expected goals in football: improving model performance and demonstrating value. PLoS ONE **18**, e0282295 (2023). https://doi.org/10.1371/journal.pone.0282295
17. Pappalardo, L., Rossi, A., Natilli, M., Cintia, P.: Explaining the difference between men's and women's football. PLoS ONE **16**(8), 1–17 (2021). https://doi.org/10.1371/journal.pone.0255407

18. Peñas, C.: The influence of match location, quality of opposition, and match status on possession strategies in professional association football. J. Sports Sci. **27**, 1463–1469 (2009). https://doi.org/10.1080/02640410903131681
19. Lago-Peñas, C., Lago-Ballesteros, J., Dellal, A., Gómez, M.: Game-related statistics that discriminated winning, drawing and losing teams from the Spanish soccer league. J. Sports Sci. Med. **9**, 288–93 (2010)
20. Reep, C., Benjamin, B.: Skill and chance in association football. J. R. Stat. Soc. Ser. A **131**(4), 581–585 (1968)
21. Singh, k.: Introducing expected threat (xt) (2018). https://karun.in/blog/expected-threat.html
22. Spearman, W.: Beyond expected goals. In: Proceedings of the 12th MIT Sloan Sports Analytics Conference, pp. 1–17 (2018)
23. StatsBomb: Statsbomb open data (2022). https://github.com/statsbomb/open-data.git
24. Swaby, S.: Pep guardiola calls tiki-taka 'rubbish,' admits that he loathes all the passing — bleacherreport.com. https://bleacherreport.com/articles/2234051-pep-guardiola-calls-tiki-taka-rubbish-admits-that-he-loathes-all-the-passing. Accessed 21 Nov 2023
25. Tenga, A., Holme, I., Ronglan, L., Bahr, R.: Effect of playing tactics on goal scoring in Norwegian professional soccer. J. Sports Sci. **28**, 237–244 (2010). https://doi.org/10.1080/02640410903502774

A Generic Virtual Template for Camera Calibration in Soccer Broadcast Footage

Gerhardt Breytenbach(✉) and Jacomine Grobler

Department of Industrial Engineering, Stellenbosch University, Stellenbosch, Western Cape, South Africa
breytenbachgerdo@gmail.com, jacominegrobler@sun.ac.za

Abstract. Camera calibration is an underlying process for pivotal sports analytics tasks such as augmented reality, player tracking, and scene reconstruction. Camera calibration in soccer aims to estimate the geometrical relationship between the pitch and broadcast footage, however, the international pitch guidelines allow for a variance of up to $1850\,\mathrm{m}^2$ in physical soccer pitch size. The objective of this paper is to determine if a generic virtual template can be used as the calibration object for camera calibration in all soccer broadcast footage from internationally approved pitches. An experiment is therefore conducted to determine if the *Federation Internationale de Football Association* (FIFA) recommended-sized pitch can be morphed into any internationally approved pitch. Four extreme soccer pitches are created in a virtual space to resemble the minimum, maximum, min-max, and max-min pitch dimensions accordingly. The direct linear transform is employed to find a homography between the generic template and extreme image planes. It is concluded that the generic template is well grounded for accuracies up to at least 96%, calculated with respect to the camera's perspective. This accuracy method, however, considers the total area of the field and not different segments of the playing field within that area. Therefore, in addition to the standard metric used in the literature, a novel metric is proposed to calculate the combined *intersection over union* (IoU) as the average IoU per field segment in the visible plane.

Keywords: Camera calibration · Soccer · Broadcast footage · Homography estimation · Calibration object · IoU · Virtual template

1 Introduction

In the computer vision domain, camera calibration is a fundamental process and precedes pivotal sports analytics tasks such as augmented reality, player tracking, *three-dimensional* (3D) scene reconstruction, and virtual refereeing [6,9,15]. The purpose of camera calibration is to estimate a set of camera parameters which describe how a camera perceives objects, with respect to a world coordinate system, and may be limited to pan, tilt, focal length, and a 3D position [2]. World coordinates refer to points in virtual space that directly relate to reality,

J. S. Dong et al. (Eds.): ISACE 2024, LNCS 14794, pp. 18–32, 2024.
https://doi.org/10.1007/978-3-031-69073-0_2

whereas image coordinates refer to the same coordinates transformed by a set of camera parameters. Image coordinates are, therefore, a collection of points on an image plane, measured in pixels rather than meters. As a result, camera parameters effectively define the viewpoint of a virtual camera, allowing 3D world coordinates to be displayed on an image plane as *two-dimensional* (2D) image coordinates.

Camera calibration necessitates a known calibration object that is visible in both the world coordinate system and the image plane, *e.g.* a soccer pitch can be modelled and is visible in broadcast footage [15]. Calibration objects are therefore often modelled in 3D virtual space to represent the world coordinate system. Considering that a soccer pitch can be seen as a 2D plane in a 3D space, the task of camera calibration may be reduced to finding the homography matrix, which describes the relationship between two 2D planes [7].

The first publicly available benchmark dataset, tailored to camera calibration in soccer broadcast footage, was provided by Homayounfar *et al.* [13] in 2017. This benchmark dataset was specifically designed to estimate the homography matrix between a provided *pitch template* and images from broadcast footage of the 2014 FIFA World Cup—a pitch template refers to a set of world coordinates representing a physical soccer pitch. Cioppa *et al.* [5] released another benchmark dataset called SoccerNetV3 in 2022. They also provide a pitch template according to FIFA's recommended pitch dimensions [8]. Both of the aforementioned templates have the exact same dimensions, even though soccer law permits a vast array of pitch sizes [14]. The guidelines for international soccer pitches state that the field length has to be between 100 m and 110 m long, while the width has to be between 64 m and 75 m wide. These guidelines allow for a variance in area of up to 1850 m^2 between the theoretical largest and smallest soccer pitches. The pitch templates of both datasets are provided under the assumption that they accurately resemble the physical pitches of their data, however, there is no proof nor validation that their templates could be used outside their given data. The aim of this article is therefore to determine if FIFA's proposed pitch template can be accurately deployed for any internationally-approved soccer pitch. If their template is generic it would imply that the literature pertaining to automatic camera calibration is scalable and would not need to be redesigned per stadium (or group of stadiums), nor would stadiums need to be verified for automatic camera calibration algorithms if they are already internationally accredited. Automatic camera calibration algorithms aim to receive real-time broadcast footage as input and estimate the camera parameters with respect to a virtual template. These algorithms do not need any additional input parameters, therefore, they would be highly scalable if a generic virtual template could be used.

To determine the usability of FIFA's template as a generic template, an experiment was conducted to map their template to four theoretically extreme pitches. These four pitches were initialised by exploiting the international guidelines. The first pitch design is constrained to a minimum length and width, whilst the second pitch design attributes a maximum length and width. The third and fourth pitch designs were combinations of the previous two. A random set of camera parameters were also initialised with which each pitch template was projected onto an image plane, according to the synthetic guideline stipulated by Chen and Little [2]. The *direct linear transform* (DLT) was then deployed to estimate a homography between the generic template and each subsequent image plane projection [1]. The resulting matrices were evaluated by projecting FIFA's template onto an image plane and calculating the *intersection over union* (IoU) with the image points of the corresponding extreme image plane. Satisfactory results were obtained to conclude that the generic template is usable for all internationally approved pitches with an IoU accuracy of up to at least 96%. For the four extreme pitches the IoUs were 96.2%, 96.6%, 96.5%, and 97.6%, respectively.

A common approach adopted by the seminal literature is to calculate the IoU with respect to the total area of projection [2,13,17]. This approach insinuates that if the outer area of the pitches align, the dependent lines within the pitch would also align. This assumption is challenged and it is shown that there is a difference when calculating the IoU of the outer perimeter versus calculating the average IoU per segmented pitch area. It is further suggested that it may be more suitable to implement IoU per segmented pitch area in the image plane.

The research contributions of this paper is primarily two-fold: (1) A generic pitch template is defined and compared with the most extreme international pitches, and (2) a new standard for calculating IoU in this application is proposed. The proposed metric is also applicable for camera calibration in other sports broadcast footage with clearly visible pitch segments. The rest of this paper is organised according to a brief literature review in Sect. 2, a detailed explanation of the experimental setup in Sect. 3, followed by a report and discussion of the results obtained, along with an evaluation of multiple IoU methods in Sect. 4. The paper is then concluded and recommendations for proceeding literature are also provided in Sect. 5.

2 Literature Review

This brief literature review provides background to camera calibration in Sect. 2.1, the DLT algorithm in Sect. 2.2, benchmark datasets for camera calibration in soccer broadcast footage in Sect. 2.3, and a short overview of various approaches for calculating the IoU in Sect. 2.4.

2.1 Camera Calibration

Traditionally camera calibration is employed to estimate the camera's internal and external parameters [19]. These can then be combined into a single matrix called the *projection matrix* ($\mathbf{P}$), or camera matrix, which is of shape 3×4 [11]. The shape of this matrix, however, renders it impossible to multiply 3D or 2D coordinates as unique vectors. A solution to this problem is to use homogeneous coordinates, for both the 3D and 2D coordinates. Homogeneous coordinates refer to a plane of coordinates one dimension higher than the coordinate of interest [10]. By using homogeneous coordinates the coordinate (u, v) can be expressed as (ku, kv, k), where $k \in \mathbb{R}$, and implies that a single 3D coordinate has multiple corresponding 4D points which all lie on a plane within the 4D space. Therefore, $\mathbf{P}$ may be used to transform homogeneous world coordinates $(\boldsymbol{X})$ to homogeneous image coordinates $(\boldsymbol{x}')$ according to

$$\boldsymbol{x}' = \mathbf{P}\boldsymbol{X}. \tag{1}$$

The projection matrix is of rank three, which suggests that each of the three dimensions of a world coordinate may be multiplied with an independent vector inside the projection matrix. Consequently, if the column responsible for depth is removed, a new matrix can be extracted of shape 3×3 which maps 2D homogeneous world coordinates to 2D homogeneous image coordinates [2,20]. This is, in fact, a well-known matrix within the domain of computer vision referred to as the *homography* matrix, denoted by $\mathbf{H}$ [12]. The reformatted equation is

$$\boldsymbol{x}' = \mathbf{H}\boldsymbol{x}, \tag{2}$$

where $\boldsymbol{x}$ is a 2D homogeneous world coordinate. Modern camera calibration algorithms typically employ deep learning to solve for either $\mathbf{P}$ or $\mathbf{H}$, however, in these scenarios only the world coordinates are known and the corresponding image coordinates are unknown. Recently, deep learning techniques have been adopted successfully to predict corresponding image points in order to utilise the DLT to determine the geometric relationship between the world and image coordinates [3,16]. The DLT is, accordingly, a well-established and computationally efficient method to solve for either $\mathbf{P}$ or $\mathbf{H}$, provided there exists a theoretical set of world coordinates with corresponding image coordinates [15].

2.2 Direct Linear Transform

The DLT states that an equation, like the aforementioned equations, should be rewritten as a system of linearly independent equations and subsequently use singular value decomposition to compute the solution with the least squared reprojection error [12,21]. The algorithm, for this reason, does not guarantee an exact solution but an estimation that minimises the reprojection error. When using the DLT to solve for $\mathbf{P}$, it is important to note that if all 3D coordinates are on a single plane, the system of equations will not provide enough linearly independent equations to solve, regardless of the number of point correspondences, and will result in an inaccurate solution [12].

The task of camera calibration in sports broadcast footage is commonly reduced to estimate the homography matrix rather than the projection matrix [15,20]. This alteration may be due to multiple reasons, one of which is that the pitch is typically seen as a 2D plane in 3D space. This would imply that either z coordinates are randomised to solve for $\mathbf{P}$, or the DLT would not find a solution and therefore solving for $\mathbf{H}$ may be the more effective solution.

2.3 Benchmark Datasets

The two primary benchmark datasets pertaining to camera calibration in soccer broadcast footage are the 2014 World Cup dataset by Homayounfar *et al.* [13], and the SoccerNetV3 dataset by Cioppa *et al.* [5]. The former was only released in 2017 with target labels strictly being homography matrices. In 2022, the SoccerNetV3 dataset was updated for camera calibration, having previously been released for action detection. It allows for the evaluation of homography and projection matrices. Both these datasets present a single soccer pitch as the virtual template to map across multiple stadiums, assuming that the physical pitches in their datasets do not vary significantly. The assumption is consequently justified as a result of high recorded accuracies [4,20], however, there is no certainty regarding the scalability of the templates beyond these datasets.

2.4 Intersection over Union

Various methods for calculating the IoU have been applied across the literature. The metric used by Homayounfar *et al.* [13] is commonly referred to as IoU_{whole}, whilst, in 2018, Sharma *et al.* [18] proposed to rather use IoU_{part}. The former metric refers to the IoU of the entire template used, whereas the latter refers to the IoU of only the visible image plane. The literature typically presents both methods in parallel since 2019 [2,17].

Upon analysing the code implementation of Chen and Little [2], as well as Theiner and Ewerth [20], it is revealed that the IoU is calculated by first warping two homography matrices to a bird's-eye view of the image space, and then the two resulting views are compared with respect to the intersection over their union. For IoU_{whole}, the entire outer perimeter of the true and predicted pitches are warped into two bird's-eye view instances as binary images. The resulting images are rectangles representing the outer area of a soccer pitch. The intersection is then calculated by multiplying the non-zero values of both images, while the union is computed by summing the non-zero values. The IoU is obtained by dividing the intersection over the union. The only difference between IoU_{whole} and IoU_{part} is how the binary images in bird's-eye view are created. For IoU_{part}, only the visible area of the pitch is mapped to the bird's-eye view. The resulting images in effect highlight the area of the pitch covered by the camera. Both these methods indirectly assume that the inner pitch lines, *e.g.* the penalty or goal areas, will also align if the area of the pitch aligns.

Cioppa *et al.* [5], on the other hand, did not follow the same standard when creating the SoccerNetV3 dataset. They defined a new method based on the Euclidean distance between the true pitch lines and the predicted pitch lines. Their method, however, is not a form of IoU because they do not calculate an intersection over any union. They label predicted pixel points as either true positives, false positives, or false negatives. If a projected line is within a certain *threshold* distance of the true line, it is recorded as a true positive. If it is within the threshold distance of a different ground truth line, however, it is recorded as a false positive. If any ground truth lines are visible without any associated projected lines, they are recorded as false negatives, while there are no true negatives. They calculate an accuracy per threshold, by dividing the total number of true positives by the sum of true positives, false positives, and false negatives.

3 Experimental Approach

The research question at hand is: Can FIFA's recommended pitch dimensions be used as a generic calibration object for camera calibration in soccer broadcast footage? To classify this virtual template as generic, there needs to exist a homography (or projection) matrix that can accurately map this template to any theoretical pitch. This section details the experimental setup concerning the theoretical pitch designs in Sect. 3.1 and the methodology relating to relevant accuracy measures in Sect. 3.2.

3.1 Theoretically Extreme Pitches

The International Football Association Board's guideline [14] stipulates that a pitch can vary in total length and width, but no other pitch dimension may vary. Consequently, four extreme pitches can be created to exploit all possible pitch designs within the international guidelines. In the first pitch design the length is set to 100 m and the width to 64 m, whereas in the second design the length and width are set to 110 m and 75 m, respectively. The third pitch is characterised by a length of 100 m and width of 75 m, while the fourth pitch is characterised by a length of 110 m and width of 64 m. All four extreme pitches can be viewed by an arbitrary set of camera parameters in Fig. 1.

Considering that the pitch coordinates of the FIFA template [8] are known, the method explained by Chen and Little [2] may be used to create a synthetic camera matrix, denoted as $\mathbf{P}_0$, which can then be used with Eq. (1) to calculate corresponding image points. The image points can then be connected via lines to illustrate the soccer pitch. This method is applied to the FIFA template as well as all four extreme pitches to create five sets of world (pitch) coordinates and corresponding image coordinates.

Let $\boldsymbol{x}'_{pitch}$ denote the set of image points for all four extreme pitches, and let $\boldsymbol{x}_{FIFA}$ denote the set of world coordinates, according to FIFA's template. Since world coordinates represent a 2D plane in 3D space, the corresponding sets of points can be solved via a 2D-to-2D mapping. Therefore, Eq. (2) is selected to model these point correspondences to apply the DLT algorithm. To hinder ambiguity from hereon, "the template" will refer to FIFA's template. Consequently, let $\mathbf{H}_{pitch}$ denote the homography matrix that maps the template to the respective extreme pitches according to

$$\boldsymbol{x}'_{pitch} = \mathbf{H}_{pitch}\boldsymbol{x}_{FIFA}, \quad pitch \in \{Min, Max, MinMax, MaxMin\}. \tag{3}$$

All obtained homography matrices have to be measured according to some accuracy metric to validate their usability. The implemented DLT returns an

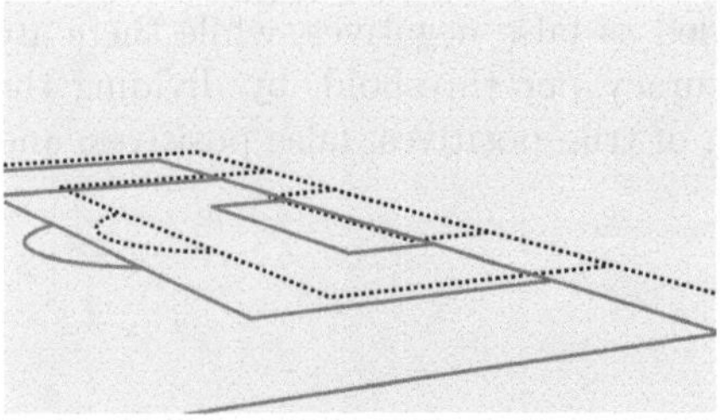

(a) First extreme template, with minimum length and width.

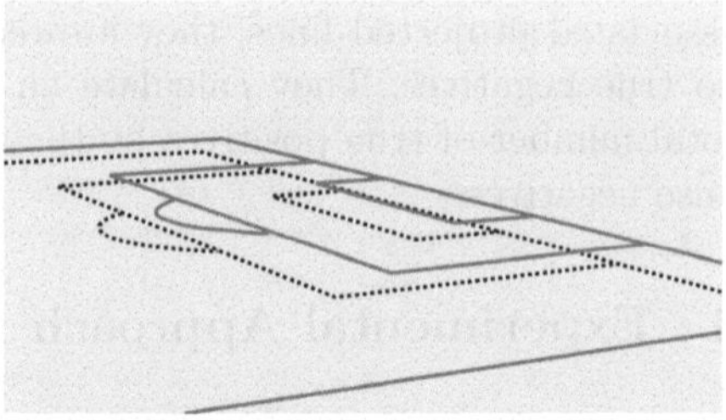

(b) Second extreme template, with maximum length and width.

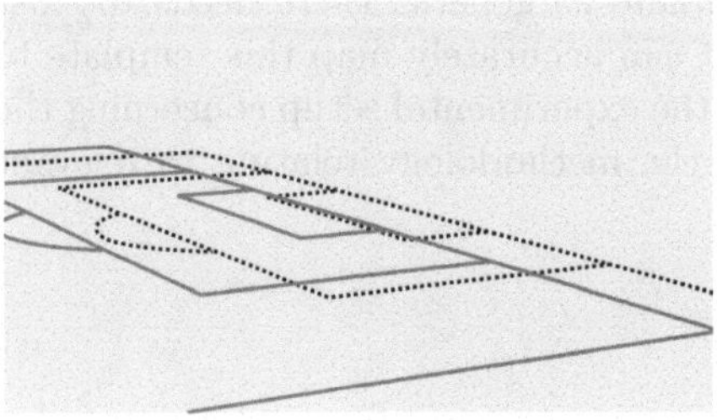

(c) Third extreme template, with minimum length and maximum width.

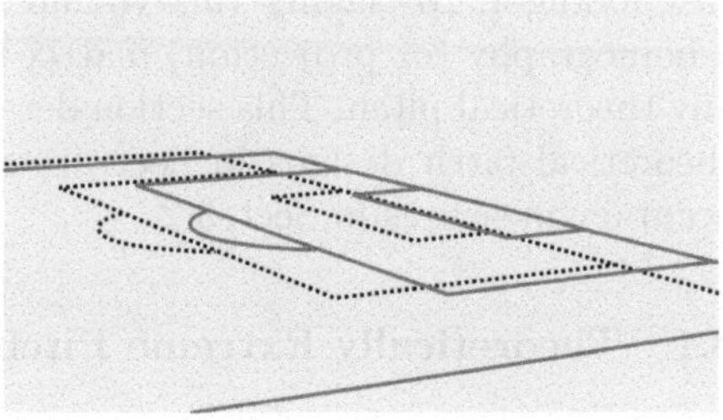

(d) Fourth extreme template, with maximum length and minimum width.

Fig. 1. The extreme pitches (red/solid) are plotted over FIFA's recommended pitch (black/dotted), with an arbitrary set of camera parameters. (Color figure online)

error calculated from the least squared distances between mapped points which can be used as a form of accuracy, however, the IoU is viewed as the standard metric due to measuring the area of overlapping planes and not just specific points. As mentioned in Sect. 2.4, the standard approaches to calculate the IoU do not necessarily consider the overlapping of soccer pitch segments, but rather only the greater perimeter of the pitch. Therefore, in this paper, the IoU_{part} is analysed in addition to different variations of calculating the IoU.

3.2 IoU Variances

The IoU variations detailed in this experiment are calculated with respect to the visible image plane and not transposed to a bird's-eye view. The reason is two-fold: The aim is to preserve the integrity of the pitch lines, and it is less cumbersome. The visible image plane in this context mimics the pitch orientation of soccer broadcast footage, as illustrated in Fig. 1. For this reason, the initial image plane of an extreme set is viewed as the true set of points and lines, whereas the reprojected template points, via $\mathbf{H}_{pitch}$, are referred to as the predicted points and lines. The IoU calculations, consequently, measure the quality of overlapping between the true and predicted image planes. Due to the accuracy measures being specific to the visible image plane, the IoU_{part} is also calculated as a reference. All image planes are $720px$ in height and $1280px$ in width.

A total variety of eight IoU calculations are reported and can be grouped into two distinctive methods, namely *line-based* IoU calculations and *area-based* IoU calculations. Line-based IoU calculations are computed as the percentage of true lines covered by predicted lines in the visible image plane, whereas area-based refer to the percentage of true polygons covered by predicted polygons within the projected lines. The line-based approach was applied five times, where the predicted lines' thickness increases with each iteration. The true lines are $5px$ thick in the image plane, whereas the predicted lines vary in thickness between $5px$, $10px$, $20px$, $30px$, and $40px$. The sixth variant is IoU_{part} which is a form of area-based IoU.

The difference between line-based and area-based IoU is illustrated in Fig. 2. For both images, the green (top/light) projection represents the template projected with $\mathbf{H}_{MinMax}$ onto the image plane, whereas the red (bottom/dark) projection indicates the true projection of $\boldsymbol{x}'_{MinMax}$. In Fig. 2(a), an example of line-based projection is illustrated where the true and predicted lines are $5px$ and $10px$ thick respectively. On the right-hand side, in Fig. 2(b), an example of area-based projection is illustrated, *i.e.* the outer perimeter of the pitch projections are filled polygons. This specific example illustrates the seventh IoU variant, called IoU_{mask}, where the IoU is calculated with respect to the outer pitch area of the true and predicted projections. This metric is the same as the standard metric IoU_{part}, however, IoU_{mask} is calculated in a different image plane, namely the visible image plane that imitates broadcast footage.

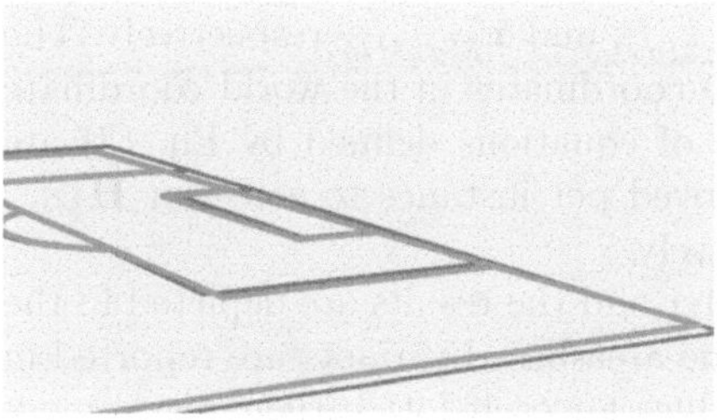

(a) Line-based IoU, $5px$ thick

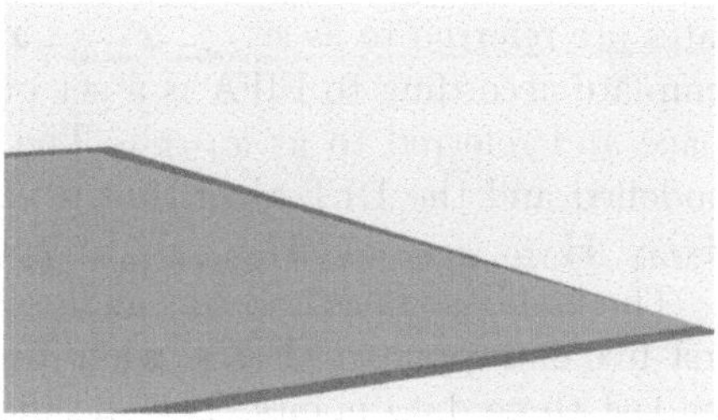

(b) Area-based IoU, specifically IoU_{mask}

Fig. 2. A comparison of the two IoU calculation methods implemented in the image plane. The red (bottom/dark) plot represents the true pitch obtained via $\boldsymbol{x}'_{pitch}$. The green (top/light) plot represents the predicted pitch via $\mathbf{H}_{pitch}\boldsymbol{x}_{FIFA}$. (Color figure online)

The final variant considered in this experiment is an adaptation of the previously mentioned IoU, where the IoU_{mask} per visible pitch segment was calculated and divided by the total number of visible segments. This last IoU variance is called the segmented IoU denoted, by IoU_{seg}. The visible pitch segments are illustrated by different colours in Fig. 3.

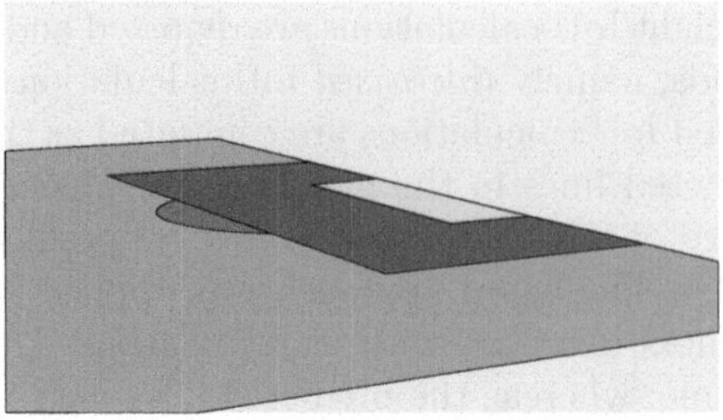

Fig. 3. Different pitch segments as obtained via the camera matrix $\mathbf{P}_0$.

4 Results

The experimental setup defined in Sect. 3 is analysed and reported on in this section. The four extreme pitches are designed exactly as stated and depicted in Fig. 1, and relevant IoU methods are constructed. A concise report of the analysis is disclosed in Sect. 4.1 which is followed by a discussion thereof in Sect. 4.2.

4.1 Numerical Results

The four extreme templates in world coordinate space are referred to as $\boldsymbol{x}_{Min}$, $\boldsymbol{x}_{Max}$, $\boldsymbol{x}_{MinMax}$, and $\boldsymbol{x}_{MaxMin}$, respectively. The camera matrix used to calculate the true image points is referred to as $\mathbf{P}_0$, and the resulting image coordinates are referred to as $\boldsymbol{x}'_{Min}$, $\boldsymbol{x}'_{Max}$, $\boldsymbol{x}'_{MinMax}$, and $\boldsymbol{x}'_{MaxMin}$ respectively. The template according to FIFA is a set of 2D coordinates in the world coordinate space and referred to as $\boldsymbol{x}_{FIFA}$. The set of equations defined by Eq. (3) are modelled and the DLT algorithm is employed per instance to solve for $\mathbf{H}_{Min}$, $\mathbf{H}_{Max}$, $\mathbf{H}_{MinMax}$, and $\mathbf{H}_{MaxMin}$, respectively.

The line-based method was analysed first and the results are depicted in the first five data points of Fig. 4, wherafter the area-based variants are reported in the last three data points. The specific values for each IoU variant per homography matrix is recorded in Table 1.

Regarding the line-based method there is a clear correlation between the line thickness and the yielded IoU. The $40px$ line-based method obtains accuracies up to 99.75%, however, a vertical line of thickness $40px$ is also equal to 5.6% of the total image plane width, which is not an accurate representation of a line on a pitch. Experiments are not conducted with greater line thicknesses.

A difference of nearly 10% in accuracy is visible between $\mathbf{H}_{Min}$ and $\mathbf{H}_{Max}$ at a line thickness of $30px$. The projection of $\boldsymbol{x}_{FIFA}$ by both these matrices are represented in green (top/thick) over the true field templates represented in red (bottom/thin), as illustrated in Fig. 5. By analysing this figure it can be seen that the bottom predicted line (green/thick) in Fig. 5(b) separates from the true line (red/thin), whilst in Fig. 5(a) the lines overlap continuously. For this reason it is stated that the bottom line's projection of the pitch by $\mathbf{H}_{Max}$ is further from parallel to the true projection, when compared with the projection of $\mathbf{H}_{Min}$. It is

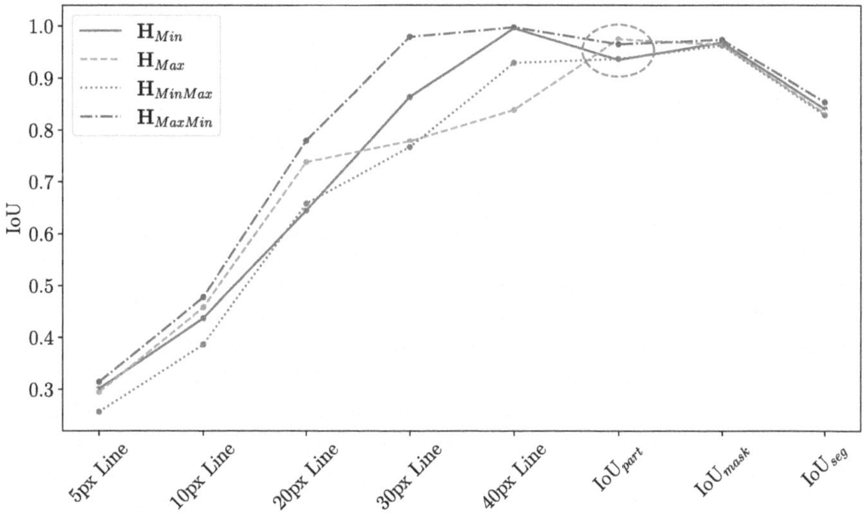

Fig. 4. A comparison of the eight IoU variations for the homography matrices that map the FIFA template to the respective extreme pitches. The circle marks the results of the standard metric used in the literature, namely IoU_{part}.

further determined that this line separation is the reason why the reported accuracies of $\mathbf{H}_{Max}$ do not increase in tandem with the other homography matrices over line thicknesses of $30px$ and $40px$.

The area-based method obtained a stronger pairing of results in general, as can be viewed in the last three data points of Fig. 4. The grey dotted circle in the figure indicates the results obtained from the standard metric, IoU_{part}. To calculate this metric, two bird's-eye views of the distinct pitch templates were created, one for the template and one for the true pitch. The dimensions were then adjusted to determine the IoU. This implementation is, however, different to the implementation by Chen and Little [2], since they only used one template. The calculated IoU_{part} accuracies range from 93.5% to 97.5% with an average of 95.3% accross the four homography matrices. The calculated IoU_{mask} accuracies are similar and range from 96.3% to 97.4% with an average of 96.7%. The proposed metric IoU_{seg}, however, is drastically lower than the previous two ranging from 82.9% to 85.4% with an average of 83.9%.

The reason for the abrupt drop in accuracy between IoU_{seg} and the other two area-based methods is due to the segments not aligning equivalently with the outer perimeter. In Fig. 6(a) the predicted segments are placed over the true segments and in Fig. 6(b) the overlapping error is emphasised by changing all overlapping pixels (per segment) to green, while changing all non-overlapping pixels to black.

Referring to Fig. 6(a), the outer segment (green) was predicted with 90.7% accuracy, the penalty arc (red) was predicted with 84.3% accuracy, the penalty area (blue) was predicted with 87.4%, and the goal area (yellow) was predicted

Table 1. All eight IoU variant accuracies for each homography matrix estimation, *i.e.* $\mathbf{H}_{pitch}$, with respect to each extreme pitch are presented. The line-based IoU variants only consider lines in the image plane, whereas the area-based variants only consider the encapsulated areas of these lines. The IoU_{part} metric refers to the total area in a bird's-eye view, IoU_{mask} refers to the total area in the camera's perspective, and IoU_{seg} refers to the average IoU_{mask} per pitch segment.

	Line-based					Area-based		
	$5px$	$10px$	$20px$	$30px$	$40px$	IoU_{part}	IoU_{mask}	IoU_{seg}
$\mathbf{H}_{Min}$	30.07	43.64	64.45	86.35	99.56	93.50	96.82	84.04
$\mathbf{H}_{Max}$	29.44	45.71	73.75	77.84	83.86	97.47	96.40	83.20
$\mathbf{H}_{MinMax}$	25.64	38.58	65.78	76.66	92.93	93.68	96.26	82.90
$\mathbf{H}_{MaxMin}$	31.38	47.68	77.94	97.90	99.75	96.51	97.36	85.36

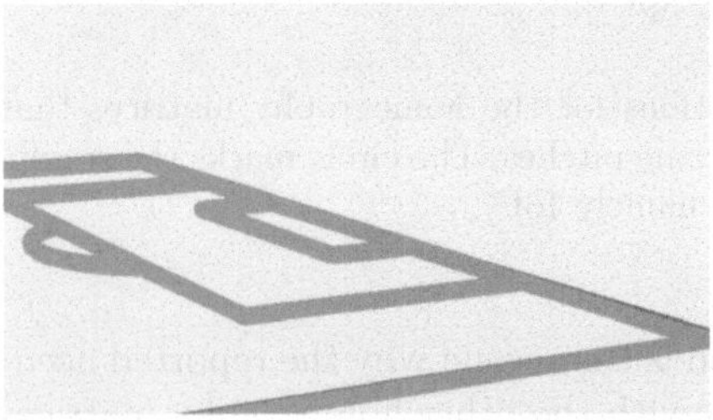

(a) The red (bottom/thin) lines connect the true image coordinates, $\boldsymbol{x}'_{Min}$.

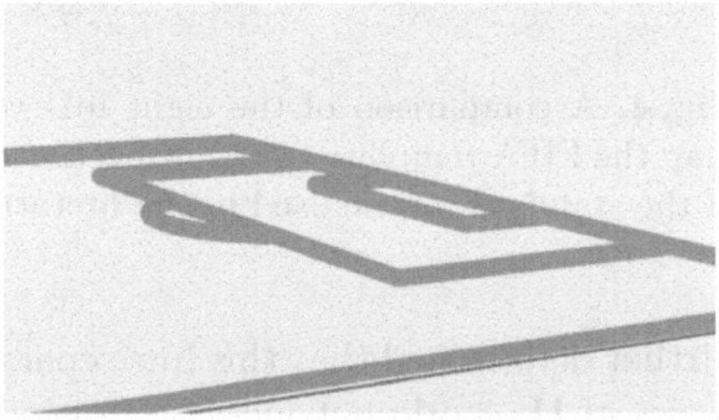

(b) The red (bottom/thin) lines connect the true image coordinates, $\boldsymbol{x}'_{Max}$.

Fig. 5. A comparison of $30px$ thick line-based IoU between $\mathbf{H}_{Min}$ and $\mathbf{H}_{Max}$, where the FIFA template is projected via both homography matrices as the green (top/thick) lines in (a) and (b), respectively. (Color figure online)

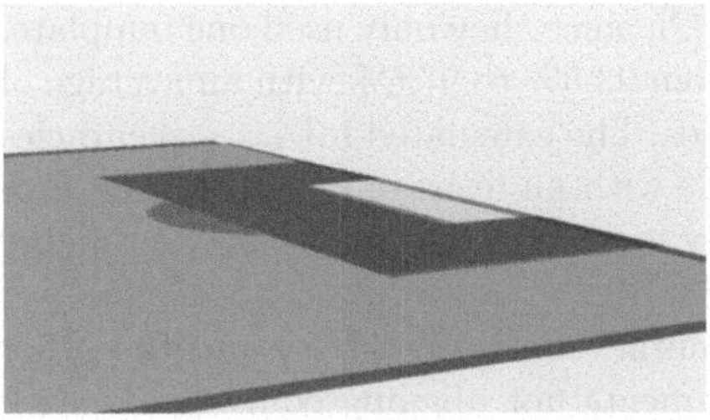

(a) Predicted pitch over true pitch

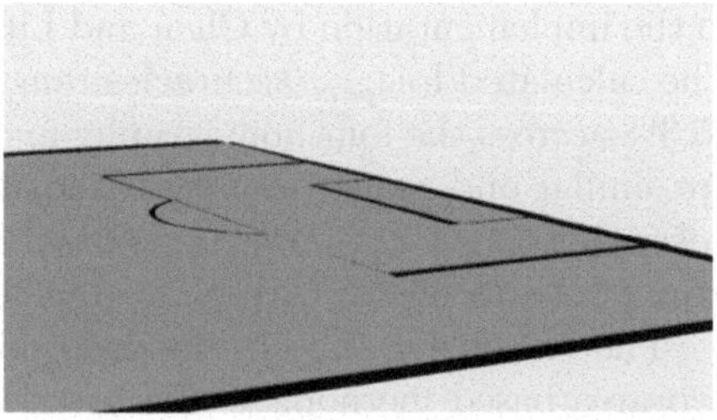

(b) Ephasised overlapping error

Fig. 6. Combining the IoU_{mask} per pitch segment, referred to as IoU_{seg}, constitutes first dividing the pitch into segments and then projecting the predicted segments onto the true segments as depicted in (a). The areas where specific segments do not overlap are blacked out, whilst the overlapping segments are made green, to emphasis the overlapping error as depicted in (b). (Color figure online) with 70.4% accuracy. These predictions were calculated according to the IoU_{mask} per segment and yielded a total IoU_{seg} accuracy of 83.2%. The relatively low accuracy of the goal area is illustrated in Fig. 6(b) where the black lines account for a large portion of total goal area.

4.2 Discussion

The experiment was verified by calculating the homography transform between the template and its known image coordinates using the DLT, *i.e.* estimating $\mathbf{H}_0$ as the relationship between $\boldsymbol{x}_{FIFA}$ and $\boldsymbol{x}'_{FIFA}$. The predicted matrix was then compared with the original matrix that created $\boldsymbol{x}'_{FIFA}$, and reported 100% for IoU_{part}, 99.9% for IoU_{mask}, and 99.5% for IoU_{seg}.

Regarding the line-based IoU variants reported in this paper, the accuracies were very low when computed with thin lines and high accuracies were only attained with exceedingly thick lines. These variants are highly sensitive and should be deployed in relevant scenarios, such as with certain applications of augmented reality where the added visuals have to precisely align with the objects in reality. An example may be to draw the offside line in broadcast footage.

The area-based IoU variants, on the other hand, are less sensitive and the accuracies are more holistic representations of the overlapping predicted and true image coordinates. The proposed metric, IoU_{seg}, aims to provide a balance between the sensitive, as well as precise, nature of the line-based methods and the holistic nature of the area-based methods. The proposed IoU_{seg} is consequently applicable to any sport with visible pitch segments, *e.g.* basketball, hockey, netball, and rugby. This metric, however, can be fine-tuned by adding weighted scales to each of the segments with respect to their total number of true pixels.

An important point to note regarding this paper is that 2D-to-2D mapping was tested and not 3D-to-2D, as may be desirable in some situations, since the data used for testing only represented a 2D plane in 3D. Furthermore, the homography matrices obtained do not represent the true mapping between the actual pitch and actual camera. Instead, the experiment validated that a fictional homography matrix exists which maps a generic pitch to any international pitch, as if the true camera and pitch coordinates were known, up to the accuracies provided in Table 1.

If the exact camera parameters are provided by the owner of the broadcasting cameras, and the exact pitch dimensions are not known, the operator should definitely not assume that $\boldsymbol{x}_{FIFA}$ may be used as the virtual template because the result may resemble the four examples in Fig. 1. These examples were created by plotting two different pitch templates with the same camera parameters. In a case where the camera parameters are known but not the pitch dimensions, the dimensions should be obtained or at least estimated accurately.

5 Conclusion

The objective of this paper was to determine if FIFA's recommended pitch guidelines could be used to create a generic virtual pitch template to use as the calibration object for camera calibration in soccer broadcast footage. The international guidelines for soccer allow for a variance in soccer pitches of up to $1850\,\mathrm{m}^2$, and no similar experiment has been conducted to the best of the authors' knowledge. An experiment was therefore designed to find a fictitious homography matrix that maps the recommended pitch template to the image coordinates of an actual pitch, when the true pitch can take any form that adheres to the international guidelines.

The lowest IoU_{mask} accuracy reported is 96.2%—which implies that for any given international soccer pitch the virtual template according to FIFA recommendations can be used to determine the outer perimeter of the playing field from the camera's perspective up to at least 96.2% accuracy. This finding is significant because (1) this result is comparable with state-of-the-art camera calibration accuracies [4,17,20], (2) it implies that the related literature for automatic camera calibration is scalable for any international soccer pitch, and (3) it implies that methods relying on camera calibration, *e.g.* player tracking, are also theoretically scalable for any international soccer pitch. Furthermore, it is revealed that the accuracies reported by seminal literature do not necessarily imply accurate aligning of inner pitch lines and, therefore, a new metric is proposed that combines the holistic characteristics of the current standard IoU metrics whilst taking into account the alignment of inner pitch lines. The proposed metric is also applicable for camera calibration in Basketball and other sports broadcast footage, where pitch segments are clearly visible.

In order to use this template one of two assumptions must hold: Either the camera parameters are unknown, or the template precisely matches the true pitch. If the camera parameters are known and the template does not accurately represent the true pitch, then the result will resemble Fig. 1, where two dissimilar pitches are projected with the same camera parameters. In most scenarios, however, both the camera parameters and true pitch dimensions are unknown and, therefore, the use of a generic pitch is warranted.

For future work, this experiment can be extended to determine the relationship between extreme pitch scaling and the projection accuracy of the generic template. Additional work could also consider the relationship between IoU_{mask} and IoU_{seg} accuracies with regards to extreme pitch scaling. Furthermore, this experiment can be conducted for multiple sports with symmetric pitches, such as rugby and Australian rules football, which have different international guidelines. Australian rules football, specifically, may be an interesting study since the pitch dimensions are circular of nature, but not perfectly circular, whilst the pitch scaling allows for independent scaling in multiple dimensions. Finally, for future work, a similar experiment can be conducted for 3D-to-2D transformation of world coordinates to image coordinates and specifically to determine if a subset of known camera parameters, for instance the position of the camera, would aid the analysis or not.

Disclosure of Interests. The authors have no competing interests with the work discussed in this paper.

References

1. Abdel-Aziz, Y.I., Karara, H.M.: Direct linear transformation from comparator coordinates into object space coordinates in close range photogrammetry. In: Proceedings of the Symposium on Close-Range Photogrammetry, pp.1–19. Urbana (IL), USA (1971)
2. Chen, J., Little, J.J.: Sports camera calibration via synthetic data. In: Proceedings of the IEEE/CVF Conference on Computer Vision and Pattern Recognition (CVPR) Workshops, pp. 2497–2504. IEEE/CVF, Long Beach (CA), USA (2019). https://doi.org/10.1109/CVPRW.2019.00305
3. Chu, Y.J., et al.: Sports field registration via keypoints-aware label condition. In: Proceedings of the IEEE/CVF Conference on Computer Vision and Pattern Recognition (CVPR) Workshops, pp. 3523–3530. IEEE, New Orleans (LA), USA (2022). https://doi.org/10.1109/CVPRW56347.2022.00396
4. Cioppa, A., et al.: Camera calibration and player localization in SoccerNet-v2 and investigation of their representations for action spotting. In: Proceedings of the IEEE/CVF Conference on Computer Vision and Pattern Recognition (CVPR) Workshops, pp. 4537–4546. IEEE/CVF, Nashville (TN), USA (2021). https://doi.org/10.48550/arXiv.2104.09333
5. Cioppa, A., Deliege, A., Giancola, S., Ghanem, B., Van Doogerenbroeck, M.: Scaling up SoccerNet with multi-view spatial localization and re-identification. Sci. Data **9**, 355 (2022). https://doi.org/10.1038/s41597-022-01469-1
6. Dzialowski, K., Forczmanski, P.: Football players movement analysis in panning videos. In: Paszynski M., Kranzlmüller D., Krzhizhanovskaya V.V., Dongarra J.J., Sloot P.M.A. (eds.) Computational science - ICCS 2021, vol. 12746, pp. 193–206. Springer, Cham (2021). https://doi.org/10.1007/978-3-030-77977-1_15
7. Farin, D., Krabbe, S., De, W.P., Effelsberg, W.: Robust camera calibration for sport videos using court models. In: Proceedings of SPIE 5307, Storage and Retrieval Methods and Applications for Multimedia, pp. 80–91. SPIE, San Jose (CA), USA (2004). https://doi.org/10.1117/12.526813
8. FIFA pitch dimensions and surrounding areas. https://publications.fifa.com/en/football-stadiums-guidelines/technical-guideline/stadium-guidelines/pitch-dimensions-and-surrounding-areas/#. Accessed 22 Mar 2024
9. Ghassab, V., Maanicshah, K., Bouguila, N., Green, P.: REP-MODEL: a deep Learning framework for replacing ad billboards in soccer videos. In: 2020 IEEE international symposium on multimedia, pp. 149–153. IEEE, Italy (2020). https://doi.org/10.1109/ISM.2020.00032
10. Hartley, R., Zisserman, A.: Multiple View Geometry in Computer Vision (Chapter 1: Introduction - A Tour of Multiple View Geometry), 2nd edn. Cambridge University Press (2003)
11. Hartley, R., Zisserman, A.: Multiple View Geometry in Computer Vision (Chapter 3: Projective Geometry and Transformations of 3D), 2nd edn. Cambridge University Press (2003)
12. Hartley, R., Zisserman, A.: Multiple View Geometry in Computer Vision (Chapter 4: Estimation - 2D Projective Transformations), 2nd edn. Cambridge University Press (2003)

13. Homayounfar, N., Fidler, S., Urtasun, R.: Sports field localization via deep structured models. In: Proceedings of the IEEE Conference on Computer Vision and Pattern Recognition (CVPR), pp. 4012–4020. IEEE, Honolulu (HI), USA (2017). https://doi.org/10.1109/CVPR.2017.427
14. IFAB Law 1 - The field of play. https://www.theifab.com/laws/latest/the-field-of-play/#field-surface. Accessed 24 Mar 2024
15. Manafifard, M.: A review on camera calibration in soccer videos. Multimedia Tools Appl. **83**, 18427–18458 (2024). https://doi.org/10.1007/s11042-023-16145-8
16. Oo, Y.M., Jamsrandorj, A., Chao, V., Mun, K.R., Kim, J.: A residual attention-based EfficientNet homography estimation model for sports field registration. In: Proceedings of the 49th Annual Conference of the IEEE Industrial Electronics Society (IECON), pp. 1–7. IEEE, Singapore (2023). https://doi.org/10.1109/IECON51785.2023.10312494
17. Sha, L., Hobbs, J., Felsen, P., Wei, X., Lucey, P., Ganguly, S.: End-to-end camera calibration for broadcast videos. In: Proceedings of the IEEE/CVF Conference on Computer Vision and Pattern Recognition (CVPR), pp. 13624–13633. Seattle (WA), USA (2020). https://doi.org/10.1109/CVPR42600.2020.01364
18. Sharma, R.A., Bhat, B., Ghandi, V., Jawahar, C.V.: Automated top view registration of broadcast football videos. In: Proceedings of the IEEE/CVF Winter Conference on Applications of Computer Vision (WACV), pp. 305–313. IEEE, Lake Tahoe (NV), USA (2018). https://doi.org/10.1109/WACV.2018.00040
19. Stein, G.: Accurate internal camera calibration using rotation, with analysis of sources of error. In: Proceedings of the IEEE International Conference on Computer Vision, pp. 230–236. IEEE, Cambridge (MA), USA (1995). https://doi.org/10.1109/ICCV.1995.466781
20. Theiner, J., Ewerth, R.: TVCalib: camera calibration for sports field registration in soccer. In: Proceedings of the IEEE/CVF Winter Conference on Applications of Computer Vision (WACV), pp. 1166–1175. IEEE/CVF, Waikoloa (HI), USA (2023). https://doi.org/10.1109/WACV56688.2023.00122
21. Zhao, Z., Ye, D., Zhang, X., Chen, G., Zhang, B.: Improved direct linear transformation for parameter decoupling in camera calibration. Algorithms **9**(2), 1 (2016). https://doi.org/10.3390/a9020031

Smart Stadium: A Testbed for Research, Development, and Deployment of Sports Analytics Systems

Edward J. Coyle(✉)

VIP Program, Georgia Tech, 777 Atlantic Dr, Atlanta, GA 30332, USA
ejc@gatech.edu

Abstract. The Smart Stadium VIP team conducts research on sports analytics, machine learning, venue sensing, and fan engagement. The results are integrated and implemented in the Smart Stadium testbed during football games in the stadium at Georgia Tech.

Keywords: Sports Analytics · Machine Learning · Conflation · Sensor Networks · Infotainment · Apps · Testbed

1 Introduction

The Smart Stadium VIP team [1] has developed a testbed for research, design, development, and deployment of innovative approaches to sports analytics, venue sensing, and fan engagement. The focus has been on American Football (AF), but the approach can be applied to any sport.

The Smart Stadium Testbed at Georgia Tech (GT) is shown in Fig. 1. It captures and integrates many data sources: video clips of plays, official annotations of plays, accelerometer measurements from a sensor network that monitors the stadium's structure, and information gathered from fans. Time-synchronization of these sources, machine learning algorithms for identifying plays from video clips, conflation to fuse independent data sources for identifying plays, computation of the crowd's level of excitement, and solicitation of fans' predictions for the game enable: automated identification of plays; rankings of plays by fans' level of excitement; on-demand viewing of any play that has happened so far in the game; and phone apps that enhance fans' engagement with the game, the venue and other attendees [2–6].

This paper provides an overview of the testbed, focusing on new results on Machine Learning (ML) for automated play identification and annotation, structural vibration monitoring to measure fans' reactions, and phone apps for fan engagement.

2 Related Work

American Football (AF) teams at all levels are adopting the latest technologies to enhance both their performance and their fans' enjoyment of the game. There has thus been significant interest in the use of machine learning (ML) algorithms to analyze and classify

J. S. Dong et al. (Eds.): ISACE 2024, LNCS 14794, pp. 33–45, 2024.
https://doi.org/10.1007/978-3-031-69073-0_3

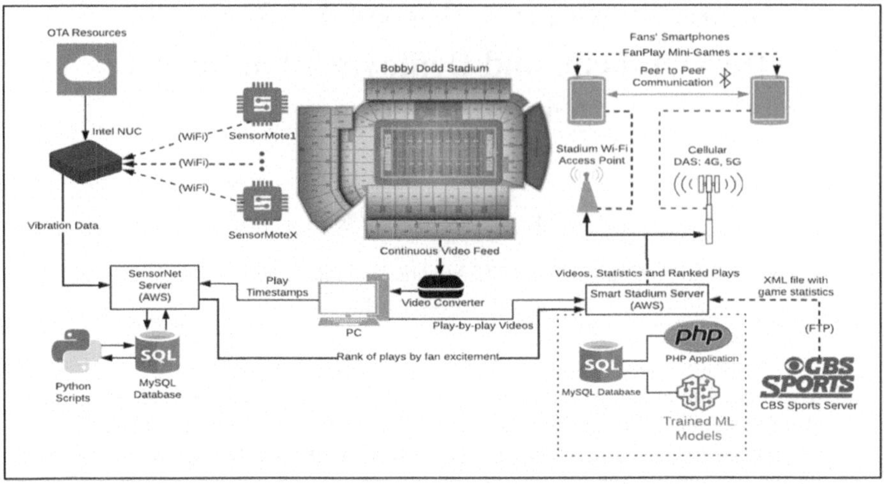

Fig. 1. The Smart Stadium Testbed. It enables integration of video clips of plays, official annotations of plays, accelerometer measurements from the stands, and input from fans. The Smart Stadium team worked with the GT Athletics Association to deploy these systems, capture 5000+ video clips of plays, and acquire play annotations for GT games since 2000.

plays in video of AF games. This is challenging in a team sport like AF due to the many players involved, their close contact, and their complex interactions.

Siddiquie, et al., presented a novel method for recognizing AF plays by utilizing a combination of player tracking and modeling techniques [7]. They developed a probabilistic framework that incorporated spatial and temporal relationships among players, enabling the identification of distinctive play patterns that achieved an average accuracy of 71.9%.

Ötting used Hidden Markov Models to predict the next play [8]. Using 300K observations, a prediction accuracy of 71.5% was achieved.

Chen et al. proposed a two-stage Convolutional Neural Network (CNN) architecture to recognize offensive and defensive play types in AF videos [9]. In the first stage, they used a CNN to extract spatial features from video frames, while the second stage utilized temporal CNNs to capture the temporal relationships between frames. The study achieved an overall recognition accuracy of 75.3% in distinguishing between offensive and defensive play types.

These studies demonstrated the benefits of fusing machine learning models and play predictions. We use a similar approach: a neural net for play classification from video clips and fusion of these classifications with predictions of the next play. Our innovation is the use of conflation for the fusion process, which increases the accuracy from 75.3%, mentioned above, to 87.2%.

3 Datasets

Our ML training dataset was built in-house. During GT home football games, we manually recorded video clips containing each play and tagged each with its official annotation. After data-cleaning we had 4722 plays clips. (See Appendix A.2.A, A.2.B.) for more details.

Our Markov model of play sequences is based on XML files containing play annotations and NCAA game statistics that are hosted by CBS Sports. This dataset included annotations for each play in 277 GT football games. We parsed these files to extract contextual and statistical data for 56,596 plays (see Appendix A.2.C).

4 Methods and Results

4.1 Computer Vision Model

Our objective is to automatically classify videos of football plays into 5 categories: Rushing Play, Passing Play, Extra Point or Field Goal, Punt, and Kickoff.

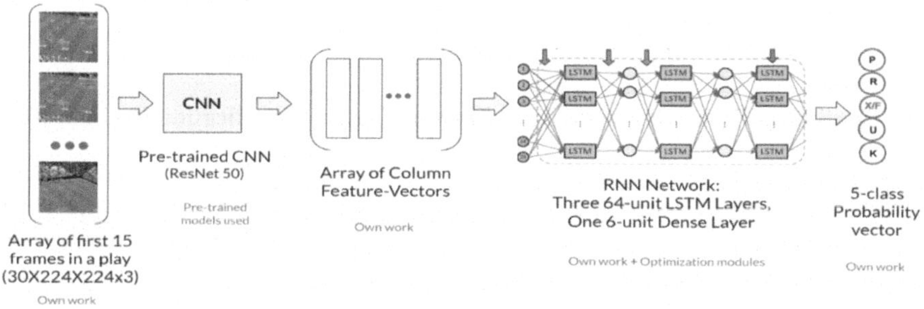

Fig. 2. Architecture of the Computer Vision Pipeline for classifying plays from Video clips

Our computer vision pipeline (Fig. 2) for classifying plays uses a pre-trained Convolutional Neural Network (ResNet50) to extract feature vectors from frames from the play clip.

The early layers of the ResNet50 architecture detect lines, edges and hence, general objects from the frames, making each of the hidden units in the network semantically significant [10]. Leveraging this ability to generate feature vectors for each static frame of our play clip, our system inputs the collection of feature vectors to a custom Recurrent Neural Network (see Appendix A.2.D) that outputs a final prediction for the 5 play types. We are currently exploring more modern and powerful architectures, such as 3D-CNNs [11].

4.2 Markov Model of Play Sequences

To ensure that the sequence of classifications from the Computer Vision model are consistent with the "grammar" of play sequences in football, we developed a Markov

Chain (MC) that contains the probabilities associated with all possible state transitions that can occur from one play to the next. The characteristics that label each state are: **Down (4):** 1, 2, 3, 4; **Play type (7):** run (R), pass (P), PAT (X), field goal (F), punt (U), kickoff (K), other (O); **Field Position (10):** 100-yard field divided into 10-yd buckets on the home side: [0, 9], [10, 19]… [40, 50] and opposition side: [50, 40], [39, 30]… [9, 0]; **Distance (yards) to 1st-down (6):** [1, 3], [4, 6], [7, 9], [10, 14], [15, 19], [20, 99]. This yielded 4 * 7 * 10 * 6 = 1680 states and a 1680 x 1680 state transition matrix. Each row maps a current state to all possible next states with the corresponding probability of moving to each state (See Appendix A.2.E) (Table 1).

Table 1. 4×4 MC based on Downs. P ($1^{st} \rightarrow 2^{nd}$) = 0.597; P ($1^{st} \rightarrow 3^{rd}$) = 0.00. Kickoffs + PATs are considered 1st-down plays, increasing P ($1^{st} \rightarrow 1^{st}$) to 0.403.

Down	1	2	3	4	*Total*
1	0.403	0.597	0.000	0.000	1
2	0.375	0.005	0.619	0.000	1
3	0.454	0.000	0.003	0.543	1
4	1.000	0.000	0.000	0.000	1

4.3 Conflating Computer Vision and Markov Chain Classification Probabilities

We considered several strategies for fusing the classification probabilities produced from the video clips by the Neural Network and the vector of conditional probabilities from the MC: confidence/belief thresholds, weighted averages, and encoding the previous play as an input to our Recurrent Neural Network itself.

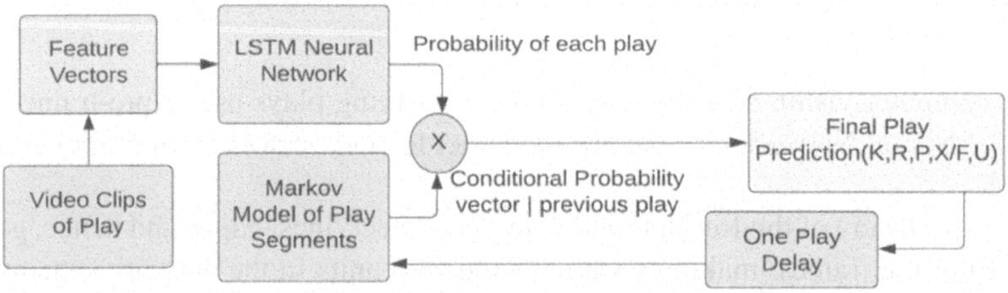

Fig. 3. Final Architecture: Conflation (entry-wise multiplication of classification probabilities) of the ML model output with clips as input with the predictions of MC based on the prior play minimizes effects of bad video clips, such as those contain the end of an ad instead of the play.

We found conflation [12], implemented as shown in Fig. 3, to be the optimal fusion strategy. Specifically, we created a final Neural Network that optimally calculates the specific weights to assign to each element of the 5-class probability vectors. This approach allowed us to use the full dataset and incorporate MC information in a unified model that performs optimal conflation. As for the tuning process, we performed hyper-parameter tuning once again to obtain the final conflated output. This led to an overall accuracy of 87.2%, with play-specific accuracies of [89.29, 89.65, 83.42, 87.36, 83.10] shown in Fig. 4.

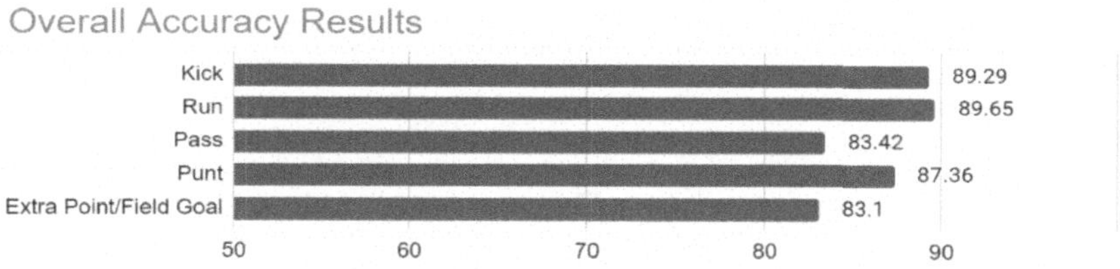

Fig. 4. Accuracy for the conflated Neural Net + Markov Model system. The overall accuracy achieved was 87.2%, compared to prior work that achieved 75.3%. With additional data sources, we believe our approach will be able to achieve an accuracy of ~95%, which would equivalent to ~1 classification error per game.

5 SensorNet Data – Measuring Fans' Excitement in Real-Time

We developed and deployed the Smart Stadium SensorNet to collect accelerometry data from the stands during games at GT's stadium. Figure 5 shows the data from a Miami vs GT game. Spikes correspond to significant plays as well as other events.

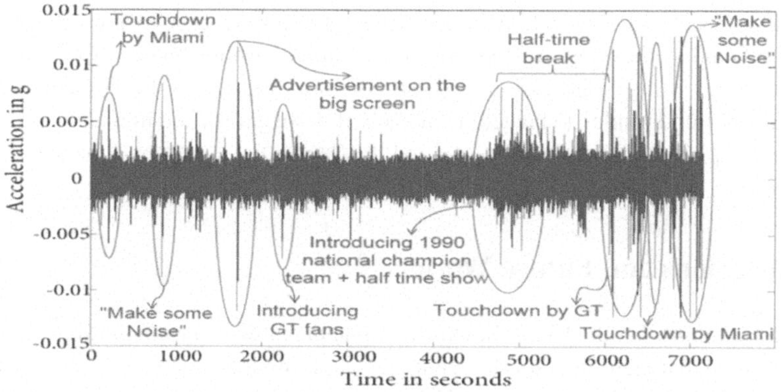

Fig. 5. Accelerometer data from the girders supporting the north stands of the stadium at GT. The spikes result from sudden increases in fan reactions – suddenly jumping up during an exciting plan, dancing to music, swaying to an ad, etc.

Time-stamped accelerometer data is collected by our wireless sensor nodes (see Appendix A.3), relayed to a ClusterHead, and forwarded it to a server that computes the "hype" - the energy that fans impart to the stands during each play. We will integrate this data into the ML model to improve the play classification accuracies.

Our SensorNet "hype" data predicts changes in momentum in the game. During Duke vs. GT 2016, Fig. 6 shows that our top 5 most "hype" plays matched changes in ESPN's probability of GT winning [6]. These analytics make it possible to share real-time win percentages with fans in the stands.

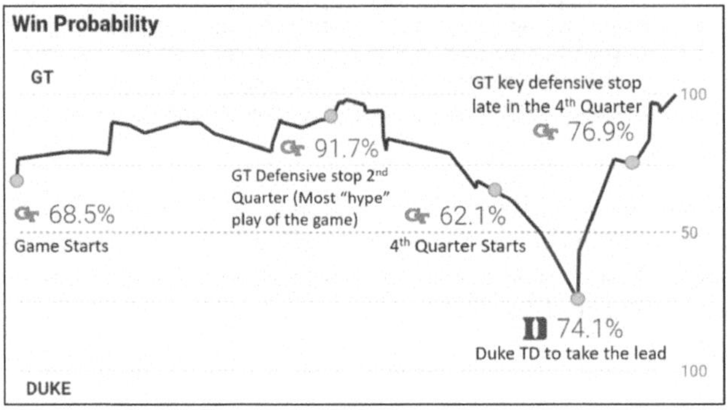

Fig. 6. The graph shows ESPN's estimation of the probability of GT winning as the game against Duke University progressed. The yellow circles show the times of the five plays during which fans generated the most "Hype". (Color figure online)

6 The FanPlay Suite of Applications – Engaging Fans

The FanPlay Suite aims to redefine the fan experience for Georgia Tech football fans at the Bobby Dodd stadium by making use of Machine Learning Models and SensorNet data. The Apps in the Suite include Play Prediction, Tap-Drive, Field-Goal Kicking games, and a Friend Finder. (The details of each of these games and how they utilize the data from the play classification systems and the SensorNet system will be the topic of a later paper).

7 Conclusions and Future Work

The Smart Stadium Testbed has shown the advantages of fully integrating the many sources of data available in a sports venue into a comprehensive sports analytics system. We have so far integrated game video, play annotations, fan reactions during the game, and fan input from apps. There are many additional data sources we are currently exploring. The challenge is always how to best fuse them with our existing systems to enhance coaches' and fans' analysis of and enjoyment of the game.

Acknowledgments. We thank the prior members of our Smart Stadium VIP team for gathering the ground truth data we used and for their initial efforts on the Computer Vision model and the SensorNet. We thank the leadership and staff of Georgia Tech Athletics for allowing our team access to the stadium to deploy our system to gather video and other data during games. This work was supported in part by Texas Instruments, Verizon, and Cisco Systems.

Disclosure of Interests. The authors have no competing interests relevant to this article's content.

A Appendix

A.1 List of Authors: Members of the Smart Stadium VIP Team

Subteam Leaders (alphabetical by surname): Ayman Ismail, Greg Lanier, Shail Patel, Pranav Raj, Saahil Sharma.

Team Members (alphabetical by surname): Diya Bhatia, Li-Chen Chang, Niranjan Deepak, Nick Eliacin, Andrew Gao, Ananya Garg, Aakash Gupta, Archie Goli, Yousef Ibrahim, Tiffany Jensen, Supratim Kundu, GinWook Lee, Henry Lin, Daniel Lowenthal, Rylan Klein, Kathryn Metheny, Sacchit Mittal, Srikar Narayan, Mit Patel, Sahil Punwani, Rugved Rajendra, Rahul Rajesh, Ryan Rodriguez, Brianna Rudolph, Jack Sherling, Rushil Sudunagunta, Nyshad Williams.

Advisers (alphabetical by surname): Edward Coyle, Deepa Phanish, Pedro Pinto.

A.2 Machine Learning

A. **Data Cleaning Details**
During Georgia Tech home football games for the NCAA Football seasons from 2010 through 2017, past and current members of our team manually recorded video clips containing each play labeled with the official NCAA annotation of the play. This gave our team a dataset of 6,056 football videos. Exploring this dataset, we immediately noticed errors with some recordings, including some that began significantly before or after the play, others with overlaid graphics/ads, some with changing camera angles during the play, and even a few recordings that contained no play.

Fig. 7. A frame from a video clip with an overlaid graphic during a play. This is an example of an unusable play clip that was removed from our original dataset.

Figure 7 shows one of the 1,000+ play clips we cleaned from our original dataset. Like this recording error, many of the errors found in our independent manual recording of videos reflect common problems associated with the current state of college football play delivery and analysis. Specifically, our data cleaning process included visual inspection of all 6,056 Georgia Tech football plays in our dataset to identify recording errors. Each video clip is typically 7–15 s long and consists of one single football play, such as a completed pass or a field goal kick (or potentially no play at all). The result of this intensive process was a cleaned dataset of usable plays for training.

Plays with fundamental recording errors, like "No play", or "Duplicate", that were deemed unusable were excluded from the dataset. Minor errors like "Late" or "Minor graphic" were reviewed on a case-by-case basis: in some cases, the error was deemed not significant enough to affect how the play was classified. For the plays labeled "Early", the video was simply trimmed to the actual start of the play to mitigate the issue. After scrubbing the data set of all recording errors, the size of the cleaned dataset was 4,722 plays.

B. **Data Exploration Process**

Fig. 8. A frame from video of a play that our model correctly classified as a pass.

To gain a better general understanding of our dataset, while watching each play clip to identify recording errors, we also identified complex/rare play clips that would be harder to classify. For example, Figs. 8 and 9 both show frames from video clips that were classified as a pass; while the play in Fig. 8 was a forward pass, the play in Fig. 9 was a backwards pitch, where the ball is "passed" backwards. While this is technically a run play, it was understandably misclassified as a pass.

Figure 10 below lists the possible labels for each play clip, with some labels corresponding to recording errors and others corresponding to complex plays that we believed to be inherently difficult to classify.

The motivation to label and review these rare play types, such as Lateral and Interception, was to identify potential weaknesses of the existing Computer Vision pipeline we had in place. To test our hypotheses, we measured the model accuracy for each irregular play type, for which results are shown in Fig. 11.

Fig. 9. A frame from a video of a pitch run that our model incorrectly classified as a pass.

Normal	No notable errors
Early	The recording started too far before the snap
Late	The recording started too far after the snap
No Play	The ball was not snapped or extraneous footage like a crowd closeup
Duplicate	The recording is a copy of another video
Quarterback Scramble	An improvised run by the quarterback outside of the pocket
Sack	The quarterback was tackled behind the line of scrimmage without throwing a pass
Interception	A pass was caught by the opposing team
Lateral	A backwards pass
Fumble	A loss of possession during the play not due to an interception
Long Kick Return	A kick return longer than fifteen yards
Long Run	A run longer than fifteen yards
Fake Kick	A false punt or field goal attempt where the ball is run or thrown instead
Minor Graphic	A graphic covering part of the screen
Full-Screen Graphic	A graphic covering the majority of the screen
Miscellaneous	A recording error not covered by another label

Fig. 10. The labels used for video clips during the Data Cleaning process.

As shown in Fig. 11, we observed that the accuracy of the model on play clips containing most irregular play types performs similarly, if not better, than the accuracy of the model on play clips containing normal (Simple Run, Simple Pass, etc.) plays. We noticed that our standalone Computer Vision model performs worse on the Long Run, Lateral, and Fake Punt/FG play types, which are all inherently confounding play types, even to a trained human eye. As the play develops, Laterals and Long Runs show many similarities to a typical pass play and Fake Punts/FGs may appear similar to realistic Punts/FGs. From this experiment, we hypothesized that the sequential context provided by the Markov Model can assist in our classification

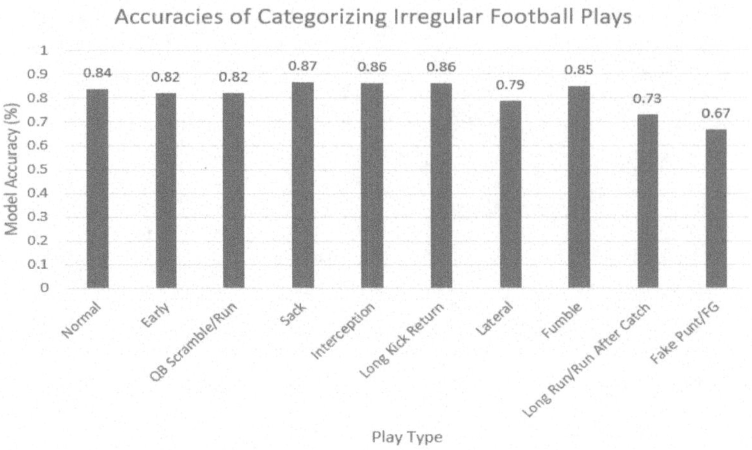

Fig. 11. Overall Model Accuracy for Problematic/Complex Play Types.

task. For example, it is much more likely for a Fake Punt to occur while on the opponent's 40-yard line than on a team's own 10-yard line.

C. **XML Entry Example**

The text below shows the header and and example row of the CSV files of play annotations:

```
playID,type,clock,token,context,text
24,"4,5,27",P,,"PASS:1,I,82,*","H,3,6,H42","Dantzler, Woodr
pass incomplete to Robinson, Jacki."
```

D. **Hyperparameter Tuning: Computer Vision Model**

Initially, we created and tuned our Computer Vision pipeline on our local systems with an 800-play sample. However, to utilize the entire dataset, we migrated all our models to the Partnership for an Advanced Computing Environment (PACE) [9] Instructional Cluster Environment (ICE) at Georgia Tech. We used The Open OnDemand interface for our Jupyter notebooks, because it allows access to PACE clusters through a web browser. On this cluster, our model is trained using a 24-core node hosting Dual Intel Xeon Gold 6226 CPUs @ 2.7 GHz, 192 GB RAM and the Nvidia Tesla V-100 GPU. Our software stack mirrors commercial setups as it consists of locally built Anaconda3 Python 3.9 environments with OpenCV, FFmpeg, Pandas, TensorFlow, Keras, ScikitLearn, and CUDA Toolkit.

Wanting to maximize the performance of our Computer Vision architecture, we implemented a Grid Search algorithm for hyperparameter tuning. The specific parameters we included were the duration of the play clip, batch size, frames per second, epochs, activation function, loss function, and optimization algorithm. We tested all combinations of these hyperparameters on both the pre-trained ResNet50 and VGG16 Convolutional Neural Network architectures, along with the images in Grayscale or

RGB, respectively. Hence, there were 9 parameters we tuned in combination. We performed this extensive hyperparameter tuning process locally on the 800-play sample dataset, and eventually on the entire dataset.

E. **Markov Chain**

The matrix is built in row-major order, meaning that an entry M[i, j] represents P(i → j), the probability of going from state i to state j, and the sum of each row must be 1. Each row maps a current state to a list of possible next states with the corresponding probability of moving to each state. Rows will have entries that are 0 because certain play transitions, such as a kickoff on 2nd down, are impossible. Other play transitions that are unlikely, such as a field goal or punt before 4th down, will generally have lower transition probabilities.

Starting with the Down matrix, a 4×4 matrix of transition probabilities between the 4 Down states, we gradually added new states to our matrix to decrease relevance. From the Down matrix, we then built the Down-Type, Down-Type-FieldPosition, and finally the complete 1680×1680 Down-Type-FieldPosition-DistanceToGo matrix.

From this base matrix, we then added the Type, Field Position, and Distance fields consecutively to the respective matrices. These matrices are only differentiated from each other based on the specific input parameters used to define a state. Alongside the Computer Vision model, the matrix is then used to influence the final decision by providing calculated probabilities of the most likely next state/play type.

To address the run bias due to GT's run-heavy offense, we tested the use of the general Markov Model, which was trained on all NCAA plays from 2021–2023.

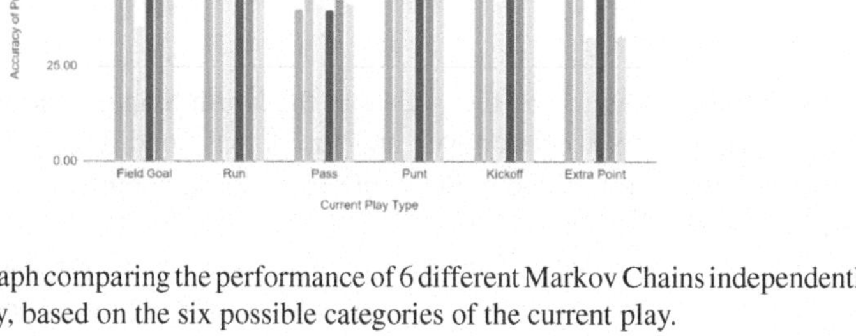

Fig. 12. Graph comparing the performance of 6 different Markov Chains independently predicting the next play, based on the six possible categories of the current play.

As shown in Fig. 12, we compared the performance of three varieties of the Original (Georgia Tech data only) Markov Chain with the same three corresponding Markov chains trained on all NCAA plays from the past 3 seasons. We tested the performance of these Markov chains on solely Georgia Tech statistical data to ensure consistency with the Computer Vision model, in which we only have Georgia Tech video data to work with. It is important to note that as we only have video data from Georgia Tech games, we cannot accurately gauge the performance of NCAA Markov chains as part of our overall Conflated model until our model incorporates video recordings representative of the entire NCAA's plays. Ideally, we would develop unique Markov chains for each NCAA football team to accurately represent their unique tendencies. For teams which are unable to develop their own Markov chains, we suggest the general NCAA chain be used as a baseline approximation. For our Conflation process, we solely use the original Georgia Tech Markov chains.

The results demonstrated in Fig. 12 are primarily for informational purposes, rather than information we use to derive key conclusions. Nonetheless, the Markov Model particularly excels in predicting certain play types such as Extra Point. This is a quality we used to increase the accuracy of predicting the Extra Point type in our final conflated model.

F. **The Hardware Comprising the Smart Stadium SensorNet**

Deployment and orientations of four Sensor Motes on the girders of the North of Bobby Dodd Stadium:

The image below shows:

- (B) A sensor mote mounted on the girders in the North Stands. The small white enclosure contains the accelerometer and the signal conditioning board. The accelerometer enclosure is held to the girder by a strong magnet.
- (C) The microcontroller, battery-pack, etc. Of the sensor mote.
- (D and E) The SensorNet CLusterHead: The Intel NUC that serves as a clusterhead; a ZigBee Coordinator; PoE for remote rebooting; and power supply.

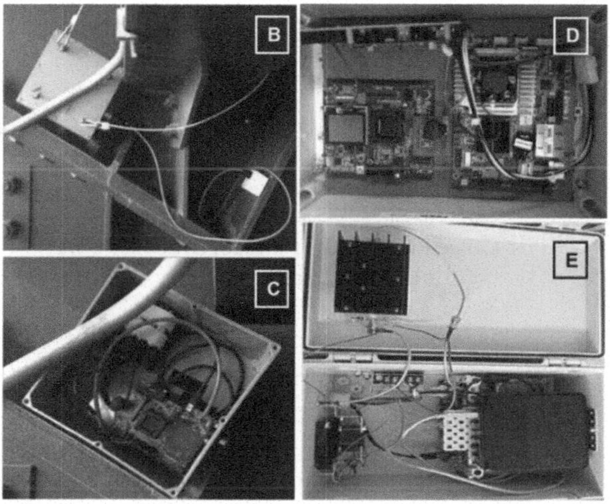

References

1. Smart Stadium | Vertically Integrated Projects. https://vip.gatech.edu/node/622
2. Zhong, X., Chan, H.-H., Rogers, T.J., Rosenberg, C.P., Coyle, E.J.: The development and eStadium testbeds for research and development of wireless services for large-scale sports venues. In: 2nd International Conference on Testbeds and Research Infrastructures for the Development of Networks and Communities, TRIDENTCOM 2006, p. 9, pp. – 348 (2006)
3. Zhong, X., Coyle, E.J.: eStadium: a wireless "living lab" for safety and infotainment applications. In: 2006 First International Conference on Communications and Networking in China, pp. 1–6 (2006)
4. Ault, A., Krogmeier, J.V., Dunlop, S.R., Coyle, E.J.: eStadium: the mobile wireless football experience. In: 2008 Third International Conference on Internet and Web Applications and Services, pp. 644–649 (2008)
5. Phanish, D., et al.: A wireless sensor network for monitoring the structural health of a football stadium. In: 2015 IEEE 2nd World Forum on Internet of Things (WF-IoT), pp. 471–477 (2015)
6. Li, H., Pinto, P.H.R., Phanish, D., Abler, R.T., Coyle, E.J.: Good vibrations: an IoPT testbed for infotainment in a football stadium. In: 2020 IEEE 6th World Forum on Internet of Things (WF-IoT), pp. 1–6 (2020)
7. Siddiquie, B., Yacoob, Y., Davis, L.: Recognizing Plays in American Football Videos (2009)
8. Ötting, M.: Predicting play calls in the National Football League using hidden Markov models. IMA J. Manag. Math. **32**, 535–545 (2021). https://doi.org/10.1093/imaman/dpab005
9. Chen, S., et al.: Play type recognition in real-world football video. In: IEEE Winter Conference on Applications of Computer Vision, pp. 652–659 (2014)
10. Zhou, B., Khosla, A., Lapedriza, À., Oliva, A., Torralba, A.: Object Detectors Emerge in Deep Scene CNNs. CoRR. abs/1412.6856 (2014)
11. Tran, D., Wang, H., Torresani, L., Ray, J., LeCun, Y., Paluri, M.: A closer look at spatiotemporal convolutions for action recognition. In: 2018 IEEE/CVF Conference on Computer Vision and Pattern Recognition, pp. 6450–6459 (2018)
12. Hill, T.P., Miller, J.: How to combine independent data sets for the same quantity. Chaos: Interdisc. J. Nonlinear Sci. **21**, 033102 (2011). https://doi.org/10.1063/1.3593373

Lending a Hand in Bringing Ballcarriers Down

Cecil Isaih Battiste IV[1], Charles Jeffrey Danoff[2(✉)], and Christopher Hanes[3]

[1] Fireball Findings, Atlanta, GA 30076, USA
isaih@fireballfindings.com
[2] Post Office Box 802738, Chicago, IL 60680, USA
contact@mr.danoff.org
[3] Lombard, IL 60148, USA
chris@chrishanes.com

Abstract. In this paper we examine National Football League (NFL) Next Gen Stats data to uncover insights on how defensive teammates collectively bring down offensive ballcarriers. Traditional defensive statistics focus on individual tacklers, which is certainly vital, but in a team game there is often more than one defender who contributes to the stop. This paper was our submission for the 2024 NFL Big Data Bowl to "create metrics that assign value to elements of tackling". We found that individuals who slowed down ballcarriers had a strong positive correlation with tackles and that the distance that defensive players were from the offensive ballcarrier was a statistically significant predictor of ballcarrier speed in its deceleration path down to zero. This paper aims to contribute to the conference topics of player evaluation and performance analysis.

Keywords: Individual Contributions · NFL Defender · Gridiron Football · Sports Analytics

1 Introduction

The importance of studying film for National Football League (NFL) coaches and players cannot be overstated. Countless hours are dedicated to the act of analyzing an opponent's every move over the course of a season. Offensive coaches self-scout their tendencies and play-calling patterns to stay one step ahead of opposing defenses. Meanwhile, defensive coaches look for anything they can learn about the offenses they will face in upcoming weeks, hoping to counter offensive game plans. High-impact players will jump off the screen with flashes of brilliance between the sidelines for all to see, but what about unheralded players who do the little things right?

These players deserve credit too, and their contributions might not be spotted on a consistent basis since their actions may not result in a tackle for themselves, but it may help set one up for a teammate. Teams currently tally assisted tackle metrics. However, this project aims to go deeper than the act of tackling. We are interested in the ballcarrier's entire journey that led to the point where they could be brought down rather than just the final action of a tackle taking place. Therefore, our goal is to add a new variable

J. S. Dong et al. (Eds.): ISACE 2024, LNCS 14794, pp. 46–59, 2024.
https://doi.org/10.1007/978-3-031-69073-0_4

that coaches can account for in their statistical evaluations aside from just tackles and assisted tackles.

This project was made possible by using NFL Next Gen Stats player tracking and Pro Football Focus data from the 2022 NFL season, weeks 1–9. In it, we aim to shine light on defenders who contribute to bringing a ballcarrier down by slowing them down in the first place. After all, the objective of every team's defense as a whole is to work together to bring ballcarriers down as soon as possible, saving every yard[1] they can, and keeping ballcarriers out of the endzone[2] on each play. Many players are taught since their youth playing days that even if they cannot make an individual tackle themselves, as long as they slow a ballcarrier down until the cavalry arrives that they have fulfilled their duties and contributed on that play.

We believe that by analyzing ballcarrier speed and defender distance data we can assign credit to individual defenders who influence a ballcarrier's speed. By doing so we can identify who can be credited with the largest deceleration on any given play. These individual credits for slowing ballcarriers down will be referred to as *slowdowns*. The data was provided as part of the 2024 NFL Big Data Bowl competition on Kaggle [1]. Our submission was for the coaching presentation track, with the purpose of augmenting coaches' defensive player evaluation as an added layer to their film study throughout the season. Although we did not win the competition [2], we believe that our insights are still valuable for coaches at all levels to consider for implementation.

Our findings may even have implications for the other game of football that we call soccer back at home. Is working collectively with your teammates to slow down the ballcarrier not important for winning the Champions League as well? Although gridiron football is played in a non-continuous fashion, separated by individual plays, we believe that the two sports have at least one important shared aspect between them. We believe that defenders who can interrupt the flow of the offense and the advancement of the ball towards the goal or endzone should be evaluated and credited accordingly. Our assumption is that they would provide value in either version of football.

2 Methodology and Findings

Our approach to this project began with ballcarrier speed data. The idea was to track the ballcarrier's speed in terms of yards per second (yds/sec), as well as miles per hour[3] (mph) from the beginning of the play until the end. We focused on the apex of speed on any given play and aimed to track the path down until the end of the play.

---

[1] Gridiron football is typically played in the United States of America, which is not on the metric system. Instead, yards (0.914 m) are used to measure the field of play. The distance between the endzones is 100 yards.

[2] The endzone is where teams aim to end up on each offensive possession. This is where touchdowns are scored, resulting in six points for the offense which is the most points possible on any singular play.

[3] Since the USA is not on the metric system, miles (1.609 km) per hour is a common form of measuring speed.

For an example of ballcarrier speed on one play, consider this completion[4] to Devin Singletary of the Buffalo Bills in the 2022 season opener against the Los Angeles Rams. Here is a screenshot from the visualization we made of the entire play (Fig. 1):

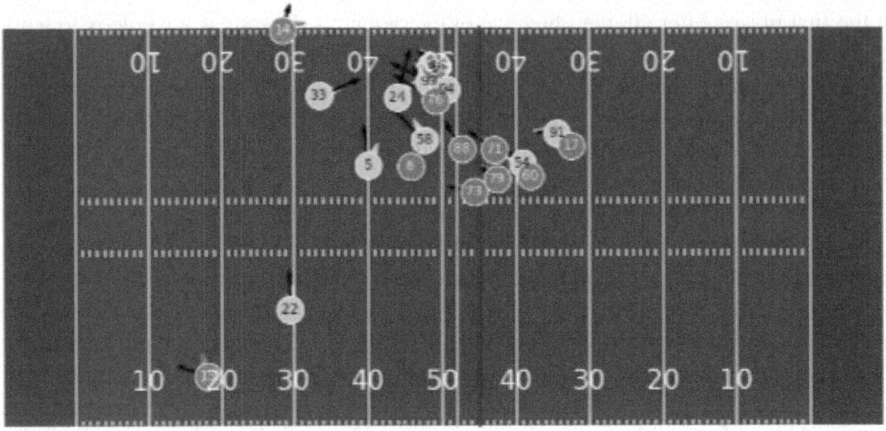

Fig. 1. This image is a representation of a single frame from an entire play where Buffalo Bills Quarterback[5] Josh Allen has passed the ball to his Running Back[6], Devin Singletary, who has evaded the defense (represented in yellow) for some positive yardage before being caught by the defense (represented in orange). Each player is represented by their jersey number in the circles, and the black arrows denote the direction that they are facing, thanks to the tracking data. This was Game #2022090800 and Play #122.

This next chart shows Singletary's speed by frame during the play (Fig. 2):

The running back (RB) Singletary's speed gradually accelerates at first, and tops out at 12.8 mph. From there it is all downhill. Our approach was to measure the decreases in speed across the frames after peak speed. Here is what that looked like on this particular play (Fig. 3):

Each of these decreases in speed, by frame, are able to be isolated and quantified. Since we wanted to assign credit for them we brought in the defender distance data as well. The idea here is that a defender should be given credit for causing a decrease in ballcarrier speed, however small the decrease might be. Just like a tackle or an assisted tackle can be recorded, we can also measure slowdowns for each defender's statistics on any given play, game, or across many games.

---

4 A completion occurs when a forward pass is transferred from one player to another and caught successfully.

5 A Quarterback in Gridiron football is a position that is viewed as the most important, as they are the conductor of the offense. They are responsible for the distribution of the football to different players and leading the team down the field into the endzone.

6 A Running Back in Gridiron football is mostly tasked with carrying the football and running forward for as many yards as possible on any given play. They also have responsibilities of blocking at times, as well as receiving the football via a pass through the air.

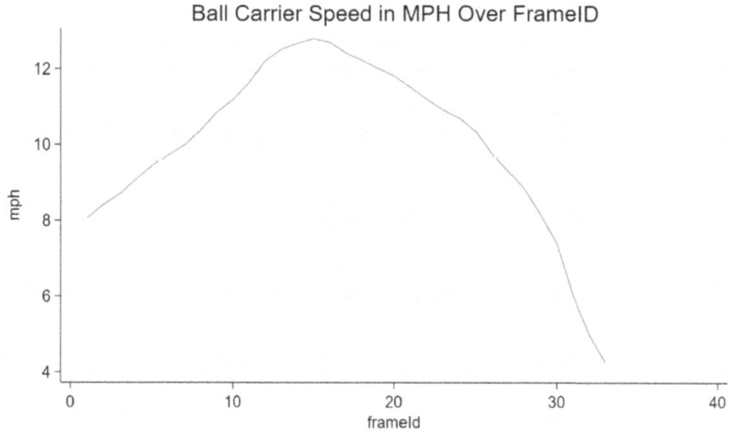

Fig. 2. This image represents what a fairly typical speed distribution would look like for a ballcarrier on a typical offensive play. In this case we are measuring Singletary's speed on play #122 of Game #2022090800.

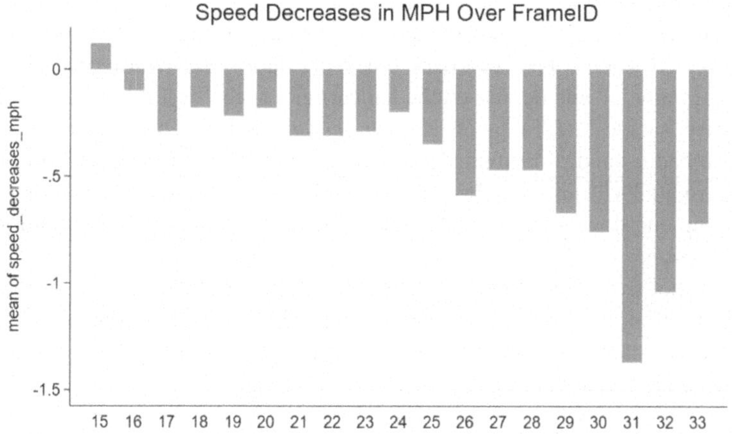

Fig. 3. Although the overall trend in this visual shows that decreases in speed were growing larger over the course of the play, the sharpest decrease was near the end, which would represent a typical play as speed should drop sharply to near zero just before a player is tackled.

In order to do so we found the distances of all eleven defenders for every frame for all plays in weeks 1–9 of the 2022 NFL season. By focusing on the post-peak ballcarrier speed, we measured the slowdowns and who should be given credit for each. Ultimately, we decided that the nearest defender who caused the ensuing slowdown should be given credit for that slowdown. The logic being that there is a natural lag effect. If a slowdown occurred in one frame the assumption is that the nearest defender in the previous frame was the one who caused the ballcarrier's speed to decrease.

For the Singletary play, the speed decreases in mph and yds/sec were tracked, and so were the slowdowns. Thus, each defender who was the closest in terms of distance was given credit for their ballcarrier slowdown contribution for the next frame, so long as it was after peak ballcarrier speed.

The defender who made the largest contribution on that play was Linebacker[7] (LB) Bobby Wagner. He contributed a speed decrease of 1.37 mph on that play. Highlighting all slowdowns and measuring the top contribution for any given play could be useful in the event that a coaching staff would want to review one play and figure out who contributed the most to slowing the ballcarrier down.

This would be especially true if that top slowdown contributor did not actually end up making the tackle or an assisted tackle. That would be a case where an unsung hero would be getting their due credit. In this case, Wagner did make the tackle, but that is not always the case.

In the next example play from the Week 1 game between the San Francisco 49ers and Chicago Bears, the description of the play from the play-by-play data on Pro Football Reference [3] is "Justin Fields pass complete short middle to David Montgomery for 16 yards (tackle by Tashaun Gipson)".

However, when watching the game tape from that play you can see multiple San Francisco 49er defenders impacted the speed of Bears running back Montgomery, not just the 49ers Safety[8] Gipson.

This is a perfect example of where a slowdown credit can highlight a contribution that would be missed when solely reviewing box score data[9]. Fred Warner had the biggest slowdown at frame 57 and decreased the ballcarrier's speed by 1.62 miles per hour.

Defensive Tackle[10] (DT) Javon Kinlaw as well as LBs Dre Greenlaw and Fred Warner also had a hand in bringing down Montgomery by getting near him. None of them were credited with an assist. Instead, Kinlaw and Greenlaw recorded missed tackles. By leveraging our slowdown metric, coaches could give them credit in addition to the tackle for Gipson.

A screenshot from our second animation highlights the players who were close to Montgomery all along the play. By parsing out the other eight defenders it becomes easier to see the main three defenders who contributed to bringing Montgomery down when viewing the full animation (Fig. 4):

[7] In Gridiron football a Linebacker is a defensive player usually tasked with making the most amount of tackles on the defense as they are in the middle of the field. They are meant to stop running plays, and at times assist in pass defense as well, making them versatile members of the defense.

[8] In Gridiron football a Safety is usually in the very rear of the defense, as they are the last line of defense preventing opposing ballcarriers from entering the endzone.

[9] Box score data is where counting statistics and some advanced statistics from the game can be seen.

[10] In Gridiron football a Defensive Tackle is typically the largest player on the defense, with their main responsibility being to create pressure at the point of attack for an offense. They are as close as possible to the ball at the beginning of each play and they use their size and strength to occupy blockers and stymying the offensive gameplan from the beginning of each play.

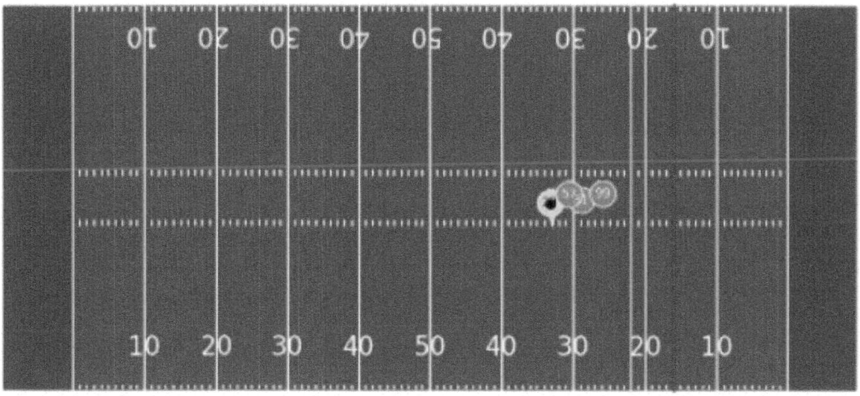

Fig. 4. This figure highlights only key defenders in Play #364 in Game #22091102. In short, the three defenders chosen were the ones who contributed the most to making the stop. The full animation can be seen here: https://www.youtube.com/watch?v=aUMYHo6KHOw. For the real play, please refer to this web page: https://www.nfl.com/videos/49ers-vs-chiefs-highlights-from-super-bowl-lviii-on-nickelodeon.

2.1 Analyzing Trends

We have gone over a couple of plays now as examples, which can be helpful for coaches' evaluation of players in a micro sense. However, it would be best to let patterns and trends emerge by reviewing slowdowns in a macro sense. In this case, that would mean over 9 weeks of games. By this point outliers would not have as strong of an effect on the final results, leading to accurate assessments of a defender's abilities.

Here we observe the relationship between the sum of slowdowns and the sum of individual tackles. We found that the correlation between total accumulated slowdowns in mph and tackles was 0.92 (Fig. 5):

Here we can see the relationship between the sum of slowdowns and assisted tackles. The correlation that we observed was 0.82 (Fig. 6):

Since we have observed such strong correlations between both tackles and assists by the sum of slowdowns in mph, slowdowns prove to be valuable in assessing a defender's contributions to the team's goals of tackling ballcarriers as soon as possible. Even if a defender does not record a lot of tackles or assists in any one game in particular, it is possible that they had a great effect on the game if they accumulated a lot of slowdowns.

2.2 Top Performers

We became interested in finding out who among all of the defenders in the NFL in 2022 were best at accumulating slowdowns across the first nine games of the season. We thought this might make for a good sanity test or proof of concept to demonstrate the value of the slowdowns metric in hopes that it not only correlated with both individual and assisted tackles, but also overall high-quality defender play. Here were the top 10 defenders in terms of slowdowns (Fig. 7):

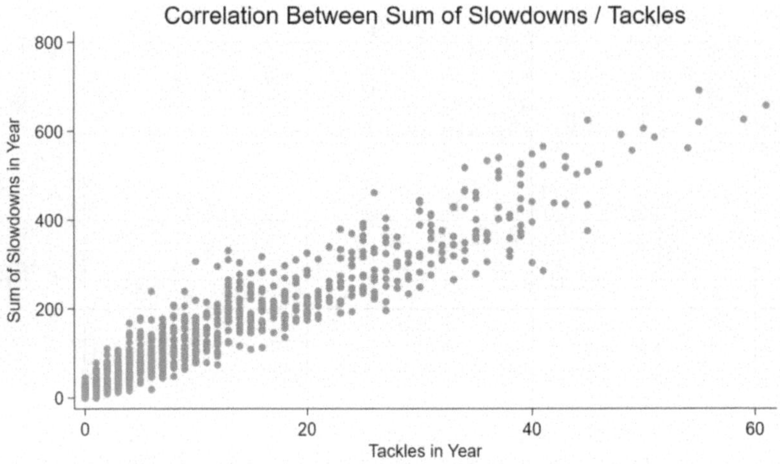

Fig. 5. This scatterplot shows the correlation between sum of slowdowns and sum of tackles over the first nine weeks of the 2022 NFL season. A strong, positive correlation has been revealed.

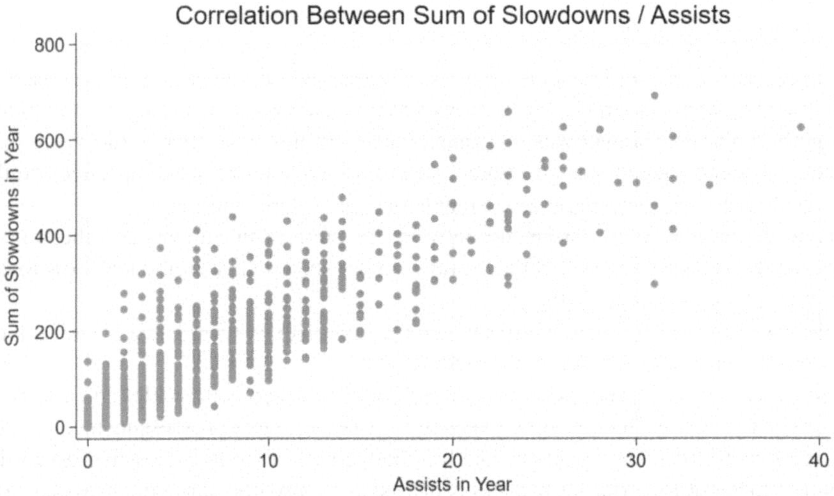

Fig. 6. This scatterplot shows the correlation between sum of slowdowns and sum of assisted tackles over the course of the first nine weeks of the 2022 NFL season. A strong, positive correlation is shown, but it is weaker than the relationship between the sum of slowdowns and sum of individual tackles across that timeframe.

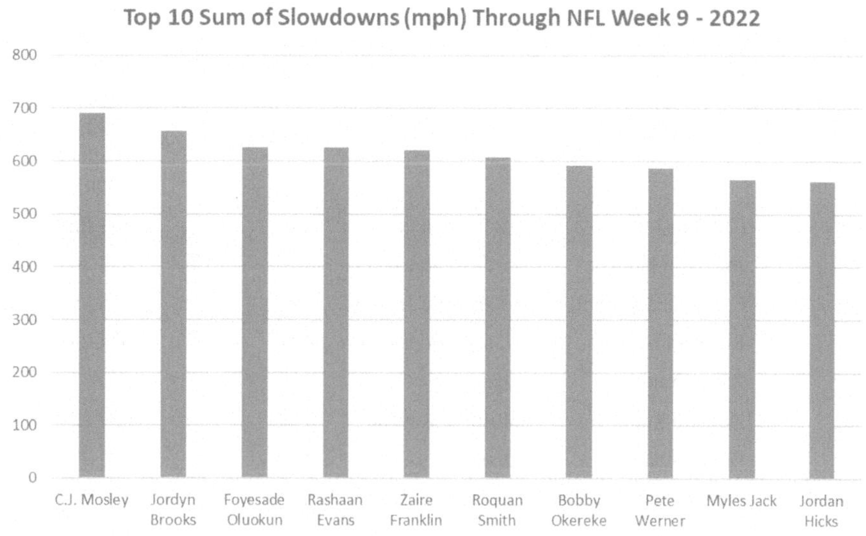

Fig. 7. This bar chart displays the top ten players by sum of slowdowns. C.J. Mosley earned first place with nearly 700 points worth of accumulated slowdowns (in mph) in the span of the first nine weeks of the 2022 NFL season.

Each of these players is clearly contributing to the defenses in a large way, and they each deserve to receive credit for doing so. Although it is unlikely that coaching staffs have not noticed their tenacity in pursuit of ballcarriers, it may be possible that other players on the complete list are hidden gems. If so, coaching staffs and general managers would do well to identify those high-value contributors early on and give them more playing time and sign them to contract extensions.

To say that the players who made the top ten sum of slowdowns list are quite accomplished would be an understatement. C.J. Mosley and Roquan Smith made the 2022 All-Pro team[11] [4]. The table below shows that every player who made the top ten sum of slowdowns list and who played 16 or more games also ended up making the top ten total tackles list by the end of the season, except for Jordan Hicks of the Minnesota Vikings, who finished 18th with 129 tackles. It appears safe to say that as long as a player stays healthy, slowdown data is a great predictor of tackles and therefore, contributions to the defense.

Not surprisingly, we found that all members of the top-ten in terms of sum of slowdowns were Linebackers. This position group is generally placed in the center of the defense and is responsible for being involved in almost every play, whether it be against the run or pass. Due to this responsibility, it is logical that Linebackers would be provided with ample opportunities to rack up lots of slowdowns over the course of nine weeks (Table 2).

[11] An All-Pro player is one who was selected by the media as the best at their respective position for that year. It is a very prestigious award due to the scarcity and the fact that fan voting is not considered.

Table 1. This table outlines the top-ten players in terms of the sum of slowdowns (mph).

Sum of Slowdowns 2022 Weeks 1–9 Rank (mph)	Player	Team	Player Position	Sum of Slowdowns 2022 Weeks 1–9 (mph)
1	C.J. Mosley	New York Jets	LB	691.02
2	Jordyn Brooks	Seattle Seahawks	LB	657.76
3	Foyesade Oluokun	Jacksonville Jaguars	LB	625.95
4	Rashaan Evans	Atlanta Falcons	LB	624.83
5	Zaire Franklin	Indianapolis Colts	LB	620.37
6	Roquan Smith	Baltimore Ravens	LB	606.22
7	Bobby Okereke	Indianapolis Colts	LB	592.47
8	Pete Werner	New Orleans Saints	LB	586.51
9	Myles Jack	Pittsburgh Steelers	LB	565.25
10	Jordan Hicks	Minnesota Vikings	LB	561.30

Table 2. This table retains the sorting from Table 1, but now displays tackling data.

Total Tackles 2022 Rank	Player	Total Tackles	Games Played	Tackles per Game
9	C.J. Mosley	158	17	9.29
6	Jordyn Brooks	161	16	10.06
1	Foyesade Oluokun	184	17	10.82
7	Rashaan Evans	159	17	9.35
4	Zaire Franklin	167	17	9.82
3	Roquan Smith	169	17	9.94
10	Bobby Okereke	151	17	8.88
99	Pete Werner	80	12	6.67
48	Myles Jack	104	15	6.93
18	Jordan Hicks	129	17	7.59

What we found interesting here is that although most of the members of the top-ten for sum of slowdowns also finished the season in the top-ten for total tackles, C.J. Mosley only finished in 9th place for total tackles as opposed to 1st for sum of slowdowns. Since he earned All-Pro honors for the 2022 season along with Roquan Smith, this suggests that there is inherent value in a metric such as slowdowns, as it captures what the eye is seeing in terms of a player being involved and influencing plays. In short, individual tackles are shown to not be the end-all and be-all. Slowdowns provide a way to actually quantify the player tracking and defensive influence data that our eyes seek out as spectators watch the games or when coaches study film (Table 3).

Table 3. This table retains the original order, while displaying salary and experience data.

Player	Years of Experience	2022 Base Salary (in Millions)	LB Base Salary Ranking 2022
C.J. Mosley	8	$1.12	69
Jordyn Brooks	3	$1.72	30
Foyesade Oluokun	5	$1.50	35
Rashaan Evans	5	$1.03	87
Zaire Franklin	5	$1.10	79
Roquan Smith	5	$0.57	240
Bobby Okereke	4	$2.54	17
Pete Werner	2	$0.91	141
Myles Jack	7	$1.50	49
Jordan Hicks	8	$1.45	50

Unfortunately for Linebackers, their position group has become devalued as of late in terms of their salary share relative to other position groups. This would explain the low salaries, but not the rankings. Curiously, the Linebacker salary rankings [5] shown here for 2022 did not correlate well with slowdown data. Experience would not be a factor for the low salaries shown here, as the years of experience listed here would suggest that many of these players are in prime earning years.

The likely answer is that Edge Rushers/Defensive Ends/Outside Linebackers[12] and Linebackers have been categorically lumped together as a recent trend in the NFL. Edge Rushers, Defensive Ends, and Outside Linebackers in certain types of defensive schemes tend to get paid much more than Interior Linebackers. With most players on this list being not being Edge Rushers or that archetype of Outside Linebacker, that would explain the discrepancy in pay relative to their Outside counterparts. Other factors for pay would include draft position and scarcity or team needs at the time. Player contracts are structured so that the position in which the player was drafted matters in terms of what they can expect to be paid, moving from different scales depending on when they were

[12] Edge Rushers are players who are primarily tasked with lining up on the outer edge of a defensive front, facing the offensive line and near the line of scrimmage. They are tasked with applying pressure on opposing Quarterbacks, and setting the "edge" so that they can contain ballcarriers within their own or their teammates reach.

selected by their teams in the NFL Draft[13] or in the Undrafted Free Agent (UDFA[14]) pool. Teams hope to discover "diamonds in the rough" when it comes to finding talent in the UDFA pool that all teams passed on, originally.

Regarding the hidden gem aspect that slowdown data might provide, a player like Pete Werner of New Orleans stands out. After the first nine weeks of the NFL season he finished 8th in sum of slowdowns, but he only had two years of experience up to that point, and in terms of Linebacker pay he was ranked #141 for the year.

Based on a profile like this we would predict that this sort of player might be one to watch out for in terms of future success at the Linebacker position with an increase in salary to compensate for his efforts. This might hinge on slowdown ability assuming that they can stay healthy. Given the 0.82–0.92 correlation between slowdowns and assisted or individual tackles, combined tackles can be a proxy for slowdowns. Werner's #74 overall ranking in combined tackles across *all* position groups was quite impressive for the 2023 season [6]. Entering the 2024 season [7], Werner will earn $1.43M, an increase of about 57%, landing him the #69 ranking for LB base salary pay. Werner provides tremendous value relative to his production.

2.3 Further Analysis

To do another check that our assumption of the speed and defender distance relationship made sense, we looked to see if there was a statistical relationship between the distance a defender is from the ballcarrier and the ballcarrier speed in yards per second. We calculated the Pearson correlation coefficient between speed and distance within one yard. There were 283,336 records and we found a weak, positive correlation between the two (0.09).

We then did an Ordinary Least Squares regression with distance under one yard as a predictive variable and discovered it was significant. The coefficient was 0.75 and the p-value was 0. So, we found that as the defender's distance away from the ballcarrier decreases by one yard, the ballcarrier's speed is expected to decrease by 0.75 yds/sec.

Next, we did the same thing for defenders less than two yards away. There again was a weak, positive correlation (0.17) and a statistically significant, positive coefficient (0.71). We repeated it for less than three and four yards. Each also had a significant coefficient (0.61 for three yards and 0.51 for four).

The main takeaway here for coaches is that players who are less than four yards away have a significant impact on slowing down the ballcarrier. So, defenders should be encouraged to get as close as they can to the ballcarrier. They may not think it matters if they are not close enough to tackle, but even if they are four yards away, it is helpful as any potential cutback lanes or ways for the ballcarrier to have an escape route would

[13] The NFL Draft is where incoming players are selected by the 32 active teams. There are seven rounds, with the best players being selected in the earlier rounds. Teams can trade their picks for players or other picks in the same draft or future drafts.

[14] Undrafted Free Agents are incoming players who were not selected in the NFL Draft. Instead, they are a part of the open market player pool. They are free to sign with any team that they wish, instead of being selected by a team, albeit to a lower wage compared to their drafted counterparts.

be taken away as options. Players who can close the gap should be rewarded using slowdown data.

A typical saying that coaches say is to "swarm" the ballcarrier and this is why that matters. Even if the defenders are on the backside of the play they can reduce any other options for the ballcarrier by increasing proximity as soon as possible. This is why everyone praises defenses where they see "11 shirts" headed towards the ballcarrier right away on a consistent basis (Table 4).

Table 4. This table shows the results of statistically testing the relationship between distance from ballcarrier and ballcarrier speed.

Distance from Ball Carrier	Coefficient	P-Value Significance of Coefficient	Correlation
<1 Yard	.7537	.000	.0918
<2 Yards	.7099	.000	.1711
<3 Yards	.6063	.000	.2227
<4 Yards	.5056	.000	.2503

3 Conclusion

It would make the most sense for coaching staffs to compare players in the same position group to see who sticks out in terms of slowdowns, assuming that all else about the players being compared to each other is about equal. This remains true whether we are talking about American gridiron football or soccer. That could be the difference between seeing the field or being offered a contract extension. Player agents could leverage slowdown data as a means to highlight the contributions that the player they represent has made to the team.

Advanced defensive statistics in most sports are notoriously hard to measure and rely on, but we believe that this straightforward approach to capturing the relationship between ballcarrier speed and defender distance data can finally shed light to those who assist other players in making tackles by hustling on each play. Slowdowns can provide insight on "hustle metrics" like "who wants it more" and "who gets after it" best, as announcers and coaches tend to praise (Fig. 8).

Fig. 8. Image of defenders swarming to slowdown the ballcarrier is from OpenAI's DALL·E 3

Acknowledgments. We would like to express our thanks to the National Football League, NFL Data & Analytics, Amazon Web Services, Kaggle, and the other competing teams for another wonderful competition!

Disclosure of Interests. The authors have no competing interests to declare that are relevant to the content of this article.

Appendix

Videos of plays were via code refactored from this 2021 Big Data Bowl submission "NFL Big Data Bowl 2021: Animating Players Movement" https://www.kaggle.com/code/ar2017/nfl-big-data-bowl-2021-animating-players-movement/notebook.

Image at the end of this submission showing players generated using OpenAI's DALL·E 3 https://openai.com/dall-e-3.

References

1. NFL Big Data Bowl 2024. https://www.kaggle.com/competitions/nfl-big-data-bowl-2024. Accessed 31 Mar 2024
2. 2024 Big Data Bowl winner and finalists. NFL Football Operations. https://operations.nfl.com/gameday/analytics/big-data-bowl/2024-big-data-bowl-winner-and-finalists/. Accessed 31 Mar 2024

3. San Francisco 49ers at Chicago Bears - September 11th, 2022 https://www.pro-football-reference.com/boxscores/202209110chi.htm#pbp_15.000. Accessed 31 Mar 2024
4. 2022 All-Pro Team. https://en.wikipedia.org/w/index.php?title=2022_All-Pro_Team&oldid=1214550881. Accessed 31 Mar 2024
5. 2022 NFL Salary Rankings. https://www.spotrac.com/nfl/rankings/player/_/year/2022/position/lb/sort/cap_base. Accessed 13 May 2024
6. 2024 NFL Salary Rankings. https://www.spotrac.com/nfl/rankings/player/_/year/2024/position/lb/sort/cap_base. Accessed 13 May 2024
7. 2023 Combined Tackles Leaders. https://www.pro-football-reference.com/years/2023/defense.htm#defense::tackles_combined. Accessed 13 May 2024

WAR Accumulation Differential: A Statistic for Identifying Undervalued Players

Willie K. Harrison(✉) and John L. Salmon

Brigham Young University, Provo, UT 84602, USA
{willie.harrison,johnsalmon}@byu.edu

Abstract. Recent emphasis on the wins above replacement (WAR) statistic in Major League Baseball (MLB) has been well documented. The benefit of classifying a player's ability to generate wins beyond what a readily-available replacement player could provide has been useful in establishing the value of position players, pitchers, and hitters alike. Unfortunately, the statistic does not adequately address the efficiency with which players accumulate WAR, but rather the total value only. Players with limited playing time are thus penalized by the statistic. This paper presents a new suite of WAR-like statistics that measure the rate (or differential) by which WAR is accumulated. The new statistics are shown to be effective in highlighting valuable players who had limited playing time during the course of a season (e.g., young or injured players). In general, a properly normalized version of any cumulative statistic will have similar value.

Keywords: Wins above replacement (WAR) · Normalization · Player analysis

1 Introduction

As early as the 1980's, people have been trying to quantify a Major League Baseball (MLB) player's value using only a single number [5]. Many attempts have been made, but arguably the most successful statistic in this category is wins above replacement (WAR). This stat is meant to estimate the number of *wins* generated by a player *above* the amount that an easily obtainable replacement player would be expected to generate over the same stretch of time [3]. Thus, WAR answers the question of which players would be the most difficult to replace.

Although several versions of WAR exist [3,12,13], each one slightly different from the others [5], the general idea for the statistic (that a player's overall contribution to his team can be summed up with a single number) is continually gaining greater acceptance in mainstream media. See, e.g., [1] where WAR is used to justify the opinion that Mike Trout was the best player in MLB from 2012–2019.

J. S. Dong et al. (Eds.): ISACE 2024, LNCS 14794, pp. 60–74, 2024.
https://doi.org/10.1007/978-3-031-69073-0_5

Since the calculation of WAR is not an exact science, however, the statistic has a significant number of critics as well (see, e.g., [9,10]). Thankfully, some of the sources of the most prominent versions of WAR have published many of their methods in great detail [3,13], and have been willing to openly defend these methods [7,8,11], resulting in an open dialogue regarding the usefulness of WAR. These same statisticians have also been careful to warn that the variance of WAR is significant [3], and therefore small differences in WAR may not be indicative of significant differences in wins generated above what a replacement player might be expected to generate.

The ingredients in each version of WAR are similar. Players who excel at batting, base running, and defense, or pitching, will find themselves rewarded with a high WAR value, as long as they play a sufficient number of games. The reason that playing time is significant in the calculation is that the statistic of WAR is cumulative; meaning, that a player accumulates wins above replacement throughout the course of a season or a career. Successes in specific games grow the stat, while failures in specific games deteriorate the stat. This cumulative nature of WAR identifies a question that is not easily answered by the application of WAR: how can promising talent in players who experience limited playing time be easily identified? Note that such a question requires a statistic that lumps quality performances in all baseball skills together, like the WAR and WAR-like statistics; however, the penalty of limited playing time must be removed.

In this paper, we explore a straightforward normalization of WAR and other WAR-like statistics so as to immediately identify players who generate WAR at a high rate (or differential). We dub the new set of statistics wins above replacement accumulation differentials (WARADs). Using the framework for WAR employed by Baseball-Reference (B-R) [3], we show the exact mechanism for applying the normalization to produce WARAD. We also employ data visualization techniques on the WAR and WARAD statistics so as to identify players whose skills are undervalued when only WAR is referenced.

The remainder of the paper is organized as follows. Section 2 motivates WARAD as a statistic for identifying undervalued players by explaining the B-R version of WAR and pointing out the proper use cases and limitations regarding evaluation of young or injured players. Section 3 introduces the new statistics and discusses their utilities, while Sect. 4 applies the new statistics to the 2019 MLB regular season data to identify the top players in each new statistic. Data visualization techniques are used to display the results in an intuitive manner, and clearly identify undervalued players. Conclusions are given in Sect. 5.

2 Motivation

In this section, we introduce Baseball-Reference.com's version of WAR [3] and show how the current version of WAR cannot identify top players with limited playing time. Both young and injured players tend to suffer from shorter seasons than other players, and are thus shortchanged if we evaluate all players simply by their raw WAR values.

2.1 WAR Overview

Baseball-Reference.com first posted WAR data on their website using Sean Smith's approach to wins above replacement in 2010 [6]. Since that time, adjustments have been made to the original version of the statistic to produce a number of newer versions. The current version in use at Baseball-Reference.com is B-R WAR 2.2 (see [5]), which has been the version of choice since 2013.

In version 2.2 of the statistic, the framework for WAR is given in [3], and can be summarized as follows. A player's runs generated over a replacement player are first calculated as

$$\texttt{Players\_Runs\_over\_Replacement} = \texttt{Player\_runs} - \texttt{ReplPlayer\_runs} \quad (1)$$

$$= (\texttt{Player\_runs} - \texttt{AvgPlayer\_runs}) + (\texttt{AvgPlayer\_runs} - \texttt{ReplPlayer\_runs}). \quad (2)$$

The first part of the equation

$$\texttt{runs\_above\_avg} = (\texttt{Player\_runs} - \texttt{AvgPlayer\_runs}) \quad (3)$$

is calculated with reference to the average MLB player, while the second part of the equation

$$\texttt{runs\_replacement} = (\texttt{AvgPlayer\_runs} - \texttt{ReplPlayer\_runs}) \quad (4)$$

is simply an adjustment comparing the average MLB player with the average replacement-level player. For position players, there are six major components to the calculation of (1):

A) batting runs,
B) baserunning runs,
C) runs added or lost due to grounding into double plays in double-play situations,
D) fielding runs,
E) positional adjustment runs, and
F) replacement level runs.

Components A) through E) are lumped into calculating `runs_above_avg` in (3), while component F) is `runs_replacement` in (4). Since components A) through E) are cumulative, component F) must be scaled to cover the amount of playing time experienced by the player.

While we could go into some detail regarding each of the six components in the calculation for position players, that is not the purpose of this paper. Suffice it to say that the curious reader can come fully up to speed on B-R WAR 2.2 using the excellent resources already posted in [3].

The calculation is quite different for pitchers, where

$$\texttt{runs\_above\_avg} = \texttt{xRA\_final} - \texttt{RA}. \quad (5)$$

Here RA is the number of runs allowed by the pitcher (both earned and unearned), and xRA_final is the expected number of runs allowed by an average MLB pitcher when placed in the same situations as the pitcher being evaluated (i.e., in the same ballparks, with the same defensive support, facing the same offensive teams). Since only pitchers in the National League have a chance to bat, and a pitcher's value is almost never linked to his ability to bat or play defense (besides pitching, of course), the pitcher WAR is devoid of the components A) through D) from the position player calculation.

In both cases (for position players and pitchers),

$$\texttt{runs\_above\_rep} = \texttt{runs\_above\_avg} + \texttt{runs\_replacement}, \qquad (6)$$

where runs_replacement is equal in magnitude to the number of runs generated by a readily available replacement player, and is expressed as a negative number.

For position players, Baseball-Reference.com also calculates offensive and defensive WAR statistics, but again the calculations are first computed in units of runs. Here

$$\texttt{runs\_above\_avg\_off} = \texttt{runs\_bat} + \texttt{runs\_br} + \texttt{runs\_dp} + \texttt{runs\_position}, \quad (7)$$

and

$$\texttt{runs\_above\_avg\_def} = \texttt{runs\_defense} + \texttt{runs\_position}, \qquad (8)$$

where runs_bat is runs above average due to batting, runs_br is runs above average due to base running, runs_dp is runs above average due to double play situations, runs_position is a positional adjustment to level the playing field between positions, and runs_defense is runs saved due to defense. Notice that

$$\texttt{runs\_above\_avg} \neq \texttt{runs\_above\_avg\_off} + \texttt{runs\_above\_avg\_def} \qquad (9)$$

in the B-R model because the positional adjustment is made for both runs_above_avg_off and for runs_above_avg_def, but only once overall in runs_above_avg. This is by design and is justified by Baseball-Reference.com with the reasoning that teams are willing to sign less superior offensive players to more skilled positions, so the adjustment should be considered for both offense and defense.

In FanGraphs' version of WAR, the positional adjustment is said to take into account the fact that some positions are more difficult to play than others, and is thought of as mainly a defensive adjustment [13]. In the B-R version of WAR, the adjustment is made in the amount of defensive degradation teams are willing to allow for players playing those positions, and is hence thought of as both an offensive and defensive adjustment [3]. For non-pitchers, the catcher gets the greatest positional adjustment, while the first baseman gets the least (or actually the greatest negative) adjustment due to position. All adjustments collectively provide zero net gain to runs above average.

Finally, four types of WAR are obtained using the Baseball-Reference.com approach, by converting *runs* to *wins*. This is done using an advanced version of the Pythagorean formula for baseball [4]. In the simplest version of this formula, runs are used to "buy" wins at the rate of 10 runs per win. But in reality, the true relationship is a bit more complicated. The true relationship is not linear, since one can only buy so many wins before there are no additional wins left to buy. Also, some ballparks "sell" wins for more or less runs than 10. All of this is taken into account in the B-R WAR 2.2 statistic.

The four WAR-like statistics that come from this process are `WAR` for position players, `WAR` for pitchers, `WAR_off` as offensive WAR for position players, and `WAR_def` as defensive WAR for position players.

2.2 WAR for Young and Injured Players

Since WAR is a cumulative statistic, a player must be playing to generate it. Suppose a player is badly injured partway through the season, and therefore is severely limited in playing time. At the time of the injury, the player's WAR value will likely reflect a reasonable estimate of the player's value; however, as the season continues that player's WAR will not change, while other uninjured players will continue to accrue additional wins above replacement. This may be good for keeping track of a player's total contribution to his team, but is certainly bad for evaluating player talent.

In a similar way, suppose a AAA player is called up to MLB sometime during the season of play. This player will begin to accrue WAR much later than most other players in the league, leaving him with a smaller total, even if his contribution to winning is substantial. To a lesser degree, consider teams with 4-men rotations and 5-men rotations for their starting pitchers. Depending on the team, a pitcher may be allowed to pitch more often or less often. Again we see a hint of unfairness if WAR is being used to evaluate player value, since it is not normalized by playing time. This aspect of WAR undervalues many players in MLB. Since WAR is now being thought of as a proper means for identifying the best players overall, an adjustment should be made to produce new versions of the WAR-like statistics.

3 Methods

In this section, we consider the four WAR-like statistics produced by Baseball-Reference.com, and show how each can be normalized to produce a *rate* or *differential* that shows how quickly a player generates WAR, rather than the total WAR generated. Such a suite of statistics avoids the issues of WAR we see in injured or young players who are naturally undervalued by WAR.

For all of our new statistics, we choose to normalize by *full games played* by the player. For a position player, one full game played is equivalent to 4.266 plate appearances (PA) and 8.939 innings of defense (Inn). For a pitcher, one full game played is equivalent to 26.816 outs pitched (IPouts). These values are the average game statistics for the regular 2019 MLB season, which can be calculated from the full-season data found at [2].

Consider 2019 MLB position player i with WAR statistic $\texttt{WAR}_i$, offensive WAR statistic $\texttt{WAR\_off}_i$, and defensive WAR statistic $\texttt{WAR\_def}_i$. Let $\texttt{PA}_i$ be the number of plate appearances for player i, and $\texttt{Inn}_i$ be the number of defensive innings played by player i. Then we calculate

$$\texttt{WARAD\_off}_i = \frac{\texttt{WAR\_off}_i}{\texttt{PA}_i/4.266}, \tag{10}$$

$$\texttt{WARAD\_def}_i = \frac{\texttt{WAR\_def}_i}{\texttt{Inn}_i/8.939}, \text{ and} \tag{11}$$

$$\texttt{WARAD}_i = \frac{\texttt{WAR}_i}{\frac{1}{2}\left(\texttt{PA}_i/4.266 + \texttt{Inn}_i/8.939\right)}. \tag{12}$$

This normalization gives half a game for a full game on defense and half a game for a full game on offense in the total WARAD calculation, but a full game for either on the offensive and defensive specific WARAD statistics.

If player i is a 2019 MLB pitcher with WAR statistic $\texttt{WAR}_i$ having pitched $\texttt{IPouts}_i$ outs, then we calculate

$$\texttt{WARAD}_i = \frac{\texttt{WAR}_i}{\texttt{IPouts}_i/26.816}. \tag{13}$$

Since each of these WARAD statistics is equal to the associating WAR statistic normalized to a full-game-played basis, players will score highly on the WARAD statistics only if they generate WAR statistics quickly (or at a high differential). Care should be taken to ensure that players have played a minimum acceptable number of games so that the statistical estimates are meaningful. Otherwise, the noise inherent in small samples will dominate the statistic. For example, a player who has a single PA and hits a homerun will have WARAD values completely off the charts compared to the other players.

4 Results

In this section, we show WAR and WARAD statistics calculated for the 2019 MLB regular season. The raw WAR data are from Baseball-Reference.com [3]. We only calculated WARAD statistics for a position player if he had at least 50 plate appearances and 100 innings of defense. For a pitcher, we only calculated WARAD numbers if he had pitched at least 40 full innings.

4.1 WAR vs. WARAD

Figure 1 shows WAR vs. WARAD for all position players in the 2019 MLB regular season who played the minimum amount of time to warrant a WARAD calculation. Here we see that the overall position-player leader for WAR was Cody Bellinger, but the overall position-player leader for WARAD was Mike Trout. Tables 1 and 2 give the top 18 position players in WAR and WARAD,

Table 1. WAR leaders for position players in the 2019 MLB regular season.

Rank	Player	WAR	WARAD	PA	Inn
1	Cody Bellinger	9.03	0.0599	661	1312
2	Alex Bregman	8.36	0.0534	690	1355.3
3	Mike Trout	8.28	0.0612	600	1159.7
4	Marcus Semien	8.13	0.0484	747	1435
5	Christian Yelich	7.07	0.0543	580	1111
6	Ketel Marte	6.94	0.0491	628	1210
7	Mookie Betts	6.82	0.0433	706	1336.3
8	Matt Chapman	6.69	0.0437	670	1336
9	Trevor Story	6.44	0.0437	656	1257.3
10	Anthony Rendon	6.33	0.0432	646	1265.3
11	George Springer	6.17	0.0502	556	1032
12	Josh Donaldson	6.07	0.0404	659	1306
13	DJ LeMahieu	6.03	0.0411	655	1250.7
14	Nolan Arenado	5.72	0.0378	662	1319.7
15	Max Muncy	5.72	0.0428	589	1157.3
16	Jorge Polanco	5.69	0.0362	704	1332
17	Ronald Acuña Jr.	5.50	0.0344	715	1364
18	Aaron Judge	5.38	0.0534	447	865.3

Table 2. WARAD leaders for position players in the 2019 MLB regular season.

Rank	Player	WAR	WARAD	PA	Inn
1	Mike Trout	8.28	0.0612	600	1159.7
2	Cody Bellinger	9.03	0.0599	661	1312
3	Christian Yelich	7.07	0.0543	580	1111
4	Aaron Judge	5.38	0.0534	447	865.3
5	Alex Bregman	8.36	0.0534	690	1355.3
6	George Springer	6.17	0.0502	556	1032
7	Fernando Tatis Jr.	4.22	0.0499	372	731.3
8	Mike Tauchman	3.63	0.0494	296	694.3
9	Ketel Marte	6.94	0.0491	628	1210
10	Tommy Edman	3.84	0.0490	349	669.3
11	Mitch Garver	3.97	0.0485	359	711.7
12	Marcus Semien	8.13	0.0484	747	1435
13	Bo Bichette	2.14	0.0454	212	397.7
14	**Kyle Tucker**	**0.75**	**0.0451**	**72**	**146.7**
15	Yordan Alvarez	3.72	0.0442	369	732
16	Trevor Story	6.44	0.0437	656	1257.3
17	Matt Chapman	6.69	0.0437	670	1336
18	**Seth Brown**	**0.84**	**0.0435**	**83**	**171**

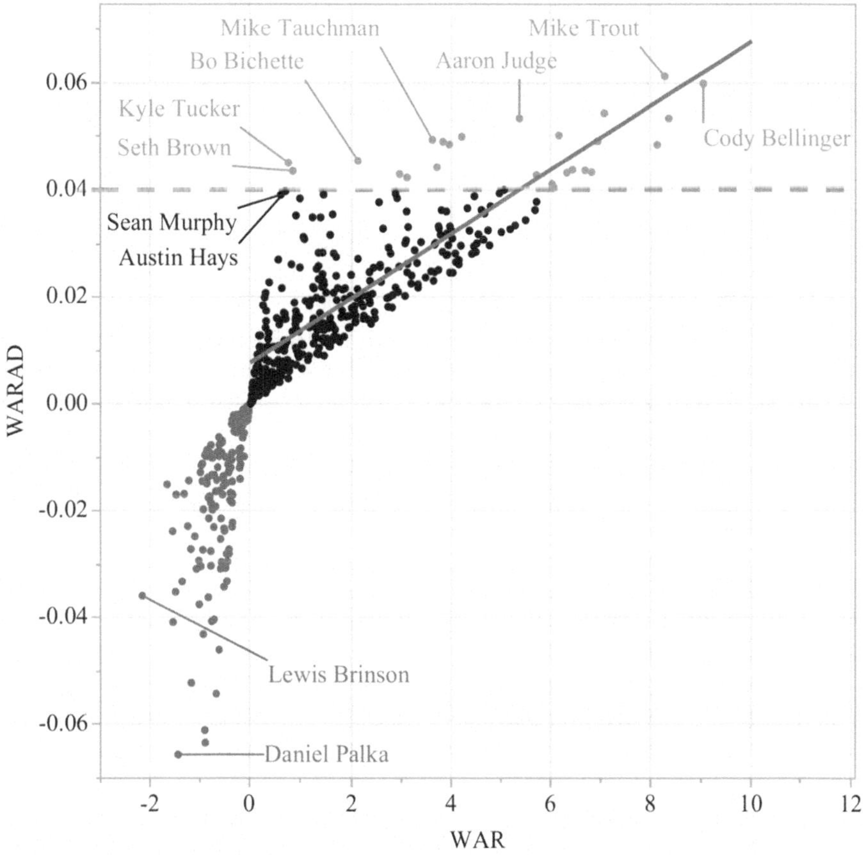

Fig. 1. WAR vs. WARAD for position players in the MLB 2019 regular season.

respectively, along with their WAR, WARAD, number of plate appearances, and defensive innings played.

Consider a vertical slice in the plot of Fig. 1. All players along such a slice generated the same number of wins above replacement; however, the players who generated their WAR the most efficiently are those with high magnitude WARAD values. For players who generated positive WAR, the most efficient generators appear at the top of the vertical slice. The 25 most efficient generators of positive WAR (highest WARAD players) are shown in green in the figure. Now, consider a horizontal slice in the same plot, e.g., the green dashed line. All players along a horizontal slice generated WAR at the same rate, but some of them had more playing time than others. The players with the most playing time who generated positive WAR will be found at the right extreme of a horizontal slice for the black data in the figure. Relationships are reversed for players generating negative WAR, meaning efficient generators of negative WAR are along the bottom and negative WAR generators with more playing time can be found along the left edge with regards to the red data in the figure.

Although WARAD ranks some of the best players slightly differently than does WAR, we consider the true value of WARAD is in properly rewarding players above the blue line in Fig. 1, which is the best-fit line to the positive data. Note that players above this line have been undervalued by the WAR statistic. They generate WAR at a much higher rate than do other players with similar total WAR values. Consider Seth Brown and Kyle Tuckers' data points in the left green portion of Fig. 1. Their data is bolded in Table 2 for convenience. These players were elite WARAD players in 2019, and yet, were only able to generate a small total WAR due to limited playing time. Consider further Fernando Tatis Jr., Mike Tauchman, and Tommy Edman from Table 2, all three crack the top 10 in WARAD for position players. They were also undervalued by WAR, although not to the extreme of Seth Brown and Kyle Tucker. Mitch Garver, Bo Bichette, and Yordan Alvarez also show up in the table with high WARAD, but not particularly high WAR. All of these undervalued players are properly identified as elite players by WARAD in Table 2.

In Fig. 2, we see a similar plot as in Fig. 1, but applied only to the defensive WAR and WARAD statistics, while Fig. 3 shows the results for the offensive WAR and WARAD statistics. These results speak for themselves, and we can readily identify a host of elite defensive and offensive players using WARAD that are not as easily identified using WAR alone. Again, players above the blue line are undervalued by WAR, and players above the green dashed line are in the top 25 of WARAD generators. These 25 players, with green points, generated WAR at the highest rates of any players in MLB during the regular season of 2019. The other black points represent positive WAR/WARAD for a player (but not in the top 25 WARAD), while the red points represent negative WAR/WARAD for a player.

In Fig. 4, we show the WAR vs. WARAD results for pitchers in the 2019 regular season. Again we easily identify elite pitchers in terms of WARAD who did not generate sufficient WAR to be considered elite by the WAR statistic alone. A few sample players are labeled at the extremes of these areas of interest.

In all of these WAR vs. WARAD discussions, we note that generating high WAR often means that a player also has high WARAD. In fact, for those players represented by either green or black points in the figures who are below the blue line, we would simply argue that they have *not been undervalued* by the WAR statistic like those players above the blue line. Their WAR and WARAD statistics may still label them as elite players, although properly rewarded by both statistics.

It is also interesting to note that many of the players who were undervalued by WAR in 2019, but had high WARAD, have since been identified as top players due to their performances over full seasons of play.

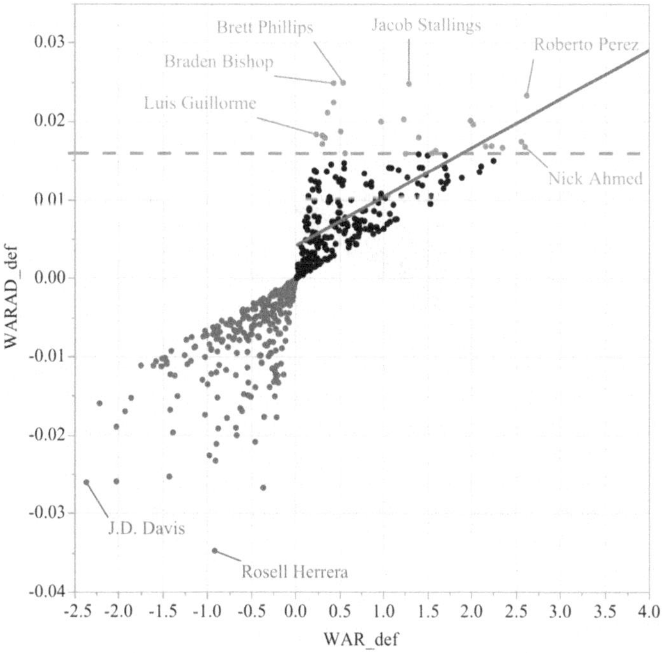

Fig. 2. WAR_def vs. WARAD_def for position players in the MLB 2019 regular season.

4.2 WAR vs. Salary

In this section of the paper, we wish to consider offensive and defensive WARAD vs. the salary of a player. This analysis is only completed for position players from the 2019 MLB regular season. The data indicate whether defense or offense is more prevalent in today's MLB players (on average) in generating WAR for position players, and also how better-paid players fare against poorer-paid players.

In Fig. 5, we see offensive WARAD vs. defensive WARAD for every position player in our analysis. The size of the circle signifies the salary of a player; the bigger the circle, the bigger the salary. Blue circles are for players who generate positive WARAD in both offense and defense. We can see from this figure that big circles seem to show up much more readily when `WARAD_off` is positive, even if `WARAD_def` is negative. Also, we note that even the best defensive players are only generating WAR from defense at a rate less than half of the best offensive WAR generators (note the tick labels on both axes). Being a good offensive player seems to be more positively correlated with generating more wins, and also generating larger player contracts at the same time.

We also see that some larger circles are present in the negative WARAD zones of Fig. 5. Since WARAD is simply a normalized version of WAR, this means the players have actually generated negative WAR for their team in either

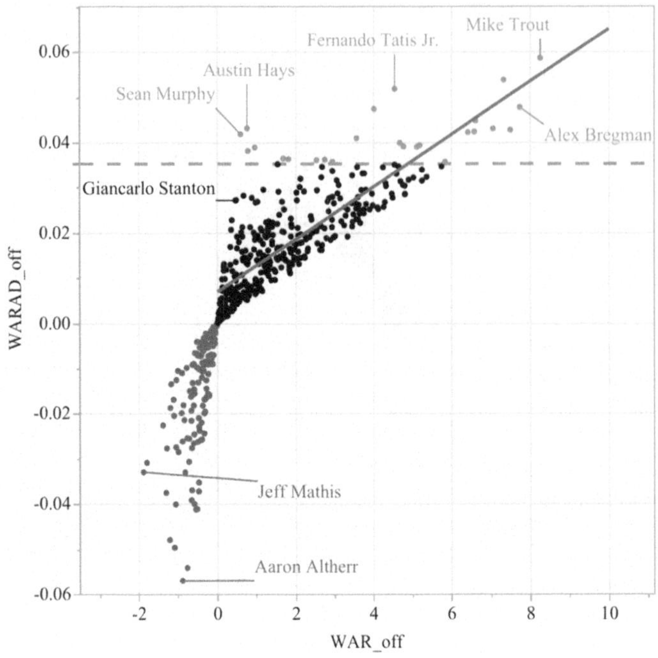

Fig. 3. WAR_off vs. WARAD_off for position players in the MLB 2019 regular season.

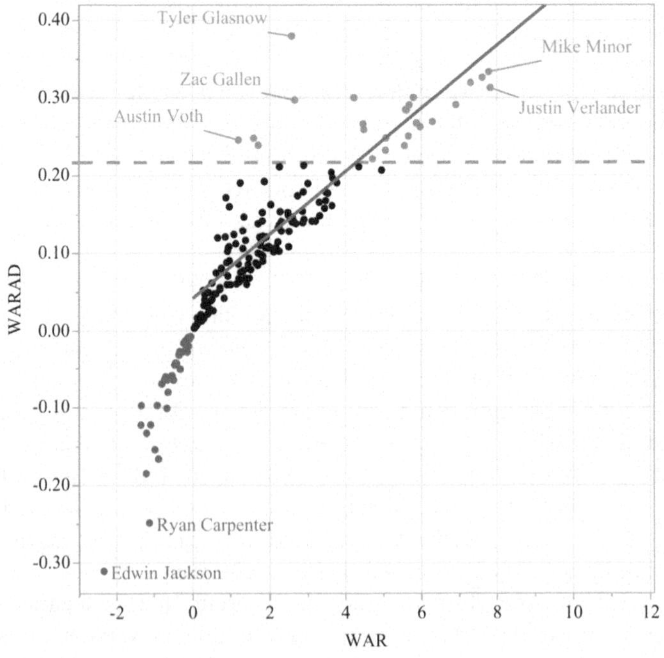

Fig. 4. WAR vs. WARAD for pitchers in the MLB 2019 regular season.

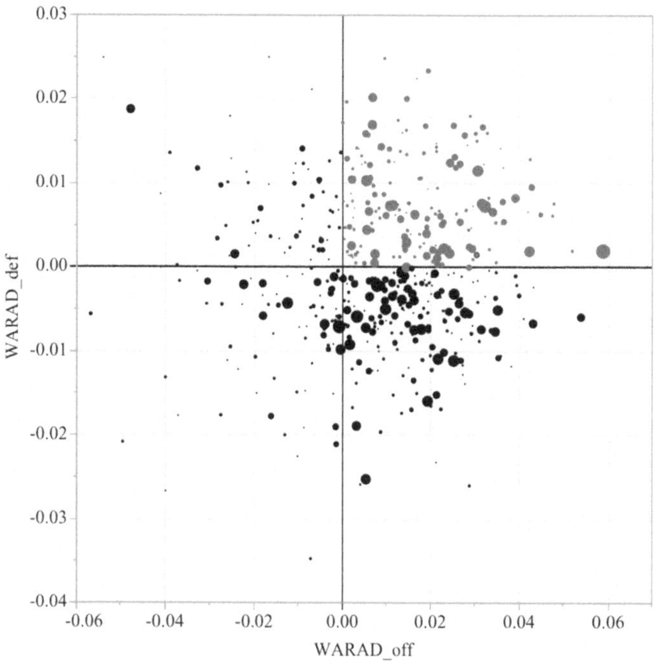

Fig. 5. `WARAD_off` vs. `WARAD_def` for position players in the MLB 2019 regular season. The size of the circle signifies the salary of the player, with larger circles indicating larger salaries. Blue circles are for players with positive `WARAD_off` and `WARAD_def`.

offense, defense, or both. The larger circles that appear in the negative offense and defense zones, are likely players who received large contracts due to past superior play, but have since regressed in their abilities. Managers may continue to play these players since their presence affects ticket sales, or simply because the managers feel a need to play the highest-paid players on their rosters.

In Fig. 6 we zoom into only the positive `WARAD_off` and positive `WARAD_def` quadrant of Fig. 5, and label some of the circles. In this zoomed-in figure, black-filled-in circles are a small selection of labeled players, while blue circles represent unlabeled players. We also equalized the scale on both axes so we can more easily see and compare the contributions from both offensive WARAD and defensive WARAD. With the absence of players with defensive WARAD in the top half of the figure, it is more obvious that offense is roughly twice as important as defense in generating WAR on a per-game basis among today's players (as is measured by WARAD). This may signify that the game naturally places greater importance on offense on a per-player basis, or that offense is simply more highly sought after, and hence players focus, and excel more, on offense.

Several dashed lines help us in analyzing this figure. Firstly, the black dashed line indicates the divide between regions of more or less offensive and defensive WARAD. Players to the left of this line generate WAR at a higher rate with

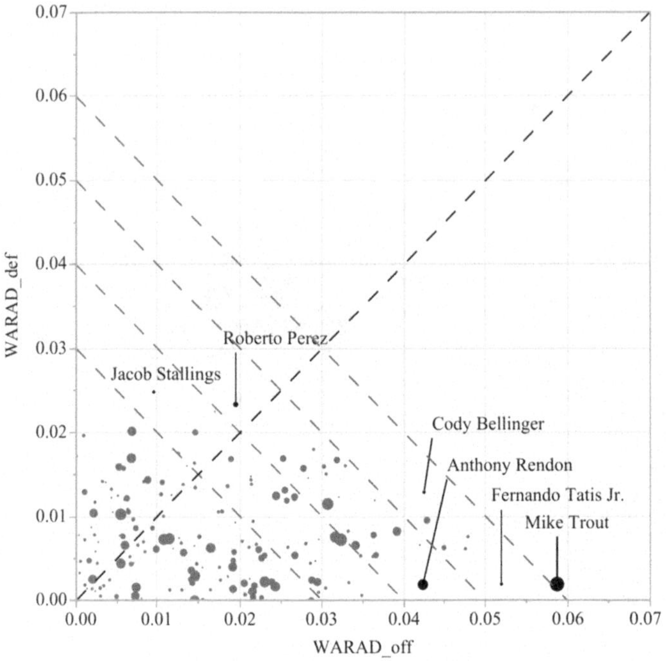

Fig. 6. `WARAD_off` vs. `WARAD_def` for position players in the MLB 2019 regular season zoomed to show only players with both positive `WARAD_off` and `WARAD_def`. The size of the circle signifies the salary of the player, with larger circles indicating larger salaries. Labeled circles are black in color.

their defense than their offense, while players to the right of the line are more valuable for their offensive capabilities. Since the scaling of the axes is made equal for this zoomed figure, players' overall WARAD values can be estimated using the L1 (Manhattan) distance from the origin. This only provides a loose estimate due to (9), but can still be useful for quick comparisons of players. The red-slanted dashed lines are such that any point along one line has the same Manhattan distance from the origin, i.e., the sum of the offensive and defensive WARAD values is constant along each line. The size of the players' circles is once again linked to salary. Since Mike Trout was the highest-paid player in MLB in 2019, his circle is the largest. Roberto Perez and Anthony Rendon are positioned at relatively equal Manhattan distances from the origin and yet the latter obtained a WARAD almost exclusively from offense, while Perez was more balanced across offensive and defensive WARAD. Cody Bellinger and Fernando Tatis Jr. are also approximately positioned at an equal Manhattan distance from the origin, both with relatively small circle sizes. However, Bellinger's salary jumped from \$605,000 in 2019 to more than \$11 million in 2020, which would grow the size of his circle considerably for future years of analysis. Fernando

Tatis Jr. experienced a similar increase in pay, and is currently (as of 2024) signed to a 14-year/$340 million contract with the San Diego Padres.

5 Conclusion

In this paper, we showed that players with limited playing time are undervalued with respect to the WAR statistic, and presented a new suite of WAR-like statistics called WARAD, with normalization so as to quantify the rate at which WAR is generated per full game played. We presented WAR vs. WARAD plots to highlight undervalued players on offense, defense, and the combination of offense and defense together for position players, as well as total WAR for pitchers. We showed that the best defensive contributions to WARAD are roughly half of the best offensive contributions to WARAD in terms of magnitude. We also showed that premier offense tends to be more highly correlated to large player contracts.

Disclosure of Interests. The authors have no competing interests to declare that are relevant to the content of this article.

References

1. Diamond, J., Beaton, A.: He's the best player in baseball. and he can't win. Wall Street Journal (2019). https://www.wsj.com/articles/hes-the-best-player-in-baseball-and-he-cant-win-11573662161
2. Forman, S.: MLB team statistics. Baseball-Reference.com (2019). https://www.baseball-reference.com/leagues/MLB/2019.shtml
3. Forman, S.: Baseball-reference.com WAR explained. Baseball-Reference.com https://www.baseball-reference.com/about/war_explained.shtml
4. Forman, S.: Baseball-reference.com WAR explained, converting runs to wins. Baseball-Reference.com https://www.baseball-reference.com/about/war_explained_runs_to_wins.shtml
5. Forman, S.: WAR comparison chart: WAR-like stats timeline. Baseball-Reference.com https://www.baseball-reference.com/about/war_explained_comparison.shtml
6. Forman, S.: 10 for 10: #7 player wins above replacement. Baseball-Reference.com (2010). https://www.baseball-reference.com/blog/archives/6063.html
7. Forman, S.: My answer to "i don't like how complicated WAR is and how it is constantly changing." "WAR is like GDP for baseball". Baseball-Reference.com (2013). https://www.sports-reference.com/blog/2013/03/my-answer-to-i-dont-like-how-complicated-war-is-and-how-it-is-constantly-changing/
8. Forman, S.: A discussion of WAR wherein i ardently attempt to avoid any WAR-related puns. Baseball-Reference.com (2017). https://www.sports-reference.com/blog/2017/11/a-discussion-of-war-wherein-i-ardently-attempt-to-avoid-any-war-related-puns/
9. James, B.: Judge and Altuve. Bill James Online (2017). https://www.billjamesonline.com/judge_and_altuve/
10. James, B.: MVP followup. Bill James Online (2017). https://www.billjamesonline.com/mvp_followup/

11. Judge, J.: Prospectus feature: Bill James vs. The Noise. Baseball Prospectus (2017). https://www.baseballprospectus.com/news/article/35455/prospectus-feature-bill-james-vs-noise/
12. McQuown, R., Pavlidis, H., Judge, J.: Prospectus feature: Updates to FRAA, BP's fielding metric. Baseball Prospectus (2015). http://www.baseballprospectus.com/article.php?articleid=27944
13. Slowinski, S.: What is WAR? FanGraphs (2010). https://library.fangraphs.com/misc/war/

Analyzing Soccer Training Sessions to Predict Player Match Performance

Leili Javadpour(✉), Mehdi Khazaeli, and Ryanne Molenaar

University of the Pacific, Stockton, CA 95219, USA
Ljavadpour@pacific.edu

Abstract. This research analyzes performance data from training sessions of male soccer players to predict player performance in subsequent matches. The model is developed based on training performance in sessions leading up to games to predict each player's match performance capabilities prior to their next match taking place. The outcome of this study will help identify how various training loads leading up to a match affect player outcome and creates a platform for coaches to optimize their starting lineup and player substitutions throughout the duration of the game based on performance predictions.

Keywords: Performance prediction · Soccer analytics · Match performance

1 Introduction

The increasing interest in sports analytics over the last two decades can be attributed to advances in technology where data has been used by teams and individuals to gain a competitive advantage. Statistics have always played a role in sport, but the use of predictive analysis has increased in recent years. The volume of data collected for each game makes a big data problem since it is not readily feasible to gain meaningful insights from raw data. Data driven decision-making is being incorporated in different aspects of sports from gambling, fantasy leagues, to improving team dynamics and performance, decision making, preventing injuries, etc.

Soccer is a high intensity sport involving various complex factors that allow a team to come together and compete. At the highest level, consistent optimized player performance is key to a successful team. However, there are many factors that affect the physical readiness of players to withstand the demands of competing. The main factor we will be focusing on is the intensity and volume of training sessions leading up to matches. Ultimately, the responsibility of monitoring this workload falls to the coaching staff. Coaching style, organization, discretion, and intentionality of the staff all can affect a team's ability to perform to maximum capacity.

In this research, we are focusing on how a coaching staff can optimize player and team performance using predictive analysis and machine learning. This is done by analyzing training session data leading up to matches as well as the resulting performance data of individual players. From this, a predictive model is developed to determine the match

J. S. Dong et al. (Eds.): ISACE 2024, LNCS 14794, pp. 75–80, 2024.
https://doi.org/10.1007/978-3-031-69073-0_6

performance of each individual prior to the game based on their training performance. This research will aid coaches in identifying how the demands of training sessions affect performance come game day, as well as determine optimal starting lineup and substitution patterns to maximize team performance.

2 Literature Review

The application of machine learning in sports analytics and prediction analysis is becoming increasingly popular. Specifically, in professional soccer, studies are employing various modeling techniques to predict a myriad of success-related parameters.

Predictive modeling in soccer aims to estimate the probabilities of possible outcomes (win, draw, lose) for a given match. The low scoring nature of the soccer game makes accurate score prediction challenging. Soccer analytics research falls in many categories such as predictive modeling of match outcomes [1–6], match performance based on training workload [7–9] and player performance specific to player role [10, 11].

Elmiligi and Saad (2022) analyzed the returns of 205,182 soccer matches of multiple teams over the period of 2000–2017. In their study they combined machine learning with statistical analysis to enhance the predictive accuracy of soccer match outcomes [1].

The study by Guerrero-Calderón et al. (2021) analyzed the relationship between the training load applied throughout the week and players' performance metrics in games [2]. As a result, match performance can be predicted based on training load during the previous training week. Training total distance negatively affected match physical output while training high intensity positively affected match output.

Joseph, Fenton, and Neil (2006) utilized Bayesian networks for predicting match outcomes [3]. They studied the importance of updating probabilities as new data becomes available. Hvattum and Arntzen (2010) explored the use of feature-based models, using logistic regression to predict match results [4]. Their work highlighted the effectiveness of simple statistical features in making predictions. Recent studies have focused on ensemble methods and more sophisticated models to enhance prediction accuracy. Berrar et al. (2019) investigated the use of ensemble learning, combining multiple machine learning models to improve predictive performance in soccer matches [5]. Kahn (2022) explored deep learning approaches, specifically recurrent neural networks (RNNs) and long short-term memory (LSTM) networks, to model the sequential nature of match events and predict outcomes with higher accuracy [6]. A study by Santos et al. (2021) emphasized the importance of integrating biometric data, including heart rate variability (HRV) and sleep quality, into training load management [7]. They showed that personalized training programs based on these data points could significantly enhance match performance by optimizing recovery and readiness. Research by Miller et al. (2022) highlighted the role of wearable technology in providing real-time data on player workload and physiological responses [8]. This study demonstrated how real-time analytics could be used to adjust training intensity, reducing injury risk and improving performance outcomes. A study by the study by Zhang and Lee (2022) focused on leveraging machine learning algorithms to predict player responses to various training loads [9]. They developed predictive models that could forecast individual players' performance and risk of injury.

Furthermore, research is being conducted on soccer player performance specific to the role they play on their team. Lago-Peñas and Gómez-Ruano (2016) conducted a systematic review focused on the assessment of offensive performance in soccer [10]. Their study used various statistical methods and performance indicators to evaluate offensive play in soccer matches. The research done by Carpita et al. (2021), used statistical analysis to determine the most impactful and effective players in each role [11]. Their methodology assesses team performance based on players' positions and contributions.

3 Data

The data used is on division I 2022–2024 seasons of one college men's soccer team. This data is directly related to physical performance and gathered using the PlayerTek technology and platform. PlayerTek is a professional grade sensor device and web-based software that is used to measure and track athletes' physical performance [12]. It uses a GPS system and a range of smart sensors to gather a series of metrics. These sensors and systems are specifically designed for high-level soccer player use.

PlayerTek categorizes the performance metrics into two groups – volume and intensity. Within the volume category, we are analyzing distance, sprint distance, energy, power plays, and sprints. Within the intensity category, we are analyzing top speed, distance per minute, power score, work ratio, and player load. Additional attributes are considered including total duration, duration within speed zone 2–5 and session player score. Session player score is an indication of how much load a player experienced compared to that typical of a full match [13]. As an example, if a player received a session player score of 75, this means that they experienced a load equal to 75% of a full match load. Further detail and description of each of these attributes can be seen in Table 1.

Table 1. Feature description.

Attribute	Description
Training Player score	Percentage of experienced load compared to that of a typical match
Duration	Total time in seconds of the training
Duration within zone 2–5	Total time in seconds of the training the player is moving with velocity greater than 1 m per second
Distance	Total distance covered over the duration of a training
Sprint distance	Distance covered while running at speeds greater than 5 m per second
Power plays	Significant action where power output is over 20 watts per kilogram of body weight

(continued)

Table 1. (*continued*)

Attribute	Description
Energy	Amount of energy expended in the duration of a training
Sprints	Total number of sprints indicated by change in speed from below to greater than 5 m per second
Top speed	Maximum speed sustained for at least half a second
Distance per minute	Meters per minute, indicates how hard and intensely a player worked
Power score	Measures power output used per kilogram of player weight
Work ratio	Percentage of time player is working compared to resting, defined as speeds greater than 1.5 m per second
Player load	Measure of instantaneous rate of change of acceleration divided by a scaling factor

4 Methodology

In this paper we introduce a new method for the field of soccer analytics by predicting how the player would perform during a match based on their training performance leading up to the match. In our binomial classification model, the ‘true class’ refers to players outperforming their performance in training sessions. By utilizing these predictions, coaches can learn how to optimize player performance to achieve the best outcomes.

After collecting data and data analysis, feature selection and extraction is performed. We built machine learning models to predict the performance based on the features listed in Table 1. We utilized supervised learning to train the model and evaluated the accuracy for each pattern recognition model and the top 4 models are described in Table 2.

Table 2. Different model methods with accuracy and total time.

Model	Accuracy	Std	Total Time	Training Time	Scoring Time
Generalized Linear Model	***79.3%***	***±7.2%***	***325 ms***	***223 ms***	***195 ms***
Naive Bayes	72.7%	±8.3%	411 ms	126 ms	146 ms
Fast Large Margin	72.7%	±8.3%	871 ms	184 ms	146 ms
Deep Learning	68.7%	±8.7%	808 ms	1 s	170 ms

Generalized Linear Model (GLM) gave the highest accuracy of 79.3% with a precision of 83.33% and recall of 71.7%. The top features based on the weight by chi statistic are presented in Table 3. According to this, the attributes that held the most weight were sprint distance, power plays and energy.

Table 3. Weight by Chi Squared statistic results.

Attribute	Normalized Weight by Chi Squared
Sprint Distance	1
Power Plays	0.87
Energy	0.80
Work Ratio	0.64
Duration within zones 2–5	0.63
Top Speed	0.63
Distance Per Minute	0.59
Sprints	0.45
Power Score	0.44
Player Load	0.41

5 Conclusion

This research creates a model to predict the performance of each player in a soccer match. We used the players' performance metrics from the training sessions leading up to the match to identify which players were likely to perform better in the match than they had during training. The outcome of this study is intended to create a platform for coaches to optimize their starting lineup and player substitutions throughout the duration of the game based on performance predictions.

The future study will focus on analyzing different sessions and their effects on player performance. We plan to break down each training session into various segments, categorizing them by features such as category, difficulty level, and progression, in order to create a recommender system that simulates the game.

References

1. Elmiligi, H., Saad, S.: Predicting the outcome of soccer matches using machine learning and statistical analysis. In: IEEE 12th Annual Computing and Communication Workshop and Conference, CCWC 2022, pp. 1–8. IEEE (2022). https://doi.org/10.1109/CCWC54503.2022.9720896
2. Guerrero-Calderón, B., Klemp, M., Morcillo, J.A., Memmert, D.: How does the workload applied during the training week and the contextual factors affect the physical responses of professional soccer players in the match? Int. J. Sports Sci. Coach. **16**(4), 994–1003 (2021)
3. Joseph, A., Fenton, N., Neil, M.: Predicting football results using Bayesian nets and other machine learning techniques. Knowl.-Based Syst. **19**(7), 544–553 (2006)
4. Hvattum, L.M., Arntzen, H.: Using ELO ratings for match result prediction in association football. Int. J. Forecast. **26**(3), 460–470 (2010)
5. Berrar, D., Lopes, P., Dubitzky, W.: Ensemble learning for soccer match prediction. Artif. Intell. Sports **2**(1), 19–28 (2019)
6. Kahn, J.: Deep learning for predictive modeling in soccer: an LSTM approach. J. Sports Anal. **8**(1), 35–47 (2022)

7. Santos, S., Jones, D., Figueiredo, A.: Integrating biometric data to enhance personalized training workload models in professional soccer. J. Sports Sci. **39**(11), 1234–1242 (2021)
8. Miller, P., Smith, A., Garret, J.: The impact of wearable technology on training load management and player performance in elite soccer. Sports Technol. **15**(1), 56–67 (2022)
9. Zhang, Y., Lee, A.: Machine learning models for predicting performance responses to training loads in professional soccer players. J. Quant. Anal. Sports **18**(4), 251–263 (2022)
10. Lago-Peñas, C., Gómez-Ruano, M.Á.: Assessment of offensive performance in soccer: a systematic review. Res. Sports Med. **24**(3), 308–329 (2016)
11. Carpita, M., Ciavolino, E., Pasca, P.: Players' role-based performance composite indicators of soccer teams: a statistical perspective. Soc. Indic. Res. **156**, 815–830 (2021)
12. GPS Player Tracking System. PlayerTek. https://www.playertek.com/us/. Accessed 25 Jan 2024
13. Understanding Playertek Metrics. https://medium.com/playertek/understanding-playertek-metrics-898c90f12127. Accessed 10 Dec 2023

Tracking Small and Fast Moving Ball in Broadcast Videos Using Transfer Learning and the Enhanced Interactive Multi-motion Model

Kan Jiang(✉), Zhaoyu Liu, Qirui Wu, Murong Ma, and Jin Song Dong

National University of Singapore, Singapore, Singapore
jiangkan@comp.nus.edu.sg

Abstract. Ball tracking is a fundamental task in sports video analytics. However, it is challenging because the ball is small and moves fast. We propose a general framework consists of a vision based ball detector and a motion based tracker to accurately track the ball in broadcast videos. Unlike usual frame by frame based detection followed by tracking, our ball detector itself is video based, which exploits both spatial and temporal information. Furthermore, instead of working in the raw image space, our ball detector works in the feature space through transfer learning. It contains few trainable parameters, and is easy to train. Our tracker complements the detector. It can find the most likely ball track based on detections by using a Viterbi based data association technique. It uses multiple motion models to associate a new detection to existing tracks even when the ball changes its direction. It can also tolerate temporary ball occlusion by introducing "null" nodes (representing miss detections) in the Viterbi algorithm and by back tracking. Our algorithm is evaluated using broadcast videos downloaded from tennis TV channels. Our experiments show that our method achieves 99.22% accuracy and is better than any existing ball tracking method. Besides, due to the modular design and the fact that our detector can be easily re-trained to detect other objects, our algorithm can be generalised to track other small and fast moving objects.

Keywords: Sports analytics · Video analytics · Object tracking

1 Introduction

In many object detection and tracking tasks, deep learning system has achieved or surpassed human level accuracy. Usually, to achieve high accuracy, it is common to design complex Deep Neural Network (DNN) architecture targeted for the specific application and to train it with large amount of data. We argue it is more cost effective to simply reuse existing DNN with transfer learning to obtain reasonable but less than ideal accuracy, and then improve the accuracy with a Bayesian estimation approach. We use sports ball tracking as a case study to show the effectiveness of our method.

Supported by National University of Singapore.

J. S. Dong et al. (Eds.): ISACE 2024, LNCS 14794, pp. 81–96, 2024.
https://doi.org/10.1007/978-3-031-69073-0_7

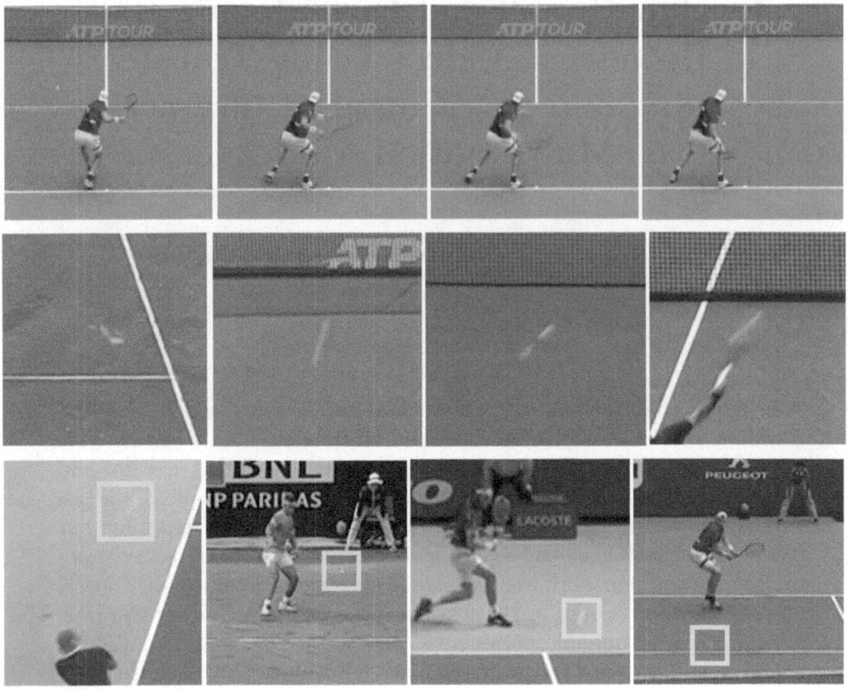

Fig. 1. (a) Successive occlusion (the player blocks the ball); (b) deformation; (c) motion blur (yellow bounding boxes denote true ball positions). (Color figure online)

Ball tracking is one of the essential components in sports video analytics. An accurate and efficient ball tracking algorithm helps us to collect ball direction and speed information at each event. For example, in tennis, we would like to collect such detailed information at each serve, return and stroke, in order to build player profiles which represents the player's choice of actions and the success rates. Such player profiles allow us to anticipate the opponent's move and to reason if a different choice of action improves our player's winning chance. [2,3,8,11,13,14] Although highly desirable, such detailed information is completely missing for many sports, such as tennis and soccer. This is because collecting such data usually requires multiple ceiling mounted high speed cameras working in tandem in order to obtain a clear view of the entire court. It is expensive to setup and to operate, and is only available for top tie tournaments. Even if such data is recorded, it is owned by the tournament organizer and is not available to the public. This motivates us to use Computer Vision (CV) and DNN techniques to automatically track ball in broadcast videos.

We refer broadcast videos as those downloaded from TV channels or YouTube with a resolution of either 1280×720 or 1920×1080, and a frame rate ranging from 25 to 50 frames per second. A typical tennis broadcast video stream starts from a close-up view to show the player is getting ready, and then, the main camera view to show actions from both players until one of them wins the point,

Fig. 2. The ball falls on the complex background.

Fig. 3. Ball-shaped objects (yellow bounding boxes are true balls, while red bounding boxes are false balls). (Color figure online)

and then, another close-up view to show the player or the audience's reaction. There are various techniques to segment such a long video into many short clips and to filter out close-up and irrelevant clips. In the remaining clips, we can assume they are from the main camera view showing both players and only one ball. In this paper, we focus on tracking the ball in these clips. In other words, given a short clip from the main camera view, we aim to locate the (x, y) image coordinates of the ball at each time step. One additional requirement is that the same method should be applicable to other sports, such as table tennis, badminton and soccer.

However, it is a challenging task to detect balls in broadcast videos for the following reasons: (1) balls are small objects, which do not contain a lot of information for detection; (2) motion blur, deformation, and successive occlusion often occur as shown in Fig. 1; (3) complex backgrounds such as the advertisement boards or audiences, make the detection very difficult when the ball falls on such backgrounds as shown in Fig. 2; (4) there often exists ball-shaped objects or irrelevant balls as shown in Fig. 3; (5) due to hitting and camera movement, ball trajectory is not completely predictable.

To solve these problems, we propose a framework consists of vision based ball detectors, and motion based ball tracker. Taking the video frames as the input, the detectors output the (x, y) positions of ball candidates at each time step. The tracker takes many possible sequences of noisy ball candidates as the input and estimates the true ball position for the most likely track.

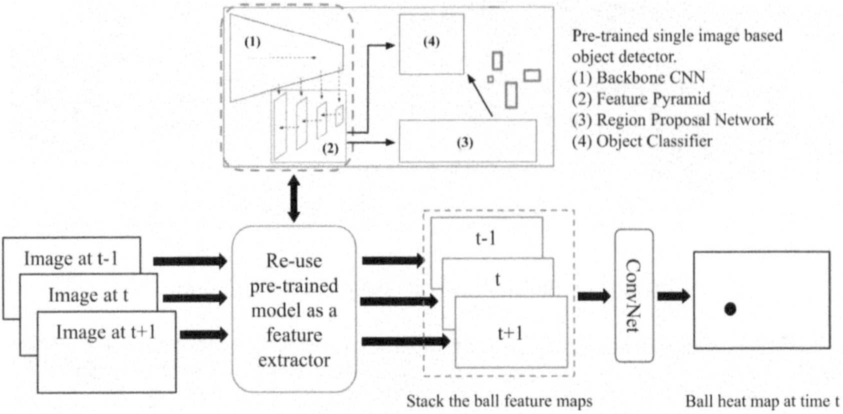

Fig. 4. Our 3-frame ball detector.

In order to detect small balls, instead of zooming in the original image, we adopt the Feature Pyramid Network (FPN) technique proposed by [7] shown as component (2) in Fig. 4. Small balls can be detected at the last up-scaled (referred as the p2 scale) feature map. To detect fast moving balls, we stacked the p2 scale feature maps together for 3 connecting frames and train a simple ConvNet as shown in Fig. 4. This simple transfer learning detects 96.50% ball candidates correctly.

The missed ball candidates can be predicted using a constant acceleration motion model in our tracker. Besides the constant acceleration, our tracker also contains a sudden change motion model. These two motion models are integrated to track flying ball with changing directions. There are also false ball candidates, which will be identified by our tracker because they clearly deviate from the two motion models. Essentially, these two motion models assign a probability score for each ball candidate given the ball state in the previous time step. Searching among all possible sequences of ball states, the most likely sequence, which has the highest track probability, is the optimal Bayesian estimation.

Since we are processing the recorded video clips, we use the information in the future to back track the ball position in the earlier time steps to further improve the tracking accuracy. Overall, we can track 99% balls correctly in our tennis videos. We have published our source code and training data labels in this site, https://github.com/jiangkansg/ball_tracking.

Our contributions are: (1) We argue, instead of designing more complex DNN, it is more cost effective to reuse existing DNN with transfer learning, and then improve the tracking accuracy by finding the most likely track based on Bayesian estimation. (2) Our ball detector itself is a video based small object detector, which exploits both spatial and temporal information to detect the ball reasonably accurately. Furthermore, instead of working in the raw image space, our ball detector works in the feature space (via transfer learning), and contains few

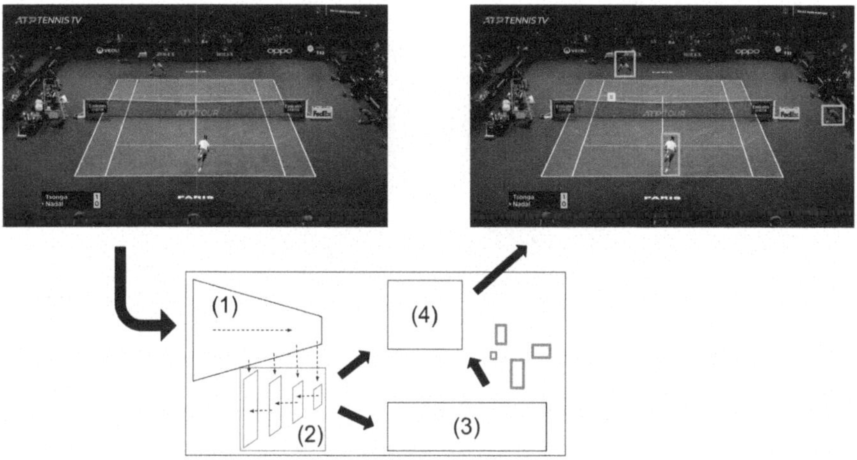

Fig. 5. Detectron2 framework. (1) Backbone Network (ResNet); (2) Feature Pyramid Network; (3) Region Proposal Network; (4) Classifier.

trainable parameters. It is easy to train and has better performance and generalizability compared to other existing methods. (3) We proposed an enhanced multi-motion model tracking algorithm, which tracks the true ball with changing flying patterns and filters out false balls. It utilizes multiple detectors, data association algorithm and back tracking to achieve high tracking accuracy.

2 Background and Related Work

Traditional computer vision detection methods [17,18] will detect all foreground moving blobs using frame difference and then classify them into ball candidates and non-ball candidates according to their shape, size, color, and location. However, these methods have several drawbacks: (1) the parameters need to be tuned carefully based on different source videos because the ball properties (shape, size, color, etc.) may vary; (2) classification is performed on every moving blob. As a result, the detection speed becomes very slow especially when there is a significant movement in the video scene; (3) many false candidates could be reported because there are many ball-like moving objects/patterns in the frames (e.g. the rackets, some patterns on players' clothes, wristband).

2.1 General Object Detector

Detectron2 [16] is a general-purpose region-based single image object detection network. It was trained on the COCO dataset with over 330,000 images for 80 object categories. There are mainly four components in Detectron2 as shown in Fig. 5: (1) Backbone Network to extract features using ResNet; (2) Feature Pyramid Network to obtain feature maps in different scales. This step is important for small object detection because the small object can hardly be recognized

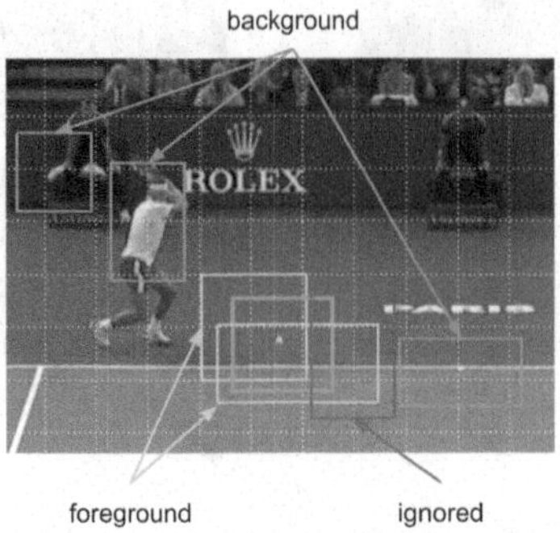

Fig. 6. An illustration of the anchor labelling. The green box is the ground truth region, the blue boxes are positive anchors with IOU to ground truth box >0.7, the brown boxes are negative anchors with IOU <0.3, the red box is ignored. (Color figure online)

in a low-resolution feature map; (3) Region Proposal Network to propose possible object regions (i.e. bounding boxes) from the multi-scale feature maps; (4) Classifier to predict the object class in each region.

After the feature maps are generated by components (1) and (2), Detectron2 measures Intersection Over Union (IOU) distances between all predefined anchors and the ground truth bounding boxes, and automatically label anchors close to the ground truth as positive (foreground) training samples and anchors far as negative (background) samples [10]. This step is illustrated in Fig. 6. Effectively, this step turns a single image into "hundreds of" training samples, which makes the Detectron2 training very data efficient. However, the shortcoming of Detectron2 is that it takes a single image as input, therefore, does not utilize the temporal correlation between connecting frames.

2.2 TrackNet

TrackNet [5] is a spatial-temporal tennis ball detector trained on broadcast videos. When detecting the tennis ball in given frame t, it takes a stack of consecutive frames as input (i.e., frames at time step $t-1$, t, $t+1$) and outputs a heatmap indicating the ball's most probable position. The architecture of TrackNet is shown in Fig. 7. It first extracts features from three consecutive frames using VGG16 [12] as the backbone network , followed by a De-Convolution network [19] to upsample the feature map to the same resolution as the input images. Finally, it generates a heatmap through pixel-wise dense classification. The main advantages for TrackNet are: (1) it utilizes temporal correlations on consecutive raw images, and (2) it uses pixel-wise dense classification to predict the object heatmap, which is efficient because it performs conv operation using local feature map.

However, it has some shortcomings: (1) it does not perform well on matches that are different from training samples; (2) it requires a large amount of train-

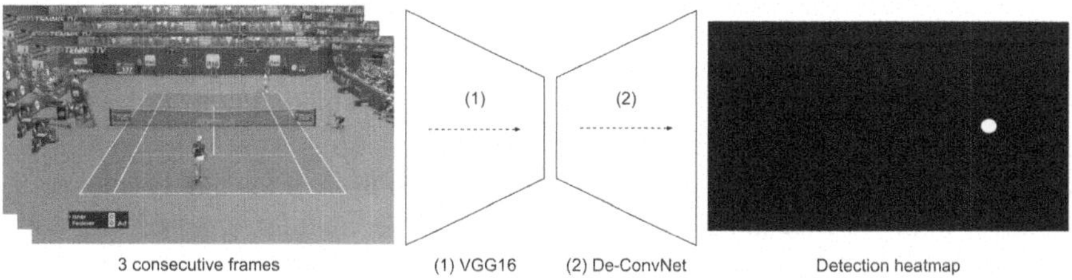

Fig. 7. TrackNet framework.

ing data. Likely, it is because TrackNet does not use the pre-trained VGG16 backbone network weights (i.e., no transfer learning), and there is no skip connection between backbone layers and De-Convolutional layers, which leads to information loss.

2.3 Different Scaling Method

Small object detection is challenging because the target object usually takes up only a small portion of the entire image and contains limited information. Therefore, scaling is one of the crucial steps which can be adopted on either original images or feature maps. Some existing works such as [15] try to crop and zoom in to a smaller area on the original image which contains the target object; while others [5,16] focus on obtaining information from scaled-up feature maps through Feature Pyramid Network (FPN) [7]. We choose to use FPN instead of image cropping for the following reasons: (1) Image cropping is a 2 stage method, which is less efficient. (2) The cropped image only contains local information, while the scaled-up feature maps (obtained from FPN) includes both global and local information.

2.4 Single Object Tracking, Kalman Filter

In this case, the input is a sequence of single detections $(z_1..z_t)$. In other words, at each time step, we have one and only detection z_t. The goal is to estimate the sequence of ball states $(S_1..S_t)$ based on a motion model. Assume Markov property, this problem is simplified to, given a motion model F, last known state S_{t-1} and a ball detection z_t, estimate S_t.

For example, z_t is the ball (x, y) coordinates reported by a ball detector, and ball state S is $[x, y, \dot{x}, \dot{y}, \ddot{x}, \ddot{y}]^\top$, i.e., the ball (x, y) position, their respective velocities and accelerations. A constant acceleration model is written as:

$$S_t = FS_{t-1} + \mathcal{N}(0, Q) \tag{1}$$

F is the motion model, and $\mathcal{N}(0, Q)$ is a noise term. The motion model F projects the ball state from the previous step to the current step. Given a very small Δt, such a motion model is reasonable in many cases, but is imperfect. The 2nd term represents the uncertain position, velocity and acceleration change at each step. We assume S_{t-1}, S_t are Gaussian distributions, i.e., $S_{t-1} \sim \mathcal{N}(x_{t-1}, P_{t-1})$

Such a problem has been solved by [6] based on Bayes theorem. It consists of two steps, (1) prediction and (2) update. In the prediction step (referred as $KalmanPredict(S_{t-1}, F, Q)$ function), the ball **state prior** (denoted as $\hat{S}_t$), because it is an estimation without evidence (z_t), is calculated according to:

$$\begin{aligned} \hat{x_t} &= F x_{t-1} \\ \hat{P_t} &= F P_{t-1} F^\top + Q \end{aligned} \tag{2}$$

In the update step, both the likelihood $P(z_t \mid S_t)$ and the prior are used to calculate the ball **state posterior** (denoted as S_t). In reality the true ball state is only partially observable, therefore, a measurement function (H) is used to reflect the fact that the ball detector can only detect the (x, y) position of the ball. Furthermore, such detection contains some noises, which is assumed to follow a Gaussian distribution $\mathcal{N}(0, R)$.

$$\begin{aligned} z_t &= H S_t + \mathcal{N}(0, R) \\ H &= \begin{bmatrix} 1\,0\,0\,0\,0\,0 \\ 0\,1\,0\,0\,0\,0 \end{bmatrix} \end{aligned} \tag{3}$$

The update step, $KalmanUpdate(\hat{S}_t, H, R, z_t)$ function is:

$$\begin{aligned} x_t &= \hat{x_t} + K(z_t - H\hat{x_t}) \\ P_t &= (I - KH)\hat{P_t} \\ K &= \hat{P_t} H^\top (H \hat{P_t} H^\top + R)^{-1} \end{aligned} \tag{4}$$

2.5 Single Object Back Tracking, RTS Smoother

Since we are detecting the ball from the recorded video, we can also use future information to improve the current state estimation. In other words, given improved future state (denoted as S^*_{t+1}), and S_t, we want to compute an improved current state estimation S^*_t. This is known as RTS smoother and was proposed by Rauch et al. [9].

RTS smoother also consists of 2 steps. The first step is to find the reverse motion model, i.e. $S^*_t = P(S_t \mid x_{t+1})$. Consider S_t as the prior and S^*_t as the posterior based on the observation x_{t+1}. The likelihood $P(x_{t+1} \mid S_t)$ is based on the forward motion model, which is described by the linear transformation F and the noise term $\sim \mathcal{N}(0, Q)$. Therefore, the posterior $S^*_t = KalmanUpdate(S_t, F, Q, x_{t+1})$, is:

$$\begin{aligned} x^*_t &= x_t + K_k(x_{t+1} - F x_t) \\ P^*_t &= (I - K_k F) P_t \\ K_k &= P_t F^\top (F P_t F^\top + Q)^{-1} \end{aligned} \tag{5}$$

The second step is to project the improved future state back to current state using the reverse motion model, i.e. $S_t^* = P(S_t \mid S_{t+1}^*)$:

$$\begin{aligned} x_t^* &= x_t + K_k(x_{t+1}^* - Fx_t) \\ P_t^* &= P_t + K_k(P_{t+1}^* - P)K_k^\top \\ P &= FP_tF^\top + Q \end{aligned} \tag{6}$$

2.6 Assign Ball Candidates to Tracks

At each time step t, we may have multiple m_t ball candidates, i.e., $z_t = \{z_t^i, i = 1..m_t\}$. Let $i = 0$ represents the miss detection case, clearly, we need to choose one out of the $m_t + 1$ options first before applying the Kalman update. This is known as the Data Association problem [1].

The Data Association problem can be viewed as to find $\arg\max_i P(i \mid z_t, \hat{S}_t)$. In other words, we are finding the most likely i (i.e., detection z_t^i is the correct detection) given the ball state prior and the set of candidates. Based on Bayes theorem, $P(i \mid z_t, \hat{S}_t) \propto P(z_t \mid i, \hat{S}_t) \times P(i \mid \hat{S}_t)$.

(1) If all candidates are far away from the center of $\hat{S}_t$, then $P(i \mid \hat{S}_t) \approx 0$ for all $i = 1..m_t$, therefore the best choice is $i = 0$. This idea is known as the "Gating Window". A gating window of $\hat{S}_t$ is typically at least 3 standard deviations from the center of $\hat{S}_t$.
(2) If there are m candidates within the gating window, a simple solution is to choose the z_t^i which is closest to the center of $\hat{S}_t$ (Nearest Neighbour) measured by the Mahalanobis distance $d(z_t^i, \hat{S}_t)$. An alternative is to choose all candidates within the gating window and then calculate an average weighted on $P(i \mid \hat{S}_t) \propto e^{-d(z_t^i, \hat{S}_t)}$.

Note that the gating window is adaptive. If we miss detect the ball at any step, we have no detection to update the ball state posterior. Hence, we have to carry the ball state prior over to be the posterior. This means the uncertainty is increased at this step. The consequence is that the gating window will be increased in the next step which reflects this growing uncertainty.

2.7 Viterbi Algorithm

Suppose G is a directed graph with N nodes and E directed edges, G is a trellis if N nodes can be partitioned into ordered subsets (stages) $N_1, N_2, ..., N_k$, such that edges only connect nodes in stage N_{i-1} and N_i for $i \in [1, k]$ as shown in Fig. 8. Viterbi algorithm [4] is a dynamic programming algorithm which aims to find the most likely sequence of states. It can be used to find the best track in a trellis given the initial node, end node, and edge weights. The best track represents the track with the maximum accumulated weights. The key idea of the Viterbi algorithm is that, for each node at each stage, it only keep the current best track to that node as well as the corresponding score. The forward process will repeat until the final state and the global best track can then be identified by back tracing.

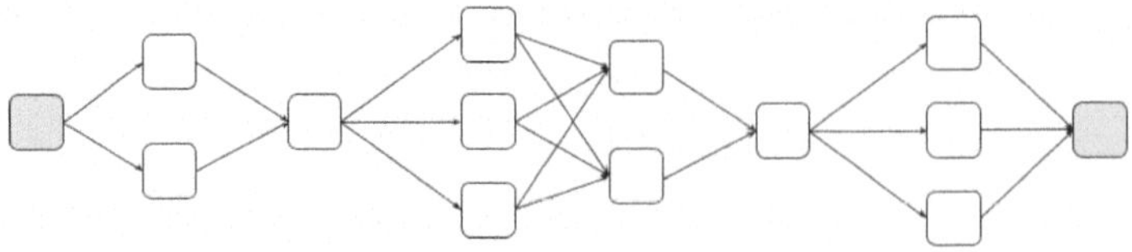

Fig. 8. Example of a trellis.

3 Our Method

Our solution consists of 2 ball detectors and a tracking algorithm. The first detector (referred as Detector1) is a single frame based ball detector. It is a re-trained Detectron2 to detect a single class of object, which is the ball. The second detector (referred as Detector2) is a 3-frame based ball detector as shown in Fig. 4, which detects the ball candidate at the time step t (given frames at time step $t-1$, t, and $t+1$). The tracking algorithm (referred as Tracker, and we name it the EIMM algorithm) takes the sequence of noisy detections as the input, and outputs the most likely ball track based on 2 predefined motion models.

3.1 Reusing Existing DNN via Transfer Learning

Detector1 is simply re-trained using manually labelled images. Besides using it to output ball candidates frame by frame, we also use Detector1 as a feature map extractor. It is reasonable to assume that the ball will not travel very far within a short duration. Therefore, we can simply stack the feature maps together and expect the feature map at the true ball position will be amplified even if the ball is occluded in one of the frames. This temporal information increases the possibility of detecting the moving ball. The ConvNet in the Detector2 simply consists of a 3×3 conv followed by a 1×1 conv layers. The ball candidates detected by Detector1 and Detector2 are the input for the tracker.

3.2 Tracker, EIMM Algorithm

Given a sequence of detections, we first construct a trellis (Fig. 9) in such a way that each frame corresponds to a stage in the trellis, and each node n_k^i corresponds to a detection at stage k. There are also multiple "null" nodes in each stage representing the cases where the ball is not detected in frame k. Each node needs to store (1) **best track**: the most likely track from the initial to the current node; (2) **best track score**: the maximum accumulated weights following the best track; (3) **best state**: the ball state which consists of two Gaussian distributions with their corresponding model probabilities. One Gaussian is the ball state following a constant acceleration model and the other is the ball state following a sudden change model. Both are used to capture

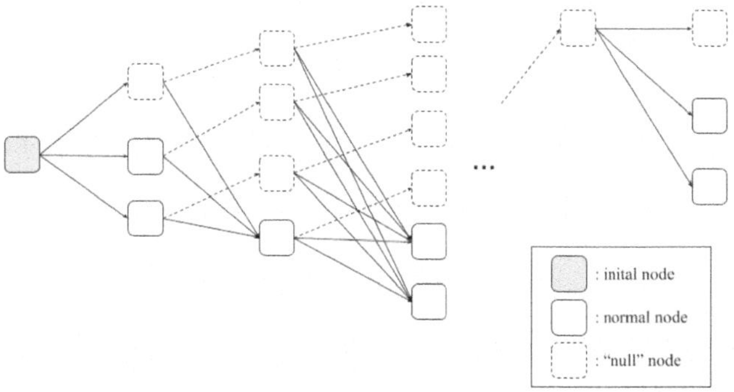

Fig. 9. Construct the trellis from detections. Each normal node represents a detection in a frame, and the "null" node represents the true ball is not detected.

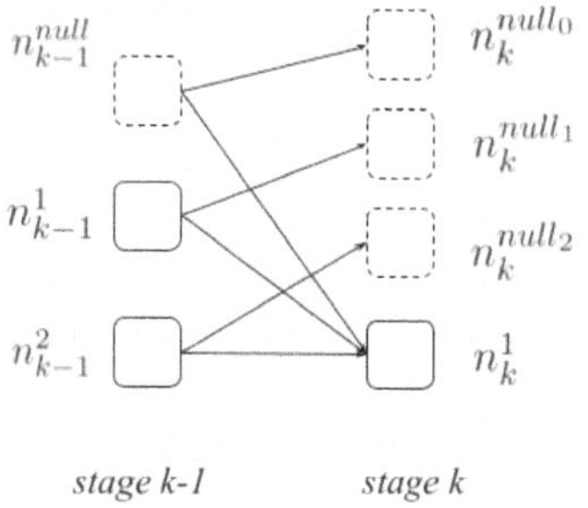

Fig. 10. Illustration of Viterbi algorithm.

the ball movement and are updated along the best track. We use the Viterbi algorithm to find the most likely ball track in a sequence of frames.

For an example shown in Fig. 10, there are three nodes in stage $k-1$. n_{k-1}^1 and n_{k-1}^2 represent 2 different ball detections, and n_{k-1}^{null} represents the miss detection. Each of the node contains the current best track, the current best score (referred as s_{k-1}^1, s_{k-1}^2 and s_{k-1}^{null}), and the current best state. When updating nodes in stage k, we first calculate edge weights between nodes in two stages. For example, we want to calculate the edge weight between n_{k-1}^1 (referred as previous node) and n_k^1 (referred as current node). Figure 11 denotes the current best state in the previous node n_{k-1}^1, where the green thick solid oval is the ball state following the constant acceleration model with probability μ_{k-1}^1 and blue one is the ball state following the sudden change motion model with the remaining probability $\mu_{k-1}^2 = 1 - \mu_{k-1}^1$. Since the green and blue states represent the same ball, these two states should be mixed by adjusting the green state towards the blue, and likewise for the blue to the green as shown in Fig. 12. We then calculate the predicted state based on each individual motion model using the KalmanPredict function (Eq. 2) as highlighted in Fig. 13. In stage k, there is a detection in n_k^1.

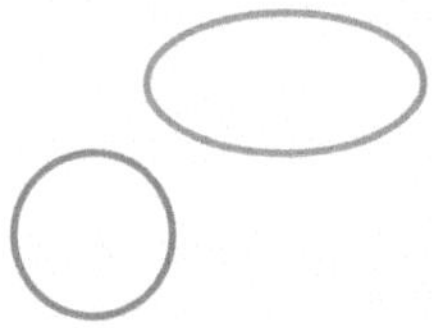

Fig. 11. Two motion models in the previous node n^1_{k-1}.

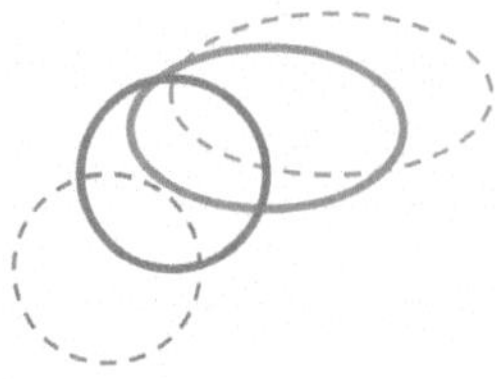

Fig. 12. Adjust two motion models n^1_{k-1} towards each other.

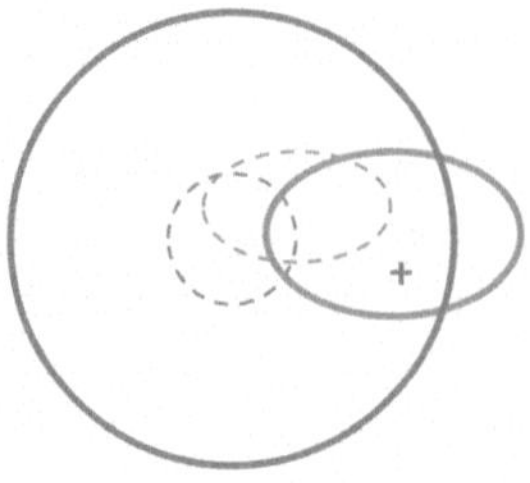

Fig. 13. Predicted n^1_{k-1} and a detection (denoted as "+") in n^1_k.

We can then compute two probabilities (likelihoods) that the detection in n^1_k belongs to either the constant acceleration model or the sudden change model based on the predicted Gaussians. We take the larger probability as the edge weight between node n^1_{k-1} and n^1_k, denoted as w_1. Similarly, we calculate edge weights between n^2_{k-1} and n^1_k as w_2, and between n^{null}_{k-1} and n^1_k as w_{null}. The best score in n^1_k is $max\{w_1 * s^1_{k-1}, w_2 * s^2_{k-1}, w_{null} * score^{null}_{k-1}, \}$. The best track is the track of the corresponding previous node that generates the best score, appended with the current node. The best state is the corresponding previous node's state updated with the detection in n^1_k using Eq. 4.

For each node in stage $k-1$, it will have certain probability transit to a different "null" node. The reason is that the current best state in each node in stage $k-1$ is different. When there is no detection in the next stage, the next state will also be different. Since there is no detection in the "null" state in stage k, after the Gaussian prediction step as illustrated in Fig. 13, we directly put the predicted Gaussian distributions in the "null" node as the current best state, and use a constant FNR (i.e., false negative rate) as the edge weight to calculate the current best score. However, if each node will lead to a possible "null" node in the next stage, the node space will grow quickly. To avoid this problem, we remove the "null" node if the best state covariance is larger than some threshold (i.e., very uncertain about the current track).

Finally, once the forward tracking is completed, we get the track with highest score in the final stage as our final best track, in other words, the most likely ball track within a sequence of frames. We then perform a backward smoothing step based on Eq. 5 and 6 to obtain a smoother ball trajectory.

4 Experiment and Results

We downloaded 33 tennis broadcast videos from TV channels and YouTube. We randomly selected 5 videos as the test set and use the remain videos as training set. Within the 5 test videos, there are 2 videos with a resolution of 1280×720

pixels and a frame rate of 25 frame per second, which are referred as half-HD videos, and the remaining 3 videos with 1920×1280 pixels resolution and 50 frames per second, referred as full-HD videos. We manually labelled 42,717 images, one ball per image, as our training data. These labelled data are used to train both the Detector1 and the Detector2.

Table 1 shows Detector1 achieves 93% accuracy, consistently for both half-HD and full-HD test videos. TP refers to True Positives. FP refers to False Positives. FN refers to False Negatives, which is also referred as miss detection. There is no True Negatives in our test data because there is one ball, visible or occluded, in each frame. $Accuracy = TP/(TP + FP + FN)$. Among the 2 types of errors, there are more FN than FP, which shows Detector1 can reject false ball candidates most of the time but fail to detect ball if it is occluded. Therefore, in the second experiment tilted "Detector1 + Detector2", if Detector1 does not detect any candidate, we use Detector2 which uses the feature maps from 3 connecting frames. Table 2 shows "Detector1+Detector2" achieves 96.5% accuracy. This shows our 3-frame transfer learning based ball detector in the feature space is indeed effective.

Table 1. Detector1 result.

	TP	FP	FN	Accuracy
Half-HD	2816	88	128	92.88%
Full-HD	3077	44	168	93.55%
Overall	**5893**	**132**	**296**	**93.23%**

Table 2. Detector1+Detector2 result.

	TP	FP	FN	Accuracy
Half-HD	2908	115	9	95.91%
Full-HD	3192	89	8	97.05%
Overall	**6100**	**204**	**17**	**96.50%**

We compare our "Detector1+Detector2" against TrackNet by [5], because TrackNet also uses 3 connecting frames ($t-1$, t, $t+1$) as the input to detect the ball candidate at time t. TrackNet is a specially designed DNN to detect tennis ball trained using more than 20,000 manually labelled images from full-HD videos. Comparatively, ours is a transfer learning network based on an existing general purpose object detection DNN. To ensure validity, we run the trained TrackNet, published by the original authors, on our full-HD test set. Table 3 shows our method is effective, because we outperforms TrackNet by about 10%.

Table 3. Comparing with TrackNet.

	TP	FP	FN	Accuracy
Our's	**3192**	**89**	**8**	**97.05%**
TrackNet	2654	129	266	87.04%

Table 4. EIMM Tracking result.

	TP	FP	FN	Accuracy
DNN only	6100	204	17	96.50%
Using EIMM	**6273**	**49**	**0**	**99.22%**

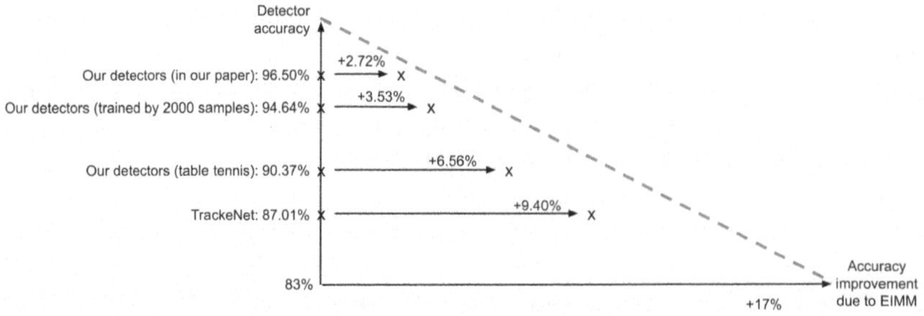

Fig. 14. Our proposed technique is a combination of object detection and tracking.

Using DNN only, i.e., "Detector1+Detector2", we can already achieve 96.50% accuracy, however, we can further improve the accuracy by adding the Bayesian estimation step explained in our EIMM algorithm. Table 4 confirms that our EIMM tracking algorithm achieves more than 99% accuracy, which is significantly better than using DNN only.

We would like to highlight that our proposed technique is a combination of object detection and tracking. It requires both components, instead of relying on the ball detection DNN alone. Referring to Fig. 14, we use y-axis to indicate accuracy achieved by the object detector DNN alone, and x-axis to indicate the improvement obtained by combining the detector with our EIMM tracking algorithm. The dashed blue line indicates our goal (100% accuracy). Such a goal can be achieved by a very accurate object detector alone, or a relatively weaker object detector but greatly enhanced by a tracking algorithm. However, the reality is somewhere in the middle as indicated by the following 3 additional experiments.

Table 5. Detectors trained by 2000 samples

	TP	FP	FN	Accuracy
1-frame Detectron2	5469	140	467	90.01%
3-frame CNN	5708	293	30	94.64%
Detectors + EIMM	**6208**	**113**	**9**	**98.07%**

Table 6. TrackNet (and EIMM)

	TP	FP	FN	Accuracy
TrackNet	2654	129	266	87.01%
TrackNet + EIMM	**2980**	**108**	**3**	**96.41%**

(1) In Table 5, we retrain Detectron2 freshly with 2000 randomly sampled training data. Due to the smaller training data size, the accuracy is only 90.01%. Using our 3-frame ball detector (retrained using the 2000 samples), the accuracy is improved to 94.64%. Combining with our EIMM tracking algorithm, it is further improved by 3.53%, reaching 98.07%.

(2) Table 6 shows, TrackNet alone achieves 87.01% accuracy. TrackNet is already a 3-frame based ball detector. We then combine it with our EIMM. The accuracy is improved by 9.4%, reaching 96.41%.

Table 7. Table tennis ball detectors trained by 16639 samples.

	TP	FP	FN	Accuracy
1-frame Detectron2	2390	63	321	86.16%
3-frame CNN	2507	142	125	90.37%
Detectors + EIMM	**2588**	**82**	**0**	**96.93%**

(3) We also tested our method in a different sports using smaller ball, i.e., table tennis. As shown in Table 7, the single and 3-frame detector accuracy is up to 90.37%. Combining with EIMM, the final accuracy reaches 96.93%.

5 Summary

We have shown tracking a small and fast moving ball from the broadcast video requires both vision based algorithm and motion based algorithm. With sufficient training data, DNN based solution has proven to be accurate and generalizable. Furthermore, well-trained DNN can serve as feature extractor, which allows us to build simple and effective multi-frame ball detectors.

Vision based ball detector has it limit. There are times ball is too small or too blur to be recognized even under the multi-frame setting. However, we know the ball mostly follow certain motion model. From these observation, we conclude tracker is an important component if we want to build a highly accurate ball tracking solution. Acknowledging there are false and miss detection from time to time, we search for the best sequence of ball states by locating the most likely sequence of ball candidates. The motion models determine the likelihood of each candidate in the current time step based on the estimated ball state in the previous time step. Furthermore, our tracker can use future information to back track the ball state to further improve the tracking accuracy.

This framework also shows it is possible to avoid designing complex DNN in highly accurate object tracking tasks. Combining transfer learning using existing DNN and Bayesian estimator is an effective alternative solution.

References

1. Bar-Shalom, Y., Fortmann, T.E., Cable, P.G.: Tracking and data association (1990)
2. Dong, J.S., et al.: Sports analytics using probabilistic model checking and deep learning. In: 2023 27th International Conference on Engineering of Complex Computer Systems (ICECCS), pp. 7–11. IEEE (2023)
3. Dong, J.S., Shi, L., Jiang, K., Sun, J., et al.: Sports strategy analytics using probabilistic reasoning. In: 2015 20th International Conference on Engineering of Complex Computer Systems (ICECCS), pp. 182–185. IEEE (2015)
4. Forney, G.D.: The viterbi algorithm. Proc. IEEE **61**(3), 268–278 (1973)

5. Huang, Y.C., Liao, I.N., Chen, C.H., İk, T.U., Peng, W.C.: Tracknet: a deep learning network for tracking high-speed and tiny objects in sports applications. In: 2019 16th IEEE International Conference on Advanced Video and Signal Based Surveillance (AVSS), pp. 1–8. IEEE (2019)
6. Kalman, R.E.: A new approach to linear filtering and prediction problems (1960)
7. Lin, T.Y., Dollár, P., Girshick, R., He, K., Hariharan, B., Belongie, S.: Feature pyramid networks for object detection. In: Proceedings of the IEEE Conference on Computer Vision and Pattern Recognition, pp. 2117–2125 (2017)
8. Liu, Z., Jiang, K., Hou, Z., Lin, Y., Dong, J.S.: Insight analysis for tennis strategy and tactics. In: 2023 IEEE International Conference on Data Mining (ICDM), pp. 1169–1174. IEEE (2023)
9. Rauch, H.E., Tung, F., Striebel, C.T.: Maximum likelihood estimates of linear dynamic systems. AIAA J. **3**(8), 1445–1450 (1965)
10. Ren, S., He, K., Girshick, R., Sun, J.: Faster R-CNN: towards real-time object detection with region proposal networks. Adv. Neural Inf. Process. Syst. **28** (2015)
11. Siddharth, S., Saurav, S., Kan, J., Bimlesh, W., Song, D.J.: Model driven inputs to aid athlete's decision making. In: 2020 27th Asia-Pacific Software Engineering Conference (APSEC), pp. 485–489. IEEE (2020)
12. Simonyan, K., Zisserman, A.: Very deep convolutional networks for large-scale image recognition. arXiv preprint arXiv:1409.1556 (2014)
13. Song, S., Sun, J., Liu, Y., Dong, J.S.: A model checker for hierarchical probabilistic real-time systems. In: Madhusudan, P., Seshia, S.A. (eds.) CAV 2012. LNCS, vol. 7358, pp. 705–711. Springer, Heidelberg (2012). https://doi.org/10.1007/978-3-642-31424-7_53
14. Sun, J., Liu, Y., Dong, J.S., Pang, J.: PAT: towards flexible verification under fairness. In: Bouajjani, A., Maler, O. (eds.) CAV 2009. LNCS, vol. 5643, pp. 709–714. Springer, Heidelberg (2009). https://doi.org/10.1007/978-3-642-02658-4_59
15. Voeikov, R., Falaleev, N., Baikulov, R.: Ttnet: real-time temporal and spatial video analysis of table tennis. In: Proceedings of the IEEE/CVF Conference on Computer Vision and Pattern Recognition Workshops, pp. 884–885 (2020)
16. Wu, Y., Kirillov, A., Massa, F., Lo, W.Y., Girshick, R.: Detectron2 (2019). https://github.com/facebookresearch/detectron2. **2**(3)
17. Yan, F., Christmas, W., Kittler, J.: A tennis ball tracking algorithm for automatic annotation of tennis match. In: British Machine Vision Conference, vol. 2, pp. 619–628. University of Surrey (2005)
18. Yu, X., Sim, C.H., Wang, J.R., Cheong, L.F.: A trajectory-based ball detection and tracking algorithm in broadcast tennis video. In: 2004 International Conference on Image Processing, 2004. ICIP'04, vol. 2, pp. 1049–1052. IEEE (2004)
19. Zeiler, M.D., Krishnan, D., Taylor, G.W., Fergus, R.: Deconvolutional networks. In: 2010 IEEE Computer Society Conference on Computer Vision and Pattern Recognition, pp. 2528–2535. IEEE (2010)

Mechanomyography as a Promising Tool for Managing Physical Activity and Preventing Injuries in the Field

Juliette Reerink-Boulanger[1,2](✉), Auréanne Ferssiwi[3], Maxime Projetti[3], Matthieu Correa[3,4], and Alain Somat[2]

[1] Innovation and Research Department, Hospitalité St Thomas de Villeneuve, Rennes, France
juliette.boulanger@hstv.fr
[2] LP3C - EA1285 - Université Rennes 2, Rennes, France
[3] Moten Technologies, Puteaux, France
[4] Laboratoire CIAMS - Université Paris-Saclay, Orsay, France

Abstract. Due to manpower shortage in the healthcare and medico-social sector, Hospitalité Saint Thomas de Villeneuve has observed that a large number of musculoskeletal disorders (MSDs) affects negatively the health of employees during their physical activity. Mostly linked to the handling of residents/patients and manipulation of material and equipment in hospital's logistic department, an experiment has been set up to assess levels of physical activity of deltoid and lumbar muscles during logistics tasks with the use of mechanomyography (MMG). We will discuss how this specific measurement of muscle activity can prevent MSD hazards, reduce sport injuries and provide an interesting tool to discuss and conduct organizational changes within Hospitals.

Keywords: muscle activity · physical activity · mechanomyography · ergonomics · sports · musculoskeletal disorders · injuries

1 Introduction

Today, musculoskeletal disorders (MSDs) prevention is a major economic and healthcare issue. MSDs cost at least two billion euros to companies in France in 2017. Irreversible and severe musculoskeletal disorders affect 45% of workers. Biomechanical risk factors, such as repetitive tasks, excessive efforts and heavy loads are identified as leading causes of MSDs prevalence [1]. Theses situations induce muscle fatigue, which has been shown to play a central role in MSDs appearance [2]. In sports, a similar observation is made as fatigue and excessive load are known to be risk factors of injuries [3]. The challenge of injury prevention includes managing new decisions process and Quality of Life and Working Conditions (QoLWC). It involves testing innovative solutions to reduce accident and Musculoskeletal Disorders but also choose physical activity preparation according to data set. In this perspective, monitoring physical activity and detecting

J. S. Dong et al. (Eds.): ISACE 2024, LNCS 14794, pp. 97–103, 2024.
https://doi.org/10.1007/978-3-031-69073-0_8

muscle fatigue would constitute great opportunities for injuries prevention in the working environment and in sports. The most common method used in the literature for such tasks are through the measure of muscle activity [4].

A specific measurement of muscle activity, known as mechanomyography (MMG), could represent a relevant alternative to the current reference measure: the electromyograhy (EMG). EMG suffers several limitations, such as skin preparation and sensitivity to sweat [5] making it hardly suitable in the field. MMG, defined as measurement of muscle vibrations at the skin surface [6], can be detected with accelerometers which are cheap, lightweight, insensitive to sweat and don't require any skin preparation. MMG is a promising alternative to EMG in the field that recently shown greater sensitivity to changes in load during a dynamic tasks [7].

The aim of this study is to use MMG as a tool to assess levels of physical activity of deltoid and lumbar muscles during logistics tasks. We shall see in the discussion that this MMG measure offers at least two application perspectives: one relating to work activity and the other to sports. The first was to use the MMG tool to provoke discussion about the work activity and its difficulty, in order to prioritize work situations that are sources of hardship, and to collectively design a new organization. The other would be to use MMG as a tool to analyze sports practice, in order to help coaches and team managers to make appropriate choices for scheduling training and managing the risks of intensive sports practice.

2 Material and Method

2.1 Data Collection

A data collection campaign has been initiated in the Logistic Departement of the Hospital and in EHPAD (institution for dependent elderly people) to monitor working activities identified as physically demanding: 1) large logistics orders; 2) showering activities in nursing home; 3) linen and waste management; 4) toileting (night-time diaper changes). In total, 3 individuals (2 males, 1 female) were equipped in the period of May-August 2023. The purpose of the database obtained from this data collection was to identify hazards and work situations that are sources of hardship, MSD risks, injuries and work-related accidents to the target population. For each working situation, the performance monitored with sensors was: a) Muscular effort b) Effort intensity c) Duration of effort. In this article, only large logistics order and muscular effort will be discussed.

2.2 Sensors

To measure muscle activity, accelerometer-based mechanomyographic sensors sampled at 1000 Hz were used (Moten Technologies, Puteaux, France). For each muscle studied, the sensor was placed over the muscle belly, following recommendations. The MMG signal was band-pass filtered between 5 and 100 Hz to reject motion artifacts and a 1-second time window root mean square (RMS) amplitude was used as the extraction feature [8]. As it was not possible to measure the maximum voluntary contraction of the studied muscles, the MMG amplitude was normalized according to the maximum RMS value obtained during the recording. The normalized RMS amplitude will further be referred to as muscular effort.

2.3 Procedure

Workers involved in the large logistic order working situation were given information of the experiment by the PRAP trainer, ambassador of the MSD prevention approach. One worker (logistic operator, see Fig. 1) was then trained by an ergonomist on how and where to place the sensors before starting the physical activity, placing them on both deltoid and lumbar muscles. The ergonomist helped determining the sequencing of the working situation into tasks.

Fig. 1. Fitting the Moten sensors to the logistic operator, here on the left deltoid muscle.

3 Results

3.1 Descriptive Analysis of the Logistics Tasks

The four tasks studied during the experiment are presented in Fig. 2. In 2 h and 30 min, the two operators carried 2991.71 kg, which correspond to 739 packages distributed over 15 pallets.

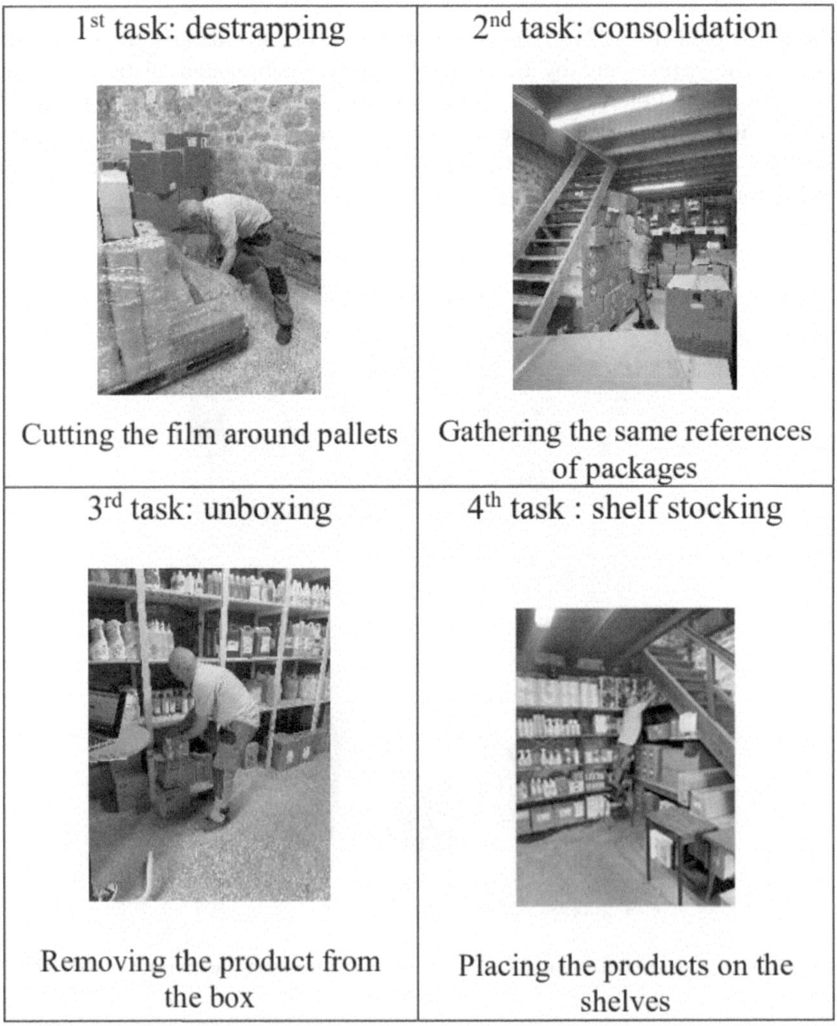

Fig. 2. Description of the tasks during the receiving of a large logistics order

3.2 Muscular Effort Data

Throughout the activity of receiving a large logistics order, the average muscular effort was 46% for the right deltoid, 41% for the left deltoid, 40% for the left lumbar, and 32% for the right lumbar. Mean muscular effort during the different activities studied are displayed in Table 1. Muscular effort was higher during destrapping and shelf stocking than during consolidation and unboxing. For each activity, muscular effort was systematically greater on the left side than the right side.

Table 1. Mean muscular effort per muscle and task

Tasks	Lumbar		Deltoid	
	right	left	right	left
1st task: Destrapping	36%	42%	41%	46%
2nd task: Consolidation	22%	29%	26%	29%
3rd task: Unboxing	20%	29%	28%	29%
4th task Shelf stocking	31%	40%	41%	47%

4 Discussion and Perspectives

The aim of this experiment was to test the MMG as a tool for measuring muscle activity during logistical tasks, in order to better manage it. According to the MMG data, the most intensive task among the four studied was destrapping for lumbars. For deltoids, destrapping and shelf stocking were identified as most demanding tasks.

This data is supported by the biomecanics of the realized tasks, as we can see in Fig. 2. Destrapping demanded the worker to band the trunk and extend their arms forward, exerting high levels of muscular effort on both lumbar and deltoid muscles, as the center of gravity is deported forward. On the other hand, shelf stocking required the worker to lift entire packages above deltoids level, inducing high muscular strain for deltoids.

From the results obtained in this study, MMG could be a relevant tool to assess muscular strain between various tasks, including lifts, as it was the context of this procedure.

As a working perspective, we observe that an increasing number of medical, social and hospital teams are testing innovative devices with their staff to improve quality of life at work and reduce musculoskeletal pain [9]. The experiment set up in Hôtel-Dieu de Pont-l'Abbé hospital supported this approach for at-risk populations with physical activity. Firstly, this measure was interesting because it encouraged a participatory discussion on physical activity. It was indeed possible to involve hospital professionals at several hierarchical levels (top management, managers, supervisors, operators) and finally allowed a collective search of optimal solutions to prevent injuries. Considering the MMG as a tool to support work discussion has been made possible due to common representations between the person carrying out the work activity and the person managing it. Secondly, by sharing these indicators, it engages working groups to collectively pilot preventing measures, analyze efforts and muscular intensity, check whether physical activities are appropriate or produce barriers in order to improve working conditions. On that perspective, collecting this data is a mean to discuss the physical activity and collectively prevent injuries and accidents. Thirdly, although results of the test are inconclusive due to limited sample size, period of use (the sensors were tested on limited periods and during spring and summer) and organizational barriers (limited time to conduct research, manpower shortage), the benefits of this pre-investigation study highlighted the need of introducing innovative devices and facilitating organizational support to measure muscular activity, discuss injuries prevention of workers engaged in real physical activities [10] and evaluate it collectively.

Associated with open innovative techniques and tools to support participation (such as: i) prepare a participatory and democratic project governance; propose focus groups, interviews, photo-reportage collection for risk factors identification; ii) involve groups to autonomously pilot preventing measures; iii) collectively engage managers and workers to evaluate solution together) this living lab co-design methodology occurs promising land to future experimental settings in MSD hazard and physical activity monitoring. Based on the current results, the living lab at Hospitalité Saint Thomas de Villeneuve and MOTEN are planning further research to make fruitful use of MMG data as a means of discussing work, improving it by testing relevant technologies (e.g. exoskeletons) and driving organizational changes within Hospitals and medical institutions where physical activities are practiced.

Even though intensities of the studied tasks were relatively low, approximately 4 kg (2991 kg/739 packages), MMG was successful at detecting differences in muscular effort between tasks and between sides (left and right). This sensitivity, even at low levels of effort, opens the application of MMG in sports where: i) lifting exercises performed at the gym such as deadlifts or shoulder presses can be heavier by an order of magnitude, ii) the assessment of muscular laterality differences, for example between an injured and a valid limb, is a major issue in rehabilitation after an injury and iii), the targeting of training sessions intensity and volume for a specific goal (strength or endurance) requires precise settings.

Indeed, MMG can be used to both i) negotiate and plan training sessions in order to prevent or heal injuries and ii) optimize performance through a precise assessment and monitoring of muscle activity during training.

References

1. Vignais, N.: From sensors to biofeedback and exoskeletons: how biomechanics may support ergonomics. thesis, Université Paris-Saclay, January 2023
2. Rashedi, E.: Localized Muscle Fatigue: Theoretical and Practical Aspects in Occupational Environments. PhD Thesis, Virginia Tech, 2016
3. Karamanoukian, A.: Développement d'un outil de quantification de la charge mécanique en football à partir de crampons instrumentés de capteurs de force: vers une application à la prévention des blessures, 2023
4. Al-Mulla, M.R., Sepulveda, F., Colley, M.: A review of non-invasive techniques to detect and predict localised muscle fatigue. Sensors (Basel, Switzerland) **11**(4), 3545–3594 (2011)
5. Laferriere, P., Chan, A.D.C., Lemaire, E.D.: Surface electromyographic signals using a dry electrode. In: 2010 IEEE International Workshop on Medical Measurements and Applications, (Ottawa, ON, Canada), pp. 77–80, IEEE, April 2010
6. Orizio, C.: Muscle sound: bases for the introduction of a mechanomyographic signal in muscle studies. Crit. Rev. Biomed. Eng. **21**(3), 201–243 (1993)
7. Correa, M., Projetti, M., Siegler, I.A., Vignais, N.: Mechanomyographic analysis for muscle activity assessment during a load-lifting task. Sensors **23**, 7969 (2023)
8. Ibitoye, M.O., Hamzaid, N.A., Zuniga, J.M., Hasnan, N., Wahab, A.K.A.: Mechanomyographic parameter extraction methods: an appraisal for clinical applications. Sensors **14**(12), 22940–22970 (2014)
9. Settembre, N., et al.: The use of exoskeletons to help with prone positioning in the intensive care unit during COVID-19. In: Annals of Physical and Rehabilitation Medicine, vol. 63, no. 4, pp. 379–382. Elsevier (2020)
10. Venkatesh, V., Morris, M.G., Davis, G.B., Davis, F.D.: User acceptance of information technology: toward a unified view. MIS Q. 425–478 (2003). Publisher: JSTOR

Exploring Team Strategy Dynamics in Tennis Doubles Matches

Zhaoyu Liu[1(✉)], Chen Dong[2], Chen Wang[2], Tian Yu Dong[3], and Kan Jiang[1]

[1] National University of Singapore, Singapore, Singapore
liuzy@nus.edu.sg
[2] Louisiana State University, Baton Rouge, USA
[3] Saint Mary's College of California, Moraga, USA

Abstract. In the dynamic and strategic environment of tennis doubles, understanding the multifaceted interactions between players is crucial for enhancing team performance. This paper introduces a novel analytical framework for tennis doubles, employing Markov Decision Processes (MDP) and probabilistic model checking (PMC) to model the intricate behaviors and interactions in doubles matches. Unlike existing studies predominantly focused on singles matches, our approach captures the complexities and uncertainties inherent in doubles, including larger state spaces and diverse action types. Through analyzing historical match data, we derive probability distributions, success rates, and transition probabilities, enabling the prediction of match outcomes and formulation of effective strategies. This work expands on previous singles match analytics, offering a comprehensive model that balances explainability and accuracy, suitable for both player and coach utilization. A preliminary evaluation using NCAA Division 1 tennis doubles matches validates our model and demonstrates its potential in strategic recommendation, thereby providing a significant step forward in the analytics of tennis doubles.

Keywords: Tennis Doubles Analytics · Markov Decision Processes · Probabilistic Model Checking

1 Introduction

A tennis doubles match involves two teams, each consisting of two players, competing against each other, contrasting with a single match where individual players face off. The complexity of tennis doubles arises from the increased number of players, leading to more dynamic and multifaceted interactions on the court. This environment necessitates a heightened strategic approach, as players must coordinate movements and tactics with their partners, manage spatial coverage more effectively, and exploit the combined skills and strengths of the team. The interplay between teammates and opponents in tennis doubles creates a nuanced game, where strategy and collaboration become as crucial as individual skill.

J. S. Dong et al. (Eds.): ISACE 2024, LNCS 14794, pp. 104–115, 2024.
https://doi.org/10.1007/978-3-031-69073-0_9

Prevailing research in racket sports predominantly concentrates on analytics of singles matches [1–3]. Terroba et al. [4] introduced an MDP-based framework employing Monte Carlo tree search to deduce optimal policies in singles tennis matches. Wei et al. [5] and Wang et al. [6] assessed individual actions in singles tennis and badminton, respectively, calculating the expected probability of winning a rally by considering player locations, movement speeds, and ball dynamics. Wang et al. [7] further analyzed actions in singles table tennis by categorizing shots as "good" or "bad" through expert assessment and video analysis. However, these studies do not delve into the doubles context, which presents increased uncertainty, variety, and complexity.

In this paper, we model a tennis doubles match using Markov Decision Processes (MDP) with shot-by-shot actions, capturing complex behaviors and interactions among players. The probability distributions, success rates, and transition probabilities are derived from historical matches. With the learned MDP model, we can conduct probabilistic reasoning such as predicting match outcomes and recommending strategy adjustments that increase winning chances.

This research augments our prior work [8] on singles tennis, transitioning to doubles matches. In comparison, our doubles model accommodates more players, a greater variety of actions, and an expanded state space. This enlargement yields a higher degree of uncertainty and possibilities in state-action transitions, such as a forehand down-the-line shot from the deuce court potentially being volleyed at the net or returned from the baseline by any opponent, indicative of the complex strategies and tactics in play. Our contributions are as follows:

- We introduce a novel tennis doubles analytics framework utilizing MDP and PMC, based on detailed shot-by-shot data.
- Our model balances explainability and accuracy, capturing the complex dynamics and interactions among four players, while remaining comprehensible and applicable for players and coaches.
- We conduct a preliminary evaluation using two NCAA Division 1 tennis doubles matches to affirm our model's validity and illustrate strategy recommendations.

2 Related Works

Recent studies in tennis doubles analytics have provided insightful perspectives into tactical variants, ranking methodologies, and the impact of ball-tracking technology on understanding game dynamics. Kocib et al. [9] investigated the frequency and efficiency of tactical formations in professional men's doubles tennis, analyzing 1067 points from 18 matches. Their findings indicated a prevalent use of the I-formation and a preference for baseline positioning by the receiving team, offering valuable insights into current strategic preferences at the elite level. This study underscores the necessity of tailored training sessions to reflect these tactical trends.

Breznik [10] explored an alternative approach to ranking male doubles teams and individual players, employing social network analysis and the PageRank

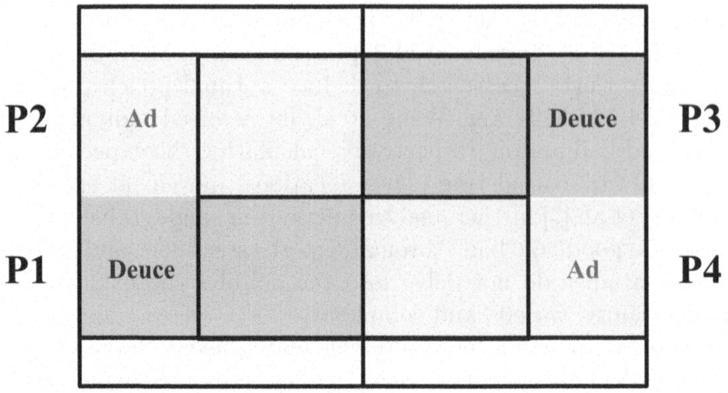

Fig. 1. Tennis court and players default locations.

algorithm on data from over 128,000 matches. The analysis highlighted the Bryan brothers and Todd Woodbridge as the foremost doubles team and individual players, respectively, suggesting the potential of network analysis as a complementary tool to the traditional ATP ranking system.

In a groundbreaking study, Martínez-Gallego et al. [11] described the structural characteristics and point-concluding patterns in professional doubles matches, revealing a distinct game structure compared to singles play, with a notable emphasis on the serve and offensive strategies. Their research filled a significant gap in the literature by quantifying the dynamics of doubles play, particularly on hard courts.

Furthering this line of inquiry, Martínez-Gallego et al. [12] utilized tennis ball tracking technology to analyze volley positions in both men's and women's doubles matches. The study identified significant differences in playing styles and positions between genders, with a higher variability in men's matches. This research emphasizes the importance of ball-tracking technology in enhancing the understanding of match dynamics and in preparing players for the competitive demands of professional doubles tennis.

However, none of these works focus on modeling tennis doubles matches as MDPs to predict match outcomes and provide strategy recommendations.

3 The Proposed Approach

In this paper, we focus on tennis doubles matches, where two players from Team 1 $T1$ are referred to as $P1$ and $P2$, and the ones from Team 2 $T2$ are $P3$ and $P4$. The default position for $P1$ and $P3$ is deuce court and ad court for $P2$ and $P4$ as shown in Fig. 1.

To forecast the match outcome, we analyze the winning probability within a simplified **tiebreak game**, serving as an abstraction of the full match. We cap the maximum score at 7 points to prevent state space explosion, positing that the team first achieving this score wins. This analysis is predicated on the assumption that the player who is most likely to win the tiebreak game also has a higher chance of winning the entire match. Such an abstraction facilitates efficient performance verification through PAT.

3.1 Modeling Tennis Doubles Matches in MDP

We formulate a tennis doubles match as a Markov Decision Process (MDP), drawing on expert tennis knowledge to define states and actions using tennis terminology. The MDP components are detailed as follows:

State Space. A state in this model captures the instance when a player strikes the ball, categorized into six types: serve, return, volley, smash, stroke, and termination states.

- 4 **serve** states: first serve on the deuce court, second serve on the deuce court, first serve on the ad court, and second serve on the ad court.
- 4 **return** states: forehand return of a deuce court serve, backhand return of a deuce court serve, forehand return of an ad court serve, and backhand return of an ad court serve.
- 4 **volley** states: forehand deuce court volley, backhand deuce court volley, forehand ad court volley, and backhand ad court volley.
- 4 **smash** states: forehand deuce court smash, backhand deuce court smash, forehand ad court smash, and backhand ad court smash.
- 4 **stroke** states: forehand deuce court stroke, backhand deuce court stroke, forehand ad court stroke, and backhand ad court stroke.

Each state records the current tiebreak game point. A termination state signifies that either player has won the tiebreak game (i.e., achieved 7 points first), with possible scores such as 7-1 ($T1$ wins), 5-7 ($T2$ wins), and 7-6 ($T1$ wins).

Action Space. In each state s, players have a set of possible actions, influenced by their position and handedness, including:

- Serving (first/second) to T, B, W locations.
- Forehand/Backhand stroke/volley/lob/smash to cross-court, down the line, inside-out, inside-in.

Transition Function. The transition function $P : S \times A \times S \rightarrow [0, 1]$ represents the probability of transitioning to a subsequent state, considering three outcomes for each state-action pair: **in** (successful action not leading to point win), **winner** (action leads directly to point win), and **error** (failed action). Winning or erroneous actions transition to a new state for the next serve, adjusting the score accordingly, while **in** actions proceed to another non-termination state with a defined probability.

Policy. The policy π is the probability distribution over possible actions for each state, expressed as $\pi(a|s) = Pr(A = a|S = s)$. This delineates the strategic choices players make in each state, exemplified by a serving probability distribution of 60% to T, 30% to W, and 10% to B.

3.2 Implementation in PCSP#

The implementation of our MDP model is demonstrated in the PCSP# language, utilizing a tiebreaker game involving four right-handed players as an example. The tennis court is segmented into four regions, corresponding to the deuce and ad courts on each side, as depicted in Fig. 1.

Serving Order. In the tiebreak game, serving commences from the deuce court with the initial server. Subsequently, a player from the opposing team undertakes the next two serves, beginning from the ad court followed by the deuce court. Serving order alternates between the teams, with each participant serving two consecutive points, transitioning after the deuce court serve. To encompass all potential serving sequences, we introduce a variable `order`, denoting the serving order (e.g., `order=[1,4,2,3]` signifies that $P1$ serves first, succeeded by $P4$, $P2$, and $P3$). Various serving orders are accommodated through alternate choices.

```
Orders = p1p3{order[0]=1;order[1]=3;order[2]=2;order[3]=4;turn=1}->Skip []
         p1p4{order[0]=1;order[1]=4;order[2]=2;order[3]=3;turn=1}->Skip []
         p2p3{order[0]=2;order[1]=3;order[2]=1;order[3]=4;turn=2}->Skip []
         p2p4{order[0]=2;order[1]=4;order[2]=1;order[3]=3;turn=2}->Skip []
         p3p1{order[0]=3;order[1]=1;order[2]=4;order[3]=2;turn=3}->Skip []
         p3p2{order[0]=3;order[1]=2;order[2]=4;order[3]=1;turn=3}->Skip []
         p4p1{order[0]=4;order[1]=1;order[2]=3;order[3]=2;turn=4}->Skip []
         p4p2{order[0]=4;order[1]=2;order[2]=3;order[3]=1;turn=4}->Skip;
```

where `turn` indicates the current server ID. We also define a `nextServer` function to find the next server based on the serving order and the current server ID. Please refer to the code for more details.

Model for Serve. Each player can serve from his deuce court or ad court and has a second serve opportunity if he fails the first one. The following example shows a right-hand player $P1$ performing his first serve from the deuce court.

```
// P1 1st serve from Deuce court
P1_DeServe = [turn==1]P1DeReady1st -> pcase {
    3: ServeT_in -> P3_DeReturn_BH
    1: ServeT_err -> P1_DeServe_2nd
    0: ServeT_win -> Ace{team1++; if (team1==points) {won=t1}
                         else {turn=call(nextServer, turn)}} -> NextPt
    4: ServeWide_in -> P3_DeReturn_FH
    0: ServeWide_err -> P1_DeServe_2nd
    0: ServeWide_win -> Ace{team1++; if (team1==points) {won=t1}
                         else {turn=call(nextServer, turn)}} -> NextPt
```

```
    1: ServeBody_in -> pcase {
        0: P3_DeReturn_FH
        1: P3_DeReturn_BH
    }
    2: ServeBody_err -> P1_DeServe_2nd
    0: ServeBody_win -> Ace{team1++; if (team1==points) {won=t1}
                        else {turn=call(nextServer, turn)}} -> NextPt
};
```

As shown in the code, three serving actions are specified: Serve_T, Serve_Wide, and Serve_Body, each with three potential outcomes: in, err, and win. The numeral preceding each action reflects its frequency in historical data (for instance, $P1$ serving to T occurs four times, with three instances resulting in in and one in err). If an err occurs, $P1$ will execute a second serve (P1_DeServe_2nd). A win outcome yields a point for team 1, transitioning to the subsequent point (NextPt), provided the game is not yet won. An in outcome instigates a transition to the succeeding state. Notably, the transition following ServeBody_in is probabilistic, potentially leading to either $P3$'s deuce court forehand or backhand return.

Model for Return. A player can return a deuce/ad court serve using forehand or backhand. For example, P2_AdReturn_BH describes how $P2$ returns serve from the ad court with his backhand.

```
P2_AdReturn_BH = P2AdReadyBHReturn -> pcase {
    2: BH_DownLine -> pcase {
        0: P3_DeVolley_FH
        0: P3_DeVolley_BH
        0: P4_DeVolley_FH
        2: P4_DeVolley_BH
    }
    2: BH_DownLine_err -> Error{team2++; if (team2==points) {won=t2}}
                       -> NextPt
    1: BH_DownLine_win -> Winner{team1++; if (team1==points) {won=t1}}
                       -> NextPt

    1: BH_DownLine_lob -> pcase {
        0: P3_DeSmash_FH
        0: P3_DeSmash_BH
        0: P4_DeStroke_BH
        0: P4_DeStroke_FH
        1: P4_DeSmash_FH
        0: P4_DeSmash_BH
        0: P3_DeStroke_BH
        0: P3_DeStroke_FH
    }
```

```
    2: BH_DownLine_lob_err -> Error{team2++; if (team2==points) {won=t2}}
                           -> NextPt
    0: BH_DownLine_lob_win -> Winner{team1++; if (team1==points) {won=t1}}
                           -> NextPt

    5: BH_CrossCourt -> pcase {
        1: P4_AdVolley_BH
        0: P4_AdVolley_FH
        1: P4_AdStroke_BH
        0: P4_AdStroke_FH
        1: P3_AdVolley_BH
        1: P3_AdVolley_FH
        1: P3_AdStroke_BH
        0: P3_AdStroke_FH
    }
    2: BH_CrossCourt_err -> Error{team2++; if (team2==points) {won=t2}}
                         -> NextPt
    0: BH_CrossCourt_win -> Winner{team1++; if (team1==points) {won=t1}}
                         -> NextPt

    0: BH_CrossCourt_lob -> pcase {
        0: P4_AdSmash_FH
        0: P4_AdSmash_BH
        0: P3_AdSmash_FH
        0: P3_AdSmash_BH
        0: P4_AdStroke_BH
        0: P4_AdStroke_FH
        0: P3_AdStroke_BH
        0: P3_AdStroke_FH
    }
    0: BH_CrossCourt_lob_err -> Error{team2++; if (team2==points) {won=t2}}
                             -> NextPt
    0: BH_CrossCourt_lob_win -> Winner{team1++; if (team1==points) {won=t1}}
                             -> NextPt
};
```

When $P2$ returns from the ad court with his backhand, he can either play a backhand down the line (`BH_DownLine`) or a backhand cross-court (`BH_CrossCourt`). Furthermore, he can also lob the ball over the opponent at the net to avoid being volleyed (`BH_DownLine_lob` or `BH_CrossCourt_lob`). The current state and action taken determine the possible next states. For example, if $P2$ returns the ball down the line, it will usually be blocked by either $P3$ or $P4$ at the net with certain probabilities; if $P2$ returns the ball cross-court back to the server side, there are more possibilities such as the ball is volleyed at the net or received by the server at the baseline; and if $P2$ lobs the ball, $P3$ or $P4$ may smash (e.g., `P3_DeSmash_FH`) or take the ball at the baseline (e.g., `P4_DeStroke_BH`).

Similarly, we can model the processes for **volley**, **smash**, and **stroke** for each player accordingly. Due to the space limit, we only provide sample codes for each state without further elaboration.

Model for Volley. Sample code for *P*4 forehand volley from the ad court.

```
P4_AdVolley_FH = P4DeReadyFHVolley -> pcase {
    3: FH_InsideIn_volley -> pcase {
        0: P1_DeVolley_FH
        0: P1_DeVolley_BH
        1: P2_DeVolley_FH
        0: P2_DeVolley_BH
        1: P1_DeStroke_FH
        0: P1_DeStroke_BH
        0: P2_DeStroke_FH
        1: P2_DeStroke_BH
    }
    0: FH_InsideIn_volley_err -> Error{team1++; if (team1==points) {won=t1}
        else {if ((team2+team1)%2==1) {turn=call(nextServer, turn)}}} -> NextPt
    0: FH_InsideIn_volley_win -> Ace{team2++; if (team2==points) {won=t2}
        else {if ((team2+team1)%2==1) {turn=call(nextServer, turn)}}} -> NextPt

    0: FH_InsideIn_volley_lob -> pcase {
        0: P1_DeSmash_FH
        0: P1_DeSmash_BH
        0: P2_DeSmash_FH
        0: P2_DeSmash_BH
        0: P1_DeStroke_FH
        0: P1_DeStroke_BH
        0: P2_DeStroke_FH
        0: P2_DeStroke_BH
    }
    0: FH_InsideIn_volley_lob_err -> Error{team1++; if (team1==points) {won=t1}
        else {if ((team2+team1)%2==1) {turn=call(nextServer, turn)}}} -> NextPt
    0: FH_InsideIn_volley_lob_win -> Ace{team2++; if (team2==points) {won=t2}
        else {if ((team2+team1)%2==1) {turn=call(nextServer, turn)}}} -> NextPt

    5: FH_InsideOut_volley -> pcase {
        0: P2_AdVolley_BH
        0: P2_AdVolley_FH
        1: P1_AdVolley_BH
        0: P1_AdVolley_FH
        1: P2_AdStroke_BH
        2: P2_AdStroke_FH
        0: P1_AdStroke_BH
        1: P1_AdStroke_FH
    }
    1: FH_InsideOut_volley_err -> Error{team1++; if (team1==points) {won=t1}
        else {if ((team2+team1)%2==1) {turn=call(nextServer, turn)}}} -> NextPt
    0: FH_InsideOut_volley_win -> Ace{team2++; if (team2==points) {won=t2}
        else {if ((team2+team1)%2==1) {turn=call(nextServer, turn)}}} -> NextPt

    1: FH_InsideOut_volley_lob -> pcase {
        0: P2_AdSmash_BH
        1: P2_AdSmash_FH
        0: P1_AdSmash_BH
        0: P1_AdSmash_FH
        0: P2_AdStroke_BH
        0: P2_AdStroke_FH
        0: P1_AdStroke_BH
        0: P1_AdStroke_FH
    }
    0: FH_InsideOut_volley_lob_err -> Error{team1++; if (team1==points) {won=t1}
        else {if ((team2+team1)%2==1) {turn=call(nextServer, turn)}}} -> NextPt
    0: FH_InsideOut_volley_lob_win -> Ace{team2++; if (team2==points) {won=t2}
        else {if ((team2+team1)%2==1) {turn=call(nextServer, turn)}}} -> NextPt
};
```

Model for Smash. Sample code for $P3$ forehand smash from the ad court.

```
P3_AdSmash_FH = P3AdReadyFHSmash -> pcase {
    0: FH_InsideIn_smash -> pcase {
        0: P1_DeStroke_FH
        0: P1_DeStroke_BH
        0: P2_DeStroke_FH
        0: P2_DeStroke_BH
    }
    0: FH_InsideIn_smash_err -> Error{team1++; if (team1==points) {won=t1}
        else {if ((team2+team1)%2==1) {turn=call(nextServer, turn)}}} -> NextPt
    2: FH_InsideIn_smash_win -> Ace{team2++; if (team2==points) {won=t2}
        else {if ((team2+team1)%2==1) {turn=call(nextServer, turn)}}} -> NextPt

    0: FH_InsideOut_smash -> pcase {
        0: P2_AdStroke_BH
        0: P2_AdStroke_FH
        0: P1_AdStroke_BH
        0: P1_AdStroke_FH
    }
    0: FH_InsideOut_smash_err -> Error{team1++; if (team1==points) {won=t1}
        else {if ((team2+team1)%2==1) {turn=call(nextServer, turn)}}} -> NextPt
    0: FH_InsideOut_smash_win -> Ace{team2++; if (team2==points) {won=t2}
        else {if ((team2+team1)%2==1) {turn=call(nextServer, turn)}}} -> NextPt
};
```

Model for Stroke. Sample code for $P1$ deuce court forehand stroke.

```
P1_DeStroke_FH = P1DeReadyFHStroke -> pcase {
    4: FH_DownLine -> pcase {
        1: P4_AdVolley_BH
        1: P4_AdVolley_FH
        0: P3_AdVolley_FH
        2: P3_AdVolley_BH
        0: P4_AdStroke_BH
        0: P4_AdStroke_FH
        0: P3_AdStroke_BH
        0: P3_AdStroke_FH
    }
    1: FH_DownLine_err -> Error{team2++; if (team2==points) {won=t2}
        else {if ((team1+team2)%2==1) {turn=call(nextServer, turn)}}} -> NextPt
    1: FH_DownLine_win -> Ace{team1++; if (team1==points) {won=t1}
        else {if ((team1+team2)%2==1) {turn=call(nextServer, turn)}}} -> NextPt

    0: FH_DownLine_lob -> pcase {
        0: P4_AdSmash_BH
        0: P4_AdSmash_FH
        0: P3_AdSmash_FH
        0: P3_AdSmash_BH
        0: P4_AdStroke_BH
        0: P4_AdStroke_FH
        0: P3_AdStroke_BH
        0: P3_AdStroke_FH
    }
```

```
        0: FH_DownLine_lob_err -> Error{team2++; if (team2==points) {won=t2}
            else {if ((team1+team2)%2==1) {turn=call(nextServer, turn)}}} -> NextPt
        0: FH_DownLine_lob_win -> Ace{team1++; if (team1==points) {won=t1}
            else {if ((team1+team2)%2==1) {turn=call(nextServer, turn)}}} -> NextPt

        11: FH_CrossCourt -> pcase {
            2: P3_DeVolley_FH
            2: P3_DeVolley_BH
            1: P4_DeVolley_FH
            0: P4_DeVolley_BH
            3: P3_DeStroke_FH
            1: P3_DeStroke_BH
            2: P4_DeStroke_FH
            0: P4_DeStroke_BH
        }
        3: FH_CrossCourt_err -> Error{team2++; if (team2==points) {won=t2}
            else {if ((team1+team2)%2==1) {turn=call(nextServer, turn)}}} -> NextPt
        0: FH_CrossCourt_win -> Ace{team1++; if (team1==points) {won=t1}
            else {if ((team1+team2)%2==1) {turn=call(nextServer, turn)}}} -> NextPt

        0: FH_CrossCourt_lob -> pcase {
            0: P3_DeSmash_FH
            0: P3_DeSmash_BH
            0: P4_DeSmash_FH
            0: P4_DeSmash_BH
            0: P3_DeStroke_FH
            0: P3_DeStroke_BH
            0: P4_DeStroke_FH
            0: P4_DeStroke_BH
        }
        0: FH_CrossCourt_lob_err -> Error{team2++; if (team2==points) {won=t2}
            else {if ((team1+team2)%2==1) {turn=call(nextServer, turn)}}} -> NextPt
        0: FH_CrossCourt_lob_win -> Ace{team1++; if (team1==points) {won=t1}
            else {if ((team1+team2)%2==1) {turn=call(nextServer, turn)}}} -> NextPt
};
```

Predict Winning Probability

```
#define Team1Win won==t1;
#define Team2Win won==t2;

#assert TieBreakGame reaches Team1Win with prob;
#assert TieBreakGame reaches Team2Win with prob;
```

To predict the winning probability of a team, we define a predicate to specify the target player as the winner of the tiebreak game (i.e., gets 7 points first), and then look for a state that satisfies the predicate using probabilistic reachability analysis.

4 Experimental Results

We conducted experiments on two NCAA tennis doubles matches:

- Louisiana State University (LSU) vs. University of Florida (UF)[1] and,
- Louisiana State University (LSU) vs. University of South Carolina (SC)[2].

[1] https://rb.gy/ueaczg.
[2] https://rb.gy/dob6no.

We collect all shot-by-shot data from video recordings. Due to limited data, we combined these two matches into one MDP model as "LSU vs. other teams" and implemented it in PCSP#. We set Julien Penzlin (LSU) as $P1$, Chen Dong (LSU) as $P2$, Jeremy Jin (UF) & Sean Daryabeigi (SC) as $P3$, and Henry Jefferson (UF) & Jelani Sarr (SC) as $P4$ based on their positions in matches. We then calculated LSU's winning probability against other teams (i.e., UF and SC). The results showed that the probability of LSU winning chance ranged from 0.73558 to 0.76943, while "other teams" had winning chances from 0.23057 to 0.26442. Our preliminary results aligned well with actual match results where LSU indeed defeated both teams with great advantages.

Beyond predicting match outcomes, we aim to formulate opponent-specific strategic recommendations to boost the winning probabilities of teams. By modifying parameters in the MDP model, such as the distribution of a player's actions, the success rate of specific skills, and the percentage of shot selection, we can gauge their effect on the overall winning chances, thereby pinpointing the most effective strategies and quantifying the potential improvement in the winning rate. For instance, if player 1 enhances their forehand cross-court shot from the deuce court by reducing errors by 5%, Team 1's overall winning probability could increase by 1.6%. Similarly, if Team 2 strategically increases their serve targeting Team 1's T area by 5%, their winning likelihood could rise by 1.9%. These strategic insights are valuable for both in-game tactics and pre-match preparation, with each recommendation being rigorously verified.

5 Conclusion and Future Work

This paper has presented a comprehensive analytical framework for tennis doubles using Markov Decision Processes (MDP) and probabilistic model checking (PMC), offering a novel approach to capturing the complex dynamics and interactions inherent in doubles matches. Our model effectively utilizes shot-by-shot action data to predict match outcomes and develop strategic recommendations, marking a significant advancement in the analytics of tennis doubles. The preliminary evaluation, conducted on NCAA Division 1 tennis doubles matches, has affirmed the model's validity and its potential in strategizing.

Future work will focus on refining the model with a larger dataset to enhance its predictive accuracy and generalizability. We aim to incorporate real-time match data to enable dynamic strategy adjustments during live matches. Moreover, we intend to investigate the effectiveness of various formations in tennis doubles, analyzing their impact on match outcomes. Further studies will also consider expanding the model's applicability to other doubles sports, such as badminton and table tennis, enhancing decision-making tools for players and coaches.

References

1. Jiang, K., Izadi, M., Liu, Z., Dong, J.S.: Deep learning application in broadcast tennis video annotation. In: 2020 25th International Conference on Engineering of Complex Computer Systems (ICECCS). IEEE, pp. 53–62 (2020)
2. Dong, J.S., et al.: Sports analytics using probabilistic model checking and deep learning. In: 2023 27th International Conference on Engineering of Complex Computer Systems (ICECCS), pp. 7–11. IEEE (2023)
3. Liu, Z., Guo, J., Wang, M., Wang, R., Jiang, K., Dong, J.S.: Recognizing a sequence of events from tennis video clips: addressing timestep identification and subtle class differences. In:2023 IEEE 28th Pacific Rim International Symposium on Dependable Computing (PRDC), pp. 337–341. IEEE (2023)
4. Terroba, A., Kosters, W., Varona, J., Manresa-Yee, C.S.: Finding optimal strategies in tennis from video sequences. Int. J. Pattern Recognit. Artif. Intell. **27**(06), 1355010 (2013)
5. Wei, X., Lucey, P., Morgan, S., Reid, M., Sridharan, S.: The thin edge of the wedge: accurately predicting shot outcomes in tennis using style and context priors. In: Proceedings of the 10th Annu MIT Sloan Sport Anal Conference, Boston, MA, USA, pp. 1–11 (2016)
6. Wang, W.-Y., Chan, T.-F., Yang, H.-K., Wang, C.-C., Fan, Y.-C., Peng, W.-C.: Exploring the long short-term dependencies to infer shot influence in badminton matches. In: 2021 IEEE International Conference on Data Mining (ICDM), pp. 1397–1402. IEEE (2021)
7. Wang, J., et al.: Tac-Valuer: knowledge-based stroke evaluation in table tennis. In: The 27th ACM SIGKDD Conference on Knowledge Discovery & Data Mining, pp. 3688–3696 (2021)
8. Liu, Z., Jiang, K., Hou, Z., Lin, Y., Dong, J.S.: Insight analysis for tennis strategy and tactics. In: 2023 IEEE International Conference on Data Mining (ICDM), pp. 1175–1180. IEEE (2023)
9. Kocib, T., Carboch, J., Cabela, M., Kresta, J.: Tactics in tennis doubles: analysis of the formations used by the serving and receiving teams. Int. J. Phys. Educ. Fit Sport **9**(2), 45–50 (2020)
10. Breznik, K.: Revealing the best doubles teams and players in tennis history. Int. J. Perform. Anal. Sport **15**(3), 1213–1226 (2015)
11. Martínez-Gallego, R., Crespo, M., Ramón Llin, J., Micó, S., Guzmán Luján, J.F.: Men's doubles professional tennis on hard courts: game structure and point ending characteristics, 2020
12. Martínez-Gallego, R., Ramón-Llin, J., Crespo, M.: A cluster analysis approach to profile men and women's volley positions in professional tennis matches (doubles). Sustainability **13**(11), 6370 (2021)

Strategy Analysis in NFL Using Probabilistic Reasoning

Zhaoyu Liu(✉), Murad Durrani, Leong Yu Xuan, Julian-Frederik Simon, and Tan Yong Feng Deon

National University of Singapore, Singapore, Singapore
liuzy@nus.edu.sg

Abstract. Many devices and cameras collect different sports data, and discovering useful insights from this data is crucial for increasing the chances of winning for professional athletes. In this paper, we introduce a novel application of probabilistic reasoning to the field of sports analytics, with a focus on the National Football League (NFL). By leveraging the Probabilistic Model Checking (PMC), we build probabilistic models using historical match data to predict the outcomes of NFL drives and generate strategy recommendations. Our approach simplifies the complex, strategic nature of NFL plays into discrete, sequential events, enabling us to explore the impact of team strategies on the likelihood of scoring touchdowns and field goals. This research not only sheds light on the intricate dynamics of American football but also opens new avenues for using probabilistic modeling in sports analytics, offering insights that could significantly influence team decision-making and resource allocation.

Keywords: Sports analytics · NFL · Probabilistic model

1 Introduction

The intersection of sports and data-driven analytics has unlocked opportunities to understand and predict the outcomes of sporting events [3,7,8,10,11]. Probabilistic Model Checking (PMC) has conventionally been used to analyze the correctness and performance of computer systems and protocols. Expanding beyond its original scope, PMC's versatility allows its application to diverse domains, including sports analytics [4,12].

The NFL presents an unparalleled level of complexity as a strategic sport, characterized by a vast array of strategies and nuanced gameplay. Current sports analytics methodologies [6,16], despite their variety, leave a gap in understanding the effect of varied strategies on NFL game results. The nuances of player decisions, team dynamics, and strategic choices are yet to be fully explored within the analytical realm. Addressing these challenges holds the promise of unlocking a wealth of information, providing a detailed comprehension of how subtle strategy adjustments can sway game results. This effort not only enriches theoretical knowledge of the sport but also offers tangible benefits for improving team performance and decision-making processes.

J. S. Dong et al. (Eds.): ISACE 2024, LNCS 14794, pp. 116–128, 2024.
https://doi.org/10.1007/978-3-031-69073-0_10

To fill these gaps, we are developing a pioneering probabilistic model using PAT (Process Analysis Toolkit) model checker [17], specifically designed for the intricacies of NFL gameplay. This model is capable of accurately forecasting the outcomes of NFL drives and delivering strategic recommendations to enhance team performance. In conjunction with our previous work [4,12], our goal is to establish a set of probabilistic reasoning models for various sports, advancing the frontier of sports analytics.

2 Related Work

In the realm of NFL sports analytics, research spans various themes, including predicting winning teams, next play selections, team rankings, and player performance analyses. For example, Lock et al. [13] employed Random Forest algorithms to estimate win probabilities before any play in an NFL game. Baker et al. [1] utilized a point process model for precise predictions of final NFL game scores. Additionally, Gifford et al. [6] developed predictive analytics models using decision trees and logistic regression to forecast outcomes of NFL season games.

While certain studies within NFL analytics have concentrated on predicting the winning team, others have delved into forecasting play calls and player performance. Joash Fernandes [9] leveraged data from multiple NFL seasons, applying various machine-learning models to predict play types. Reyers and Swartz [14] assessed quarterback performance using player tracking data, which accounts for all players' speed and locations on the field.

These existing approaches primarily focus on using machine learning to predict match outcomes and player performances. Yet, these "black-box" models often lack transparency and do not facilitate in-depth strategy analysis. In contrast, our probabilistic model excels not just in accurately forecasting match results but also in providing explainable, insightful, and formally verified strategic analyses.

3 Preliminaries of NFL

The National Football League (NFL) stands as the premier American football league in the United States, celebrated for its widespread popularity and competitive intensity.

For analytical purposes, we have streamlined the representation of the NFL field, focusing on the aspects most relevant to our model while omitting finer details (see Fig. 1).

3.1 Key Rules

The fundamental aim in American football is to score points through field goals or touchdowns, each offering a different score value.

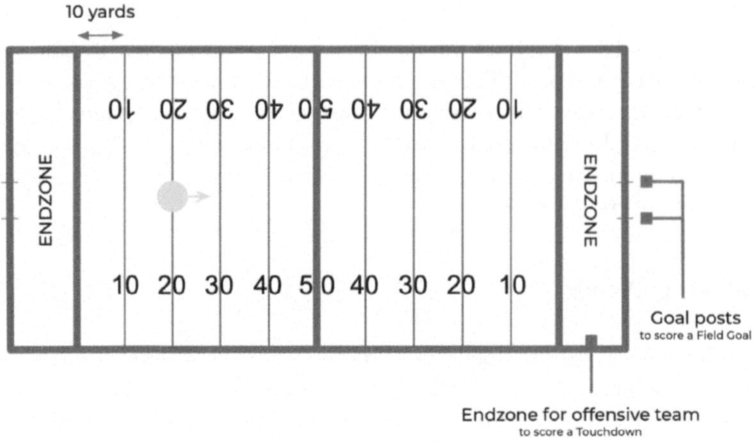

Fig. 1. Simplified representation of NFL field

The game is played between two teams: the offense, which drives the ball toward the opponent's end zone, and the defense, which aims to stop this advance. The offensive team is given four attempts, or downs, to move the ball at least 10 yards. Successfully doing so resets the count of downs, allowing them further attempts to progress. Failure to cover the required distance within four downs results in the ball being turned over to the opposing team.

3.2 Terminology

This section outlines common NFL terminologies crucial for understanding our analysis.

- **Drive**: A sequence of plays with the football under the possession of the offensive team, concluding when the ball changes hands.
- **Down**: Essentially an attempt or chance for the offensive team to advance the ball.
- **Touchdown**: Achieved when a player successfully carries the ball across the opponent's goal line or secures a catch in the end zone, rewarding the team with 6 points.
- **Field Goal**: Earned by kicking the ball through the opponent's goalposts, granting 3 points for a successful attempt.
- **Yard**: The unit of measurement used on the field to gauge distance.
- **Punt**: A strategic move usually executed on the fourth down, where the offensive team kicks the ball to push the opposing team further back, aiming to hinder their field position advantage.

These foundations and terminologies are integral to our model's understanding and analysis of the strategic dimensions within NFL games.

4 The Proposed Approach

4.1 Model Architecture

The flow of the model is contingent on two state variables: the current down and the offensive team's position on the field. These two variables inform the model's decision-making process as illustrated by Fig. 2.

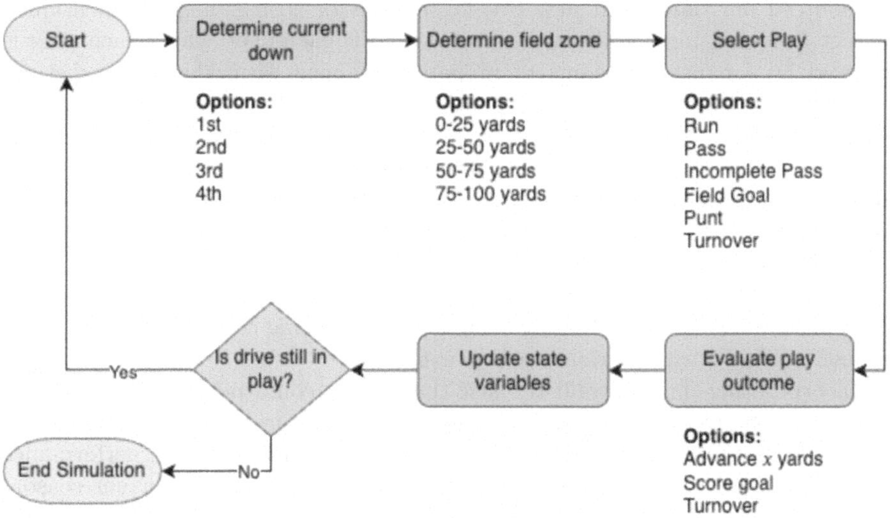

Fig. 2. Flowchart of model decision-making and state update process

Initially, the model assesses the current down, which could be any from the first to the fourth. The 100-yard football field is segmented into four distinct zones, each defined by yardage: 0–25 yards, 25–50 yards, 50–75 yards, and 75–100 yards. The model determines the offensive team's current zone based on their field position.

This combination of the current down and field zone is crucial in shaping the offensive team's play choices, compelling them to adjust their strategy according to the game's circumstances. For instance, a team on the fourth down within the 0–25 yard zone might prefer to punt, aiming to secure a better field position rather than attempting a direct score, which is less likely from such a distance.

Upon identifying the down and zone, the model employs a probabilistic approach to select the next play, which could vary among options such as a run, pass, or field goal attempt. Following the selection, the model simulates the chosen play's outcome. For run and pass plays, the progression is quantified in yards, with the chance of achieving a touchdown if the advancement crosses the 100-yard threshold. Field goals directly aim for a score, whereas punts lead to a change in possession.

The model then updates its state based on the play's outcome. The simulation concludes if the offensive team scores or if a turnover happens. If neither occurs, the process iterates with the new down number and updated field position, continually adapting the strategy until a terminal event. Please refer to here[1] for the full PCSP implementation.

4.2 Data Source

We sourced our data from play-by-play records of NFL games, as mentioned in Sect. 3, leveraging the discrete nature of NFL gameplay, where each play is followed by a pause for teams to prepare their next formation. This distinct structure simplifies data handling, providing clear start and end points for each play.

Our analysis was restricted to game data from the most recent three seasons to enhance our model's accuracy. The rationale for this limitation stems from the NFL's competitive balance, maintained through mechanisms like the "NFL Draft", where collegiate athletes are selected by NFL teams, with the lower-ranked teams receiving priority in player selection. This system allows underperforming teams to bolster their rosters, ensuring competitive parity and frequent shifts in team performance year-to-year.

Incorporating data beyond the last three years could potentially dilute our model's predictive accuracy due to the dynamic nature of team performance in the league. Our approach assumes that teams with superior performance in the preceding three seasons are more likely to excel in the current season, compared to those with weaker records. Thus, we intentionally introduce a bias by selecting game data exclusively from the last three seasons, aiming to reflect more accurately the current state of team form and performance levels.

4.3 Modeling Yardage Gains

A crucial aspect of our model was the precise depiction of yardage gains during running and passing plays. To this end, we chose to segment yardage gains into 4-yard intervals, such as 0 yards, 4 yards, 8 yards, and so forth. We then calculated the probabilities of a team advancing by 0 yards, between 1–4 yards, and so on, utilizing these probabilities to determine play outcomes.

Initially, we aimed to deduce yardage gain probabilities directly from the observational data. However, we encountered challenges due to data sparsity. Specifically, when analyzing plays from certain downs and field zones, we found a lack of sufficient observations on yardage gains, resulting in some intervals being scarcely populated with data or entirely devoid of observations (refer to Fig. 3). To overcome the data sparsity issue, we turned to a probability distribution model to fill in the gaps within our dataset. Given that NFL yardage gains typically exhibit a right-skewed distribution with a long tail, it was crucial to choose a distribution that accurately reflects this characteristic. We considered

[1] https://github.com/deeyonn/CS4211-NFL-Project/tree/main/output.

four potential distributions for this purpose: the Weibull [15], Poisson [2], Negative Binomial [5], and Gamma [18] distributions. Each candidate was rigorously tested to identify the distribution that best captured the observed pattern of yardage gains.

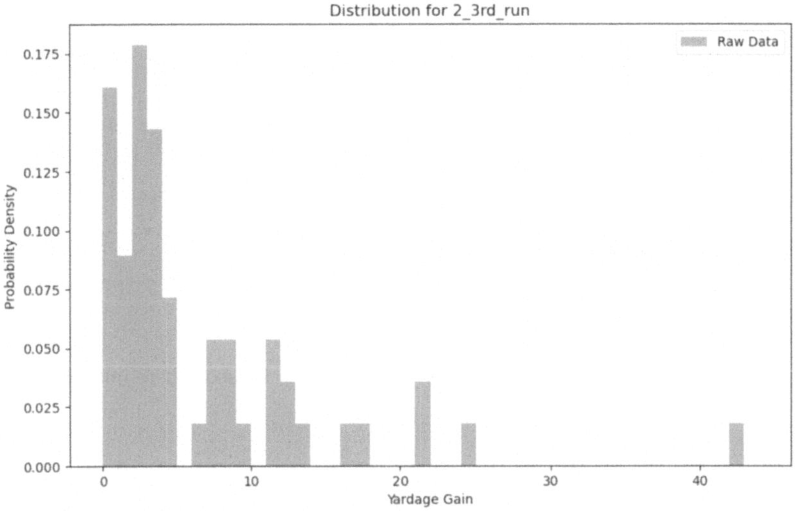

Fig. 3. Example probability distribution with empty intervals

Ultimately, the Gamma distribution emerged as the most adept at capturing the characteristics of the underlying data. While the other distributions offered varying levels of suitability, they fell short of the Gamma distribution's flexibility. For instance, the Poisson distribution is predicated on the assumption that the mean and variance are equal, an assumption rarely met by yardage gains. Yardage gains typically exhibit a relatively low mean coupled with high variance, leading to an overly pronounced peak when modeled by the Poisson distribution (refer to Fig. 4).

Another challenge we encountered was that for passing plays, a significant proportion of them resulted in incomplete passes. The outcome of an incomplete pass is a yardage gain of 0. This caused our data to skew heavily towards 0, which none of the probability distributions were able to reflect (see Fig. 5). To address this, we decided to exclude all incomplete passes from the yardage gain distribution data, instead categorizing them as a separate play with their own associated probability. This meant that the distribution for passing plays would only model yardage gains for complete passes, which did not suffer from the same zero bias. If an incomplete passing play was executed, it would result in 0 yardage gain with 100% probability.

With this adjustment, we were able to produce a much more accurate and representative distribution of yardage gains (see Fig. 6). Then, we simply derived

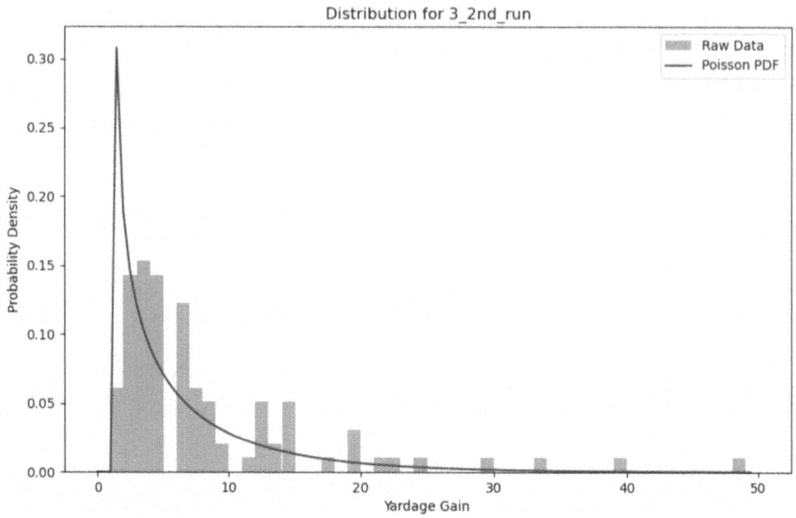

Fig. 4. Example probability distribution with Poisson distribution

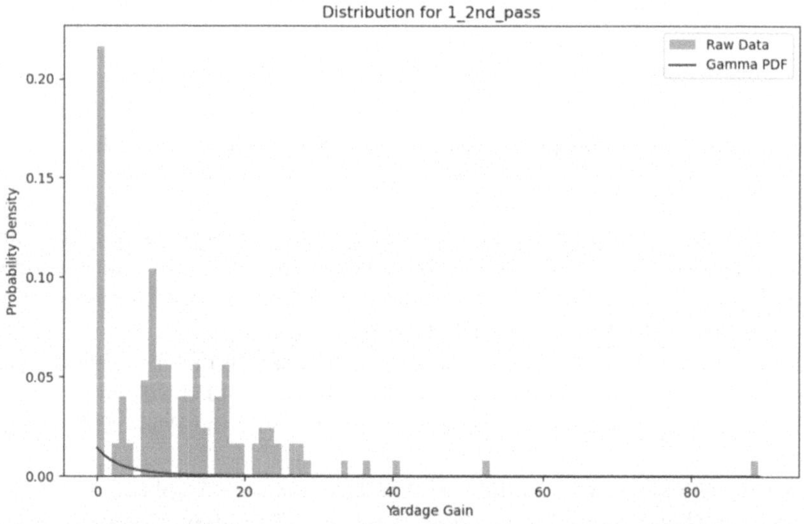

Fig. 5. Example probability distribution with incomplete passes

the probabilities of the team advancing by 0 yards, 1–4 yards, and so on, from the probability distribution and included those probabilities in the model. We elected to record intervals up to a yardage gain of 20 yards, as the probability of gaining beyond 20 yards was minimal and capturing it would provide little gain.

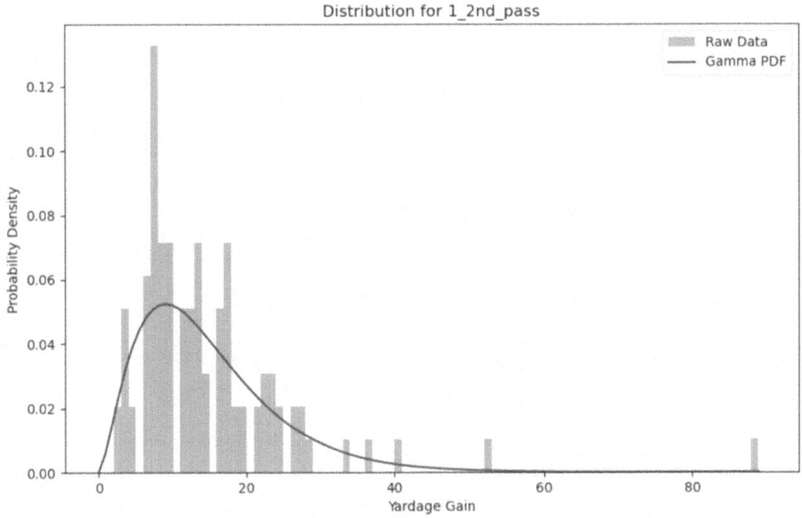

Fig. 6. Example probability distribution with incomplete passes removed

4.4 Capturing Team Skill

In our initial approach, we analyzed team performance broadly across the field. However, to more accurately reflect the dynamics of team-versus-team encounters, we integrated ELO ratings into our model. ELO ratings, a measure originally developed for chess to assess the relative skills of players based on game outcomes, have been adapted to various sports, including the NFL. These ratings assign a numerical value to each team, with higher numbers indicating superior skill.

We commenced by collecting ELO ratings for all NFL teams from a reliable online source. When simulating a matchup between two teams, we determined the ELO differential between the offensive and defensive teams. We then applied this differential to adjust observed yardage gains according to the formula:

$$\text{adjusted\_gain} = \text{original\_gain} \times (1 + \text{elo\_diff} \times \text{scale\_coefficient}),$$

where the scale coefficient set at 0.0005, a 100-point ELO advantage for the offensive team translated to a 5% increase in yardage gains. This method allowed our model to quantitatively account for the skill discrepancy between competing teams, enabling dynamic adjustments based on relative team strengths.

5 Experimental Results

Our model is designed with two key assertions: one to calculate the probability of scoring a field goal and another for the probability of achieving a touchdown. In the standard setup of our script for generating the PCSP file, the Kansas City

Chiefs (KC) are designated as the offensive team, while the New York Jets (NYJ) serve as the defensive team. Under this configuration, when Team KC initiates a drive from the 20-yard line, the calculated probabilities for scoring a field goal and touchdown within a single drive are 0.00707 and 0.13993, respectively.

Furthermore, we experimented with varying the down number and starting positions to examine how these adjustments impact the probabilities of scoring both a field goal and a touchdown (refer to Table 1).

Table 1. Results for KC (vs NYJ)

Case	Down	Position at x yard line	Probability of scoring Field goal	Probability of scoring Touchdown
1	1	20	0.00707	0.13993
2	3	20	0.00453	0.09036
3	1	50	0.01474	0.22043
4	3	50	0.09592	0.17186
5	1	80	0.01035	0.47206
6	3	80	0.2932	0.25356
7	1	90	0.00772	0.59277
8	3	90	0.29173	0.32117
9	4	90	0.72368	0.04846

Table 2. Results for KC vs NYJ compared to vs. BAL

Case	Down	Position at x yard line	Prob FG vs. NYJ	Prob TG vs. BAL	Prob TD vs. NYJ	Prob TD vs. BAL	Diff Prob TD vs. vs. NYJ & BAL
1	1	20	0.00707	0.00705	0.13993	0.11823	0.02170
2	3	20	0.00453	0.00431	0.09036	0.07314	0.01722
3	1	40	0.00928	0.00947	0.18854	0.16424	0.02430
4	3	40	0.00597	0.00579	0.12066	0.10001	0.02065
5	1	60	0.01342	0.01394	0.29299	0.26435	0.02864
6	3	60	0.09501	0.10638	0.22732	0.19791	0.02941
7	1	80	0.01035	0.01078	0.47206	0.44201	0.03005
8	3	80	0.29320	0.32706	0.25356	0.21244	0.04112

5.1 Evaluation

The three tables above provide experimental results that we used to evaluate the performance and accuracy of our model. Each table serves to verify a different aspect of our model's performance.

Table 1 illustrates how the probability of a touchdown and field goal changes based on the starting down and position of the offensive team.

Table 3. Results KC vs. CLE and Probability of KC starting at position x

Case	Down	Position at x yard line	Prob TD	Prob of starting at the position x
1	1	0	0.09472	0.1019
2	1	10	0.10078	0.151986
3	1	20	0.12713	0.476684
4	1	30	0.13087	0.119171
5	1	40	0.1743	0.056995
6	1	50	0.20836	0.027634
7	1	60	0.27634	0.020725
8	1	70	0.33824	0.022453
9	1	80	0.4547	0.015544
10	1	90	0.5794	0.006908

As we would expect in a typical NFL game, the chance of a field goal increases with each down–especially on the fourth–while the chance of a touchdown decreases. For example, from the fourth down at 90 yards, the model shows a high field goal probability (0.724) and a low touchdown probability (0.048). Additionally, starting closer to the end zone increases the probability of scoring, as indicated by higher touchdown chances from the 80-yard line (0.472) compared to the 20-yard line (0.140). This is consistent with what we would expect in a typical NFL game, and suggests that the model's modeling of decision-making is appropriate.

Table 2 displays the performance of KC against two teams, NYJ and BAL. BAL is a team with a much higher ELO rating and better performance than NYJ, and so we expect to see KC perform better against NYJ than BAL. Indeed, as indicated by the rightmost column, touchdown probabilities are higher across the board when playing against NYJ. This suggests our model is producing outcomes that change based on relative team skills. Interestingly, this performance disparity increases as yardage increases. While we did not expect this, it could be due to the fact that as the probability of scoring grows with yardage, so too does the difference between the two teams in relative proportion.

Lastly, Table 3 illustrates the probability of KC scoring a touchdown against CLE based on their starting down and position, as well as the probability of them starting from that position based on historical data. With this, we computed the probability of scoring a touchdown across all starting positions, which is 14.1%. We then, as a sanity check, compared this to the known league average to verify that our model was producing results consistent with real-life games. In 2023, the league average was 17.3% (Drive Finder). This suggests that while somewhat realistic and in the ballpark of real-world values, our model is under-predicting probabilities of touchdowns. A possible reason for this observation is that our model caps the maximum number of yards a team can advance from a play to 20 yards. In reality, there are instances where teams can advance much further than this, and so it is possible that not accounting for this placed downward pressure on the probabilities generated. However, it should be noted that the process by which the 14.1% probability was calculated also under-reports the probability. The reason for this is that when we compute the probability of a touchdown at 0 yards, we use that to represent the probability of a touchdown from 0–9 yards. This rounding down of the position to the nearest 10 causes the model to under-predict probabilities.

Based on the evaluation of the results from the three tables, it seems that the model does well to emulate the logic and decision-making flow of the game, but does not capture the real world probabilities to as high a degree. The probabilities of outcomes increase and decrease as we would expect them to based on the state of the drive, but the absolute values of the probabilities themselves seem to under-represent the true probabilities of scoring to an extent.

6 Conclusion

This study presents an innovative approach to applying probabilistic reasoning to sports analytics, particularly focusing on the National Football League (NFL). Utilizing Probabilistic Model Checking (PMC), we have developed probabilistic models based on historical game data to forecast NFL drive outcomes and provide strategic insights. By distilling the complex strategies of NFL gameplay into a sequence of discrete events, our methodology enables an in-depth examination of how various team strategies affect the chances of achieving touchdowns and field goals. The findings from this research not only illuminate the complex dynamics of American football but also pave the way for the application of probabilistic modeling in the broader field of sports analytics. Such insights have the potential to profoundly impact decision-making processes and resource management within teams, highlighting the significant implications of our work for both the academic and practical realms of sports strategy and analysis.

6.1 Potential Improvements

One way to improve our model is to include more plays. Currently, our model encompasses general plays such as run and pass. However, there are subcategories within those plays. For instance, variations of pass plays, such as slants or posts, can be incorporated. The same can be applied to other plays too. Incorporation of these plays would add a greater degree of nuance and fidelity to the model.

Additionally, it is crucial to consider yardage loss situations. Since our model only accounts for actions that increment the yardage, we are potentially overlooking factors like penalties that could lead to loss of yardage.

Lastly, the manner by which the model accounts for relative team skill by using ELO ratings fails to capture the distinct team vs team interactions that change the nature of the matchup. For example, it might be that although one team is generally strong against the field, they have a particular weakness that exposes them to another team and worsens their performance against that team specifically. ELO ratings fail to capture this nuance. A potential improvement would be to use data specifically between those two teams to bias the model to account for that specific match-up.

By incorporating the factors above, we not only broaden the scope of the model but also enhance its accuracy, offering additional valuable insights.

6.2 Extensions and Future Work

In addition to improvements that would drive better performance from the model, further work could be performed to gain new insights from our model.

One area we did not explore is how augmenting decision-making probabilities might affect the probability of a team scoring. For example, if a team were to prioritize making riskier plays by electing to run the ball more often, how would that affect their probability of scoring? By performing these experiments, we might gain insight into how a particular team can adjust its strategy to optimize performance. Because of the highly strategic and decision-driven nature of NFL, small adjustments in strategies could result in one team gaining a significant edge over another.

References

1. Baker, R.D., McHale, I.G.: Forecasting exact scores in national football league games. Int. J. Forecast. **29**(1), 122–130 (2013)
2. Clarke, R.: An application of the poisson distribution. J. Inst. Actuar. **72**(3), 481 (1946)
3. Dong, J.S., et al.: Sports analytics using probabilistic model checking and deep learning. In: 2023 27th International Conference on Engineering of Complex Computer Systems (ICECCS), pp. 7–11. IEEE (2023)
4. Dong, J.S., Shi, L., Jiang, K., Sun, J., et al.: Sports strategy analytics using probabilistic reasoning. In: ICECCS, pp. 182–185. IEEE (2015)
5. Fisher, P., et al.: Negative binomial distribution. Ann. Eugen. **11**, 182–787 (1941)
6. Gifford, M., Bayrak, T.: A predictive analytics model for forecasting outcomes in the national football league games using decision tree and logistic regression. Decis. Anal. J. **8**, 100296 (2023)
7. Jiang, K., Izadi, M., Liu, Z., Dong, J.S.: Deep learning application in broadcast tennis video annotation. In: 2020 25th International Conference on Engineering of Complex Computer Systems (ICECCS), pp. 53–62. IEEE (2020)
8. Jiang, K., Li, J., Liu, Z., Dong, C.: Court detection using masked perspective fields network. In: 2023 IEEE 28th Pacific Rim International Symposium on Dependable Computing (PRDC), pp. 342–345. IEEE (2023)
9. Joash Fernandes, C., Yakubov, R., Li, Y., Prasad, A.K., Chan, T.C.: Predicting plays in the national football league. J. Sports Anal. **6**(1), 35–43 (2020)
10. Liu, Z., Guo, J., Wang, M., Wang, R., Jiang, K., Dong, J.S.: Recognizing a sequence of events from tennis video clips: addressing timestep identification and subtle class differences. In: 2023 IEEE 28th Pacific Rim International Symposium on Dependable Computing (PRDC), pp. 337–341. IEEE (2023)

11. Liu, Z., Jiang, K., Dong, J.S.: Sports injury prediction in professional tennis. In: 2023 IEEE 28th Pacific Rim International Symposium on Dependable Computing (PRDC). pp. 304–308. IEEE (2023)
12. Liu, Z., Jiang, K., Hou, Z., Lin, Y., Dong, J.S.: Insight analysis for tennis strategy and tactics. In: 2023 IEEE International Conference on Data Mining (ICDM), pp. 1175–1180. IEEE (2023)
13. Lock, D., Nettleton, D.: Using random forests to estimate win probability before each play of an NFL game. J. Quant. Anal. Sports **10**(2), 197–205 (2014)
14. Reyers, M., Swartz, T.B.: Quarterback evaluation in the national football league using tracking data. AStA Adv. Stat. Anal. **107**(1), 327–342 (2023)
15. Rinne, H.: The Weibull Distribution: A Handbook. Chapman and Hall/CRC, Boca Raton (2008)
16. Roumani, Y.F.: Sports analytics in the NFL: classifying the winner of the superbowl. Ann. Oper. Res. **325**(1), 715–730 (2023)
17. Sun, J., Liu, Y., Dong, J.S., Pang, J.: PAT: towards flexible verification under fairness. In: Bouajjani, A., Maler, O. (eds.) CAV 2009. LNCS, vol. 5643, pp. 709–714. Springer, Heidelberg (2009). https://doi.org/10.1007/978-3-642-02658-4_59
18. Thom, H.C.: A note on the gamma distribution. Mon. Weather Rev. **86**(4), 117–122 (1958)

Identifying Team Playing Styles Across Phases of Play: A User-Specific Cluster Framework

Samuel J. Moffatt[1(✉)], Ritu Gupta[1], Suman Rakshit[1], and Brad S. Keller[2]

[1] Curtin University, Perth, Australia
samuel.moffatt@postgrad.curtin.edu.au
[2] Fremantle Football Club, Perth, Australia

Abstract. Investigating team performance at a granular level within matches allows for the analysis of phase-specific team playing styles. The cluster framework described in this paper assists in identifying phase-specific team playing styles within team invasion sports that are vital for guiding match analysis. This paper develops a novel clustering framework, proposing a composite clustering assessment index for selecting the optimal feature transformation technique, clustering algorithm and number of clusters. The proposed composite index allows the integration of subject matter expert knowledge, ensuring that the resulting clusters are chosen optimally in alignment with the analysis goals. The clustering framework is applied in the context of Australian football to identify an interpretable number of clusters that represent the inherent grouping of team playing styles during match phases.

Keywords: Clustering framework · Playing style · Team sport · Australian football

1 Background Information

Within team invasion sports, teams develop strategies within periods of the match to better manage match complexity [27]. Observing team behaviour is crucial for improving overall performance [11]. Media, coaches, and sports enthusiasts commonly refer to the overriding behaviour as a team's playing style or style of play. The pervasive and colloquial use of the playing style expression has not been matched by scientific research and measurement [11].

Current literature investigates playing styles at a whole match level. Match-level offensive and defensive playing styles have been identified within team sports such as Australian football [11,18,19], association football [9,10,23,24], netball [8], and rugby league [28,29]. To understand the complexity of team behaviour within invasion sports, a team's actions and events can be broken down into smaller periods of play [6,9,11,20]. Identifying team playing styles

Supported by Curtin University and the Fremantle Football Club.

J. S. Dong et al. (Eds.): ISACE 2024, LNCS 14794, pp. 129–136, 2024.
https://doi.org/10.1007/978-3-031-69073-0_11

within smaller periods of play expands current literature and allows for granular performance analysis, improving match analysis compared to whole match analysis.

This paper outlines a clustering framework identifying phase-specific playing styles within team invasion sports. The framework is applied to cluster team actions and identify phase-specific team playing styles within the context of Australian football.

2 Cluster Framework

The methodological framework described below objectively identifies team playing styles within Australian football. The aim of the clustering process is important, guiding decisions when implementing the clustering framework [12]. The clustering aim is to identify an interpretable number of clusters that represent the inherent grouping within the Australian football transactional match data. The framework also outlines the feature engineering process and the selection of important performance features. Summarised match possession chains are separated into the four phases of play (offence, defence, transition and out-of-play), where cluster analysis is applied and evaluated using a composite cluster assessment index. The optimal clustering hyper-parameters are identified using the composite cluster assessment index.

2.1 Data Requirements

Transactional match data, commonly available for team invasion sports, is required to identify phase-specific playing styles [7]. The data contains timestamped event information on the type of action performed and the individual performing the action. A sample of the transactional match data collected during an Australian football match is displayed in Table 1.

Table 1. Sample of the transactional match data collected during an Australian football match.

Match	Time	Team	Player	Event
100001	5	T_A	P_{17}	Gather
100001	7	T_A	P_{17}	Short kick
100001	8	T_B	P_{32}	Mark
100001	17	T_B	P_{32}	Long kick
100001	20	T_B	P_{36}	Mark

2.2 Data Preprocessing

Data preprocessing is divided into data cleaning and feature engineering, producing an analysis-ready data set. The raw data is cleaned following best practice data cleaning processes [30]. The important stage of feature engineering, guided by subject matter experts (SMEs), creates new features identifying performance indicators and the state of possession [13,17]. The data is summarised into possession chains, represented regarding chain duration.

Feature Engineering

Performance Features: Absent/present calculations are performed to engineer performance indicator features (defined in [21]) from the cleaned raw data. When an event that reflects a performance indicator occurs, a one or otherwise, a zero is coded for the respective feature (Table 2).

Table 2. Sample of transactional match data displayed in Table 1 with engineered performance features (bold).

Match	Time	Team	Player	Event	Gather	ShortKick	Mark	LongKick
100001	5	T_A	P_{17}	Gather	**1**	**0**	**0**	**0**
100001	7	T_A	P_{17}	Short kick	**0**	**1**	**0**	**0**
100001	8	T_B	P_{32}	Mark	**0**	**0**	**1**	**0**
100001	17	T_B	P_{32}	Long kick	**0**	**0**	**0**	**1**
100001	20	T_B	P_{36}	Mark	**0**	**0**	**1**	**0**

Possession State Features: The state of possession is identified for each event during a match. A rolling possession status is then calculated, with the rolling possession status not changing until a new event results in a change of possession. A chain of possession is defined as a group of events that occur while one team is in possession, the ball is in dispute or out-of-play. The chain duration is calculated from the time elapsed during the possession chain. The engineered performance features are summated to summarise the actions performed during the possession chain (Table 3).

Table 3. Sample of the transactional match data (Table 1) summarised into possession chains. The performance features (bold) represent the total number of actions performed within the possession chain.

Match	Chain	Duration	Team	Phase	Gather	ShortKick	Mark	LongKick
100001	C_2	3	T_A	Offence	**1**	**1**	**0**	**0**
100001	C_3	12	T_B	Offence	**0**	**0**	**2**	**1**

Chain Duration Representation: Representing performance features as total counts of actions causes issues because the features correlate with the duration of the possession chain. For example, a possession chain of 120 s typically contains more actions than a possession chain of 10 s. The rate of each feature is calculated to overcome the correlation with chain duration by dividing features by the chain duration. The rate at which performance indicators are performed (number of actions per second) will reflect the intent and strategy of a team (Table 4).

Table 4. Sample of the summarised possession chain data (Table 3) with each performance feature transformed concerning the duration of the chain.

Match	Chain	Duration	Team	Phase	Gather	ShortKick	Mark	LongKick
100001	C_2	3	T_A	Offence	**0.33**	**0.33**	**0**	**0**
100001	C_3	12	T_B	Offence	**0**	**0**	**0.17**	**0.08**

2.3 Mathematical Notation

The analysis-ready data set is notated as $\mathbf{X} = \{x_{ij} : i = 1, ..., n, j = 1, ..., p\}$. x_{ij} is the observation corresponding to row i and column j. $\mathbf{X}$ has n rows (each row is a chain of possession) and p columns (reflecting engineered performance features). Column j reflecting the engineered performance features is defined as $\mathbb{C}_j = \{x_{ij} : i = 1, ..., n\}, j = 1, ..., p$ where p is the number of engineered features. As the clustering goal is to reflect playing styles within specific phases of play, $\mathbf{X}$ is separated into phase-specific data sets based on the possession state feature. This results in $\mathbf{X}_{\text{off}}$, $\mathbf{X}_{\text{def}}$, $\mathbf{X}_{\text{tran}}$ and $\mathbf{X}_{\text{out}}$.

2.4 Feature Selection

In discussion with SMEs, the process of feature selection is applied to $\mathbf{X}_{\text{off}}$, $\mathbf{X}_{\text{def}}$, $\mathbf{X}_{\text{tran}}$, $\mathbf{X}_{\text{out}}$ to create user-informed data sets with features assisting in the description of team playing styles. Removing irrelevant features will reduce the required data storage and improve computation time without negatively impacting the analysis [5]. The filter feature selection method [5] is applied to a subset of $\mathbb{C}_j$ selected by SME. All features with $\text{var}(\mathbb{C}_j) = \epsilon$ ($\epsilon < \delta$, a threshold close to zero) are removed as these features have constant variance and will not impact the results.

2.5 Clustering Process

No optimal clustering algorithm exists for all possible data sets as different clustering algorithms provide different solutions [26]. To account for the different clustering results, three cluster algorithms, k-means clustering, k-medoids clustering and hierarchical agglomeration clustering using Ward's linkage, are applied to each $\mathbf{X}$. The clustering process, guided by the clustering aim, investigates the discovery of similar possession chains across $\mathbf{X}_{\text{off}}$, $\mathbf{X}_{\text{def}}$, $\mathbf{X}_{\text{tran}}$, $\mathbf{X}_{\text{out}}$. The clustering process involves the application of multiple clustering algorithms ($\mathcal{C}$) across a range of cluster numbers ($\mathcal{K}$) to identify the optimal $\mathcal{C}$ and k for each $\mathbf{X}$.

Individual assessment indexes (I_j) characterise the separate characteristics of cluster results and are used to assess the results of $\mathcal{C}$ across $\mathcal{K}$. There are a number of I_j within literature, specifically within-cluster sum of squares (I_{wcss}) [15], separation index (I_{sep}) [3], distance to the cluster centroid (I_{distcc}) [1], and density index (I_{dens}) [15] which are used within the clustering framework. To develop a composite cluster assessment index ($\mathcal{A}(\mathcal{C})$), indexes are normalised (I_j^*) because different I_j have different optimal directions and value ranges to point in the same direction across a range of [0,1], where larger index values are considered better. Equation 1 is applied to I_j where larger values are better, and Eq. 2 is applied to I_j where smaller values are better.

$$I_j^* = \frac{I_j - \min I_j}{\max I_j - \min I_j} \tag{1}$$

$$I_j^* = 1 - \frac{I_j - \min I_j}{\max I_j - \min I_j} \tag{2}$$

Using the four assessment indexes highlighted above, a composite cluster assessment index with equal I_j^* weights, $\mathcal{A}(\mathcal{C})_1$ is defined. The maximum $\mathcal{A}(\mathcal{C})_1$ for each $\mathbf{X}$ is used to identify the optimal clustering method $\mathcal{C}$ and k number of clusters.

$$\mathcal{A}(\mathcal{C})_1 = \frac{I^*_{\text{wcss}} + I^*_{\text{sep}} + I^*_{\text{distcc}} + I^*_{\text{dens}}}{4} \tag{3}$$

2.6 Clustering Process Extensions

Feature Standardisation. Feature standardisation techniques such as z-score and variance-to-range standardisation can be applied before clustering [12,25]. In addition to $\mathbf{X}$, $\mathcal{C}$ can be applied across $\mathcal{K}$ for the transformed versions of $\mathbf{X}$. $\mathcal{A}(\mathcal{C})$ can be used to assess the effect of the feature transformation on the data and used to select the optimal feature transformation technique.

Index Normalisation. A more robust index normalisation method outlined in [4,14] can be implemented when creating I_j^*. Normalisation involves applying randomised clustering techniques to generate multiple clusterings on the same data. I_j^* for all clusterings are then calibrated using z-score transformation to their expected variation over clusterings of the same data, where a higher number is optimal.

Weighted $\mathcal{A}(\mathcal{C})$. When creating $\mathcal{A}(\mathcal{C})$, [2] recommends the consideration of the dynamics of I_j^* in relation to the clustering goal. I_j^* are weighted (w_j) in discussion with SMEs to bias individual indexes, with a higher weight reflecting a greater importance. For instance, I^*_{distcc} assists in explaining information reduction, reflecting how well-represented the cluster is by the cluster centroids. SMEs determined the information reduction to be of full importance, with $w_{\text{wcss}} = 1$. $\mathbf{X}$ is required to be clustered into a small number of groups of similar profiles, prioritising within-cluster homogeneity over cluster separation. SMEs determined $w_{\text{wcss}} = 1$ and $w_{\text{sep}} = 0.5$. The characteristic that the density of the cluster reduces from the cluster centroid to the outer regions is required to augment $\mathcal{A}(\mathcal{C})$, however, with less impact than the other indexes, defined as $w_{\text{dens}} = 0.25$. This results in $\mathcal{A}(\mathcal{C})_2$, specific to the goal of clustering playing styles of Australian football. The heuristic weighting of indexes can be further extended by formalising w_j through methods such as the Analytical Hierarchical Process [22].

$$\mathcal{A}(\mathcal{C})_2 = \frac{1 \cdot I^*_{\text{wcss}} + 0.5 \cdot I^*_{\text{sep}} + 1 \cdot I^*_{\text{distcc}} + 0.25 \cdot I^*_{\text{dens}}}{1 + 0.5 + 1 + 0.25} \tag{4}$$

3 Deployment

Transactional match data was provided by Champion Data©, Melbourne, Australia, the official statistical provider of the AFL. Following Sect. 2.2, chain summary data was created to summarise team performance within specific phases of play. For the offensive phase of play, in discussion with SMEs informed by the clustering aim, an interpretable range of possible clusters is determined, $\mathcal{K} = \{2, ..., 10\}$. The R package `fpc` [16] was used to implement the cluster algorithms and assessment indexes to create $\mathcal{A}(\mathcal{C})$. Selecting the maximum $\mathcal{A}(\mathcal{C})_2$ across $\mathbf{X}_{\text{off}}$ identified five offensive playing styles (Fig. 1).

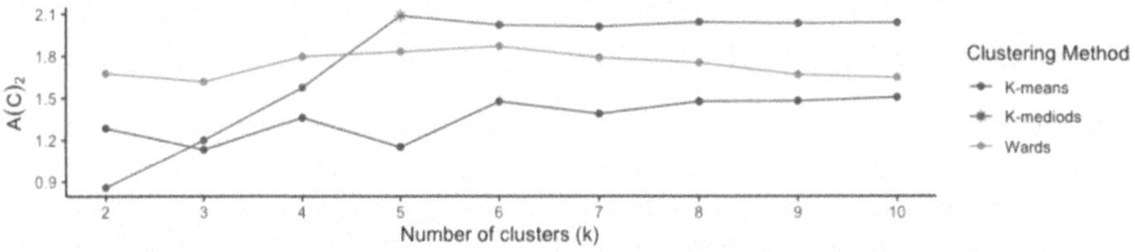

Fig. 1. $\mathcal{A}(\mathcal{C})_2$ assesses the results of three clustering methods across $\mathcal{K}$ for $\mathbf{X}_{\text{off}}$. The maximum $\mathcal{A}(\mathcal{C})_2$ identifies the k-mediod clustering algorithm with five clusters to produce the best clustering result.

4 Conclusion

The clustering framework can be implemented within any team invasion sport to analyse performance. Implementing the framework within Australian football results in the identification of team playing styles within specific periods of a match. The optimal hyper-parameters identified by the maximum $\mathcal{A}(\mathcal{C})$ results in the identification of k playing styles for each specific phase of play within

Australian football. The cluster centroids of the optimal clusters can then be used to characterise data points within each cluster, defining the team playing styles within the phase of play. Coaches and analysts can use the identified playing styles to assist with team and opposition analysis, identifying the specific styles of play that teams implement at specific periods of games. This can lead to the adaption of team tactics and strategies within specific periods of a match to maximise the likelihood of success.

References

1. Agarwal, S.: Data mining: data mining concepts and techniques. IEEE (2013)
2. Akhanli, S.: Distance construction and clustering of football player performance data. UCL (University College London) (2019)
3. Akhanli, S., Hennig, C.: Comparing clusterings and numbers of clusters by aggregation of calibrated clustering validity indexes. Stat. Comput. **30**, 1523–1544 (2020)
4. Akhanli, S., Hennig, C.: Clustering of football players based on performance data and aggregated clustering validity indexes (2022)
5. Alelyani, S., Tang, J., Liu, H.: Feature selection for clustering: a review. Data Clust. (2018)
6. Alexander, J.P., Spencer, B., Mara, J.K., Robertson, S.: Collective team behaviour of Australian rules football during phases of match play. J. Sports Sci. **37**, 237–243 (2019)
7. Born, Z.: Tactical performance insights for Australian rules football using deep learning. The University of Western Australia (2022)
8. Croft, H., Willcox, B., Lamb, P.: Using performance data to identify styles of play in netball: an alternative to performance indicators. Int. J. Perform. Anal. Sport **17**, 1034–1043 (2017)
9. Diquigiovanni, J., Scarpa, B.: Analysis of association football playing styles: an innovative method to cluster networks. Stat. Modell. **19**, 28–54 (2019)
10. Fernandez-Navarro, J., Fradua, L., Zubillaga, A., Ford, P.R., Mcrobert, A.P.: Attacking and defensive styles of play in soccer: analysis of Spanish and English elite teams. J. Sports Sci. **34**, 2195–2204 (2016)
11. Greenham, G., Hewitt, A., Norton, K.: A pilot study to measure game style within Australian football. Int. J. Perform. Anal. Sport **17**, 576–585 (2017)
12. Hennig, C.: Clustering strategy and method selection. Handb. Clust. Anal. **9**, 703–730 (2015)
13. Hennig, C., Meila, M., Murtagh, F., Rocci, R.: Handbook of Cluster Analysis. CRC Press, Boca Raton (2015)
14. Hennig, C.: Cluster validation by measurement of clustering characteristics relevant to the user. In: Data Analysis and Applications 1: Clustering and Regression, Modeling-Estimating, Forecasting and Data Mining (2019)
15. Hennig, C.: An empirical comparison and characterisation of nine popular clustering methods. Adv. Data Anal. Classif. **16**, 201–229 (2022)
16. Hennig, C.: FPC: flexible procedures for clustering. R (2023). https://CRAN.R-project.org/package=fpc
17. Kuhn, M., Johnson, K.: Applied Predictive Modeling. Springer, Heidelberg (2013). https://doi.org/10.1007/978-1-4614-6849-3

18. Lane, J.C., Van Der Ploeg, G., Greenham, G., Norton, K.: Characterisation of offensive and defensive game play trends in the Australian Football League (1999–2019). Int. J. Perform. Anal. Sport **20**, 557–568 (2020)
19. Moffatt, S.J., Gupta, R., French Collier, N., Keller, B.S.: Classifying and quantifying team playing styles in the Australian Football League. Int. J. Perform. Anal. Sport (2024)
20. Rennie, M.J., Kelly, S.J., Bush, S., Spurrs, R.W., Austin, D.J., Watsford, M.L.: Phases of match-play in professional australian football: distribution of physical and technical performance. J. Sports Sci. **38**, 1682–1689 (2020)
21. Robertson, S., Gupta, R., Mcintosh, S.: A method to assess the influence of individual player performance distribution on match outcome in team sports. J. Sports Sci. **34**, 1893–1900 (2016)
22. Saaty, R.W.: The analytic hierarchy process-what it is and how it is used. Math. Modell. **9**, 161–176 (1987)
23. Tenga, A., Sigmundstad, E.: Characteristics of goal-scoring possessions in open play: comparing the top, in-between and bottom teams from professional soccer league. Int. J. Perform. Anal. Sport **11**, 545–552 (2011)
24. Travassos, B., Davids, K., Araújo, D., Esteves, T.P.: Performance analysis in team sports: advances from an ecological dynamics approach. Int. J. Perform. Anal. Sport **13**, 83–95 (2013)
25. Visalakshi, N.K., Thangavel, K.: Impact of normalisation in distributed k-means clustering. Int. J. Soft Comput. (2009)
26. Wang, K., Wang, B., Peng, L.: CVAP: validation for cluster analyses. Data Sci. J. **8**, 88–93 (2009)
27. Wedding, C., Woods, C., Sinclair, W., Gomez, M., Leicht, A.: Exploring the effect of various match factors on team playing styles in the National Rugby League. Int. J. Sports Sci. Coaching **16**, 976–984 (2021)
28. Wedding, C., Woods, C., Sinclair, W.H., Gomez, M.A., Leicht, A.S.: Analysis of styles of play according to season and end of season rank in the National Rugby League. J. Sci. Med. Sport. **24**, 206–210 (2021)
29. Wedding, C., Woods, C.T., Sinclair, W.H., Gomez, M.A., Leicht, A.S.: Exploring the effect of various match factors on team playing styles in the National Rugby League. Int. J. Sports Sci. Coaching **16**, 976–984 (2021)
30. Wickham, H.: Tidy data. J. Stat. Softw. **59**, 1–23 (2014)

Data-Driven Smart Living Lab: Enhancing Community-Based Rehabilitation and Sports Participation for Individuals with Disabilities

Kwangtae Moon, Jin-i Hong, and Jongbae Kim(✉)

Department of Occupational Therapy, College of Software Digital Healthcare Convergence, Yonsei University, Seoul, South Korea
{otbuilder,Jongbae}@yonsei.ac.kr

Abstract. This study introduces a groundbreaking Smart Living Lab to foster community-based rehabilitation and sports participation for individuals with disabilities. Utilizing a data-driven approach, the lab integrates innovative technology to create a customizable and interactive environment. Our research outlines the development process, from conceptualization to implementation, highlighting the pivotal role of data analytics in tailoring rehabilitation exercises and sports programs to individual needs. The results demonstrate significant advancements in accessibility, engagement, and overall well-being for participants, setting a new benchmark for disability support services. This work paves the way for scalable solutions adapted across diverse community settings, ultimately enhancing the quality of life for people with disabilities.

Keywords: Community Participation · Data-Driven · Disabilities · Personalized Programs · Quality of Life · Rehabilitation · Smart Living Lab · Technology Integration

1 Introduction

The paradigm of rehabilitation has evolved significantly over the past few years, emphasizing the critical role of data-driven, user-centric approaches to address the diverse needs of individuals with disabilities. Central to this evolution is the concept of living labs, which represent an innovative framework for the co-creation, testing, and validating of new technologies, methodologies, and services in real-life settings. The living lab approach fosters an environment of collaborative innovation, where patients, healthcare providers, researchers, and technologists work together to develop solutions that are not only technologically advanced but also closely aligned with the users' needs and preferences.

Recent studies underscore the potential of living labs to revolutionize pediatric rehabilitation [1] and community-based programs for individuals with disabilities [2]. These initiatives demonstrate how data-driven insights and smart technologies can be leveraged to tailor rehabilitation exercises and sports programs, thus enhancing participants'

J. S. Dong et al. (Eds.): ISACE 2024, LNCS 14794, pp. 137–148, 2024.
https://doi.org/10.1007/978-3-031-69073-0_12

participation, engagement, and overall well-being. Furthermore, integrating advanced sensor technologies and deep learning frameworks, as highlighted by [3], offers promising avenues for recognizing and evaluating rehabilitation exercises, making personalized rehabilitation more accessible and effective.

The emergence of remote and telerehabilitation models, particularly in response to global challenges such as the COVID-19 pandemic, as discussed by [4, 5], further illustrates the adaptability and resilience of the living lab approach. These models ensure the continuity of rehabilitation services during crises and expand the reach of such services to underserved populations.

Moreover, the development of low-cost, automated rehabilitation systems, such as the one described by [6], represents a significant step toward democratizing access to effective rehabilitation solutions, particularly for individuals in low-resource settings.

As we embark on this project, we aim to harness the full potential of the living lab model to enhance community-based rehabilitation and sports engagement among people with disabilities. By fostering cross-disciplinary collaboration, leveraging cutting-edge technology, and placing users at the heart of the innovation process, we aim to develop a smart living lab that not only meets the current needs of individuals with disabilities but also anticipates future challenges and opportunities in rehabilitation.

This introduction aims to provide a comprehensive overview of the current state of living labs in rehabilitation, highlighting key studies and technological advancements that align with and inspire our project's objectives.

2 Method

This section provides an overview of our approach to developing the Smart Living Lab, emphasizing the key stages from design and construction to data integration and rehabilitation program implementation.

2.1 Developing a Smart Living Lab for Rehabilitation Exercises and Sports

2.1.1 Living Lab Design and Construction

While previous studies have highlighted the benefits of living labs in rehabilitation settings, our work uniquely integrates data-driven approaches and innovative technologies to create a customizable and interactive environment specifically tailored to the needs of individuals with disabilities. Our contributions include the development of a comprehensive big data platform for personalized rehabilitation, implementing advanced sensor technologies, and creating a standardized model for rehabilitation exercises and sports within a smart living lab environment. The development process involved careful planning and execution to ensure the Living Lab adequately supports its users' diverse needs. By integrating customized exercise programs and the required equipment, the initiative aimed to facilitate an accessible and effective environment for rehabilitation activities. This step was crucial in ensuring that individuals with disabilities could engage in rehabilitation exercises and sports within a supportive and realistic setting.

2.1.2 Literature Review and Research on Rehabilitation and Sports Programs by Disability Type

A comprehensive literature review covering the last five years (2018–2023) of domestic and international research and programs from the National Rehabilitation Center (2021–2023) was conducted to inform the development of the Living Lab's exercise programs. This review helped formulate guidelines for rehabilitation exercises and sports programs tailored to different disability types, ensuring the programs' relevance and effectiveness [7].

2.1.3 Investigation of Exercise Equipment and Programs

An extensive analysis of preceding studies, both domestically and internationally, focused on exercise equipment and programs for rehabilitation and sports. The research aimed at developing operational strategies for the Living Lab, ensuring that the facility would accommodate and enhance the rehabilitation process for individuals with disabilities through the thoughtful selection and implementation of exercise equipment and programs [8].

2.2 Development and Implementation of a Big Data Platform for Rehabilitation Exercises

2.2.1 System Overview and Data Flow Configuration

A comprehensive system was developed to collect, store, and analyze vast rehabilitation data. The platform's architecture includes a cloud-based server infrastructure (Naver Cloud Platform) to manage the data effectively. Users input essential health, exercise, and biometric information via a user-friendly app. This data is then stored on the cloud server and readily available for ongoing analysis and application. An app designed based on user and administrator permissions allows users to enter their basic health, exercise, and biometric information and accumulate this data for graphical visualization. This setup is intended to facilitate self-management of rehabilitation by enabling users to check feedback from medical professionals periodically. Administrators can enhance the efficiency of rehabilitation exercise programs by utilizing functionalities to review user information and manage feedback through registration, modification, and deletion.

2.2.2 Data Input APP Configuration

The flow from data collection and input stages to the registration and storage of data on a cloud server was meticulously designed for each user. This infrastructure lays the groundwork for recommending and implementing disability-specific customized rehabilitation exercise programs through big data analysis and labeling.

2.2.3 Data Storage and Server Registration

A server was established using the Naver Cloud Platform, and functionality was implemented to allow the continuous accumulation of data to be downloaded in Excel format. This enables the systematic management and utilization of big data related to rehabilitation exercises.

2.2.4 Enhancement Direction and Expected Effects of Utilizing Accumulated Data for the Disability Rehabilitation Exercise Platform

Based on the accumulated data, an intelligent interactive agent-centered service was developed to recommend the most suitable rehabilitation exercise equipment and programs. This service aids individuals with disabilities in quickly and easily finding the appropriate exercise equipment tailored to their specific type and situation, supporting a more personalized and effective rehabilitation process.

2.3 Developing a Standardization Model for Rehabilitation Exercises and Sports

2.3.1 Operational Guidelines Development

A comprehensive set of operational guidelines for the Living Lab was derived, incorporating the 4P (Private-People-Public Partnership) model specifically tailored for rehabilitation exercises and sports (4P-REPELLM). These guidelines were formulated to cater to various disability types, ensuring the programs were medically relevant and could be seamlessly integrated into the Living Lab operations. The guidelines also provided feedback mechanisms for exercise equipment and outlined the laboratory's operational protocols for pilot testing.

2.3.2 Safety Guidelines Development

Based on the Canadian Patient Safety Institute (CPSI) framework, safety protocols were established to safeguard participants within the Living Lab environment. These guidelines emphasized the necessity of comprehensive safety measures tailored to the specific needs of individuals with disabilities engaging in rehabilitation exercises and sports activities.

2.3.3 Smart Living Lab Usability Evaluation and Demonstration

The usability evaluation aimed to determine the effectiveness and satisfaction of users using Smart Living Lab's rehabilitation program. Participants in this phase were meticulously selected with the help of medical institutions and Seoul public health centers to ensure a comprehensive mix of individuals across the three main disease groups: 5 with cardiovascular disease, 5 with musculoskeletal disease, and 5 with spinal cord injury. The selection process emphasized informed consent, with 15 final participants participating in the study (9 men, 6 women, mean age 46.2 years). These groups are further segmented based on specific health conditions to provide a balanced representation of Smart Living Lab's target user base. We developed a structured usability evaluation scenario to collect detailed feedback on the Living Lab service. This scenario was designed as a customized task for the actual application evaluation and rehabilitation training of the device developed based on collecting basic information and interviews related to the Living Lab service [9].

This study's on-site demonstration and usability evaluation of the living lab focused on the actual operational feasibility and adequacy of the living lab for rehabilitation exercise for disabled people with musculoskeletal and spinal cord injuries.

The study subjects consisted of 15 people with cardiovascular disease, 15 people with spinal cord injury, and one patient with musculoskeletal disease admitted to the National Rehabilitation Hospital. Additionally, 15 people with final stroke and three people with incomplete spinal cord injury also participated.

The study procedure was designed as a 4-week program including pre-and post-tests to evaluate the effectiveness of rehabilitation exercises. The main measurement and exercise equipment include automatic height and weight meter (InBody, Korea), body composition analyzer (BWA 2.0, InBody, Korea), isometric muscle strength meter (Powerlink, Germany), grip strength meter (TKK5401, TAKEI, Japan), and walking ability measurement equipment (HUCA-GAS100, Huka System, Korea).

Field testing tools (myFitNote, Exercowork, Korea), aerobic exercise equipment (Elephant, MLP, Korea), and flexibility and resistance exercise equipment (JOYnT, Good Playground, Korea) were used. These devices have been used to construct and evaluate exercise programs appropriate for each type of disability [10].

The rehabilitation exercise program was applied to stroke patients and spinal cord injury patients, respectively. Both spinal cord injury patients had incomplete damage and were able to walk spontaneously. As the development of exercise equipment to be placed in the Smart living lab, walking robot devices (Huka), upper limb complex exercise equipment (Elephant), and upper limb flexibility and strength exercise equipment (JOYnT) were mainly used.

2.3.3.1 Walking Robot Device (Huka)

Footrest-based end-effector-type device. Based on the rocker and crank, the rotation of the crank causes the movement of the coupler link and is designed to realize the trajectory of the ankle joint. As a result, the movements of the pelvis, knees, and ankles were ensured to match the actual walking pattern, and the stride length was adjusted according to the crank link length. The device operates in 100% automatic mode driven by an electric motor and the patient's voluntary effort. Two gait training methods are set up in a manual mode where walking is possible. In addition, for evaluation, quantitative values such as speed, stride length, time, and distance were calculated and stored on the equipped PC, and the real-time status could be checked on the monitor. In weeks 1 and 2, the exercise was performed for 10 min at 50% of Heart Rate Reserve (HRR), and in weeks 3 and 4, it was performed for 13 min at 60% to 70% of HRR. HRR is calculated as the difference between the maximum and resting heart rates, providing a measure of exercise intensity. During exercise, your perceived exertion (RPE) and heart rate are monitored in real-time.

2.3.3.2 Upper and Lower Limb Complex Exercise Equipment (Elephant)

Performs upper and lower extremity movements independently. Alternatively, the upper and lower extremities can be exercised simultaneously, improving the user's muscle atrophy and cardiorespiratory capacity. It is possible to collect exercise time, distance, and rotation data. It has been improved compared to the pilot test by installing a force plate on the footrest to evaluate muscle strength and balance ability of the left and right lower extremities during exercise. Therefore, subjects' muscle strength, heart rate, and RPE were recorded during each exercise session during left and right lower extremity extension. If the handle is stiff or difficult to grip, wear gloves to maintain side-to-side balance as much as possible. To exclude pain in the knee joint when pedaling the lower extremities, the height and depth of the chair were adjusted for each subject.

2.3.3.3 Upper Limb Exercise Equipment (JOYnT)

JOYnT is equipment for upper body flexibility and resistance exercises. It has a wide range of uses, including older people, people with stroke, and people with spinal cord disabilities. A rehabilitation exercise program developed for flexibility and resistance exercises was built into a smart device (tablet PC) so subjects could watch it and follow the movements to perform the exercises. Depending on the type of disability and motor ability, the intensity was adjusted using bare hands or a rubber band.

2.4 Collaborative Operation for the Construction of a Smart Medical Exercise Living Lab

This study reports on the collaborative operation method for constructing a smart medical exercise living lab. For this, regular collaborations were conducted through meetings of medical professionals, disabled sports professionals, sports measurement experts, and a living lab advisory board. Furthermore, focus groups were operated for various groups, such as the musculoskeletal system, cardiovascular system, and spinal cord injuries, and specific contents for each group were derived through this. This method provides an important model for constructing and operating a smart medical exercise living lab.

3 Results

3.1 Development of a Rehabilitation Exercise and Sports Center in a Smart Living Lab

In developing a living lab dedicated to rehabilitation exercises and sports, a strategic approach was taken to create a realistic environment that mirrors real-life scenarios for individuals with disabilities. This environment, depicted in Fig. 1, is meticulously designed and constructed to enable these individuals to participate in physical activities tailored to their specific needs and abilities, thereby enhancing their rehabilitation process.

Furthermore, leveraging the unique capabilities of the living lab, personalized rehabilitation exercises and sports service programs were developed. As outlined in Table 1, these programs are crafted to ensure effective and personalized rehabilitation paths, illustrating the living lab's commitment to providing comprehensive support for the recovery and well-being of individuals with disabilities. This integration of environment and programmatic support showcases an innovative approach to rehabilitation, emphasizing the importance of tailored and accessible exercise opportunities.

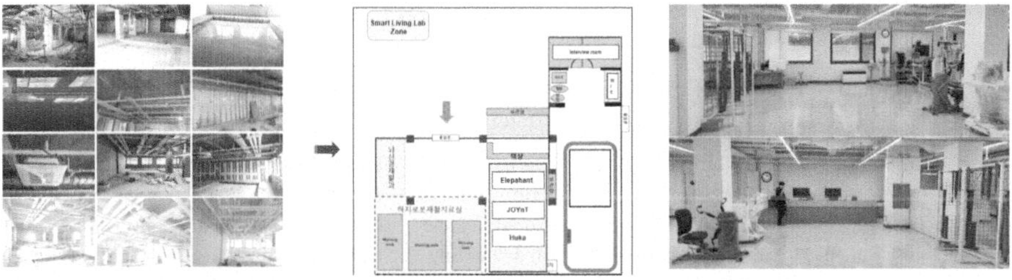

Fig. 1. Smart Living Lab

Table 1. Smart Living Lab rehabilitation exercise program

Week	Warm-up	Aerobic Exercise	Strength Training	Balance Exercise	Cool Down
1	Stretching (Duration: 5 min, Frequency: 3 times/week, Movement: 10–15 s each)	Walking/Full-body Exercise using HUCA/Elephant (Intensity: 40–50% HRR, Duration: 10 min)	Bridge, Hip Flexion & Extension with JOYnT in a lying position focusing on lower limbs and core muscles (Intensity: Level 1–3, Reps/Sets: 10 reps/2 sets, Duration: 10 min)	Feet Apart, Center Shifting (Forward/Backward, Left/Right) (Intensity: Level 1–3, Duration: 20 s/2 sets, Total Time: 5 min)	Stretching (Movement: 10–15 s each, Total Time: 5 min)
2	Stretching (Same as Week 1)	Walking/Full-body Exercise with HUCA/Elephant (Same as Week 1)	Trunk Lateral Flexion, Biceps Curl with JOYnT in a seated position focusing on upper body (Intensity: Level 1–3, Reps/Sets: 10 reps/2 sets, Duration: 10 min)	Feet Together, Center Shifting (Forward/Backward, Left/Right) (Intensity: Level 1–3, Duration: 20 s/2 sets, Total Time: 5 min)	Stretching (Same as Week 1)

(*continued*)

Table 1. (*continued*)

Week	Warm-up	Aerobic Exercise	Strength Training	Balance Exercise	Cool Down
3	Stretching (Same as Week 1)	Walking/Full-body Exercise with HUCA/Elephant (Intensity: 60–70% HRR, Duration: 13 min)	Sit to Stand, Hip AB & AD, Squat, Lunge in a standing position focusing on lower limb strength (Intensity: Level 2–3, Reps/Sets: 10 reps/2 sets, Duration: 10 min)	Feet Inline, Maintain & Upper Body Rotation (Left/Right) (Intensity: Level 1–3, Duration: 20 s/2 sets, Total Time: 10 min)	Stretching (Same as Week 1)
4	Stretching (Same as Week 1)	Walking/Full-body Exercise with HUCA/Elephant (Intensity: 60–70% HRR, Duration: 13 min)	Trunk Rotation, Overhead Shoulder Press, Squat, Lunge Variations with JOYnT in a standing position focusing on upper body strength (Intensity: Level 2–3, Reps/Sets: 10 reps/2 sets, Duration: 10 min)	Stand on One Leg, Y Balance (Intensity: Level 1–3, Duration: 20 s/2 sets, Total Time: 10 min)	Stretching (Same as Week 1)

3.2 Development and Implementation of a Big Data Platform for Rehabilitation Exercise

The development and implementation of a Big Data platform for rehabilitation exercises encompassed creating a comprehensive system for collecting, storing, and analyzing vast amounts of rehabilitation data. A user-friendly app was developed, allowing individuals to input essential health, exercise, and biometric information. Utilizing cloud technology, a server infrastructure was established to manage this data effectively, making it readily available for ongoing analysis and application. This accumulation of data informed the enhancement of the rehabilitation exercise platform, incorporating an intelligent interactive agent designed to recommend the most appropriate exercise equipment and programs tailored to each individual's specific needs and conditions, marking a significant advancement in personalized rehabilitation efforts (Fig. 2).

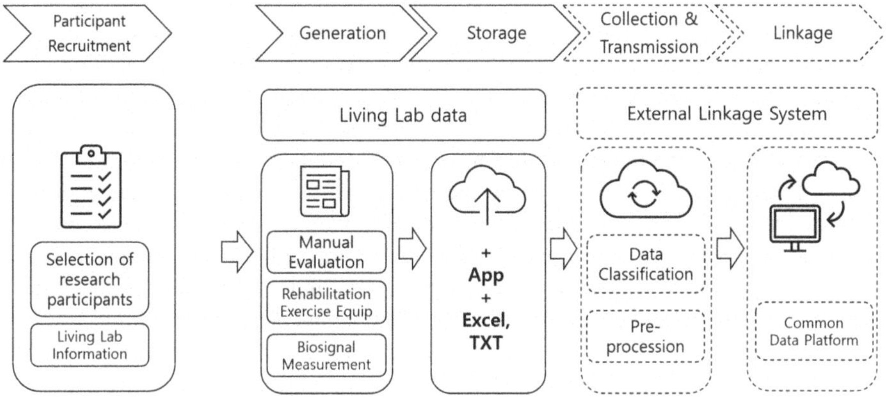

Fig. 2. Smart Living Lab Platform

3.3 Standardization of Rehabilitation Exercise and Sports Model

Smart Living Lab's approach to standardizing rehabilitation exercise and sports models included a comprehensive process to ensure the effectiveness and safety of the programs. The lab conducted two rounds of usability evaluation and field verification. The results of these assessments were instrumental in understanding the practicality of the proposed exercise and sports programs, which led to the development of detailed operational and safety guidelines [9, 10]. These guidelines have been carefully crafted, incorporating assessment feedback to create a safe and supportive participant environment. Additionally, a satisfaction survey of living lab participants revealed high levels of satisfaction with the program, highlighting the success of the tailored approach and the overall supportive atmosphere within the lab. These three strategies underline the commitment to providing an optimized, safe, and satisfying rehabilitation experience for people with disabilities and demonstrate the Living Lab's commitment to improving quality of life through tailored physical activity.

4 Discussion

This study proposed a living lab model for a fitness center specifically tailored for individuals with disabilities, aiming to offer safe and effective rehabilitation exercise services that consider their physical limitations. Despite various facilities and services available for disabled individuals in hospitals and communities, comprehensive fitness centers are not yet integrated with smart technology. Addressing this gap, the necessity for living labs emerged, and the pilot rehabilitation exercise center living lab at the National Rehabilitation Center is anticipated to be a crucial initial step in supporting individuals with disabilities to continue safe and effective rehabilitation exercises post-community reintegration.

This research delves into the advanced rehabilitation paradigm, accentuating the pivotal role of data-driven, user-centric approaches in catering to the multifaceted needs of individuals with disabilities. Echoing the sentiments of [1, 2], our study further illuminates the transformative potential of living labs in revolutionizing pediatric and community-based rehabilitation programs. By integrating user feedback, these studies validate the effectiveness of smart technologies in personalizing rehabilitation exercises, thereby significantly enhancing participant engagement and overall well-being.

In light of the challenges posed by the COVID-19 pandemic, the adaptability of rehabilitation services through remote and telerehabilitation models, as discussed by [4, 5], further demonstrates the resilience and flexibility of the living lab approach. These models have proven instrumental in ensuring the continuity of rehabilitation services during crises, extending the reach of these services to underserved populations.

Furthermore, the development of low-cost, automated rehabilitation systems, highlighted by [6], marks a significant milestone in democratizing access to effective rehabilitation solutions, especially in low-resource settings. This approach mirrors our project's aim to leverage the living lab model in enhancing community-based rehabilitation and sports engagement among people with disabilities. By fostering cross-disciplinary collaboration and leveraging cutting-edge technology, we aspire to create a smart living lab that not only addresses the current needs of individuals with disabilities but also anticipates and adapts to future challenges in the field of rehabilitation.

Our investigation reaffirms the essentiality of living labs in rehabilitation, showcasing how these innovative environments can serve as fertile grounds for the co-creation and validation of user-centered rehabilitation solutions. This research contributes to a growing body of literature that supports the adoption of living labs to improve the quality and accessibility of rehabilitation services, underscoring the importance of such collaborative, innovative approaches in meeting the evolving needs of individuals with disabilities.

This research introduces a novel approach by combining walking robot devices and aerobic equipment for both upper and lower limbs, distinguishing it from previous studies. Notably, the improvement in isometric lower limb muscle strength holds significant meaning. Beyond physical effects, mental and emotional benefits were also observed. Using survey tools, relationships such as quality of life, depression, and exercise self-efficacy were analyzed, reaffirming the importance of rehabilitation exercise and sports programs.

The Smart Living Lab faced several challenges that affected its timely establishment and operation. First, it is necessary to quickly select the location of the living lab by streamlining the consultation process between the hospital department, administration, and research department. This allows you to effectively manage making important decisions in the early stages of building a living lab. Second, the development and introduction process of devices and equipment must be improved to minimize time delays and enable the completion and operation of living labs more quickly. This contributes to increasing the functionality and efficiency of the living lab. Third, methods must be introduced to promptly correct and improve problems discovered during the testing process of devices and equipment. This will help improve the performance of devices and equipment within the living lab. Fourth, we must devise a plan to ensure that users can fully experience and use the living lab. This helps increase user satisfaction and further ensure the usefulness of the living lab. Fifth, we must ensure that disabled people, in particular, have time to experience and test various devices and equipment to verify their effectiveness. Through this, it will be possible to predict differences in effectiveness for all living lab devices and reduce restrictions on efficient use and promotion. Lastly, more efficient data measurement methods must be developed and introduced, considering a long-term operation. This plays an important role in operating and managing the living lab.

5 Conclusion

This study established a living laboratory within a rehabilitation exercise and sports center, outlining a comprehensive plan for developing and operating a living lab service and delivery system model. The design for the necessary content, services, and facilities was completed, showcasing the potential for expansion into a community model. The living lab, centered at the National Rehabilitation Center, extended its reach by connecting with the Bandabi Gymnasium of the Korea Sports Council for the Disabled, regional sports promotion centers, and the disabled exercise program of the Ministry of Culture, Sports, and Tourism, seeking expansion and operational support.

The Living Lab introduced a variety of contents and programs, offering pilot services to individuals with musculoskeletal diseases, cardiovascular diseases, and spinal cord injuries, successfully deriving a service model and dataset for rehabilitation exercises. This initiative appears to significantly aid individuals with disabilities, underscoring the importance of establishing a living lab within an exercise center that provides special medical care. This approach supports safe and effective rehabilitation exercises and aims to deliver personalized rehabilitation exercise services by considering the physical limitations of disabled individuals. The project highlights the potential for individuals to maintain health and community life without needing to access large hospitals in Seoul. The expansion plan and service model proposed by this study call for broad dissemination and application to enhance the quality of life for people with disabilities.

References

1. Archibald, M.M., et al.: Living labs for patient engagement and knowledge exchange: an exploratory sequential mixed methods study to develop a living lab in paediatric rehabilitation. BMJ Open **11**(5), e041530 (2021)
2. Lee, S.B., et al.: Data-driven smart living lab to promote participation in rehabilitation exercises and sports programs for people with disabilities in local communities. Sensors **23**(5), 2761 (2023)
3. Zhang, W., Su, C., He, C.: Rehabilitation exercise recognition and evaluation based on smart sensors with deep learning framework. IEEE Access **8**, 77561–77571 (2020)

4. Busnatu, Ş-S., et al.: Patient perception when transitioning from classic to remote assisted cardiac rehabilitation. Diagnostics **12**(4), 926 (2022)
5. Ceravolo, M.G., et al.: Systematic rapid "living" review on rehabilitation needs due to COVID-19: update to March 31st, 2020. Eur. J. Phys. Rehabil. Med. **56**(3), 347–353 (2020)
6. Vigneshwari, N., et al.: A rehabilitation system to assist diplegia by repetitive exercise using LabVIEW. In: 2020 IEEE Bangalore Humanitarian Technology Conference (B-HTC). IEEE (2020)
7. Choi, J., Park, J., Kim, M.: Analysis of research trends related to diagnosis of ASD through keyword network analysis: focusing on domestic academic journals published from 2011–2020. J. Behav. Anal. Support **8**(1), 115–135 (2021)
8. Cho Young, H., Muncheong, C., Su Mi, K.: Research on the living lab operation plan according to the survey of exercise equipments and programs for 'rehabilitation exercise and physical education'. Asia-Pac. J. Convergent Res. Interchange **9**(2), 391–403 (2023)
9. Kwangtae, M., Jongbae, K.: Comparative usability evaluation for development of rehabilitation exercise living lab: focusing on musculoskeletal, cardiovascular, and spinal cord injury groups. J. Korea Acad.-Ind. Coop. Soc. **24**(11), 653–663 (2023)
10. Lee, M.-J.L., et al.: Effects of 4 weeks high-intensity interval training with robotic assisted on body composition, basic physical fitness, gait ability and lower muscle strength in subacute stroke patients. Korean J. Adapt. Phys. Act. **31**(4), 165–178 (2023)

Design of a Handball Tactics Observatory Based on Dynamic Sub-graphs

Alexis Mortelier[1(✉)], François Rioult[1], and John Komar[2]

[1] Normandie Univ, UNICAEN, ENSICAEN, CNRS, GREYC, 14000 Caen, France
{alexis.mortelier,francois.rioult}@unicaen.fr

[2] National Institute of Education, Nanyang Technological University, Singapore, Singapore
john.komar@nie.edu.sg

Abstract. We propose the design of an observatory dedicated to the tactical analysis of handball, involving the use of *dynamic graphs* to represent and study patterns of play. This innovative methodology was used to capture the complex interactions between players, their movements on the court and passing sequences. By using techniques for extracting frequent subsequences from a dynamic graph constructed from a *gnomonic* transformation (azimuthal map projection that transforms circles into straight lines) of the court, it was possible to identify the most recurrent and therefore significant patterns of play. The extracted sequences were valued by various measures of interest: emergence rate and *expected goal*. These measures of interest introduced a hierarchy between the sequences, enabling them to be navigated. Within the observatory, the tactics discovered were illustrated by an intuitive graphical representation, giving coaches and analysts a better understanding of the trends, strengths and weaknesses of the tactics employed.

Keywords: sports analytics · dynamic graphs · handball observatory

1 Introduction

Handball is well studied in the literature on aspects of coordination, agility, strength and power, endurance, constitution, social factors, cognition (see [57] for an extensive review). However, tactical and strategic approaches are minor. With the exception of [11,33,48,55], the collective aspects of handball are very little studied. However, it is a sport where the collective aspect dominates. In addition, it produces a large number of stereotypical positioned sequences and tactics are well documented: looking for recurring combinations should be fruitful.

The identification of these recurrences would allow an automatic indexing of sequences in the match, the automatic generation of summaries (in handball, there are a lot of goals, which ones are particularly interesting?) – see [9,52,58] for soccer – and in fine the detection of the characteristic routines or formation [28] of a team, in order to obtain a competitive advantage.

J. S. Dong et al. (Eds.): ISACE 2024, LNCS 14794, pp. 149–166, 2024.
https://doi.org/10.1007/978-3-031-69073-0_13

Here we transposed the notion of observatory to the field of handball. This notion comes from linguistics, where the corpus is an *observatory* of a theory a priori, it is also a dynamic observation that can be used to describe and then develop a posteriori models [25,36]. The various activities of the observatory can be classified into three segments of intervention: an activity of production and dissemination of knowledge; an activity of a strategic nature through the production of analysis notes, sheets or elements of language concerning the situation of the subject; and an activity of an operational nature by organizing actions and putting in place tools [35,43]. Our corpus consisted of handball data from the 2015 World Championship in Qatar. Our ambition was to analyze tactics in handball by acting on the three segments of intervention mentioned above: disseminating knowledge on tactics, producing analysis notes and implementing analysis tools.

To analyze the tactics used, it was important to consider the sequence of events in a handball match as recorded in the data available to us. In practice, we had the trajectories of the players and a succession of events (pass, shot, foul, etc.). The notion of *dynamic graphs* was used to capture the dynamic evolution of the game. A graph is a mathematical structure considering a set of *nodes* which are the entities of the game and a set of *edges* indicating the relationships between the nodes. A dynamic graph is one that evolves over time.

A tactical element is a short succession of events. This element is interesting if it tends to recur frequently, which gives it the nature of a *pattern*. This interest arises from the reproduction of the situation and the characterization it gives to the team executing this tactic. The tactics we propose to analyze were therefore the result of extracting frequent subsequences from the dynamic graph associated with the game. This method produced knowledge that could be used to activate the observatory's first intervention segment. The second segment, dedicated to the production of analysis notes, would be supported by the creation of an interface for displaying the tactics detected.

This focus on dynamic graphs is original. Even in soccer, where there are many studies on the training of players, in terms of spatial organization, the state of the art emphasizes that no method performs a real-time analysis of the dynamics of tactics. Most of the time, aggregations on possession time are analyzed. For rugby, a specific study dynamically analyzes static graphs by looking at the relationship between connectivity, assortativity, strongly connected components and clustering on the player/pass/tackle graph and looks for a correlation with the amount of progression made [6].

The automatic analysis of trajectories in search for tactics complements the expertise of the coach. The techniques implemented were agnostic in that they made no presuppositions about the activity and proposed an objective analysis of it: the trajectories were transformed into dynamic graphs within which an exploratory approach was applied in search of regularities. These regularities were provided with measures of interest to encourage interaction with the expert using the observatory. We believe that this methodology and the resulting tools enriched the expert's analysis and discovery capabilities.

The article is organized as follows: Sect. 2 sets out the state of the art, Sect. 3 presents the data studied and then Sect. 4 presents the construction of the dynamic graph based on a transformation of the court where the trajectories occur. Section 5 analyzes the results obtained from the court transformation and the creation of an interface for enhancing the extracted tactics.

2 State of the Art

The search for collective regularities is a classic task in the analysis of sports trajectories, as attested by [17], which provides a very comprehensive synthesis of research into temporal analysis for team sports. This search for regularities requires a *vector quantization* from the continuous spatial domain to a *symbolic* domain. The problem of identifying trajectory patterns then becomes a problem of searching sequences of symbols, on which qualitative spatial reasoning is possible [5]. For example, spatial relations are encoded in a logic formalism that allows the prediction of the next pass in football using inductive logic programming [56].

Discretization of the spatial domain is a two-stage process: characterization/detection of an object of interest, which makes it possible to aggregate continuous position data, then grouping of objects of interest/reduction of the dimension in order to limit their number.

For the second phase of grouping objects of interest, we can distinguish between the use of k-means or EM clustering in [1,2,10,11], dimension reduction (PCA) in [44] or optimized tensor reduction [32], the use of self-organizing cards [30]) or neural gas [34] in [15,16,21,27,40,48,55], and finally the calculation of neighbors by dynamic time deformation [18].

An optional third stage in this process of transforming the space of trajectories into a series of movements concerns the classification of the movement (a series of displacements), often by comparison with the various representatives of the clusters [16].

2.1 Handball

We will not go into the details of the many studies on the individual aspects during the practice of handball (see for example [21,22,24,37,42,45]). However, contributions on collective aspects are few and far between: in [55], eight cameras detect the position of the defender in front of the shooter in order to create self-organizing Kohonen maps [30], a clustering method which can therefore be used to characterize defensive behavior. The same technique is used in [48] but for attack: sequences of five passes before the shot are grouped together, highlighting the eight most-played sequences out of a total of 612 over 6 matches. Finally, [33] analyses a sequence of temporal patterns (T-patterns [26]) to characterize defensive behavior.

2.2 Searching for Temporal Regularities

The first step in the search for regularity in collective motion patterns is to characterize the objects of interest. This task is well identified, see for example [8] which provides an extremely precise and detailed taxonomy of collective motion patterns. Once this discretization of the spatial domain has been carried out, it is possible to undertake qualitative spatial reasoning [5]: the spatial relationships are encoded in a logic formalism which allows the next pass to be predicted using inductive logic programming [56].

Spatial collective patterns (*generic aggregation patterns* [31]), although classic in the trajectory analysis community (flock, dominance, convergence, confrontation), are little used in sport. Instead, one can find the *temporal patterns* (T-patterns [26]), which are hierarchical sequences of events, hierarchical in the sense of nesting and relationships between components, for example in [33]. Techniques derived from Kohonen's concept maps are also favored for their ability to perform spatial clustering [15,16,21,27,40,48,55].

Finally, there is the use of constellations [11], which describe the relative position of objects in relation to each other, depending on their distance. A constellation is thus invariant to rotation and dilation. This approach is applied to football in [10].

2.3 Dynamic Graph

A graph $G = (V, E)$ associates a set of nodes V with a set of edges E, which are pairs of nodes. A graph is used to model the relationships between entities in a system. This graph is said to be *static*, as opposed to a *dynamic* graph whose edges and nodes change over time.

A dynamic graph $(G_t)_{t=1..T}$ is therefore defined as a sequence of static graphs (or *snapshot*) $G_1, G_2, ..., G_T$ where each G_t represents the state of the graph at a given time t. Formally, $(G_t)_{t=1..T} = (V_t, E_t)_{t=1..T}$, where V_t is the set of nodes in G_t at time t and E_t is the set of edges at time t [23].

The time t indexing the dynamic graph depends on the representation chosen for the data. For example, for our data from the World Championship in Qatar, the trajectories are sampled at 10 Hz. The time t here could be an integer number of tenth of a second. We could also consider only the sequence of graphs corresponding to each pass, ball reception, shot or foul event. In this case, t would be an integer index of the total number of events.

The same dynamic graph can be represented in a number of equivalent ways [23]: temporal graph, dynamic or temporal network, evolutionary graph, sequence graph, chronological series of graphs, and so on.

Classical approaches use a sequential representation where each instant is modelled by an adjacency matrix $(A_t)_{t=1..T}$, describing the presence or absence of edges between nodes at time t [51]. Other temporal models capture the evolution of the graph by assigning time intervals to the edges, making it possible to follow the evolution of the connections between the nodes. In this way, each edge is characterised by a triplet $(v_i, v_j, [t_{\text{start}}, t_{\text{end}}])$, indicating that the edge exists between the nodes v_i and v_j during the time interval $[t_{\text{start}}, t_{\text{end}}]$ [12].

Evolutionary graphs combine the structure of a static graph with a sequence of states. They are suitable for modelling systems that evolve continuously, such as social networks. Evolutionary graphs $(G_t)_{t=1..T}$ incorporate the static structure of a graph G and an evolution function ϕ such that $G_t = \phi(G, t)$. This function can describe changes in the graph topology over time [46].

3 Data

There are two types of dataset for team sport: spatio-temporal data and event data. *Spatio-temporal* data are the trajectories of players or the ball; they provide location, direction and speed information for each of the entities [17]. *Event* data provides logs of player-related events (pass, shot, reception, goalkeeper save, etc.) or technical events (red card, start of time, stop of time, foul, etc.) for a match. These data are the result of manual annotations. Each of these events can be associated with a distance, duration or direction and has a time stamp.

These two ways of looking at data require different technologies and technical or financial resources. For example, sensors Indoor Position System (IPS) [50] are inexpensive but not very accurate, while video [41,47,49] is accurate but requires costly treatment.

The data analyzed here comes from 88 matches of the 2015 Handball World Championship held in Qatar. These data were obtained by video analysis and manual annotation of the events. This dataset has been little studied, and only on individual aspects [4,19,20].

This data combines spatio-temporal and event-based information: the trajectory of each player at 10 Hz and details of match events such as passes, receptions, shots and goals. For each match, a statistical summary table is available for each player. This table provides individual information, such as walking distance, running distance, shooting distance at 7 m and 9 m and the player's role for each match.

4 Handball Tactics Based on Dynamic Sub-Graphs

In this section, we present our main contribution to the construction of a dynamic graph of the handball game based on the player trajectories available to us. We begin by justifying the use of the Delaunay graph, whose dynamic is encoded by a difference dynamic graph. We then introduce a gnomonic transformation to take better account of the particular topology of the handball court. We conclude by explaining how we extracted tactics from frequent dynamic sub-graphs and indicate how the relevance of these tactics is evaluated.

4.1 Transformation of Trajectories Into Graphs

To transform the available data into dynamic graphs, we first needed to choose the entities represented by the nodes and the relationships between these entities, which would be represented by the edges. The handball entities are naturally the players and the ball.

Each player could be considered individually or according to its position. In the first case, a tactic would be personalized by a specific player and a same different tactics could be instanced by different players. In the second case, the player's position was taken into account, rather than the individual, as a collective movement involves roles rather than specific people. The interface we proposed in the next section allows to choose between these different configurations. The default setting proposed individualizing the members of the French team and grouping their opponents by position.

As for the ball, it could be considered as a particular entity and give rise to a node in the graph. We could also consider that the player entities had a particular attribute which indicated possession of the ball. We have chosen to consider the ball as a particular entity.

To construct the dynamic graphs in which we are going to explore the recurring patterns, we needed to transform the players' positions into graphs. If the choice of entities that defined the nodes was clear (the players and the ball), how should the edges that symbolize the relationships between the entities constructed? There were many possible choices for this; define the neighborhood of each player, which groups together the other closest players; consider the positions of each player and construct the graph according to the relative positions of each player in attack/defense.

However, it would be preferable for the transformation into a graph to be non-parametric and *agnostic* (i.e. not require any prior knowledge of handball, for example). We therefore recommended using the *Voronoi diagram*, which shows the zones that a player can reach before all the others if they all have the same speed. It is a tool used in many scientific contributions linked to sport, for example football [29]. Voronoi zones are bounded by the bisectors of the segments joining two players[1].

The Delaunay triangulation [7] of a set of points is presented as the dual graph of the Voronoi diagram. Each cell of the Voronoi diagram is represented by a vertex in the Delaunay triangulation, and these vertices are connected by edges when the corresponding cells are adjacent. The boundaries of the Voronoi zones are determined by the bisectors of the segments connecting two nodes. To transform the raw data into a graph structure, we calculated the zones of influence at each point in time, then used Delaunay triangulation to encode a match in the form of a dynamic graph.

[1] this definition assumes that each player evolves at the same speed. The notion of dominant regions [54] or areas of influence [53], taking into account various factors such as speed, orientation vector, etc., are closer to the reality. There are also contributions based on probabilistic models of movement and control zones [3,14].

4.2 Event Differential Encoding

To encode the dynamic graph, we chose the event difference. At each instant t, we examined the changes in the Delaunay triangulation relative to $t-1$: we noted which edge appeared or disappeared. Persistent edges were ignored.

In the end, rather than $(G_t)_{t=1..T}$, we therefore considered the *dynamic difference graph* [39] $(\Delta G_t)_{t=2..T} = (V_t, E_{t-1} \setminus E_t, E_t \setminus E_{t-1})_{t=2..T}$ where $E_{t-1} \setminus E_t$ is the set of vanishing edges and $E_t \setminus E_{t-1}$ those appearing when $t-1$ changes to t. Figure 1 provides an example of two snapshots G_{t-1} and G_t with their edge sets E_{t-1} (Fig. 1a) and E_t (Fig. 1b); their differences $E_t \setminus E_{t-1}$ and $E_{t-1} \setminus E_t$ are at Fig. 1c.

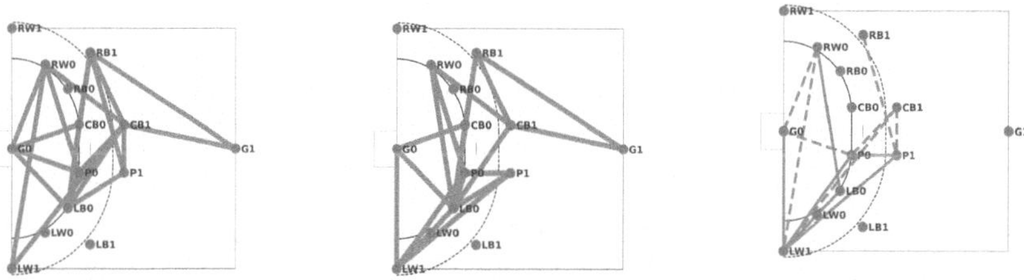

(a) E_{t-1} (b) E_t (c) $E_t \setminus E_{t-1}$ in solid lines, $E_{t-1} \setminus E_t$ in dashed lines.

Fig. 1. Difference graph.

Event difference encoding offers a fine granularity for capturing changes in the structure of the dynamic graph. In a sporting context, where interactions between players evolve rapidly, this approach provides a precise representation of the moments when new connections are formed or dissipated. This makes it easier to analyze key moments in the match, such as the formation of new tactics or the break-up of the opposing team. In addition, the event difference makes it possible to eliminate stationary edges, which would generate a large number of uninteresting frequent patterns.

Finally, as our data concerned several matches, each with two halves, extra time, stoppages in play, etc., we had to manage a dynamic graph *database*. More precisely, we considered having a dynamic graph for each series of five passes preceding a shot. This choice was justified by the desire to determine the tactics applied when approaching the shot and corresponded to the rhythm of collective movement in handball.

4.3 Conversion of the Handball Court

A handball court has an atypical topography: the area is rounded and the defenders position themselves around it to form a wall in front of the goal. This area is off-limits, unlike in football or basketball. Taking the straight line between two points, which in theory is the shortest route, is not always possible: you have to go around the forbidden zone. This prohibition changes the spatial relationships between players.

However, the aim of a Voronoi diagram is to account for the influence of the players on the court, and the conventional geometry used for this purpose does not take account of the particular topography of the handball court. In order to take better account of the spatial relationships between the players, we proposed to *transform* the initial court (Fig. 2a) by *curving* the area using a *gnomonic* transformation, so as to create a geometry in which a straight line is the shortest path between two points (see Fig. 2b). The Voronoi diagram was then calculated for this transformation. Next, the *inverse transformation* was applied, to obtain the Voronoi diagram for the initial court with *curvature* of the zone (see Fig. 2c).

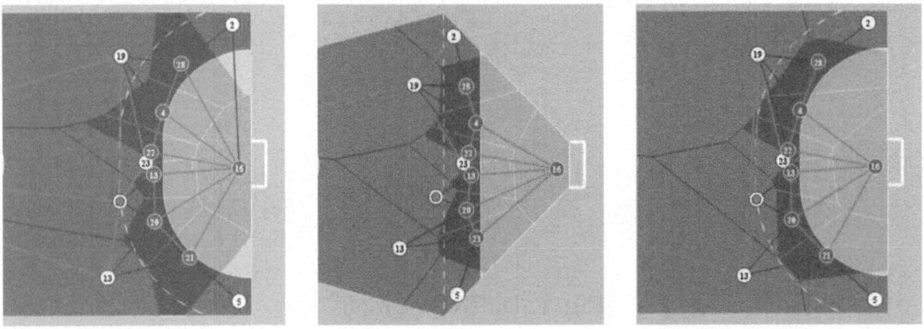

(a) Initial court. (b) Curved court. (c) Back curved court.

Fig. 2. Voronoi diagram and Delaunay triangulation for successive transformations of the court.

Let M have coordinates (x, y). Let O be the center of the quarter circle of the zone. Let $r = OM$ and θ be the angle (Ox, OM) (see Fig. 3).

The transformation of the court, which turns the quarter-circle zone into a segment, had the equation:

$$\begin{cases} x' = r \\ y' = r \cdot \frac{\theta}{\frac{\pi}{2}} \end{cases} \tag{1}$$

The level curves shown in Fig. 4 corresponded to the constant abscissa lines on the curved court.

4.4 Extraction of Recurrent Subsequences

To extract the frequent dynamic sub-graphs that represented the tactics, the dynamic graphs were converted into sequences of sets of edges. The frequent

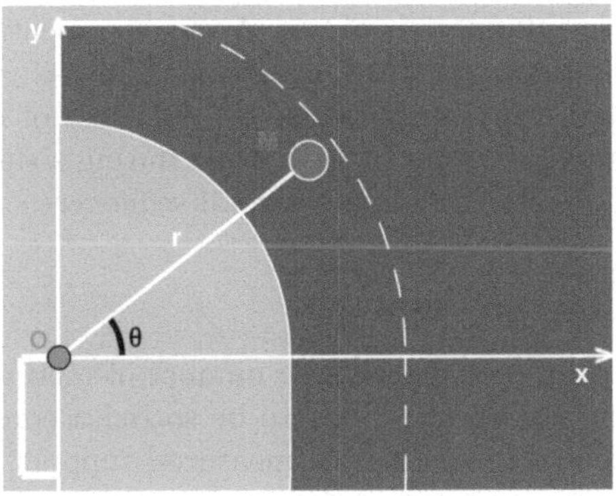

Fig. 3. Representation of a quarter of a plot.

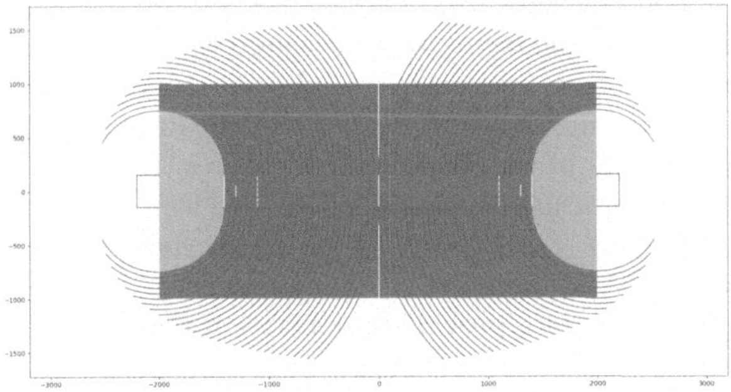

Fig. 4. Level curves (in red) on the court. (Color figure online)

closed subsequences were then extracted from these sequences [13]. A subsequence is *closed* if the addition of elements to this sequence reduces its frequency and therefore its representativeness. For example, if the algorithm determines that the sequences $\langle B, C \rangle$ (event C follows event B) and $\langle B, C, D \rangle$ has the same frequency, then $\langle B, C \rangle$ is not closed and will be ignored. And if any sequence constructed from $\langle B, C, D \rangle$, for example $\langle A, B, C, D \rangle$ or $\langle B, C, D, E \rangle$, has a lower frequency than $\langle B, C, D \rangle$, this means that $\langle B, C, D \rangle$ is closed. This technique avoids a lot of redundancy and focuses attention on the essential frequent sequences.

In addition, the algorithm was provided with temporal constraints, for example constraints on the temporal distance between the elements of the subsequences obtained. Here, we required that the elements pointed to were consecutive in the data, in order to obtain frequent sequences that represented a sequence of *consecutive* events. Otherwise, the algorithm could display sequences of events belonging to distant phases of the game, for example an event during the first quarter, followed by an event during the second, then the third, and so on. It was essential that the information obtained was representative of a sequence of consecutive events. Using temporal constraints, it was guaranteed that the subsequences extracted from our database of sequences of five passes before a shot showed a succession of events that occurred during a single sequence of five passes before a shot, and not straddling several sequences.

4.5 Measures of Tactical Interest

The extraction algorithm provided a large number of tactics. In order to facilitate access to relevant tactics, these had to be sorted according to measures of interest. Here we proposed three different measures: support, expected goal (xG) and emergence rate. *Support* counted the number of game sequences in which a tactic occurs. *Expected goal* is a statistical measure indicating the probability of scoring at the shot position at the end of a sequence. This measure was obtained using a model trained on data from Qatar 2015 and fed by the position of the shooter [38]. Finally, the *emergence rate* measured the ratio between the number of successful (giving a goal) and unsuccessful occurrences of the tactic.

Note that the emergence rate is a *forward-looking* or *anticipatory* measure, as it refers to the evolution of the situation it measures. In contrast, the expected goal is a *retrospective* measure because it is provided by a model calculated on the basis of aggregated data. The expected goal is therefore not directly influenced by developments in the situation being characterized.

While the emergence rate provided information about the profitability of a tactic, the advantage of the expected goal measure was that it did not make any assumptions about the quality of the shooter or the goalkeeper. Expected goal provided information on the quality of the situation in which the shooter was placed to take the shot, independently of the quality of the shot that follows. This measure was therefore appropriate for the objectives we had set ourselves, which ware to show the effective reasons for putting the shooter in a very favorable shooting condition.

5 Results

5.1 Relevance of the Court Transformation

In order to determine the impact of the court transformation (decurvature then recurvature), we counted the edge differentials between the initial graph and the transformed graph. To do this, we aggregated each game situation according to the player's position: Goalkeeper (G), Left Wing (LW), Right Wing (RW), Center Back (CB), Left Back (LB), Right Back (RB), Pivot (P). The defending team was marked 0 and the attacking team was marked 1. For example, CB0 indicated the center back in a defensive position.

Table 1 and 2 show the counting results, while Fig. 5a and 5b give a quantitative interpretation. The tables count the size of the reference set (initial or transformed graph), the size of the intersection (with the transformed or the initial graph) and then the difference. Comparative analysis of the dynamic graphs

Table 1. Edges lost through court deformation.

edges	initial	intersection	initial\transformed	ratio (%)
(G0, RW1)	1120	192	928	82,8
(RW0, G1)	1106	216	890	80,5
(RW1, G0)	1114	357	757	68,0
(G1, RW1)	3321	1930	1391	41,9
(RW0, G0)	3993	2999	994	24,9
(RW0, RB1)	3707	2869	838	22,6
(CB1, RB0)	5247	4370	877	16,7
(G1, CB1)	6045	5258	787	13,0
(RB0, G0)	6850	5975	875	12,8
(RW1, CB1)	2279	2213	66	2,9
(RB1, RW1)	2510	2444	66	2,6
(RW0, CB0)	3230	3153	77	2,4
(RW0, CB0)	3146	3080	66	2,1
(RW1, CB1)	3305	3237	68	2,1
(RB0, RW0)	2064	2034	30	1,4

Table 2. Edges created by court deformation.

edges	transformed	intersection	transformed\initial	ratio (%)
(RB1, RW1)	3968	2444	1524	38,4
(RB0, RW0)	3081	2034	1047	34,0
(LW1, LB1)	4659	3237	1422	30,5
(LW0, CB0)	4285	3080	1205	28,1
(LW1, CB1)	3025	2213	812	26,8
(LW0, LB0)	4113	3153	960	23,3
(LW0, RB1)	3255	2869	386	11,9
(G1, RW1)	2114	1930	184	8,7
(LW0, G0)	3256	2999	257	7,9
(LB1, RB0)	4679	4370	309	6,6
(RB0, G0)	6208	5975	233	3,8
(LW0, G1)	222	216	6	2,7
(G1, CB1)	5394	5258	136	2,5
(LW1, G0)	363	357	6	1,7
(G0, RW1)	194	192	2	1,0

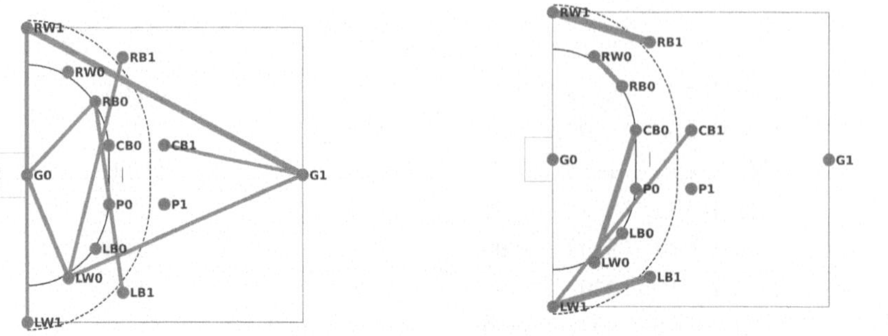

(a) Edges present in the initial graph but absent from the deformed graph.

(b) Edges present in the deformed graph but absent from the initial graph.

Fig. 5. Differentiation between edges lost and gained through deformation.

generated from the Qatar dataset revealed significant differences between the two modeling approaches.

Initially, we observed that the edges removed by our transformation (present in the initial graph and absent from the transformed graph, see Fig. 5a) were not very useful for understanding handball. These were, for example, the links between the goalkeeper and his defenders (G0-RB0 and G0-LW0), or the links between the goalkeeper and his attackers (G1-RW1 and G1-CB1).

The transformation of the court also revealed edges in the transformed graph that were absent in the initial graph (see Fig. 5b). These edges, for example, involved the relationships between wingers and defenders, which were therefore better accounted for in the transformed version of the graph.

This comparison between the initial graph and the transformed graph suggested that the transformation of the court added value by capturing more relevant links and eliminating those considered less crucial.

5.2 Tactics Visualization Interface

The data from the 2015 World Championship in Qatar resulted in a dataset of 760 dynamic graphs of five passes before a shot. The tactic extraction algorithm in the form of closed sequences was utilized with a minimal support threshold of 5% (the algorithm pruned sequences with support below this threshold). It yielded 6,820 tactics, the characteristics of which (number, average support, emergence rate ρ, and expected goal) are listed in Table 3.

Dynamic frequent subgraph extraction yielded such a significant number of tactics that it is unrealistic to attempt exhaustive examination of them. Therefore, it was necessary to provide the expert responsible for their analysis with a

Table 3. Tactics and relevancy measure by size.

length	number	support	ρ	xG
2	4,836	26.88	1.56	0.58
3	1,420	26.82	1.68	0.58
4	392	26.22	1.30	0.56
5	172	25.23	0.97	0.58
all	6,820	26.88	1.55	0.58

visualization interface, both to select a tactic for scrutiny and to contextualize it within the match. This interface enabled activation of the observatory's second intervention segment by generating analysis notes.

The knowledge produced by the tactics extractor was *objective*, as no assumptions were made about the activity in question. Our method did not use any model for handball interaction: trajectory segmentation was performed using the Delaunay graph, and tactics were obtained by extracting regularities. To involve the expert in the analysis of our results and bridge the semantic gap between our disciplines, it was important to favor a holistic approach by situating the obtained results within the framework of handball activity: edge sequences should be visualized on a player position diagram, integrated into the course of a match.

The interface should offer the expert considerable freedom to choose among the many discovered tactics. While the currently analyzed tactic naturally occupies a central position within the interface (zone 1), it is possible to select priority orders for the whole set (zone 2): attack or defense, associated interest measure (xG, emergence, support), pattern length, place attack or counter-attack, triggering position within the data sequences. The currently visualized tactic then has statistical measures (zone 3) relative to the entire data set, associated with the order selector: xG, emergence, support, triggering position. More sports-oriented semantic measures (zone 4) allow the expert to diversify potential explanations for the pattern's interest and to place it within the sequence from which it originates: xG, triggering, opponent pressure (number of links between the ball and opponents in the Delaunay graph), and richness of the solution offered by teammates (number of links between the ball and teammates in the Delaunay graph).

Finally, occurrences of the analyzed tactic are located in the complete corpus of matches (zone 5). It is possible to display a two-dimensional representation of the Delaunay graph where the tactic's edges are highlighted (zone 6), or to access video footage (zone 7). The expert can navigate within the complete sequence or from one occurrence to another (zone 8).

Numerous interactions between different parts of the visualization interface are available. Firstly, by selecting the tactic to analyze, a context transfer is made to the parts of the interface providing measures or visualization, ensuring coherent navigation. Navigation within tactics is dynamic through actions on priority order selection or tactic filtering.

It's also worth noting that the measures of interest used to sort tactics were just as useful for scrutinizing those that performed well as those that were unsuitable or had a low success rate. It was therefore just as possible to analyze the strengths and weaknesses of one's own team, as part of match preparation feedback, as it is to analyze the strengths and weaknesses of a future opponent.

Figure 6 presents in the observatory the analysis of the following tactic: [['28 Valentin Porte = Left Back_1'], ['Pivot = Left Wing_1']] which indicates a relationship being created between Valentin Porte and the opponent Left Back, then one pass later a relationship being created between the opponent Pivot and Left Wing. This pattern appears 22 times (support), and scores 6.33 times more than not scoring (*rho*), gives a favorable shooting position with a 63% chance of converting shots into goals (xG). This was a placed attack pattern, generally triggered 4 passes before the shot is fired. This pattern appeared in game sequences of around 14″ and gives an average xG at the moment of the shot of 0.63 even with the pressure of 3 opponents on the shooter.

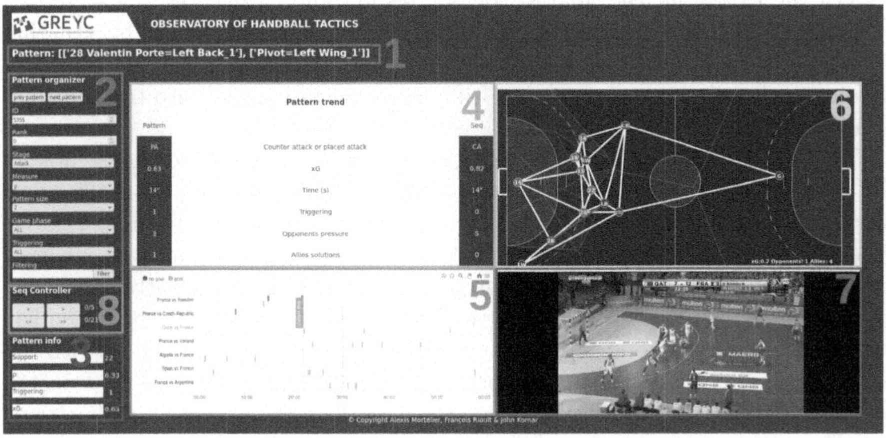

Fig. 6. Handball tactics observatory. (https://morteli211.users.greyc.fr/observatory/)

5.3 Interest of the Observatory for the Expert

The tactics observatory helped identify recurring patterns in the highly dynamic sport of handball. This tool enabled to analyze the own style of play, to ensure that the match preparation was correct. It was intended to complement traditional video analysis, which was carried out by humans who made choices on the extracts and introduced numerous biases. The automatic analysis proposed here had the merit of being exhaustive and objective. The objectivity of the tactics displayed was enhanced by the accompanying prospective or retrospective measurement, which complemented the focus that a coach would like to give to his fetish tactics.

The observatory was also invaluable for understanding an opponent's tactics, both from the point of view of successes, which could be countered, and failures, which could be exploited or encouraged. Dynamic graphs potentially provided information on deeper aspects of the activity, which were not easily and at first sight accessible to a more traditional analysis.

6 Conclusion

In this article, we presented a method for designing an observatory dedicated to the tactical analysis of handball, implementing the use of dynamic graphs to visualize and study patterns of play. This approach added a temporal dimension to the exploration of game patterns, going beyond the simple snapshots that had been observed until now. By capturing the complex interactions between players, their trajectories on the court and passing sequences, this representation offered a better understanding of the dynamics of the game. Our choice of event-difference graph encoding provided the fine granularity essential for capturing changes in the structure of the dynamic graph. Using an approach based on the Voronoi diagram to create the relationships between players, we adapted this method to take better account of the specific topography of the handball court. This sequential graph structure then allowed us to extract recurrent tactical subsequences, which were evaluated according to measures of interest such as the emergence rate and the expected goal. These measures introduced a hierarchy of tactics, making it easier to navigate the observatory. The tactics discovered were then graphically illustrated in the observatory, providing coaches and analysts with a better understanding of the trends, strengths and weaknesses of the tactics employed.

For future prospects, it would be interesting to further explore the possibilities of integrating additional data, such as player physiological data or individual performance data, to enrich tactical analysis and offer deeper insights. In addition, extending this methodology to other sports could open up new avenues of research and enable enriching interdisciplinary comparisons. Ultimately, it would be advantageous to engage in ongoing collaboration with coaches and sports analysts to further develop and tailor this approach with a refined focus on UX design, thereby ensuring its applicability and effectiveness in the practical realm of handball and beyond.

Acknowledgements. The research described here was funded by the ANR and the Normandy Region as part of the HAISCoDe project.

References

1. Andrienko, G., Andrienko, N., Budziak, G., von Landesberger, T., Weber, H.: Coordinate transformations for characterization and cluster analysis of spatial configurations in football. In: Berendt, B., et al. (eds.) ECML PKDD 2016. LNCS (LNAI), vol. 9853, pp. 27–31. Springer, Cham (2016). https://doi.org/10.1007/978-3-319-46131-1_6

2. Bialkowski, A., Lucey, P., Carr, P., Yue, Y., Sridharan, S., Matthews, I.: Large-scale analysis of soccer matches using spatiotemporal tracking data. In: 2014 IEEE International Conference on Data Mining, pp. 725–730. IEEE (2014)
3. Brefeld, U., Lasek, J., Mair, S.: Probabilistic movement models and zones of control. Mach. Learn. **108**(1), 127–147 (2019)
4. Cardinale, M., Whiteley, R., Hosny, A.A., Popovic, N.: Activity profiles and positional differences of handball players during the world championships in Qatar 2015. Int. J. Sports Physiol. Perform. **12**(7), 908–915 (2017)
5. Chen, J., Cohn, A.G., Liu, D., Wang, S., Ouyang, J., Yu, Q.: A survey of qualitative spatial representations. Knowl. Eng. Rev. **30**(1), 106–136 (2013)
6. Cintia, P., Coscia, M., Pappalardo, L.: The haka network: evaluating rugby team performance with dynamic graph analysis. In: 2016 IEEE/ACM International Conference on Advances in Social Networks Analysis and Mining (ASONAM), pp. 1095–1102. IEEE (2016)
7. Delaunay, B.: Sur la sphère vide. Bull. l'Acad. Sci. l'URSS **6**, 793–800 (1934)
8. Dodge, S., Weibel, R., Lautenschütz, A.-K.: Towards a taxonomy of movement patterns. Inf. Vis. **7**(3–4), 240–252 (2008)
9. Ekin, A., Tekalp, A.M., Mehrotra, R.: Automatic soccer video analysis and summarization. IEEE Trans. Image Process. **12**(7), 796–807 (2003)
10. Feuerhake, U.: Recognition of repetitive movement patterns–the case of football analysis. ISPRS Int. J. Geo Inf. **5**(11), 208 (2016)
11. Feuerhake, U., Sester, M.: Mining group movement patterns. In: Proceedings of the 21st ACM SIGSPATIAL International Conference on Advances in Geographic Information Systems, pp. 520–523 (2013)
12. Fournier-Viger, P., et al.: A survey of pattern mining in dynamic graphs. Wiley Interdisc. Rev.: Data Min. Knowl. Discov. **10**(6), e1372 (2020)
13. Fournier-Viger, P., Nkambou, R., Nguifo, E.M.: A knowledge discovery framework for learning task models from user interactions in intelligent tutoring systems. In: Gelbukh, A., Morales, E.F. (eds.) MICAI 2008. LNCS (LNAI), vol. 5317, pp. 765–778. Springer, Heidelberg (2008). https://doi.org/10.1007/978-3-540-88636-5_72
14. Fujimura, A., Sugihara, K.: Geometric analysis and quantitative evaluation of sport teamwork. Syst. Comput. Jpn. **36**(6), 49–58 (2005)
15. Grunz, A., Memmert, D., Perl, J.: Analysis and simulation of actions in games by means of special self-organizing maps. Int. J. Comput. Sci. Sport **8**(1), 22–37 (2009)
16. Grunz, A., Memmert, D., Perl, J.: Tactical pattern recognition in soccer games by means of special self-organizing maps. Hum. Mov. Sci. **31**(2), 334–343 (2012)
17. Gudmundsson, J., Horton, M.: Spatio-temporal analysis of team sports. ACM Comput. Surv. (CSUR) **50**(2), 1–34 (2017)
18. Haase, J., Brefeld, U.: Finding similar movements in positional data streams. In: MLSA@ PKDD/ECML, pp. 49–57 (2013)
19. Hansen, C., Sanz-Lopez, F., Whiteley, R., Popovic, N., Ahmed, H.A., Cardinale, M.: Performance analysis of male handball goalkeepers at the world handball championship 2015. Biol. Sport **34**(4), 393 (2017)
20. Hansen, C., et al.: A video-based analysis to classify shoulder injuries during the handball world championships 2015. Sportverletzung Sportschaden: Organ der Gesellschaft fur Orthopadisch-traumatologische Sportmedizin **33**(1), 30–35 (2019)
21. Hassan, A., Schrapf, N., Ramadan, W., Tilp, M.: Evaluation of tactical training in team handball by means of artificial neural networks. J. Sports Sci. **35**(7), 642–647 (2017)

22. Hassan, A., Schrapf, N., Tilp, M.: The prediction of action positions in team handball by non-linear hybrid neural networks. Int. J. Perform. Anal. Sport **17**(3), 293–302 (2017)
23. Holme, P.: Modern temporal network theory: a colloquium. Eur. Phys. J. B **88**(9), 234 (2015)
24. Ivasic-Kos, M., Pobar, M.: Building a labeled dataset for recognition of handball actions using mask R-CNN and STIPS. In: 2018 7th European Workshop on Visual Information Processing (EUVIP), pp. 1–6. IEEE (2018)
25. Jacquin, J.: IMPACT: a tool for transcribing and commenting on oral data, for teaching, learning, and research. Digit. Scholarsh. Humanit. **31**(3), 493–498 (2015)
26. Jonsson, G.K., et al.: Application of t-pattern detection and analysis in sports research. Open Sports Sci. J. **3**(1) (2010)
27. Kempe, M., Grunz, A., Memmert, D.: Detecting tactical patterns in basketball: comparison of merge self-organising maps and dynamic controlled neural networks. Eur. J. Sport Sci. **15**(4), 249–255 (2015)
28. Kim, H., Kim, B., Chung, D., Yoon, J., Ko, S.-K.: SoccerCPD: formation and role change-point detection in soccer matches using spatiotemporal tracking data. In: Proceedings of the 28th ACM SIGKDD Conference on Knowledge Discovery and Data Mining, pp. 3146–3156 (2022)
29. Kim, S.: Voronoi analysis of a soccer game. Nonlinear Anal. Modell. Control **9**(3), 233–240 (2004)
30. Kohonen, T.: Self-organized formation of topologically correct feature maps. Biol. Cybern. **43**(1), 59–69 (1982)
31. Laube, P., van Kreveld, M., Imfeld, S.: Finding REMO—detecting relative motion patterns in geospatial lifelines. In: Fisher, P.F. (ed.) Developments in Spatial Data Handling, pp. 201–215. Springer, Heidelberg (2005). https://doi.org/10.1007/3-540-26772-7_16
32. Li, R., Chellappa, R., Zhou, S.K.: Learning multi-modal densities on discriminative temporal interaction manifold for group activity recognition. In: 2012 IEEE Conference on Computer Vision and Pattern Recognition, pp. 2450–2457 (2009)
33. Lopes, A., Camerino, O., Anguera, M.T., Jonsson, G.K.: Ball recovery in the handball tournament of the 2008 Beijing Olympic games: sequential analysis of positional play as used by the Spanish team's defence. In: Proceedings of the 7th International Conference on Methods and Techniques in Behavioral Research, pp. 1–4 (2010)
34. Martinetz, T.M., Berkovich, S.G., Schulten, K.: 'Neural-gas' network for vector quantization and its application to time-series prediction. IEEE Trans. Neural Netw. **4**(4), 558–569 (1993)
35. Maryl, M., et al.: A case study protocol for meta-research into digital practices in the humanities. Digit. Humanit. Q. **14**(3), 1–20 (2020)
36. Mayaffre, D.: Rôle et place du corpus en linguistique. réflexions introductives. In: Actes du colloque JETOU 2005, pp. 5–17. Université de Toulouse-Le Mirail (2005)
37. Meletakos, P., Vagenas, G., Bayios, I.: A multivariate assessment of offensive performance indicators in men's handball: trends and differences in the world championships. Int. J. Perform. Anal. Sport **11**(2), 284–294 (2011)
38. Mortelier, A., Rioult, F., Komar, J.: What data should be collected for a good handball expected goal model? In: Brefeld, U., Davis, J., Van Haaren, J., Zimmermann, A. (eds.) MLSA 2023. CCIS, vol. 2035, pp. 119–130. Springer, Cham (2023). https://doi.org/10.1007/978-3-031-53833-9_10

39. Neiger, V., Crespelle, C., Fleury, E.: On the structure of changes in dynamic contact networks. In: 2012 Eighth International Conference on Signal Image Technology and Internet Based Systems, pp. 731–738. IEEE (2012)
40. Perl, J.: Game analysis and control by means of continuously learning networks. Int. J. Perform. Anal. Sport **2**(1), 21–35 (2002)
41. Pettersen, S.A., et al.: Soccer video and player position dataset. In: Proceedings of the 5th ACM Multimedia Systems Conference, pp. 18–23 (2014)
42. Prudente, J.N., Cardoso, A.R., Rodrigues, A.J., Sousa, D.F.: Analysis of the influence of the numerical relation in handball during an organized attack, specifically the tactical behavior of the center back. Front. Psychol. **10** (2019)
43. Publique, C.P.: Évaluation externe de l'observatoire de la langue française. un rôle au-delà de l'observation? (2014)
44. Ric, A., Torrents, C., Gonçalves, B., Sampaio, J., Hristovski, R.: Soft-assembled multilevel dynamics of tactical behaviors in soccer. Front. Psychol. **7**, 1513 (2016)
45. Romero, F.P., Angulo, E.: Finding outstanding performance in handball players based on statistical analysis. In: MLSA@ PKDD/ECML, pp. 1–12 (2019)
46. Rossi, R.A., Gallagher, B., Neville, J., Henderson, K.: Modeling dynamic behavior in large evolving graphs. In: Proceedings of the sixth ACM International Conference on Web Search and Data Mining, pp. 667–676, 2013
47. Sanford, R., Gorji, S., Hafemann, L.G., Pourbabaee, B., Javan, M.: Group activity detection from trajectory and video data in soccer. In: Proceedings of the IEEE/CVF Conference on Computer Vision and Pattern Recognition Workshops, pp. 898–899 (2020)
48. Schrapf, N., Tilp, M.: Action sequence analysis in team handball. J. Hum. Sport Exerc. **8**, S615–S621 (2013)
49. Scott, A., Uchida, I., Onishi, M., Kameda, Y., Fukui, K., Fujii, K.: SoccerTrack: a dataset and tracking algorithm for soccer with fish-eye and drone videos. In: Proceedings of the IEEE/CVF Conference on Computer Vision and Pattern Recognition, pp. 3569–3579 (2022)
50. Serpiello, F.R., et al.: Validity of an ultra-wideband local positioning system to measure locomotion in indoor sports. J. Sports Sci. **36**(15), 1727–1733 (2018)
51. Šiljak, D.D.: Dynamic graphs. Nonlinear Anal. Hybrid Syst **2**(2), 544–567 (2008)
52. Stensland, H.K., et al.: Bagadus: an integrated real-time system for soccer analytics. ACM Trans. Multimed. Comput. Commun. Appl. (TOMM) **10**(1s), 1–21 (2014)
53. Taki, T., Hasegawa, J.: Visualization of dominant region in team games and its application to teamwork analysis. In: 2000 Proceedings Computer Graphics International, pp. 227–235 (2000)
54. Taki, T., Hasegawa, J., Fukumura, T.: Development of motion analysis system for quantitative evaluation of teamwork in soccer games. In: Proceedings of 3rd IEEE International Conference on Image Processing, vol. 3, pp. 815–818. IEEE (1996)
55. Tilp, M., Schrapf, N.: Analysis of tactical defensive behavior in team handball by means of artificial neural networks. IFAC-PapersOnLine **28**(1), 784–5 (2015)
56. Vercruyssen, V., De Raedt, L., Davis, J.: Qualitative spatial reasoning for soccer pass prediction. In: CEUR Workshop Proceedings, vol. 1842 (2016)
57. Wagner, H., Finkenzeller, T., Würth, S., Von Duvillard, S.P.: Individual and team performance in team-handball: a review. J. Sports Sci. Med. **13**(4), 808 (2014)
58. Zawbaa, H.M., El-Bendary, N., Hassanien, A.E., Kim, T.: Event detection based approach for soccer video summarization using machine learning. Int. J. Multimed. Ubiquit. Eng. **7**(2), 63–80 (2012)

The Velodrome - ProCyclists Data Analytics

Robert Moskovitch[1(✉)], Perry Sinai[1], Denis Rize[1], Liam Holohan[1], and Paulo Saldanha[2]

[1] Software and Information Systems Engineering, Ben Gurion University of the Negev, Beer Sheva, Israel
robertmo@bgu.ac.il, {perrys,rize}@post.bgu.ac.il, liam@cyclingacademy.org
[2] Department of Kinesiology, McGill University, Montreal, Canada
paulo.saldanha@powerwatts.com

Abstract. Cycling is an important field of sport, and a great example of a sport that is highly measured due to cycling computers that monitor and document workouts in detail. Having the data of each cyclist stored in a centralized database enables us to perform analytics in order to support the team's decision-making, such as who to send to which race, coaching decisions, and directuer sportifs preparation towards races. We describe here The Velodrome, a web based online tool that we developed with the Israel Premier Tech pro-cycling team to facilitate decision-making in the team. The Velodrome stores the data of all the cyclists' activities and enables to analyze multiple cyclists' data in parallel, unlike existing analytics frameworks that enable to analyze a single cyclist.

Keywords: Sports Analytics · Cycling · Visualization

1 Introduction

Analytics and data science, or as it is often generally called AI, is in use in various domains in real life, and recently it is being increasingly adopted into sports. Statistics on ball games were gathered and aggregated for years and were in use when broadcasting games on television in live. However, recently with the increasing adoption of wearable devices, such as smartwatches, or cycling computers, which enables to document workouts and races in details and store them, enables later to perform analytics to gain insights and ideally decide better. Decide better how were the workouts, and what can be done better, decide better who to send to which race, how to prepare for a race, and how to perform in a race, and more. Road bicycle racing has been an organized competitive team sport for 150 years [7]. Teams of cyclists are competing in a set of races held throughout the year. In each race the cyclists from the same team work together, while the result of the race is dictated by the first team member to cross the line, for which the entire team is working towards. There are one day races, as well as multiple days races, which are called stage races. A team is typically composed of about thirty cyclists, while typically 6 to 8 are allowed in a race, chosen based on their properties and expertise, and the particular race conditions.

J. S. Dong et al. (Eds.): ISACE 2024, LNCS 14794, pp. 167–172, 2024.
https://doi.org/10.1007/978-3-031-69073-0_14

Modern cyclists use various gadgets and wearable devices to monitor a vast amount of data, such as the overall elevation gain and distance, their continuous measurements of heart rate, cadence, power, and more. This data is typically uploaded to an online service, such as TrainingPeaks[1] or STRAVA[2], which can be accessed by the coach. Additional source of information about races and cyclists' performance in races, is available through the Pro Cycling Stats (PCS) website[3].

The main long term goal of our work is to develop an analytics framework that enables to build a decision support system that assists the team's coaches, Director Sportifs, and decision makers in various tasks, such as cyclists' allocation to races, as well as for the coaches. In this paper, however, we make a first step towards this ambitious goal, by analyzing the decision process of a particular team—the Israel-Premier Tech (IPT) team[4]. We introduce The Velodrome, a web based cycling data online analytics framework that enables to customize various views of the data which enables to compare multiple cyclists, unlike common analytics frameworks that focus on a specific athlete. We describe here the framework, the types of data, and optional views, as well as customization, and provide a demonstration. We are now performing a user study whose results we will be able to report at the conference.

The contributions of this paper are the following: we introduce the needs in pro cycling data analytics, and present The Velodrome, a framework for pro cycling data analytics that enables coaches and decision makers to analyze specific cyclist's data, as well as comparison of multiple cyclists. We describe the framework in high level and its optional views of the analyzed data.

2 Related Work

2.1 Cycling Analytics

Much sport-related research was done in recent years. Some of the research focuses on the physiological domain, such as estimating oxygen uptake during workout [14]. Some studies focus was on prediction tasks; For example, Hilmkil et al. [3] trained a model to predict the heart rate of a cyclist during a workout, and Kataoka et al. [4] focused on predicting power performance at the Tour de France 2017 grand tour using GPS data, in addition to physical and environmental measurements. Other studies focused on predicting the cyclists' performance in races using their ranking points results [5]. Some works related to cycling analysis, focused on analyzing cyclist's physical measurements during a ride. Vogt et al. [12] showed that intensity and workload estimation for professional road cyclists during a ride is better to be measured with power, rather than heart rate which was common before. This was later extended to explore power in flat or mountain stages [13], and Lucía et al. [6] compared grand tours' difficulty.

[1] https://www.trainingpeaks.com/.
[2] https://www.strava.com/.
[3] https://www.procyclingstats.com.
[4] https://israelpremiertech.com/.

Additional works were done for assisting coaches and athletes in taking tactical decisions during races [9] or predicting race results using machine learning techniques [8].

2.2 Sports Analytics Frameworks

As mentioned earlier, recent advancements in wearable devices, such as smart watches, and cycling computers, provide rich longitudinal measurements on each workout, or race, which is uploaded after each workout to the mobile phone, and typically later stored through TrainingPeaks's application on their cloud. The data includes various continuous parameters, including the workout geographical coordinates, distance, elevation, and the cyclist's measurements, such as heart rate, cadence, power produced, speed, and more. Accumulating such rich and detailed data, provides opportunities to analyze the data for athletes, which can be then viewed and analyzed by their coaches. There are several analytics applications that were developed, such as TrainingPeaks's WK05, and Golden Cheetah, who enables analytics. WKO5, developed by TrainingPeaks, is a specialized performance analytics software tailored for cyclists and triathletes, offering a wide range of analytics for a single athlete for effective management of training load and intensity. For instance, in research examining the preparation of a world-class male triathlete for the Olympic Games, WKO5 facilitated the analysis of heart rate, rate of perceived exertion (RPE), speed, and power data to control workout intensity across low, moderate, and high levels [1]. Others employed the power duration curve in conjunction with heart rate data to characterize training and racing profiles, assessing the demands placed on athletes [2,11]. Additional WKO5 presents a distinct approach for creating Individualized Training Levels (iLevels), such as power zones that are based on fixed percentages of an athlete's Functional Threshold Power (FTP). It uses Chronic Training Load (CTL), Acute Training Load (ATL), and Training Stress Balance (TSB) to model an athlete's condition. Thus, overall TrainingPeaks enables an infrastructure for data based coach athlete efficient communication, from inserting workouts instructions, and later analytics.

Another analytics platform is Golden Cheetah, which differentiates itself as an open-source performance analysis tool, appealing to a wide audience including athletes, coaches, and data scientists. It offers extensive analytical capabilities, with features like aerodynamic drag analysis (CdA) and muscle oxygen saturation (SmO2) analysis. Although it lacks a dedicated workout monitoring application similar to WKO5's integration with TrainingPeaks, it is compatible with a wide variety of data file types exported from other devices or platforms, such as Garmin Connect, Polar Flow, and more. Additionally, its Train Mode facilitates interactive indoor training sessions by syncing with bike trainers and sensors to adjust resistance according to workout plans. Benefiting from community-driven development, Golden Cheetah ensures rapid updates and is available on Windows, macOS, and Linux, it provides comprehensive performance analysis free of charge, allowing accessibility and community contribution. It's well-suited for users who enjoy a hands-on approach to data analysis and training.

3 The Velodrome

While as mentioned above analytics tools exist for a single athlete, teams need the ability to view multiple athletes for various purposes of decision making and coaching. We developed The Velodrome as a web based online tool to enable the analysis of workouts and races' data of the team's professional cyclists for the use of Israel Premier Tech's decision makers, coaches and Directeur sportifs. It enables users to explore and compare various cyclists, over time periods, and options for display of aggregated cycling data. The Velodrome consists on a database that stores all the aggregated data at the level of a workout/race, cyclists' daily questionnaire's answers about their physiological properties, and how they feel, and on top of that an analytics application that we implemented. The analytics layer enables to show data on specific cyclists, over a period of time, based on the user's choice, and various parameters in different charts. There are default charts, and the user can customize charts and save them at his profile. Due to the limited space, we describe here the main page of The Velodrome, and its various functionalities, and we discuss later how we use it now.

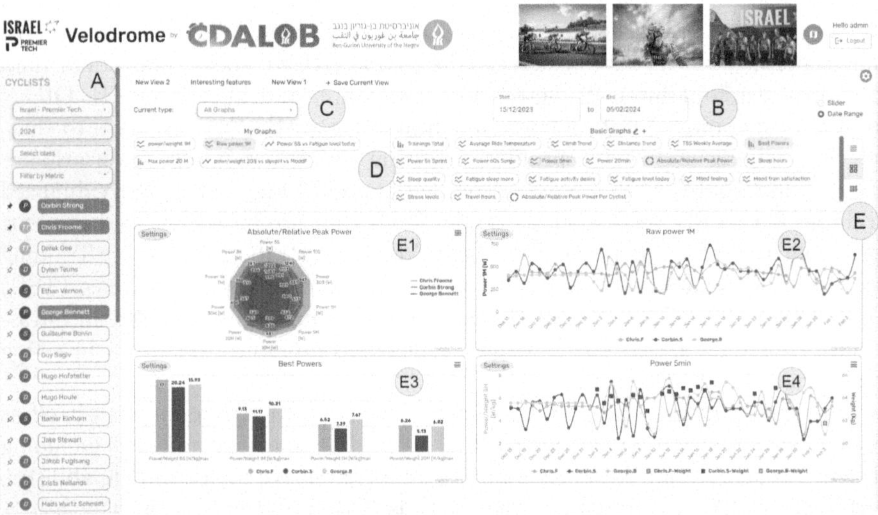

Fig. 1. The Velodrome's main page. The team's cyclists are presented, given the selected year (A), while the top right pane includes the selection of graph types (C) and allows to determine the time period start date and end date (B). (D) offers on the right default graphs, and on the left the graphs that were customized by the specific user. The bottom right pane (E) includes four different types of graphs: a radar chart of several power metrics (E1), a user-customized line chart comparing Absolute power over 1 min (E2), a basic bar graph comparing their best power metrics (E3), and a basic graph comparing the Relative power over 5 min (E4).

3.1 Cyclists Data Visual Analytics

Figure 1 presents the main visual interface of The Velodrome, in which the user can choose several charts that display multiple cyclists over a period of time. We describe here the panes of the interface. The left pane (A) enables to choose the year, which upon that presents the relevant cyclists on that year. The user can select multiple cyclists to view in the chosen graphs. This enables to compare cyclists based on their performances across different power metrics for example. In the figure here 3 cyclists were selected. Another important aspect typically required is a period of time, for which in (B) the start date and end date of the workouts analysis period can be chosen. Throughout training and races, various health, power, and environmental data are collected, alongside daily questionnaires filled out by cyclists. Velodrome categorizes these metrics into four main groups (C), each providing different basic charts when selected (D): Training - featuring charts of environmental data such as temperature and climb trends; Performance - including charts of various power metrics collected from bikes and riders' power outputs, such as power at 5 s, or power at 5 min. Two variations of power are provided: Absolute power, representing the power generated by the cyclist, and Relative power, which is calculated by dividing the absolute power by the rider's last known weight. Metrics - comprising charts of daily questionnaire data filled out by cyclists, such as sleep and stress levels; Rider comparison - offering charts that facilitate comparison between selected riders based on their power metrics. The Velodrome provides basic charts that are shown at the right part of (D), and those that were created by the user are shown on the left part of (D). In (E) four selected charts are displayed. Chart (E1) presents a basic radar chart comparing the Absolute/Relative power of each cyclist across various power metrics during the selected period and chosen cyclists. Chart (E2) is a user-customized line chart comparing Absolute power over 1 min for the chosen riders. Chart (E3) is a basic bar chart comparing the riders' best powers across different metrics. Chart (E4) is a basic chart comparing the Relative power over 5 min for different riders, with their weights displayed over time. The Velodrome has also an advanced interface to create new graphs.

4 Discussion and Conclusions

We described The Velodrome, a framework for pro cyclists' data storage that enables analytics through visualization of the cyclists' aggregated workouts and races' data. The framework was developed to store data retrieved from TrainingPeaks, as well as personal questionnaires, to have a central database of the team, which will allow the visual analytics offered by The Velodrome, as well as more advanced data science projects [10]. We are designing now a user study that will evaluate the use of the various features of The Velodrome, and how to operate it most intuitively and efficiently, which will be ready to present in the conference.

Acknowledgements. This project was funded by a donation from SYLVAN ADAMS FAMILY FOUNDATION ISRAEL.

References

1. Cejuela, R., Sellés-Pérez, S.: Road to Tokyo 2020 Olympic games: training characteristics of a world class male triathlete. Front. Physiol. **13**, 835705 (2022)
2. Gallo, G., et al.: Cross-sectional differences in race demands between junior, under 23, and professional road cyclists. Int. J. Sports Physiol. Perform. **17**(3), 450–457 (2022)
3. Hilmkil, A., Ivarsson, O., Johansson, M., Kuylenstierna, D., van Erp, T.: Towards machine learning on data from professional cyclists. arXiv preprint arXiv:1808.00198 (2018)
4. Kataoka, Y., Gray, P.: Real-time power performance prediction in tour de France. In: Brefeld, U., Davis, J., Van Haaren, J., Zimmermann, A. (eds.) MLSA 2018. LNCS (LNAI), vol. 11330, pp. 121–130. Springer, Cham (2019). https://doi.org/10.1007/978-3-030-17274-9_10
5. Kholkine, L., et al.: A learn-to-rank approach for predicting road cycling race outcomes. Front. Sports Act. Living **3** (2021)
6. Lucía, A., Hoyos, J., Santalla, A., Earnest, C., Chicharro, J.L.: Tour de France versus vuelta a Espana: which is harder? Med. Sci. Sports Exerc. **35**(5), 872–878 (2003)
7. Mignot, J.-F.: The history of professional road cycling. In: Van Reeth, D., Larson, D.J. (eds.) The Economics of Professional Road Cycling. SEMP, vol. 11, pp. 7–31. Springer, Cham (2016). https://doi.org/10.1007/978-3-319-22312-4_2
8. Ofoghi, B., Zeleznikow, J., MacMahon, C., Dwyer, D.: A machine learning approach to predicting winning patterns in track cycling omnium. In: Bramer, M. (ed.) IFIP AI 2010. IAICT, vol. 331, pp. 67–76. Springer, Heidelberg (2010). https://doi.org/10.1007/978-3-642-15286-3_7
9. Ofoghi, B., Zeleznikow, J., MacMahon, C., Dwyer, D.: Supporting athlete selection and strategic planning in track cycling omnium: a statistical and machine learning approach. Inf. Sci. **233**, 200–213 (2013)
10. Sagi, M., Saldanha, P., Shani, G., Moskovitch, R.: Pro-cycling team cyclist assignment for an upcoming race. PloS One **19**(3) (2024)
11. Spragg, J., Leo, P., Swart, J.: The relationship between training characteristics and durability in professional cyclists across a competitive season. Eur. J. Sport Sci. **23**(4), 489–498 (2023)
12. Vogt, S., et al.: Power output during stage racing in professional road cycling. Med. Sci. Sports Exerc. **38**(1), 147 (2006)
13. Vogt, S., et al.: Cycling power output produced during flat and mountain stages in the giro d'italia: a case study. J. Sports Sci. **25**(12), 1299–1305 (2007)
14. Zignoli, A., et al.: Estimating an individual's oxygen uptake during cycling exercise with a recurrent neural network trained from easy-to-obtain inputs: a pilot study. PLoS One **15**(3), e0229466 (2020)

Service and End of Rally Detection in Badminton Videos

Shin Yue See, Mohd Fikree Hassan, Ganesh Krishnasamy, Junn Yong Loo, and Raveendran Paramesran(✉)

Monash University Malaysia, Subang Jaya, Malaysia
raveendran.paramesran@monash.edu

Abstract. Video analysis of points won and lost in a badminton match has become a valuable tool for coaches and players to analyze their matches. The analysis requires someone to annotate manually the start and end of the rally for each point for the coaches and players to determine the badminton strokes employed during that rally. Hence, to eliminate manual annotation, we present a technique to detect the start of service and end of rally. It utilizes court details and poses to accurately identify the service action from the other badminton actions. The characteristics of service action are utilized to obtain the features and arranged in a 2D format for a convolutional neural network (CNN) to detect the service and non-service. Gradients are used to detect the flight of the shuttlecock till it eventually comes to rest which signifies the end of the rally. In computing the end of the rally, the algorithm considers the missing shuttlecock flight coordinates and when the shuttlecock is out of camera view. Two videos of 4 and 12 min comprising 12 and 23 consecutive points are used to determine the accuracy of the proposed algorithm. The experimental results show 88.6% accuracy for a total of 35 rally points.

Keywords: Badminton video analysis · Convolutional Neural Network (CNN) · Detection of service and end of rally

1 Introduction

Due to the increasing popularity of video analysis in recent years, researchers and technologists have turned their attention to sports fields, in particular, badminton. To better understand and analyze the players, coaches often observe the matches to identify their strengths and weaknesses. The utilization of video analysis has become essential for coaches and players alike in assessing their performances. Advancements in sequential pattern mining have demonstrated substantial promise in uncovering valuable subsequences, whether through statistical methods [12] or machine learning algorithms [13, 14].

The concept of an automated analysis tool has consistently sparked interest within the badminton community [9]. The current landscape of video badminton analysis encompasses various techniques, including service detection [1], trajectory reconstruction [2], action recognition [15, 16], and court detection [2].

J. S. Dong et al. (Eds.): ISACE 2024, LNCS 14794, pp. 173–180, 2024.
https://doi.org/10.1007/978-3-031-69073-0_15

Cooke [4] delved deeply into the study of shuttlecock aerodynamics, conducting various experiments to ascertain the shuttlecock's drag coefficient. In the ensuing years, several researchers [6–8] also contributed their research on shuttlecock aerodynamics, which was later consolidated by Cohen et al. [5]. The trajectory of the shuttlecock holds significant importance in video segmentation. The analysis of the trajectory offers valuable insights into various aspects, including tactics formulation and post-game analysis [21]. The trajectory of the shuttlecock after executing a serve has become an important assessment as it indicates a likelihood of winning the point [20].

Skeleton data obtained from pose estimation has been widely employed for human action recognition due to its capability to capture the details of human motion [17]. The feature set extracted from the skeleton models was used to accurately distinguish between various actions in the classification of badminton actions from videos [13, 14]. In [18], researchers presented a novel action recognition model leveraging skeleton-based data, incorporating temporal transformer layers.

Service detection in badminton videos was initially introduced by Fumito et al. [19], who developed an automatic method for detecting service scenes in badminton game analysis. However, their dataset was restricted to a single ceiling camera perspective. Researchers [22] introduced a slice-based optical flow weightage (SOFW) algorithm to identify service activity. We introduced a service detection algorithm [1] in our previous work. This algorithm is utilized to filter all segments related to service in input videos by employing skeleton keypoints detection to compute nineteen by twelve features. These features are then fed into a convolutional neural network for classification.

The researchers are motivated to develop techniques that can be utilized by the coaches and players to formulate successful strategies by pinpointing crucial attributes while enabling the exploration of athletes' characteristics through the visualization of their sequence of playing actions [10, 11]. Therefore, coaches often obtain official recordings of the match process after the game and study both their own players and their opponents. However, the official recordings often record the entire match, including some unnecessary segments such as picking up shuttlecocks, challenges, halftime breaks, court cleaning, etc., which means coaches need to spend more time skipping these unimportant segments when watching the videos. Additionally, coaches encounter significant challenges with unprocessed live videos provided by officials. They must invest considerable time and effort in processing, trimming, and categorizing these videos for each scoring segment. Therefore, this paper proposes a method to detect the start of service and end of rally played at each point that will eliminate the manual time needed to annotate them in a badminton video.

2 Proposed Method

In every badminton match, there is a beginning and an end of points. Badminton follows a 21-point scoring system, when there is no deuce, which implies that within a badminton match, there will be at least 21 service and end-of-rally instances. It begins by identifying the start of service pose, followed by the detection of the end of the rally. The player's position and pose are utilized in the start of service, while the flight of shuttle cock is utilized in the end of rally. Figure 1 shows the flowchart of the proposed method.

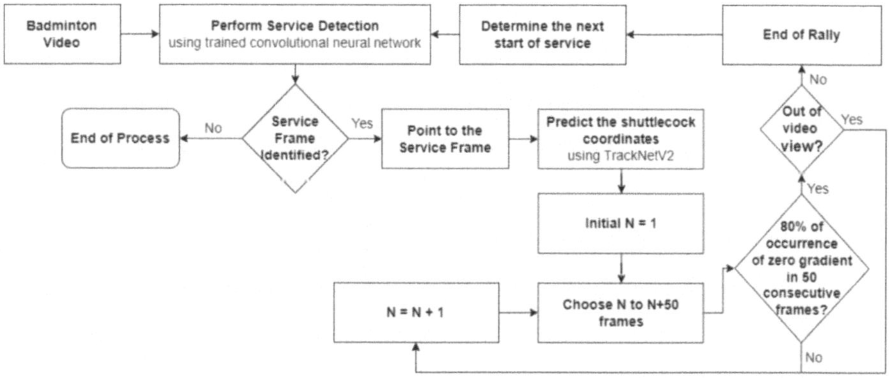

Fig. 1. Flowchart of our proposed method

2.1 Detection of Start of Service

Based on the rules of badminton and the habits of different players, we can observe the different serving poses by players, as illustrated in Fig. 2a. When serving, a player needs to stand on one side of the court and deliver the service either as a low service or high service. In contrast to the serving pose, other types of actions vary greatly from the service pose. These poses include jumping smash, net play, playing from the backcourt, defensive strokes, etc. as shown in Fig. 2b. Therefore, by observing the differences between the two, we can utilize the players' poses to classify service and non-service. This methodology has been explored in our previous study [1], wherein we take in twelve frames at a time, with nineteen features obtained from each frame. The data was acquired using skeleton keypoint detected by OpenPose. Subsequently, it was utilized as input for training a convolutional neural network, as depicted in Fig. 3.

Fig. 2. (a.) Serving Poses of different players, (b.) Different Hitting Poses

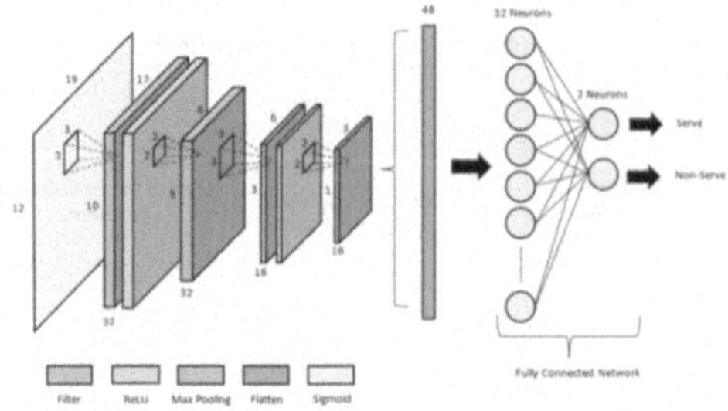

Fig. 3. Convolutional Neural Network for service detection.

2.2 Detection of End of Rally

In the paper [5], Cohen et al. studied the trajectories of shuttlecocks and different hitting poses in badminton. Figure 4 shows seven different shuttlecock trajectories. We can observe that the shuttlecock generally follows different forms of parabolic shape, as shown by all the numbers except six. For number six, it descends sharply in a straight line for a period until it lands on the court. This implies that before the service starts and after the shuttlecock lands on the court, its gradient is slowly approaching zero.

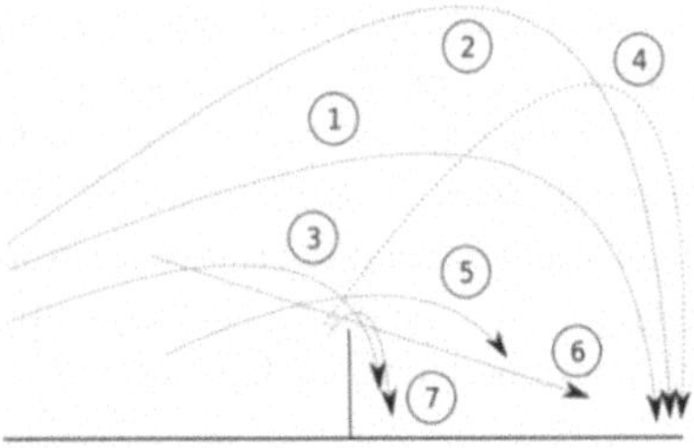

Fig. 4. Different shuttlecock trajectories in a game [5].

Once the service is executed, the rally begins with the opposing player responding to the service. The number of strokes executed by both players continues until the shuttlecock cannot be retrieved by one of the players, which marks the end of rally for that point played. The proposed method examines the gradient of the distance traveled by the shuttlecock in two consecutive frames. If the gradient is non-zero, it means that the shuttlecock is still in motion until a point where 80% of the gradient is zero over fifty consecutive frames.

To obtain the flight trajectory of the shuttlecock, we utilized a shuttlecock tracking algorithm called TrackNetV2 [3], developed by Nien-En Su et al. TrackNetV2 employs an encoder-decoder architecture to detect the shuttlecock and then processes the frames through a CNN model to predict its x and y-coordinates. Consequently, we can analyze and determine whether the shuttlecock has landed on the court based on its coordinates. One noteworthy point is that in a 2D badminton match video, the y-coordinates not only represent the position but also encompass the height of the shuttlecock. To have a better visualization, we plotted a graph with the y-coordinates on the y-axis and the frame number of shuttlecock flights on the x-axis, as shown in Fig. 5.

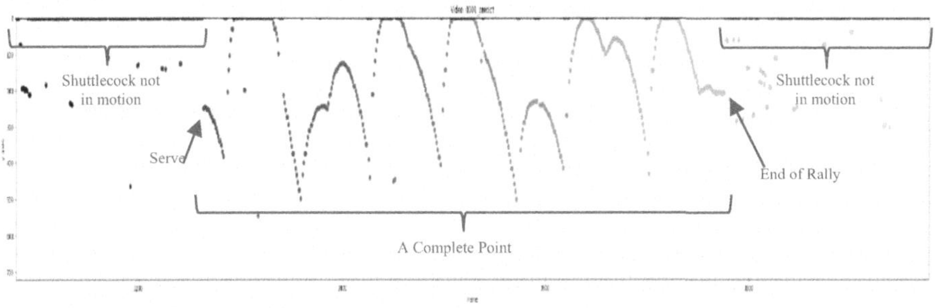

Fig. 5. Shuttlecock coordinates plotted in y-coordinates vs frames.

3 Implementation of Proposed Method and Experimental Results

A 4-min and 12-min video which consists of 12 points and 23 points respectively, operating at 30 frames per second has been used as our testing data. We notice that, due to the high-speed shuttlecock, the videos may not accurately capture the position of the shuttlecock in every frame, resulting in some false detections, which we refer to as noise. Therefore, to eliminate most of the noise, we only retain shuttlecock coordinates with a probability value exceeding 0.7. Subsequently, we aim to identify fifty consecutive frames where the shuttlecock remains stationary for that period. We use the gradient as shown in (1) to determine the occurrences of zero values.

$$\sum_{i=0}^{Consecutive\ Frames=50} \frac{(y_i - y_{i+1})}{(f_i - f_{i+1})} \quad (1)$$

where y is the y coordinates and f is the frame number. Once the service is detected, we begin by extracting fifty gradient values spanning from 0 to 50 using (1). If 80% of the gradients exhibit zero values, we then confirm it as the end of the rally. If not, we proceed to the next 50 frames from 1 to 51. This process of extraction, calculation, and classification is iterated until we identify the end of the rally. Once the end of the rally is determined, we then partition the video segment from the detection of service to the end of rally. Figure 6 illustrates a shuttlecock trajectory graph of a complete point. As shown in the graph, the service is detected using the trained convolutional neural network. The trajectory in some instances is broken due to the shuttlecock coordinates not being captured by the TrackNet. The detection of the end of rally begins from frames 3224 to 3840. The red box indicates the detection of the end of rally, which was correctly detected.

Due to the poses in detecting the service, there may be some false detections of service within the sequence of non-service before service. Table 1 provides an illustration of

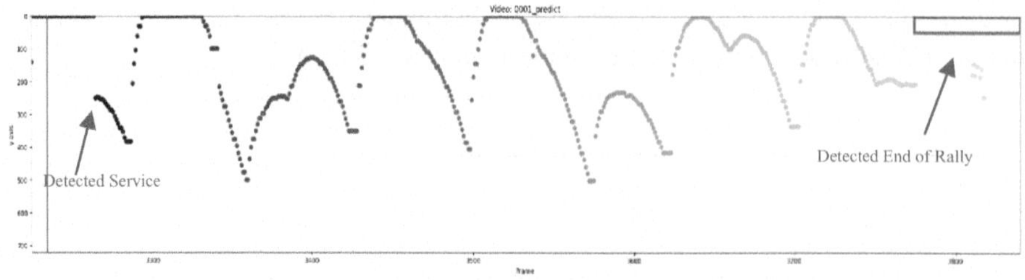

Fig. 6. Detection of service and end of rally in the Shuttlecock trajectory.

an incorrect service pose detected. We can observe that the 15th column represents the actual service, while the previous are all non-service. However, due to false detection, the 6th column was mistakenly predicted as a service, resulting in the service frame being detected prematurely. This happens when the players change the shuttlecock as well as when the court gets cleaned to remove excessive sweat.

Table 1. Chance of false detection of service.

Number of 12 frames	1	2		6		14	15
Detected	Non-Service	Non-Service	…	Service	…	Non-Service	Service
Actual	Non-Service	Non-Service	…	Non-Service	…	Non-Service	Service

Table 2 shows the result of the detection of service and end of rally for two videos of 4-min and 12-min length. In the case of incorrectly detected by the end of rally, it is because it didn't meet the criteria set to detect it.

Table 2. Results of detection of service and end of rally.

Length of Video	Detection of	Correctly detected	Incorrectly detected	Total
4-min	Service	12	0	12
	End of Rally	11	1	12
12-min	Service	23	0	23
	End of Rally	20	3	23

4 Conclusion

The players and coaches have to manually segment the start and end of rally to review the players' match performances from badminton videos. This paper shows a method of detecting service and end of rally. The service is detected using CNN uses the court details and openpose to obtain nineteen features that were unique to classify service and non-service. The result shows on rare occasions non-service have been detected as service. This happens when the court gets cleaned to remove excessive sweat and the pose and position of the cleaners are similar to the players in serving position. Besides that, it also happens when the players are preparing themselves to serve and then not serving. To correctly detect the end of rally, we analyzed fifty consecutive frames where 80% of the gradient must be zero value. The experimental results using 4 and 12 min of video with a total of 35 end of rally points achieved 88.6% accuracy. The errors are due to the immediate retrieval of the shuttlecock after hitting the ground which was detected as shuttlecock in motion. For our future work, we are going to address some of the shortcomings, and also determine the number of strokes executed after the service and before the end of rally.

References

1. See, S.Y., Paramesran, R., Krishnasamy, G.: Ready-to-serve detection in badminton videos. In: 2024 International Conference on Electronics, Information, and Communication (ICEIC), pp. 1–5. IEEE (2024)
2. Liu, P., Wang, J.H.: MonoTrack: shuttle trajectory reconstruction from monocular badminton video. In: Proceedings of the IEEE/CVF Conference on Computer Vision and Pattern Recognition, pp. 3513–3522 (2022)
3. Sun, N.E., Lin, Y.C., Chuang, S.P., Hsu, T.H., Yu, D.R., Chung, H.Y., İk, T.U.: Tracknetv2: Efficient shuttlecock tracking network. In: 2020 International Conference on Pervasive Artificial Intelligence (ICPAI), pp. 86–91. IEEE (2020)
4. Cooke, A.J.: Shuttlecock aerodynamics. Sports Eng. **2**(2), 85–96 (1999)
5. Cohen, C., Texier, B.D., Quéré, D., Clanet, C.: The physics of badminton. New J. Phys. **17**(6), 063001 (2015)
6. Verma, A., Desai, A., Mittal, S.: Aerodynamics of badminton shuttlecocks. J. Fluids Struct. **41**, 89–98 (2013)
7. Alam, F., Chowdhury, H., Theppadungporn, C., Subic, A.: Measurements of aerodynamic properties of badminton shuttlecocks. Procedia Eng. **2**(2), 2487–2492 (2010)
8. Chan, C.M., Rossmann, J.S.: Badminton shuttlecock aerodynamics: synthesizing experiment and theory. Sports Eng. **15**, 61–71 (2012)
9. Wu, J., Guo, Z., Wang, Z., Xu, Q., Wu, Y.: Visual analytics of multivariate event sequence data in racquet sports. In: 2020 IEEE Conference on Visual Analytics Science and Technology (VAST), pp. 36–47 (2020)
10. Perin, C., Vuillemot, R., Fekete, J.D.: SoccerStories: a kick-off for visual soccer analysis. IEEE Trans. Vis. Comput. Graph. **19**(12), 2506–2515 (2013)
11. Xie, X., et al.: PassVizor: toward better understanding of the dynamics of soccer passes. IEEE Trans. Vis. Comput. Graph. **27**(2), 1322–1331 (2020)
12. Malik, S., Du, F., Monroe, M., Onukwugha, E., Plaisant, C., Shneiderman, B.: Cohort comparison of event sequences with balanced integration of visual analytics and statistics. In: Proceedings of International Conference on Intelligent User Interfaces, pp. 38–49 (2015)

13. Guo, R., et al.: Comparative visual analytics for assessing medical records with sequence embedding. Vis. Inform. **4**(2), 72–85 (2020)
14. Liu, H., Jin, S., Yan, Y., Tao, Y., Lin, H.: Visual analytics of taxi trajectory data via topical sub-trajectories. Vis. Inform. **3**(3), 140–149 (2019)
15. Martin, P.E., Benois-Pineau, J., Péteri, R., Morlier, J.: Sport action recognition with siamese spatio-temporal cnns: application to table tennis. In: 2018 International Conference on Content-Based Multimedia Indexing (CBMI), pp. 1–6. IEEE (2018)
16. Soomro, K., Zamir, A.R.: Action recognition in realistic sports videos. In: Computer Vision in Sports, pp. 181–208. Springer International Publishing, Cham (2015). https://doi.org/10.1007/978-3-319-09396-3_9
17. Tejero-de-Pablos, A., Nakashima, Y., Sato, T., Yokoya, N., Linna, M., Rahtu, E.: Summarization of user-generated sports video by using deep action recognition features. IEEE Trans. Multimed. **20**(8), 2000–2011 (2018)
18. Ibh, M., Grasshof, S., Witzner, D., Madeleine, P.: TemPose: a new skeleton-based transformer model designed for fine-grained motion recognition in badminton. In: Proceedings of the IEEE/CVF Conference on Computer Vision and Pattern Recognition, pp. 5198–5207 (2023)
19. Yoshikawa, F., Kobayashi, T., Watanabe, K., Otsu, N.: Automated service scene detection for badminton game analysis using CHLAC and MRA. Int. J. Comput. Inf. Eng. **4**(2), 331–334 (2010)
20. Vial, S., Cochrane, J., Blazevich, A.J., Croft, J.L.: Using the trajectory of the shuttlecock as a measure of performance accuracy in the badminton short serve. Int. J. Sports Sci. Coach. **14**(1), 91–96 (2019)
21. Chu, X., et al.: TIVEE: visual exploration and explanation of badminton tactics in immersive visualizations. IEEE Trans. Vis. Comput. Graph. **28**(1), 118–128 (2021)
22. Teng, S.L., Paramesran, R.: Detection of service activity in a badminton game. In: TENCON 2011–2011 IEEE Region 10 Conference, pp. 312–315. IEEE (2011)

Sweaty, but Not Hot: Gamers' "Cool" Hands

Jan Rejthar(✉)

Prague University of Economics and Business, 120 00 Prague, Czech Republic
rejj02@vse.cz

Abstract. This research paper investigates the existence of the Hot Hand phenomenon by leveraging a unique dataset, which implicitly addresses many of the issues prevalent in the existing literature. In this study, two definitions of the Hot Hand phenomenon, streakiness, and clustering of successes, are presented and tested jointly and at the individual level. Streakiness is measured using conditional probabilities, and clustering of successes is measured using entropy of inter-event times. Monte Carlo permutation tests are subsequently used to determine the presence of the hot hand. Since individual-level testing leads to simultaneous inference, the family-wise error rate is controlled, and a false discovery rate is set. Neither simultaneous nor joint testing found any evidence for the existence of the Hot Hand at 5%. The results suggest that while the players of KovaaK's aim trainer may be sweaty, their hands do not get hot.

Keywords: the hot hand · momentum · streakiness · aim trainers · permutation tests

1 Introduction

The term hot hand has long been a staple part of the sports lexicon [1]. The belief in the hot hand is widespread among coaches, players, and [1–3], which is also evinced by bettors and betting houses [4, 5]. It is a manifestation of psychological momentum, which has been considered an important contributor to success [6]. It has garnered considerable attention in the literature ever since [1, 7, 8] called its existence into question and classified it as a cognitive fallacy.

While research initially focused on basketball, the presence of the hot hand has been tested in many sporting and even non-sporting domains, such as finance or marketing [9], yielding mixed results [2, 10]. However, recent studies tend to lean towards supporting the legitimacy of the hot hand [2, 11, 12].

For illustrative purposes, I will use an example of a shooter who can either hit or miss their shots further in the section. It will make the explanations clearer, more concise, and fit nicely with the data I used for the analysis.

Many articles, starting with [1], have looked at the hot hand as an excess of streakiness [12–14]. Some authors have gone as far as using streakiness and hot hand interchangeably [10]. In this approach, a shooter is believed to have hot hands if they hit their last shot or are on a streak of hits. Consequently, the probability of the shooter hitting the following

J. S. Dong et al. (Eds.): ISACE 2024, LNCS 14794, pp. 181–189, 2024.
https://doi.org/10.1007/978-3-031-69073-0_16

shot is perceived to heighten merely due to them being on a streak or hitting the last shot [1, 4, 10, 15–17]. As a result, this approach looks at heat as a binary variable, where the shooter is either hot or cold.

A different way to look at the hot hand is to view it as a clustering of hits rather than streakiness [18, 19]. In this approach, a shooter would be considered to have hot hands either when they have been recently hitting more than usual or if the shooter's hit rate gets temporarily elevated. While [18] used regression to test how the probability of hitting depends on the recent level of success, [19] looked at the size of gaps between hits, which can also detect non-streaky spikes in hit rates. This approach looks at heat as a continuous variable, which can be higher or lower depending on the recent performance, which does not have to be streaky. The approach of [19] looks at the hot hand as a departure from stationarity rather than independence. While the streakiness approach would categorize players as streaky or not, the clustering of hits approach might be closer to what is colloquially described as having momentum or being in the zone, which some authors use as the definition of the hot hand [9].

Figure 1 illustrates the major difference between how the two approaches conceptualize heat. In this example, under the streakiness approach, the shooter could be viewed as hot after a streak of 3 hits, as suggested by [20]. Therefore, they should get fully hot after the fourth and eighth shots. However, the shooter missed the fifth and ninth shots, which would fully cool the shooter's hands down.

On the other hand, under the clustering of hits approach, the shooter could be seen as slowly heating up as they hit more shots. The missed fifth and ninth shots cool the shooter only partially, temporarily, and proportionally to how well the shooter hit before. Following the last hit, the shooter cools down entirely after a few consecutive misses.

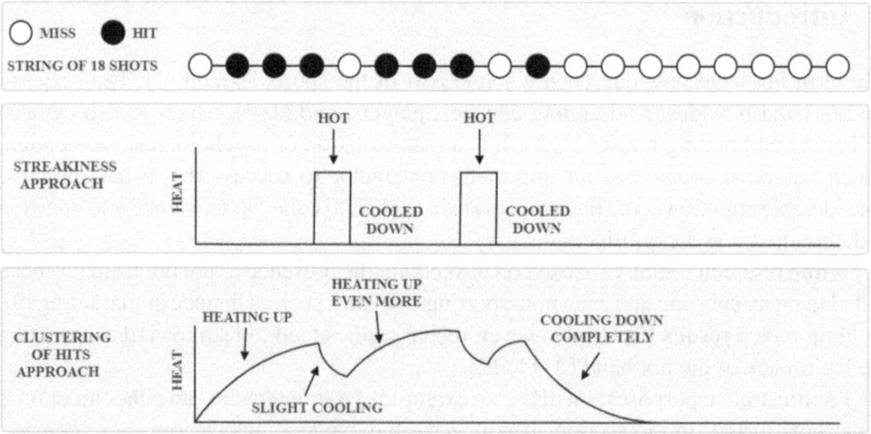

Fig. 1. Comparison of streakiness and clustering of hits approaches on a sequence of 18 shots.

Non-experimental data used in the literature have suffered from 4 major shortcomings. Firstly, many studies have relied on data from sports like basketball, football, or volleyball, where player interaction introduces complex endogeneity issues [10, 12, 21].

Secondly, the heterogeneity of shots has often been ignored [12]. Thirdly, due to the nature of the sports analyzed, many articles used short sequences of shots, which is a limiting factor for many of the employed methods [10, 19, 22–26]. Lastly, time dimensions and potential momentum disruptors such as timeouts or breaks have often been ignored, potentially overlooking a cooling effect [12].

Efforts have been made to address these challenges. For instance, [25] used bowling, and [16] used darts to avoid player interactions. [27] aggregated data from multiple tournament days to increase the number of shots in sequences. [12, 15, 18] took the heterogeneity of shots into account. Additionally, [11, 15, 18] incorporated the time dimension into their analysis. However, [18] did not consider the time between shots nor the effect of momentum disruptors. While [11] took the time between shots into account by using a state-space model, they did not consider the effect of momentum disruptors either.

The articles of [15, 28] are the closest to this article. [15] tackled all the aforementioned issues by using a complex regression analysis to test the dependence of consecutive shots. Unlike them, I tackled the issues implicitly by using data from a KovaaK's aim trainer (KovaaK's), as suggested by [28]. Data obtained from an aim trainer possess the capacity to address all the previous limitations, and therefore, aim trainers can offer data of almost experimental quality while circumventing the drawbacks associated with conducting an experiment. As a result, I could build upon the work of [13, 14, 19] and test both the definitions of the hot hand.

2 Aim Trainers

An aim trainer is a specialized software designed primarily to enhance players' aiming abilities in shooter games and improve their mouse control. It is also used as a tool where players benchmark their aim abilities and compete. I chose KovaaK's among the available aim trainers because it locally stores data from each run of a scenario. Moreover, all runs are assigned scores, and players' records are displayed on leaderboards, introducing a competitive element. KovaaK offers a selection of tens of thousands of practice scenarios, each differing in various aspects. Unfortunately, only a few of those scenarios are viable for the analysis. In the chosen scenarios, players aim at balls of the same size and aim to hit as many of them as possible. After each shot, hit or within a predefined time frame, the target vanishes and is replaced by a new one. Each scenario lasts 60 uninterrupted seconds, producing an average of over 56 hits per run.

Since the players play only against a timer, no player interactions occur. The targets are of the same shape and size and are at the same or almost the same distance from the center, resulting in entirely or almost entirely homogenous shots. Moreover, shots are evenly distributed over time, avoiding potential momentum disruptors.

3 Data and Methodology

I collected the data from players via the official KovaaK's Discord platform. Players were instructed to upload their data voluntarily and anonymously using a Dropbox link. 53,345 runs were gathered, but only 107 (about 0.2%) runs were used in the analysis.

First, only some scenarios are usable, and second, only runs with accuracy levels ranging from 20% to 80% were used. I asked players to provide all their data rather than just the usable data for three reasons. First, this approach simplifies the data collection process for the players, increasing the likelihood of players' cooperation. Second, it helps reduce or eliminate sampling bias by reducing self-selection. Third, it makes it extremely difficult for players to manipulate or edit the relevant data. Table 1 presents a summary of relevant statistics.

Table 1. Summary statistics of the runs

	Number of runs	Mean	Median	St. Dev.	Min	Max
Number of shots	107.000	56.439	67.000	21.957	31.000	94.000
Accuracy	107.000	0.502	0.516	0.141	0.219	0.778

I examined the presence of the hot hand, considering both the streakiness and clustering of hits. Additionally, I assessed the hot hand jointly and individually, as suggested by [14], since the hot hand can be detected by one but not the other.

3.1 Streakiness

Starting with streakiness, I followed [13, 14]. Let us define a vector X_i of a run i of length n representing the sequence of shots, where $X_i = 1$ indicates a hit and $X_i = 0$ indicates a miss. This article tests the null hypothesis H_0: X_i is i.i.d., assuming that the shots came from a Bernoulli process. According to [13], for a player to exhibit the hot hand either the probability they hit after a streak of 3 consecutive hits starting at shot j is higher than the marginal probability of them hitting in run i, that is

$$t_P(X_i) = P_i\left\{X_{i,j+3} = 1 | \prod_{l=0}^{2} X_{i,j+l} = 1\right\} - P_i\{X_{i,j+3} = 1\} > 0, \tag{1}$$

or the probability they hit after a streak of 3 consecutive hits starting at shot j is higher than the probability they hit after a streak of 3 consecutive misses starting at shot m, that is

$$t_D(X_i) = P_i\left\{X_{i,j+3} = 1 | \prod_{l=0}^{2} X_{i,j+l} = 1\right\} - P_i\left\{X_{i,j+3} = 1 | \prod_{l=0}^{2} (1 - X_{i,m+l}) = 1\right\} > 0. \tag{2}$$

This calculates whether players are *extraordinarily streaky*. To get the estimates $\widehat{t_P(P_i)}$ and $\widehat{t_D(P_i)}$, I utilized empirical probabilities, i.e., proportions.

3.2 Clustering of Hits

In the case of clustering of hits, I followed [19] and employed entropy as the metric to quantify the degree of clustering. Let us define a vector d_j of length m to represent the inter-event times of vector X_i. For uniformly discrete shot distributions, the time between shots can be calculated as the difference between their respective indices in vector X_i. Consequently, d_1 corresponds to the distance between the starting point and the first hit; d_m denotes the distance between the last hit and the endpoint, and d_j, where $j \in \{2, 3,\ldots, m - 1\}$, represents the distance between two closest hits. Figure 2 illustrates how the vector d_j can be constructed based on a vector X_i of length 10, where black dots represent hits and white dots represent misses.

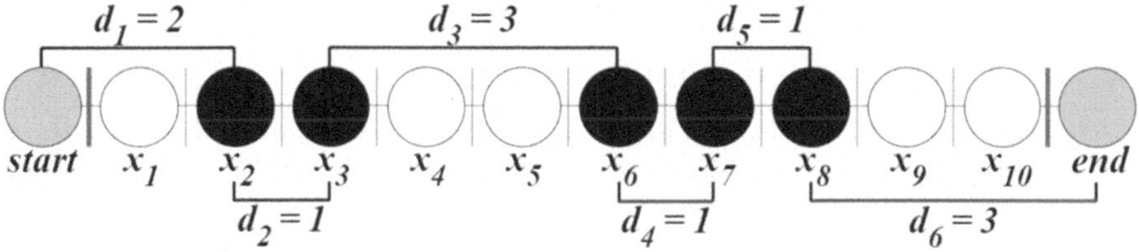

Fig. 2. Example of inter-event times calculation for a vector of length 10.

For instance, $d_1 = 2$ because the second shot corresponds to the first hit, $d_2 = 1$ because the second hit immediately follows the first one, and $d_3 = 3$ because the second and third hits occur on the third and sixth shots respectively, resulting in $d_3 = 6 - 3 = 3$, and so on resulting in $d_j = [2, 1, 3, 1, 1, 3]$. The entropy of vector d_j can then be calculated using the following formula (as devised by [29]:

$$H(X_i) = -\sum_{j=1}^{m} (d_j) \log(d_j). \tag{3}$$

Subsequently, a player can be seen as having the hot hand if the entropy is *extraordinarily* low, as that indicates overly uneven gaps between shots, showing the existence of regions of high hit clustering.

3.3 Permutation Tests and Inference

In addition to the individual estimates $\widehat{t_P(X_i)}$, $\widehat{t_D(X_i)}$, or $H(X_i)$, I also tested the hot hand jointly. To do so, I used the average of the estimates for the individual runs, denoted as $\overline{t_P(X_i)}$, $\overline{t_D(X_i)}$ and $\bar{H}(X_i)$. To test whether players are too streaky or whether their performance is too clustered, I used Monte Carlo permutation tests with 1,000,000 repetitions as a compromise between granularity and computation intensity for all six estimates. Permutation tests implicitly avoid any small sample bias [14]. I used the standard 5% level of statistical significance for inference.

Testing at the individual level involves repeatedly testing the same null hypothesis, which leads to simultaneous inference and a higher likelihood of false positives. To tackle the issue, I controlled for the Family-wise Error Rate (FWER) at 5% by employing the step-down Holm-Šidák procedure, which maintains the FWER at 5% precisely when all null hypotheses are true [14].

However, controlling for FWER is a highly conservative approach that greatly reduces statistical power [30]. Therefore, I also set a False Discovery Rate (FDR) of 5%, a less conservative approach that increases statistical power by allowing an expected rate of false discoveries to be 5%. To achieve this, I used the Benjamini-Hochberg procedure.

4 Results

Let us start with an example of a run that potentially exhibits the hot hand when measured by entropy. Equation 4 represents vector X_i with shots from run number 94.

$$\begin{aligned} X_{94} =&[0, 1, 0, 0, 0, 0, 0, 0, 0, 1, 0, 0, 0, 0, 0, 1, 1, 0, 0, 0, 1, 0, 1, 1, 1, 0, 1, 1, 1, 0, \\ &1, 1, 0, 0, 0, 0, 0, 0, 0, 0, 0, 0, 0, 0, 0, 0, 0, 0, 0, 0, 1, 0, 0, 1, 0, 1, 1, 1, 0, 0, \\ &0, 1, 0, 0, 1] \end{aligned} \tag{4}$$

Figure 3 shows a histogram of entropies calculated for 1,000,000 permutations of X_{94} and the entropy of the run itself. The entropy of the run is -107.9, which falls below 99.4% of the permuted entropies. Therefore, the run is statistically significant at 5% and 1%.

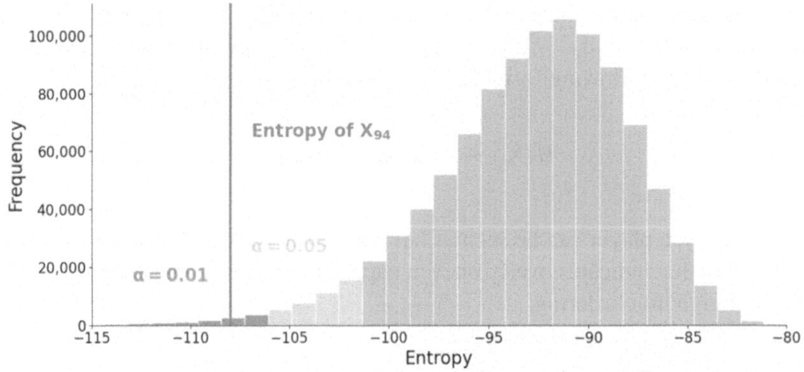

Fig. 3. Distribution of the entropy estimator for a sequence number 3.

Table 2 presents the outcomes of the significance tests conducted on the 107 individual hypotheses. Out of the 107 individual hypotheses examined, 5, 6, and 7 were statistically significant at 5% for $\widehat{t_P(X_i)}$, $\widehat{t_D(X_i)}$, and $H(X_i)$ respectively. However, none retained their significance once simultaneous inference was controlled, suggesting that no player was extraordinarily streaky, nor did success cluster more than if it was generated by a Bernoulli process. Similarly, the p-values for the joint tests were above 5%, suggesting that shooting is neither streaky nor clustering for KovaaK's players in general.

Table 2. Results of the permutation tests.

Estimator	Number of runs	Number of hypotheses rejected at 0.05			Joint testing p-value
		Individual testing	Simultaneous testing		
			FWER	FDR	
$\widehat{t_P(X_i)}, \overline{t_P(X_i)}$	107	5	0	0	0.41
$\widehat{t_D(X_i)}, \overline{t_D(X_i)}$	107	6	0	0	0.59
$H(X_i), \bar{H}(X_i)$	107	7	0	0	1.00*

*: The non-rounded p-value was 0.999993.

5 Discussion

The results of the article provide insights on two levels. First, the results suggest that while players of KovaaK's aim trainer may be sweaty, their hands do not get hot. Thus, this article reaches the opposite conclusion to e.g. [11–13]. While any extrapolation is challenging, the results corroborate that the hot hand might not exist as a universal principle of success breeding success. It is in line with, for instance, [6, 9], as it suggests that if the hot hand exists, certain conditions must be present for it to occur.

However, it may be that players not facing each other decreases the chance of momentum emerging [6]. Also, playing KovaaK's might not provoke large enough hormonal and psychological responses that would increase the level of testosterone, arousal, or anxiety, which have been linked to increased performance and to the feeling of being in the zone [31]. It might also be argued that there is too little time for people to perceive that they got the hot hand in KovaaK's. However, this is unlikely to be the case since it is a response in type 1 processing mode, for which seconds are a long enough time frame [32].

The article is not free of methodological caveats. As discussed by [14], the tests of the streaky joint hypotheses still likely lack power, especially if the elevation of probability given a streak of 3 hits is very small. As [21] noted, however, if the probability of elevation given a streak was so small, the hot hand may still have been considered a fallacy since people could not detect it regardless.

Continuing with the second insight, the article demonstrates the significant potential of video games as a platform for studying human behavior. Even in situations where the advantages of video games may not be immediately apparent, such as the absence of human error in refereeing, they offer unique advantages over other data sources. The utilization of KovaaK's data in this article showcases the quality and value that even non-experimental data from video games can provide, surpassing the capabilities of non-experimental data used in the hot hand literature. This highlights the promising opportunities that video games offer for studying various aspects of human behavior.

In their aptly named article, [2] argue that sports offer a unique opportunity to test economic theories, or as they put it, an excellent laboratory to study human behavior in real competitive environments. While the classification of video games as sports remains a topic of ongoing debate [33], I refrain from taking a stance and instead adhere to the conventional differentiation, treating video games and sports as separate domains of human endeavor. Therefore, I propose that video games may present even greater opportunities than sports, as this article indicates, which somewhat complements the idea of [34] that the role of video games in the 21st century embodies the role sports had in the 20th century. I also agree with the closing remarks of [35, 36] asserting that data from video games and esports remain underutilized, even though they are often readily available and easily obtainable.

References

1. Gilovich, T., Vallone, R., Tversky, A.: The hot hand in basketball: on the misperception of random sequences. Cogn. Psychol. **17**(3), 295–314 (1985)
2. Bar-Eli, M., Krumer, A., Morgulev, E.: Ask not what economics can do for sports - ask what sports can do for economics. J. Behav. Exp. Econ. **89**, 101597 (2020)
3. Steeger, G.M., Dulin, J.L., Gonzalez, G.O.: Winning and losing streaks in the National Hockey League: Are teams experiencing momentum or are games a sequence of random events? J. Quant. Anal. Sports **17**(3), 155–170 (2021)
4. Arkes, J.: Revisiting the hot hand theory with free throw data in a multivariate framework. J. Quant. Anal. Sports **6**(1), 1 (2010)
5. Paul, R.J., Weinbach, A.P., Humphreys, B.: Bettor belief in the "hot hand": evidence from detailed betting data on the NFL. J. Sports Econ. **15**(6), 636–649 (2014)
6. Iso-Ahola, S.E., Dotson, C.O.: Psychological momentum: why success breeds success. Rev. Gen. Psychol. **18**(1), 19–33 (2014)
7. Tversky, A., Gilovich, T.: The cold facts about the "hot hand" in basketball. Chance **2**(1), 16–21 (1989)
8. Tversky, A., Gilovich, T.: The "hot hand": statistical reality or cognitive illusion? Chance **2**(4), 31–34 (1989)
9. Morgulev, E.: Success breeds success: physiological, psychological, and economic perspectives of momentum (hot hand). Asian J. Sport Exerc. Psychol. **3**(1), 3–7 (2023)
10. Bar-Eli, M., Avugos, S., Raab, M.: Twenty years of "hot hand" research: review and critique. Psychol. Sport Exerc. **7**(6), 525–553 (2006)
11. Mews, S., Ötting, M.: Continuous-time state-space modelling of the hot hand in basketball. AStA Adv. Stat. Anal. **107**(1–2), 313–326 (2023)
12. Pelechrinis, K., Winston, W.: The hot hand in the wild. PLoS ONE **17**(1), e0261890 (2022)
13. Miller, J.B., Sanjurjo, A.: Surprised by the hot hand fallacy? A truth in the law of small numbers. Econometrica **86**(6), 2019–2047 (2018)
14. Ritzwoller, D.M., Romano, J.P.: Uncertainty in the hot hand fallacy: detecting streaky alternatives to random bernoulli sequences. Rev. Econ. Stud. **89**(2), 976–1007 (2022)
15. Lantis, R., Nesson, E.: Hot shots: an analysis of the 'hot hand' in NBA field goal and free throw shooting. J. Sports Econ. **22**(6), 639–677 (2021)
16. Ötting, M., Langrock, R., Deutscher, C., Leos-Barajas, V.: The hot hand in professional darts. J. R. Stat. Soc. Ser. A Stat. Soc. **183**(2), 565–580 (2020)
17. Rabin, M., Vayanos, D.: The Gambler's and hot-hand fallacies: theory and applications. Rev. Econ. Stud. **77**(2), 730–778 (2010)
18. Bocskocsky, A., Ezekowitz, J., Stein, C.: The Hot Hand: A new approach to an old "fallacy". In: 8th Annual MIT Sloan Sports Analytics Conference, pp. 1–10 (2014)
19. Zhang, Y., Bradlow, E.T., Small, D.S.: New measures of clumpiness for incidence data. J. Appl. Stat. **40**(11), 2533–2548 (2013)

20. Carlson, K.A., Shu, S.B.: The rule of three: how the third event signals the emergence of a streak. Organ. Behav. Hum. Decis. Process. **104**(1), 113–121 (2007)
21. Avugos, S., Bar-Eli, M., Ritov, I., Sher, E.: The elusive reality of efficacy–performance cycles in basketball shooting: an analysis of players' performance under invariant conditions. Int. J. Sport Exerc. Psychol. **11**(2), 184–202 (2013)
22. Wardrop, R. L.: Statistical tests for the hot-hand in basketball in a controlled setting. Unpublished Manuscript **1**, 1–20 (1999)
23. Miyoshi, H.: Is the "hot-hands" phenomenon a misperception of random events? Jpn. Psychol. Res. **42**(2), 128–133 (2000)
24. Frame, D., Hughson, E., Leach, J.: Runs, regimes, and rationality: the hot hand strikes back. Unpublished Manuscript, University of Colorado, Leeds School of Business (2003)
25. Dorsey-Palmateer, R., Smith, G.: Bowlers' hot hands. Am. Stat. **58**(1), 38–45 (2004)
26. Arkes, J.: Misses in "hot hand" research. J. Sports Econ. **14**(4), 401–410 (2013)
27. Cotton, C.S., McIntyre, F., Nordstrom, A., Price, J.: Correcting for bias in hot hand analysis: an application to youth golf. J. Econ. Psychol. **75**, 102091 (2019)
28. Rejthar, J.: Unlocking the untapped potential of video game data: a case study of aim trainers. In: Vale Costa, L., et al. (eds.) Videogame Sciences and Arts. VJ 2023. Communications in Computer and Information Science, vol. 1984, pp. 315–321. Springer, Cham (2024). https://doi.org/10.1007/978-3-031-51452-4_22
29. Shannon, C.E.: A mathematical theory of communication. Bell Syst. Tech. J. **27**(3), 379–423 (1948)
30. Benjamini, Y., Hochberg, Y.: Controlling the false discovery rate: a practical and powerful approach to multiple testing. J. Roy. Stat. Soc. Ser. B (Methodol.) **57**(1), 289–300 (1995)
31. Morgulev, E., Avugos, S.: Beyond heuristics, biases and misperceptions: the biological foundations of momentum (hot hand). Int. Rev. Sport Exerc. Psychol. **16**(1), 155–175 (2020)
32. Frankish, K.: Dual-process and dual-system theories of reasoning: dual-process and dual-system theories of reasoning. Philos Compass **5**(10), 914–926 (2010)
33. Tjønndal, A.: 'what's next? Calling beer-drinking a sport?!': virtual resistance to considering eSport as sport. Sport Bus. Manag. Int. J. **11**(1), 72–88 (2020)
34. Hinnant, N.: Practicing Work, Perfecting Play: League of Legends and the Sentimental Education of E-Sports (2013)
35. Shengjie, Y.: For Love of the Game: A Study of Tournament Theory and Intrinsic Motivation in Dota 2 [PhD Thesis]. Duke University Durham (2019)
36. Xenopoulos, P., Doraiswamy, H., Silva, C.: Valuing player actions in counter-strike: global offensive. In: 2020 IEEE International Conference on Big Data (Big Data), pp. 1283–1292 (2020)

The Two-Point Dilemma: Does Going for Two Win Close Football Games?

Darren Rowe, Willie K. Harrison(✉), and John L. Salmon

Brigham Young University, Provo, UT 84602, USA
{willie.harrison,johnsalmon}@byu.edu

Abstract. Upon scoring a touchdown late in a college football game to cut the lead to one, teams are faced with the decision of either tying the game with a point after touchdown (PAT) or attempting a two-point conversion. A PAT typically leads to overtime, whereas a two-point attempt usually results in a win if successful and a loss if failed. In some cases (such as when a team is on the road or the underdog), it is often believed that a two-point attempt is advantageous. This comes from the belief that winning in overtime on the road or as an underdog is unlikely, and the chance of winning is greater by converting a single play for two points. In this paper, we show that there are no situations with statistically significant support for a two-point attempt with a data sample that includes all NCAA games from 2002–2019. Furthermore, there are several circumstances where the data indicates that a team should kick a PAT, including situations where popular sports culture supports going for two.

Keywords: End of Game Strategy · NCAA College Football · Two Point Dilemma

1 Introduction

1.1 Historical Background

In college football, two-point attempts are not common. This is because PATs are successful nearly every time they are attempted, so two-point attempts would need to be successful around 50% of the time or greater in order to be statistically advantageous in terms of expected points added [4]. There has never been a year with a two-point conversion rate greater than 50%, and the most recent season where two-point conversions yielded a higher points-per-attempt than PATs was 1974 [10].

Due to the general advantage of kicking a PAT, two-point attempts are most common when a team clearly needs to score two points. For example, when a team is down by eight and scores a late touchdown to cut the lead to two, kicking a PAT would nearly guarantee a one-point loss. There are other situations where a two-point attempt is clearly better, and many of these are presented as conventional wisdom amongst coaches in [9].

J. S. Dong et al. (Eds.): ISACE 2024, LNCS 14794, pp. 190–201, 2024.
https://doi.org/10.1007/978-3-031-69073-0_17

1.2 Scope of Research

This paper will not further analyze or discuss the legitimacy of two-point attempts in situations where they are clearly the smarter option. The focus of this research is to address a more controversial situation, where a team is down by seven late in the game, and scores a touchdown to cut the lead to one. A two-point conversion usually results in a win if successful and a loss if unsuccessful, whereas a PAT typically results in overtime.

Consequently, the decision between a two-point attempt versus a PAT largely depends on whether a team thinks their chances of winning are higher by succeeding on a single play (a two-point attempt), or by succeeding in an entire overtime period (by tying with a PAT). A couple of basic statistics give the general edge to kicking a PAT: two-point conversions are successful 40.5% of the time, whereas overtime is generally close to a 50–50 tossup since the teams have played equally, although home teams maintain a slight advantage. Even road teams win 44% of the time, giving a statistical advantage over a two-point attempt [10].

Our research will compare the win percentage of teams that kick a PAT to the win percentage of teams that go for two when down by one late in a game. This analysis will be performed for various factors and combinations of factors. Our data set is comprised of all NCAA football games from 2002–2019 where the situation of interest occurs in the final six minutes of regulation or overtime.

2 Motivation

2.1 BYU vs Boise State, 2012

In 2012, BYU played Boise State on the road in a close game. The defenses were dominating the game so strongly that, with only a few minutes remaining, Boise State led 7–0, with the only score being a defensive touchdown. Boise State had even missed a 33-yard field goal, and had another possession begin at BYU's one yard line after recovering a fumble, but couldn't gain a yard and was stopped with a turnover on downs. BYU's offense was even worse, turning the ball over five times and accumulating only 200 yards.

BYU's struggling offense managed to score a touchdown with 3:37 remaining in the game, making the score 7–6. Rather than tie the game with a PAT and play for overtime, BYU decided to go for two. BYU's decision seemed like a fairly normal decision to most people, given that they were playing on the road and an underdog to a ranked team.

However, given the defensive nature of the game, the seemingly inevitable result would be a failed two-point attempt, which would then lead to a victory for Boise State. Furthermore, the proceedings of the game would seem to suggest an advantage in overtime for BYU, since the Boise State kicker was proving unreliable.

BYU would go on to fail the two-point attempt and wouldn't get the ball back again, losing 7–6. Did BYU, in fact, make the wrong tactical decision, or was the choice to go for two justified in some way?

2.2 Recent Trends

It is becoming increasingly common for coaches to decide to go for two in the situation of interest. Much of this increased aggression may stem from data analytics surrounding fourth-down conversions. Research over the last few decades has encouraged teams to go for it on fourth down in more circumstances than many would consider wise [7], and teams have slowly started to adopt some of the more aggressive strategies suggested by the research [5]. In our data set, within the 2002–2019 seasons, we observed 2.25 two-point attempts per season on average when teams trail by one in the last six minutes of regulation. Since 2010, there have been 6.6 such attempts per season on average.

However, although analytics results on fourth-down conversions suggest that teams should be more aggressive, the existing literature on two-point conversions indicates a more conservative approach is best in most situations. In [8], optimal strategies for the point-after-touchdown decision were deduced based on a dynamic programming approach for a fictitious "average" NFL team in 1998. Kicking the PAT was deemed optimal regardless of how much time was left in the game. Nearly a decade later, a more exhaustive study was carried out in [9] using 10 seasons of NCAA data and 13 seasons of NFL data. The authors accounted for differences in team abilities and suggested that going for two may be optimal for some teams, but not for most teams. This study included all point-after-touchdown decisions when a team trailed by one within the last two minutes of regulation, but did not further analyze the decision based on time remaining in the game. Finally, a more modern study given in [6] breaks down the decision based on team ability, time remaining, and the margin in score after the touchdown. This work did not address college football, however, and no works were found to address some of the conventional thinking regarding how the decision should be made for road teams, underdogs, etc.

The increasing frequency of two-point attempts, combined with our suspicion that going for two is a poor decision, and the unavailability of a recent detailed analysis on the subject for NCAA football, was the primary motivation for this research.

2.3 Conventional Thinking

Popular sports culture has produced a set of rules for going for the win or the tie depending on a number of factors. As a result, our intuition before performing this research was that there are three main situations where it is generally believed that two-point attempts when down by one are advantageous. Our data collection has confirmed that they are by far the most common circumstances for an attempt. Below is a brief explanation of these situations:

As the Road Team. Coaches often think it is better to go for two because overtime will be difficult to win on the road. Concerns such as the crowd getting louder, fatigue due to travel, weather, altitude, etc. make some coaches prefer having the game come down to one play rather than drawing it out longer.

As an Underdog. Just like road teams, underdogs often feel a lack of confidence in their chance of winning overtime. The belief is that an underdog will generally be more likely to succeed against a better team on one play than on many successive plays in overtime.

In High Scoring Games. This situation is different from the previous two. While road teams and underdogs usually go for two out of a belief that they will lose in overtime, teams in high-scoring games often go for two because they are very confident they will convert the attempt, since the offenses have been dominating the game.

2.4 Factors Included in Research

Because of the frequency of two-point attempts in these three situations, we included these three factors, as well as time remaining, which we felt was possibly significant and worth investigating. The following list shows the four factors in this study. Note that the name of a factor describes the situation for the team that is down by one with the decision to kick or go for two (for example, Road means the road team was down by one and making the decision).

1. Home vs Road vs Neutral
2. Underdog vs Favorite vs Heavy Underdog (We based these off the Vegas betting spread, [3], with Heavy Underdog defined as a 10+ point underdog)
3. High Scoring vs Low Scoring (We base this on the final score of the winning team. High Scoring is defined as 29+ points, with low scoring being less than 29 points)
4. Overtime vs Late in Regulation (defined as 0–3 min left) vs 4–6 min left (at the time of the attempt, rounded to the nearest minute)

While there may be other possible factors to consider (momentum, key injuries, etc.), these are very rare and are difficult to find and quantify, so they are not evaluated in this research.

3 Methods

3.1 Scope of Games Studied

Before performing a detailed analysis, it was vital to eliminate irrelevant games to maximize efficiency. Because overtime was instituted in college football in 1996 [11], the decision between a PAT or two-point attempt was fundamentally different prior to that season. In that time period, a PAT usually ended in a tie rather than overtime. Additionally, two-point and PAT conversion rates were significantly different in comparison to recent years [10]. Consequently, all games prior to 1996 were not considered in this research.

Although the initial intent was to start by analyzing the 2019 season and work backward to 1996, it was discovered over the course of collecting data that two-point attempts when down by one were very uncommon before 2010. In addition, accessibility of the necessary data became very limited prior to the 2002 season. These discoveries led to a decision to investigate all college football games ranging from the 2002–2019 seasons.

The final method of narrowing down the data set was to remove all games with a margin of victory greater than eight points. While it is technically possible for a one-point game with not much time left to end up with a margin of victory greater than eight, this is extremely rare, and was determined to be a negligibly small set of games.

Excluding these sets of irrelevant games increased the project's efficiency and detail while maintaining the vast majority of relevant games.

3.2 Collecting Data from the Set of Relevant Games

Games from the 2002–2019 seasons with a margin of victory of eight or less were downloaded into Excel from Sports Reference's [1] database. Among these games, data was collected from ESPN's database [2], which includes detailed game recaps. All games with a touchdown that cut the lead to one point in the final six minutes were preserved for further analysis (there were 577 of these games). Note that the six-minute mark is a somewhat conservative cutoff, but was intended to ensure that all games relevant to our research would be included (later on we learned that almost all two-point attempts came with less than three minutes remaining).

Once the data set was reduced to only games containing the situation of interest, we performed a detailed analysis. For each game, the team that was making the decision to kick or go for two was recorded, along with data corresponding to the four factors of interest (home or road, underdog or favorite, high or low scoring, time remaining).

Once all the necessary data was collected, the spreadsheet was exported into R to perform a statistical analysis. For each factor, a two-sample z-test for proportions was conducted, comparing the win percentage of teams who went for two to the win percentage of teams who kicked a PAT. All possible combinations of two factors were also analyzed in the same way (combinations of three factors did not provide a sufficiently large data set). Each procedure was a one-sided test in favor of the decision with the higher win percentage. All tests were conducted at a level of significance $\alpha = 0.10$.

4 Results

4.1 Significant Factors

There were no tests that provided statistically significant support for two-point attempts, but several tests supported the decision to kick a PAT. When the team that is down by one is at home, in a low-scoring game, or late in regulation, their chances of winning are significantly higher by kicking a PAT. In addition, when the *low scoring game* and *late in regulation* factors are combined with the *road* or *underdog* factors, there is significant support for a PAT. All data and p-values for statistically significant factors are given in Table 1, where low p-values indicate statistically significant support for kicking a PAT, rather than going for two.

The *low scoring game* and *late in regulation* factors are clearly the most significant. They are very significant individually and when combined with several other factors. The lowest p-value of all comes when the two factors are combined with each other.

For some factors, a lack of sufficient two-point attempts resulted in a near impossibility of finding statistically significant results. The factors with the fewest two-point attempts were *favored teams* (12), *neutral site games* (9), and *4–6 min remaining* (4). There were also some combinations of two factors with a small amount of two-point attempts. It will be valuable to revisit this research several years from now to potentially find additional significant factors, assuming teams go for two in the scenario under study.

Table 1. Factors with significant support for kicking a PAT (there were no factors with significant support for a two-point attempt).

Category	PAT Games	PAT Win %	Two-Point Games	Two-Point Win %	P-Value
All Games	493	41.6%	84	32.1%	0.043
Home	232	44.8%	27	25.9%	0.047
Low Scoring	143	39.2%	23	13.0%	0.014
Late in Regulation	281	42.7%	56	26.8%	0.019
Road, Low Scoring	73	32.9%	13	7.7%	0.065
Underdog, Low Scoring	76	35.5%	21	14.3%	0.055
Road, Late in Regulation	138	38.4%	33	21.2%	0.049
Underdog, Late in Regulation	146	37.0%	46	21.7%	0.041
Heavy Underdog, Late in Regulation	45	33.3%	21	14.3%	0.093
Low Scoring, Late in Regulation	83	41.0%	16	6.3%	0.009

4.2 Binned Time Analysis

While no factors provided significant support for two-point attempts, it is at least a more debatable topic in overtime. When the *road*, *underdog*, or *high scoring game* factors are combined with *overtime*, the win percentage for two-point attempts is higher, although the lowest p-value was only 0.265 (see contingency plot in Fig. 1). While this is nowhere near enough evidence to suggest going for two based on the p-value and the sample size, it is worth noting that when these same factors occur late in regulation as opposed to overtime, there is incredibly strong support for kicking a PAT.

The data suggests that when all other factors are held constant, kicking a PAT is clearly better when the game is still in regulation, but it is more debatable in overtime. This is also evident in the left contingency plot of Fig. 1.

In regulation, a team went for two 51 times in our data set, but only succeeded 13 times, for a win percentage of just 26% (contrasted against the 42% of teams that won by going for the PAT).

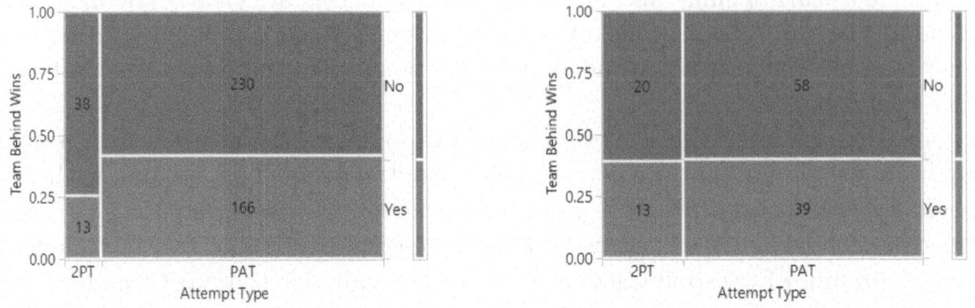

(a) Regulation Time (b) Overtime

Fig. 1. Contingency Plot of Attempt Type as a predictor of the Team Behind Wins, during regulation time (left) and in overtime (right). Red cells represent ultimate wins (i.e. Yes) for the teams that were down when facing the dilemma. Cells are sized by the relative number of occurrences in the data. (Color figure online)

As mentioned, the overtime winning probabilities for a PAT are about the same as for regulation instances, but the odds appear to be different for two-point conversions (compare left and right plots of Fig. 1). Although the data set records the same absolute number of ultimate wins from two-point attempts (i.e. 13) in both regulation time and in overtime, the number of losses is much lower, by percentage, in overtime. However, the lower sample size is still insufficient to achieve statistical significance.

A possible explanation for this discrepancy between regulation and overtime is that a two-point conversion in overtime immediately ends the game, but a two-point conversion in regulation leaves time for the opponent to go back and score. In many cases, a game-tying PAT late in regulation leads to the opponent reacting more conservatively, sometimes even willingly running out the clock to play for overtime.

Since time remains for the opponent to respond after a successful go-ahead two-point conversion in regulation, a dive into *when* this is most detrimental to that opponent is an essential question of the data. When subdividing the regulation time contingency plot (Fig. 1a) into bins of the nearest whole minute of time remaining, the contingency plots become the left and right subfigures of Fig. 2.

The 13 2PT conversions that led to victory in Fig. 1a, are divided into the Nearest Minute bins of 0, 1, and 4, with labeled values of 5, 7, and 1 (not labeled) respectively. The same process is performed for Fig. 2b.

Although it first appears that a team has a higher chance of winning (above 50%) if kicking the PAT with one minute left as opposed to zero minutes left,

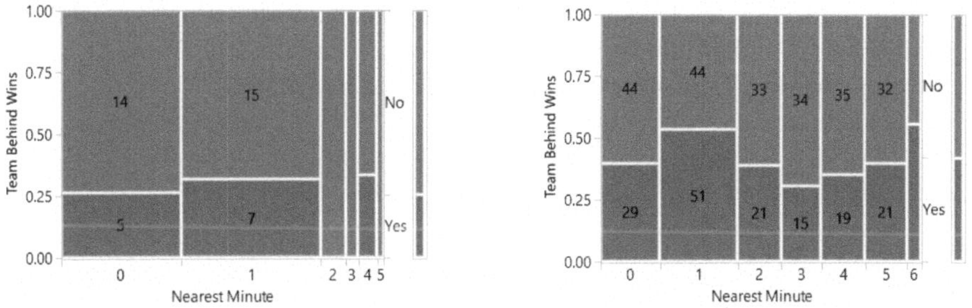

(a) Two Point Conversion (2PT) - Regulation Time

(b) Point After Touchdown (PAT) - Regulation Time

Fig. 2. Contingency Plot of time remaining (by minute) as a predictor of the Probability of the Team Behind Wins

the reader is reminded that the binning of this data results in times of 0 to 29 s remaining, being binned in the "0" min category, and times of 30 to 89 s remaining, being binned in the "1" min category. Thus, if the data was uniformly distributed, more data would be expected in the "1" min bin. Regardless, this figure is telling because it suggests a different strategy in gambling (or not) could be beneficial at different times remaining in the game.

4.3 Continuous Time Analysis

This motivates a full model analysis when these decisions were made, with time remaining as one of the key factors in predicting the outcome at the most precise resolution available (i.e. seconds). Figure 3 presents a model fitted with a neural net (with 9 hidden nodes) to predict the probability that the Team Behind will win at any time up to 350 s remaining, when selecting either strategy (i.e. PAT or 2PT). The shapes of the surfaces generally follow the binned contingency plots of Fig. 2 but with a continuous time axis.

Figure 3 suggests that at no time during regulation, based on the available data, is it better to go for two points. This is illustrated by the height of the two surfaces representing the two strategies. The surface corresponding to the PAT is always above (i.e. higher win probability) the surface corresponding to two-point conversions.

The probability of winning remains around 23% for two-point attempts until two and half minutes remaining at which time it rolls down to a lower percentage partly due to less data or two-point attempts when three minutes or more remain. This is contrasted to the almost 50% probability (48.3%) for the PAT at the end of the game (i.e. zero seconds remaining). A tie at time zero, would result in overtime where an expected 50% of winning is predicted (assuming all other things are equal). The PAT strategy surface drops too (above 100 s remaining) which is expected because the opponent has more time to respond with their own field goal or touchdown while the game is tied. This curves back up to near

50% around six minutes because multiple possessions on both teams are likely. Regardless of the individual trends, the most compelling insight from this model is that the PAT is *always* a better option over the alternative.

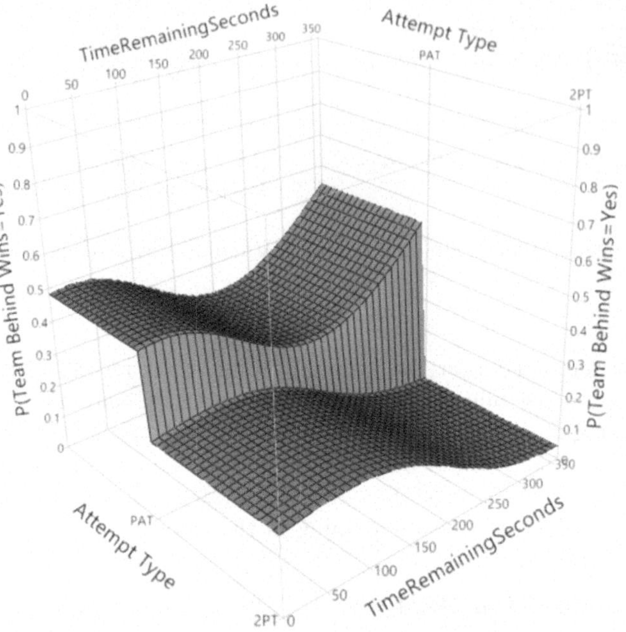

Fig. 3. Surface plot of the continuous-time predictive model of the probability of the team behind winning for PAT and 2PT.

4.4 Team-by-Team Analysis

The preceding figures aggregate the entire NCAA into the same model. Thus, one can easily advance the argument that a set of specific teams may perform above average in two-point conversions, and hence may still find that going for two improves their winning probability. Although no team has enough data points to definitely prove or disprove that position, the data is still informative when broken down by college team.

In Fig. 4, the teams are subdivided with the area of each rectangle representing one college and sized by the number of times that college faced the two-point dilemma. The colleges are ordered with the teams facing the dilemma the most in the upper left and decreasing down to the bottom right. The individual rectangles are further divided by attempt type with the number of PAT or 2PT attempts labeled in blue and red respectively. Therefore, Michigan (top left) faced the dilemma 11 times, and only once opted for the two-point conversion.

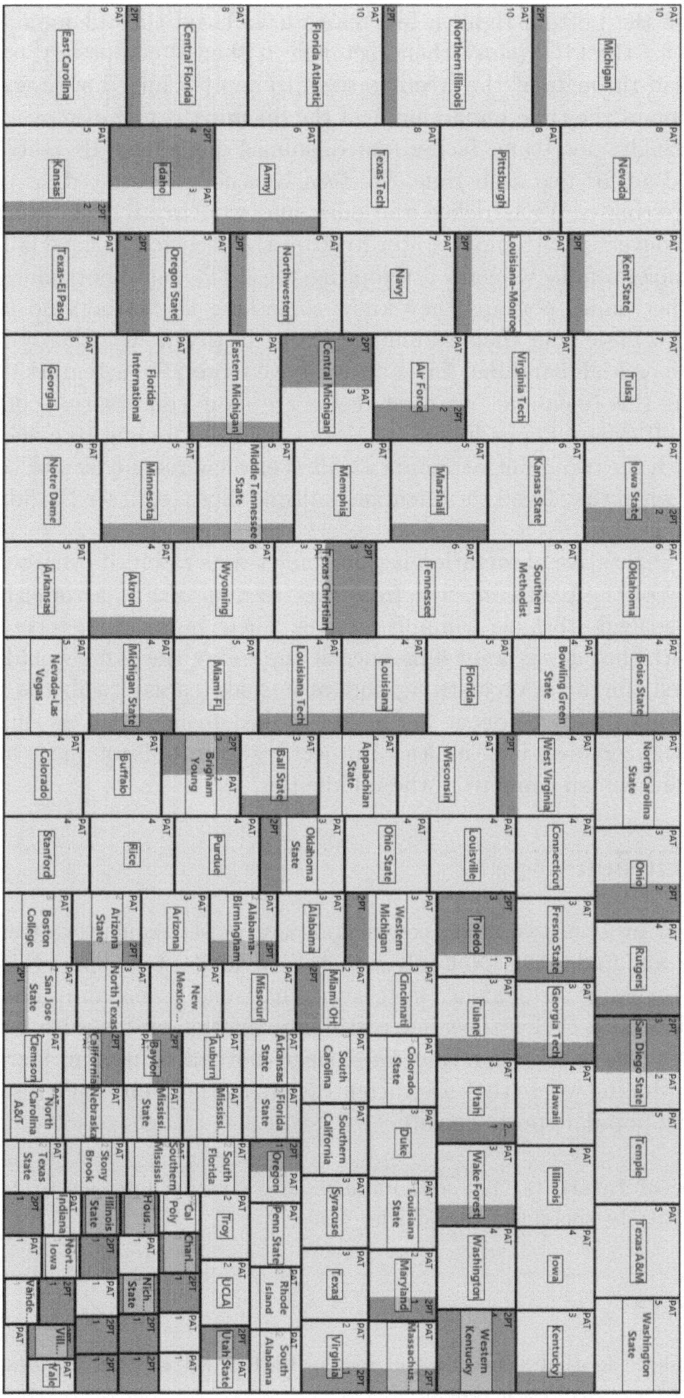

Fig. 4. Treemap of 2PT (red) and PAT (blue) attempts by college, ordered by the number of total attempts decreasing from top left to bottom right. (Color figure online)

Likewise, in the bottom right, a few teams have faced this dilemma only once but opted for the 2PT (since their rectangle is shaded completely red). Other teams spread throughout the treemap seem to apply a mixed strategy, perhaps as a function of the time remaining or if the dilemma is found in overtime.

Interestingly, one team, facing four dilemmas in the last 18 years, chose to gamble and go for two each time: Western Kentucky (see far right on Fig. 4). More interestingly, WKU defied the odds and won in each of the first three two-point conversion attempts. Later in 2016, they seemed to have fallen victim to the gambler's fallacy, again attempting the 2PT, but unfortunately losing. On the other hand, perhaps they know something that others do not or are sufficiently confident in their running plays to justify their strategy [9]. Other teams, such as Idaho and San Diego State, have more 2PT attempts than PATs when facing this dilemma, but most teams are more conservative compared to WKU overall. Many teams follow the data-supported finding to avoid the 2PT entirely with no two-point attempts at all (i.e. their rectangles are completely blue) even when they faced the dilemma multiple times (e.g., see Florida Atlantic and East Carolina).

A final qualitative observation is that some teams rarely, if ever, occur in the data. Many of the teams *missing* from the treemap of Fig. 4 are either highly ranked or struggle to have winning seasons. Their games are expectedly more lopsided such that a one-point difference at the end of the game would be a rare event indeed (for both very strong and very weak teams). Still, the two-point conversion dilemma will occur for highly ranked teams, such as during more equalized bowl games, but, at least subjectively the bulk of the teams found often in the treemap come from the middle tier.

5 Conclusion

When down by one, two-point conversions are most frequently attempted by road teams and underdogs. Not only is there no evidence to support this decision, but there is significant evidence suggesting that road teams and underdogs are better off kicking a PAT if the game is still in regulation or if it is low-scoring. By implementing these strategic changes, college football teams can increase their chances of winning where they are currently putting themselves at a disadvantage by following popular sports culture.

Disclosure of Interests. The authors have no competing interests to declare that are relevant to the content of this article.

References

1. 2019 college football schedule and results (2019). https://www.sports-reference.com/cfb/years/2019-schedule.html
2. FBS (i-a) Conference Schedule - 2019 (2019). https://www.espn.com/college-football/schedule/week/1/year/2019

3. NCAA Football Handicapping Odds and Database (2019). https://www.oddsshark.com/ncaaf/database
4. Carroll, B., Palmer, P., Thorn, J.: The Hidden Game of Football. Grand Central Pub (1988)
5. Clark, K.: Go for it: the story behind the NFL's fourth-down conversion. The Ringer (2019). https://www.theringer.com/nfl/2019/11/13/20962514
6. Morris, B.: When to go for 2, for real. FiveThirtyEight (2017). https://fivethirtyeight.com/features/when-to-go-for-2-for-real/
7. NYT 4th Down Bot: 4th down: when to go for it and why. The New York Times (2014). https://www.nytimes.com/2014/09/05/upshot/4th-down-when-to-go-for-it-and-why.html
8. Sackrowitz, H.: Refining the point(s)-after-touchdown decision. Chance **13**(3), 29–34 (2000)
9. Wenz, M., Skugrud, J.: Tackling the chart: two-point conversions and team differences in football. Chance **24**(1), 29–35 (2011)
10. Wilco, D.: The art of the 2 point conversion: when and why to go for it (2017). https://www.ncaa.com/news/football/article/2017-10-11/art-2-point-conversion-when-and-why-go-it
11. Wilco, D.: The longest overtime games in FBS college football history (2019). https://www.ncaa.com/news/football/article/2018-09-21/longest-overtime-games-fbs-college-football-history

How to Analyze Coaching: This is the WAE

Darren Rowe, John L. Salmon, and Willie K. Harrison(✉)

Brigham Young University, Provo, UT 84602, USA
{johnsalmon,willie.harrison}@byu.edu

Abstract. This paper presents a new statistic, wins above expected (WAE), for analyzing coaching in professional sports. The WAE is the first statistic of its kind, as far as we are aware. Calculating the WAE requires estimating a team's expected success under average coaching ability, and then calculating the difference between the team's actual success. The method is presented in general and then applied to the National Basketball Association (NBA) as a use case. Among other uses, the WAE can inform equitable hiring decisions and award choices for superior coaching performances, independent of player talent on a team.

Keywords: Coaching statistics · Regression · Expected value

1 Introduction

Player performance statistics have now been well-established in nearly all major sports. Advanced performance statistics help teams evaluate players and their potential contributions. This paper is perhaps the first, however, to present a serious study of coaching performance analytics. Decisions to either retain or fire coaches are often made based on win percentage and/or a team's postseason performance. Unfortunately, until now there has not been a reliable mechanism for separating coaching ability from player ability, and good coaching is therefore not always recognized or rewarded. Teams may fire an excellent coach due to a general lack of player talent, and below-average coaches may be rewarded based on an abundance of good players on a team's roster rather than actual coaching expertise. We offer the first analytical approach to rating coaches and show a use case of the method for the National Basketball Association (NBA). With time, this technique may help to establish equitable hiring decisions and influence Coach of the Year Awards across many sports.

A quick look into existing coaching statistics for the NBA (see, for example, Basketball Reference [2]) shows only a list of simple win-loss statistics in regular season and postseason play. There are no advanced statistics with which to further understand these win-loss numbers. For example, suppose a team wins 35 games in an 82-game season. If the team is comprised of mainly rookies and journeyman players, then this might be quite an accomplishment. If, however, the team is built around a number of household names, this result would likely be

J. S. Dong et al. (Eds.): ISACE 2024, LNCS 14794, pp. 202–215, 2024.
https://doi.org/10.1007/978-3-031-69073-0_18

disappointing. The context of the win-loss metrics is perhaps as important as the numbers themselves. This general dearth of quality coaching metrics exists across all major sports today. Unfortunately, a literature search on the subject returns mainly two types of articles; both of which do not solve the problem. The first type can be well summarized by [7,9,11]. Articles of this nature rely on polling a panel of experts (or even fans in some cases). The experts vote (and often write a short synopsis to justify their opinions) on who they think is the best coach. The votes are then tallied and presented as the major results of the article, often producing a list of, e.g., "top-10 coaches for the upcoming season." The problems with this technique of analyzing coaches are numerous. One problem is that the readership of these articles is often comprised of sports fans, and fans like to read about people that they already recognize. This may lead to biases in how experts place their votes. Another problem is that the experts may hold internal biases themselves, again yielding jaded results. It is very common for the panel of experts to disagree, and also common for either a lack of (or perhaps only a shallow) reference to any sort of data or legitimate analysis in articles of this nature. Finally, it may take years of above-average coaching on below-average teams for a coach to get recognized for his/her coaching acumen, particularly when the team does not advance to the postseason. The second type of article in the literature is comprised of papers like [3,6,8,10]. These works attempt to study the effects of coaching techniques on player development, diversity in sport, etc., and the studies are often focused on youth leagues.

In this paper, we detail a new approach for assessing and ranking coaches and their staffs in professional sports leagues. Our approach measures a coach's ability by comparing the actual results of the season to the expected results for his/her team given the level of talent available to the coach. Our methods are outlined in general, and outlined in detail for the use case of the NBA, in Sect. 2. The major results for NBA coaches are then shown in Sect. 3, and the paper is concluded in Sect. 4.

2 Methods

In this section, we outline the general method of producing our new coaching metric, which we call *wins above expected* (WAE). We also detail the necessary calculations and modeling techniques when the problem is applied to the NBA.

2.1 Overview of WAE

Initial Remarks. Before embarking on the methodology for producing the new WAE statistic, we must first specify what is actually measured by WAE. After all, many intangible elements may contribute to the success or failure of a team independent of player talent. For example, team camaraderie, player health, unexpected gains or losses due to the age and development of players on the team, coaching ability, expertise in coaching and training staff, etc., all play a part in determining the success level of a team. Our new metric measures all of the aspects of building a good team outside of expected player talent, but does not punish a coach for player injuries or age-related performance changes. Thus, the coach is made responsible for generating wins above or below an expected number of wins, independent of the availability of players due to health, potential boosts/declines in individual player performance due to age, or general player talent. This places responsibility for player development, team camaraderie, the impact of the coaching staff, etc. squarely on the head coach; thus, the WAE can also be thought of as a metric that measures "the system" that governs all of these aspects of the team. We believe it is fair to call WAE a coaching metric, however, since a good coach can be expected to establish positive impacts across all of these elements.

Furthermore, our approach attempts to decouple coaching ability from player talent, a task that may not be fully possible since baseline coaching and player data are never produced in isolation. To justify our model, however, we adopt the notion that all previous coaching experiences levied on a player have contributed to the player's current abilities. Changes in those abilities from year to year (outside expected changes due to age trends) are then ascribed to the new coach. We believe it is unfair to judge a coach based on the talent available on his/her roster, but rather the judgment should be levied by considering what the coach was able to achieve *given* the talent available on the roster. To use a gambling metaphor, the WAE measures a coach's ability to "get the most out of the hand he/she is dealt." The correlation between WAE and player talent, i.e., team ratings to be specific (see below), for the NBA dataset considered in this paper is −0.00028, which is essentially zero. The standard hypothesis test for a correlation coefficient of zero yields a p-value of 0.9919, and the confidence interval on the correlation coefficient at the 95%-level of confidence is [−0.0537, 0.0532], which indicates that the WAE has been adequately decoupled from player talent.

The WAE is calculated using only regular-season data. While good coaching in the postseason should be rewarded, not all teams can be evaluated in the postseason, making the inclusion of such data unfair when comparing all coaches across a league for a given season.

Finally, we also recognize that the WAE is a noisy measurement affected by several factors outside a coach's control, such as luck. Although these elements are present, we still believe the WAE has immense value, especially when calculated over a whole season, or even over a coach's entire career.

General Approach to the WAE. The general approach to generating WAE for any sport is based on the idea present in some player evaluation statistics. For example, consider the baseball statistics of Wins Above Replacement (WAR) and Wins Above Average (WAA). These statistics seek to measure a player's individual contribution above and beyond what could be reasonably expected from a readily available replacement player, or an average player across the league, respectively [4,5]. Our approach to analyzing coaching is similar to these statistics, in that we first calculate the expected wins under the assumption of average coaching for each team given the player roster. The difference between actual wins over the season and the expected wins then provides the WAE. That is,

$$\text{WAE} = w - \mathbb{E}[W; R_T], \tag{1}$$

where WAE is the new wins above expected statistic, W is a random variable that represents the number of wins accrued by a team during an entire season, w is the actual number of wins accrued by the team over the season, and $\mathbb{E}[W; R_T]$ is the expected value of W as a function of R_T, an overall team rating statistic, where the expectation operator is taken over the distribution of coaching performance in the league. A league model is required to calculate $\mathbb{E}[W; R_T]$ as a function of R_T, which amounts to a lookup table or function that simply maps the team rating to the needed expected value. Thus, we require an overall team rating R_T, and then a model to map R_T to $\mathbb{E}[W; R_T]$. We will show how this can be done for the NBA in the next subsection of the paper.

Notice that WAE does not compare coaches to a fictitious "readily available replacement," and thus, even a negative WAE may not justify replacing a coach since a better coach may not be available. If the statistic were reformulated to consider a coach's "wins above replacement," the threshold for maintaining a positive metric value would certainly be reduced.

2.2 Team Rating for the NBA

To calculate the team rating R_T for the NBA use case, we use the *player efficiency rating* (PER) and *minutes played* (MP) data available at basketball-reference.com. The PER is one of the best individual player statistics that estimates an NBA player's true worth to his team. The PER is given as a per-minute-played statistic, and was originally developed by ESPN.com's John Hollinger [1]. Other statistics could eventually replace PER in our team rating calculation if/when a better statistic becomes available. For our purposes, PER is more than sufficient for illustrating the process of producing the WAE and rating NBA coaches. Multiplying the PER by a player's MP yields a player's total accrued PER for the entire season.

We use the PER and MP data to derive an expected PER for each player on a team, as a function of the players' past performances. During the modeling aspects of this project, it was determined that using up to three of the most recent years of PER (if available) is sufficient to predict a player's PER for the next season; i.e., adding a fourth year to the model produces a negligible effect on the prediction. Since we cannot be sure how much playing time a player will receive in a season before the season is complete, we also require the actual MP for the season under question for each player. Thus, the team rating R_T (and the WAE itself) cannot be calculated for a season until the season is finished. If a player is injured and has a low MP as a result, the coach will not be penalized for the player's lack of availability to the team. If the last three years of PER data are not available, then alternate models are used that employ only the available data. Rookies are treated as a special case. To be clear, the team rating for year j is calculated as

$$R_T(j) = \sum_{i=1}^{n} \mathrm{MP}_i(j) \times \mathbb{E}[\mathrm{PER}_i(j); \mathrm{PER}_i(j-1), \mathrm{PER}_i(j-2), \mathrm{PER}_i(j-3), \mathrm{AA}_i], \tag{2}$$

where the sum is taken over all n players on a team's roster, and AA_i is an age adjustment for player i. The age adjustment allows the model to more accurately predict a player's future contribution to his team, in that younger players are expected to improve in general, and older players are expected to decline. Each subscript identifies a specific player, and the function notation with variable j represents time as measured in seasons. (Notice that the expectation is calculated itself as a function of the last three years of PER for each player and the age adjustment. We leave off the functional parameters in the expectation notation below for the sake of making further equations more concise.) The expectation is determined using a linear regression model on the available PER data for each player and each player's age. To be specific,

$$\mathbb{E}[\mathrm{PER}_i(j)] = 0.31 + 0.56\mathrm{PER}_i(j-1) + 0.28\mathrm{PER}_i(j-2) + 0.09\mathrm{PER}_i(j-3) + \mathrm{AA}_i, \tag{3}$$

when the three most recent years of data are available. When only two years of data are present (say due to a full-season injury, or when evaluating a player with only two previous years in the NBA), then

$$\mathbb{E}[\mathrm{PER}_i(j)] = 0.60 + 0.58\mathrm{PER}_i(j-1) + 0.33\mathrm{PER}_i(j-2) + \mathrm{AA}_i. \tag{4}$$

The one-year model is

$$\mathbb{E}[\mathrm{PER}_i(j)] = 2.04 + 0.82\mathrm{PER}_i(j-1) + \mathrm{AA}_i, \tag{5}$$

and the rookie model is

$$\mathbb{E}[\mathrm{PER}_i(j)] = 8.63 + 0.0026\mathrm{MP}_i(j). \tag{6}$$

Note that the last model indicates that rookies who play more minutes should be expected to be better than other rookies in general. All of these models were produced using all data from the 1969–1970 NBA season to the 2020–2021 NBA season. While each of these models could potentially be improved, we found that the impact on overall team rating R_T from further adjustments is negligible; thus, the above model is sufficient to produce reliable team ratings.

On the surface, it may seem better to simply use the current season's PER for each player in our team rating calculation rather than the expected PER, but this action would remove the effect that the coach would produce during the course of the season. Good coaches should make players more efficient than they have been in the past, and below-average coaches may have a reverse effect on player efficiency. Even when a player is coached by the same coach over the last several seasons, this fact should still remain true. A good coach could presumably find even better ways to improve a player's efficiency over the course of another season. For this reason, we will see that even long-term good coaches with very little player turnover can be expected to consistently produce positive WAE. Since all data from the league are included in the modeling, our technique produces a true average (i.e., expected) team rating that is calculated over the distribution of all coaching abilities (and across all playing abilities) in the league.

2.3 Calculating the WAE from the Team Rating for the NBA

In this section, we finally show how one calculates $\mathbb{E}[W; R_T]$ for our NBA dataset so that the WAE can be determined using (1). The modeling task is straightforward enough, in that we simply require a means to map from the team rating R_T to the expected number of wins $\mathbb{E}[W; R_T]$ assuming average NBA coaching ability. We considered a number of possible functions to do this mapping, and three options are shown in Fig. 1 overlaid on the dataset of actual wins versus team ratings. All shortened seasons have been rescaled to assume a standard 82-game season.

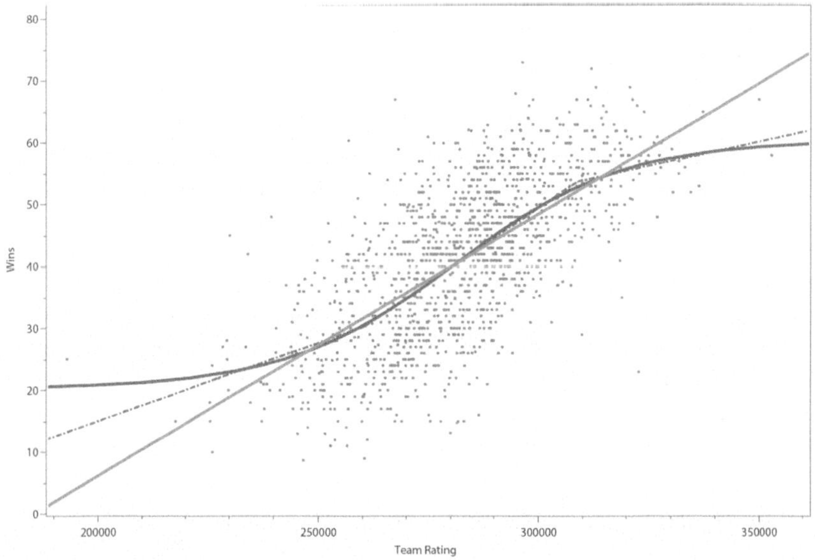

Fig. 1. Wins versus team rating R_T for each team over the span beginning with the 1969–1970 NBA season, and ending with the 2020–2021 NBA season. Three potential models for classifying $\mathbb{E}[W; R_T]$ are overlaid on the data. The green line is a linear model, the blue line is a three-piece linear model, and the red line is a model based on the Probit 4p logistics curve. The model used to generate our results is the red line. (Color figure online)

In Fig. 1, we see a basic linear regression model (green), a three-piece linear regression model (blue), and a Probit 4p logistics curve (red), all fit to the available data. Many additional curves were tried including fitting using neural nets, and the curve that minimizes the overall root mean squared error (RMSE) in the dataset is the Probit 4p logistics curve. At first glance, it may seem that the models are not accurately tracking through the dataset, but remember these models are producing best-fit estimates of $\mathbb{E}[W; R_T]$. In other words, the models should track averages when the data are binned in vertical slices in the figure. For some reason, this dataset presents an optical illusion for some, making it appear as if the data should be binned according to horizontal slices in the figure; but this would produce a curve that gives $\mathbb{E}[R_T; W]$, which is not what we require for the calculation of WAE.

In summary, each team in the NBA has a team rating R_T, which is calculated using (2)–(6). The ratings are then plotted versus wins, and a model is produced to estimate $\mathbb{E}[W; R_T]$. Thus, each team now has an expected number of wins for a season as a function of the team rating. The WAE is then calculated for each team (coach) using (1).

3 Results

In this section, we present the results of applying WAE to 21 years of NBA data. We rate and rank the 30 coaches who began the 2020–2021 season as head coaches, and note disparities between the best coaches according to WAE and coaches winning the Coach of the Year Award throughout the dataset. We also present an accumulation of WAE over the course of coaches' careers. Any head coach who coached at least one season within the span between the 2000–2001 NBA season and the 2020–2021 NBA season is included in the analysis. When necessary, we went back as far as 1970 to retrieve each coach's total career dataset to show the accumulation of WAE throughout each coach's career. Certainly, this analysis could be taken back as far as the data allows, but for this paper we drew the line arbitrarily at the 2000–2001 season. One may be quick to assume that the WAE is just measuring the variability inherent in the results of games over the course of a season. However, our accumulated results definitely show trends among coaches, and easily identify the best coach over the 21-year database.

3.1 The Best Coach in the 2020–2021 NBA Season

To analyze the latest NBA season in our database (2020–2021), we calculated the WAE for each head coach. The results are shown in Fig. 2. To those who follow the NBA, the number one coach according to WAE for 2021, Quin Snyder, will probably not come as a huge surprise. The Utah Jazz won the most games of any team in the regular season during 2020–2021, finishing with a league-best record of 52–20 in a shortened 72-game season. What some may forget is that nobody expected the level of dominance displayed by the Jazz prior to the start of the season. In fact, not even the team rating could have predicted that level of performance. Based on the Jazz team rating R_T, only 39 wins would be predicted by an average coach with that roster (or roughly 44 wins in a regular

82-game season). But the Jazz won 52 games under Snyder (or roughly 59 wins in an 82-game season), resulting in a league-best 14.9 WAE.

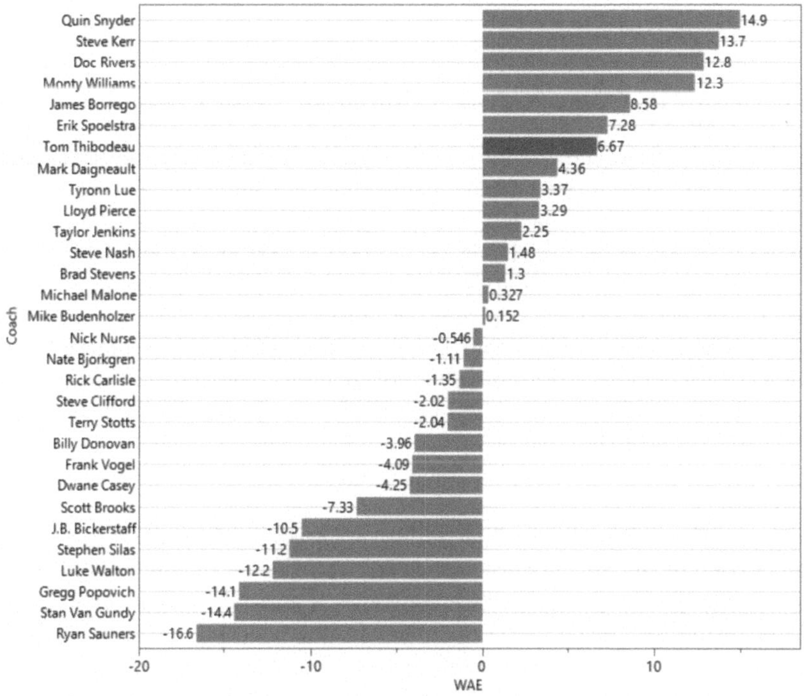

Fig. 2. WAE for all head coaches in the 2020–2021 regular NBA season. Tom Thibodeau is highlighted in green because he won the Coach of the Year Award. (Color figure online)

Other notes of interest are the presence of well-respected coaches on the positive side of the WAE spectrum including Steve Kerr, Doc Rivers, Erik Spoelstra, and so on. Some of these coaches' teams made the postseason and had successful years, while others did not. However, given the hands they were dealt, all of these coaches performed admirably. Of some surprise is the presence of Mark Daigneault, the coach of the Oklahoma City Thunder, near the top of the list. The Thunder missed the postseason with a record of 22–50 (which equates to roughly 25 wins in an 82-game season). Given the Thunder's personnel, this was actually a very good result. It is interesting to note that Daigneault has more recently coached his young squad through an impressive season of NBA play. As of the writing of this paper, the Thunder are in first place in the Western Conference, and second place in the NBA overall, with only a few games left to play in the 2023–2024 regular season. Daigneault's WAE from the 2020–2021 season was a good predictor of future success for the Thunder.

Finally, it is interesting to see where the winner of the Coach of the Year Award finished in WAE. While Thibodeau was certainly towards the top of the list, six coaches technically did better during 2020–2021 than he did according to WAE. This result makes one wonder how the award winners have fared over time in terms of WAE.

3.2 Coach of the Year Awards Compared to WAE Results

Given the results from the previous section, in this section we analyze the annual choices for the Coach of the Year Award in the NBA and compare the results to the WAE statistics of all coaches in the league. Did the committee ever choose the leader in WAE to receive the award? Who was the most snubbed coach over the 21 years spanned by our dataset? Has the committee ever awarded a coach for average or below-average coaching? Figure 3 shows us the answers to these questions, among others. Note that the year label on the figure marks the year in which the award was given; meaning, for example, the 2001 data corresponds to the 2000–2001 NBA season, etc. The WAE leaders are marked and labeled in red. The Coach of the Year Award winners are marked and labeled in green. Finally, the blue line marks the average WAE for each season, which should be close to zero.

To begin to highlight some of the interesting aspects of Fig. 3, we first consider that the Coach of the Year Award was given to the leader in WAE only five times in the 21 years of our dataset. Since the WAE is a recent invention, committee members voting for Coach of the Year would not have had access to our data. In hindsight, the committee selections were reasonable choices roughly 15 times over 21 seasons in question, but there are a number of significant snubs that are extremely obvious from the data in Fig. 3. Perhaps the most obvious is Steve Kerr in the 2014–2015 NBA season. This was Kerr's first year as head coach of the Golden State Warriors, which may have had something to do with the snubbing. Mike Budenholzer won the award with a solid second place ranking in WAE, but notice that Kerr's WAE that season was the highest in our dataset of any coach in any season. This is due to the fact that the Warriors were not expected to do anything special that year. Only after that season's championship victory did Kerr and his Warriors become expected contenders for championships. Coach of the Year Awards in 2004, 2013, and 2018 were given to coaches with barely above-average seasons according to WAE, leaving Rick Carlisle, Kevin McHale, and Brad Stevens as the snubs for each of those years; and while we're talking about Brad Stevens, the WAE data marks him as the number one coach for three years in a row, and yet he was never honored as Coach of the Year. Nate McMillan topped WAE twice, and does not have a Coach of the Year Award either. Other honorable mentions for the biggest single-season snub are George Karl in 2007, Jeff Hornacek in 2014, and Quin Snyder in 2021.

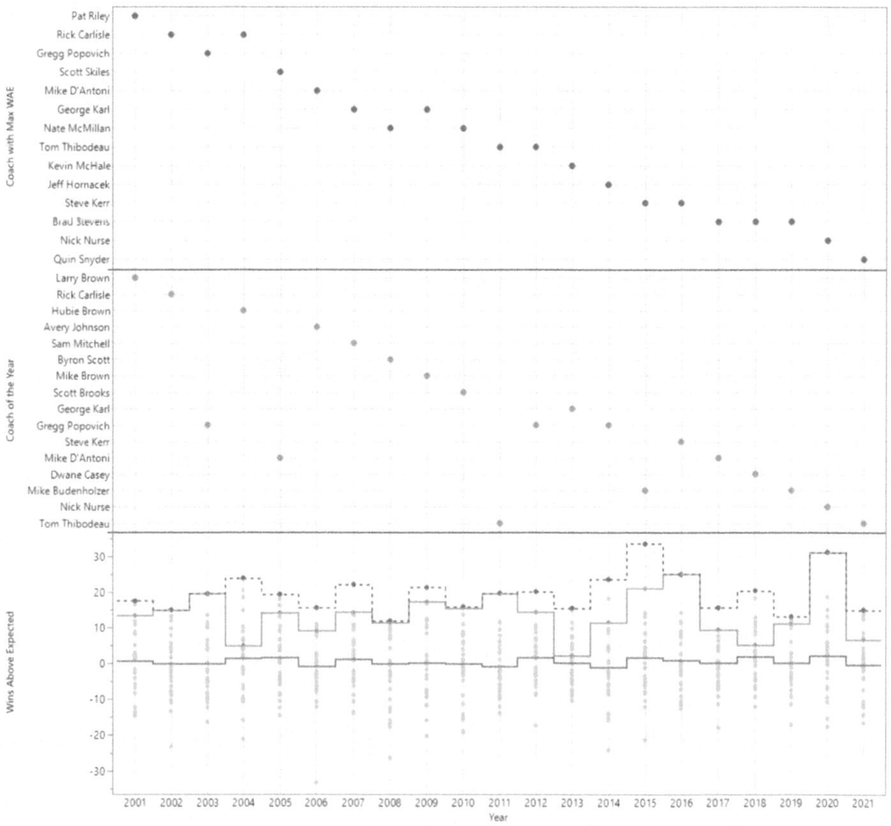

Fig. 3. WAE as a function of season. Note that a label of 2001 applies to the 2000–2001 NBA season, and so on. The WAE leaders are marked/labeled in red; the Coach of the Year Award winners are marked/labeled in green; the average WAE for each season is marked in blue. (Color figure online)

3.3 Cumulative WAE

Finally, it is of note that we can use WAE to identify the greatest coaches of all time. Notably, our current analysis falls short in that we only include coaches who coached at least one season from the 2000–2001 NBA season and onward, but the results we are able to show are still significant and interesting.

Consider Fig. 4, where all coaches from our dataset are plotted in terms of their cumulative WAE as a function of the number of years serving as head coach. Above-average years result in positive cumulative gains, while below-average years result in negative cumulative gains. Although Gregg Popovich has not been doing particularly well of late, he is clearly the greatest NBA coach in our dataset, and perhaps the best coach of all time. Other elite coaches include Phil Jackson, George Karl, and Pat Riley. While none of this is particularly surprising, the fact that well-known and well-respected head coaches immediately jump to the top of our analysis lends credibility to our methods. Note that it is common for even elite coaches to finish their careers with below-average seasons. Phil Jackson avoided this by retiring younger than many other coaches. The best head coach in his first year from our dataset is clearly Steve Kerr, and we note that it is particularly rare for coaches to last more than 8–10 years if they accumulate negative WAE. Again, this lends credibility to our approach and the WAE statistic.

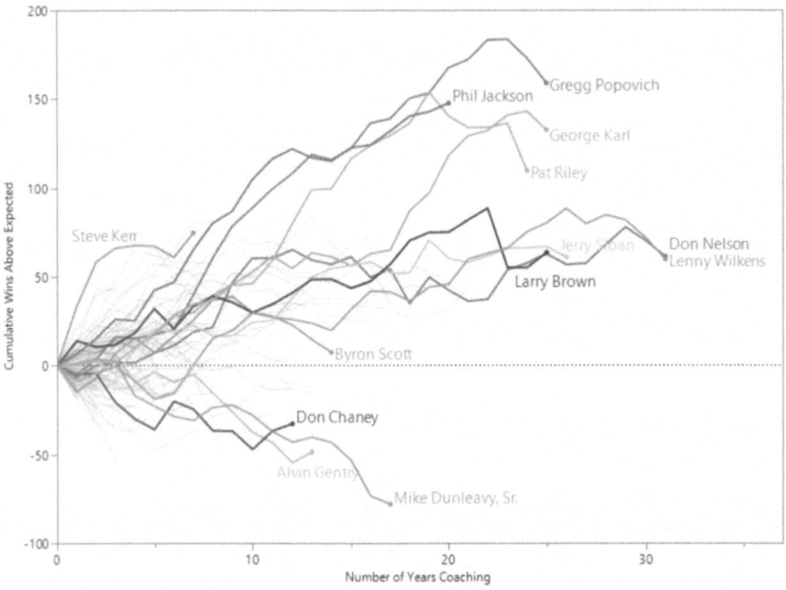

Fig. 4. Cumulative WAE for all head coaches who coached at least one year from the 2000–2001 NBA season and onward. The WAE from each season is kept as a running total for each coach through his career up to retirement or through the 2020–2021 NBA season if still active.

In the case of Steve Kerr, we need to recall that the Golden State Warriors under Mark Jackson were a perennial playoff bubble team. During this time, Stephen Curry and Klay Thompson were not considered elite players. Replacing Jackson with Kerr had an amazing impact on the Warriors' performance with little change to the player roster, and WAE detects this fact very well.

In the case of Mike Dunleavy, Sr., we see a below-average coach lasting for 17 years in the league. Dunleavy inherited Pat Riley's Lakers team (including Magic Johnson and James Worthy in the prime of their careers) and went to the finals in his first year as head coach. He was beaten by Michael Jordan's Chicago Bulls that year, but was clearly elevated in the minds of many as an elite coach. Notice that WAE only rates that season as slightly above average. It appears that other coaches could have done more with the player talent on that Lakers team. Dunleavy went on to miss the playoffs in four of his next five seasons and 10 of his next 16 seasons. He never made the NBA finals again, and won only 46% of games over his career. He ended up resigning twice and being fired once over the course of his 17-year coaching career in the NBA. His career appears to be a constant cycle of teams picking him up thinking they would have success, only to experience very little success leading to a resignation/firing of Dunleavy. It is interesting to note that the WAE correctly identifies Dunleavy as a substandard coach, but general managers struggled to recognize this fact for 17 years.

Let us prune Fig. 4 to leave only the set of active coaches in the 2020–2021 NBA season. This plot is shown in Fig. 5. Notice many of the current highly-regarded coaches within the positive section of the graph. Gregg Popovich clearly stands out as the master veteran coach among active coaches as of 2020–2021. His reign of excellence appears to have really taken off following his sixth season. Doc Rivers and Rick Carlisle are also generally positive, and have clearly been in the league for a large number of years. Notice that the last 10 years in our database for these two coaches have been mostly average or even below average, however.

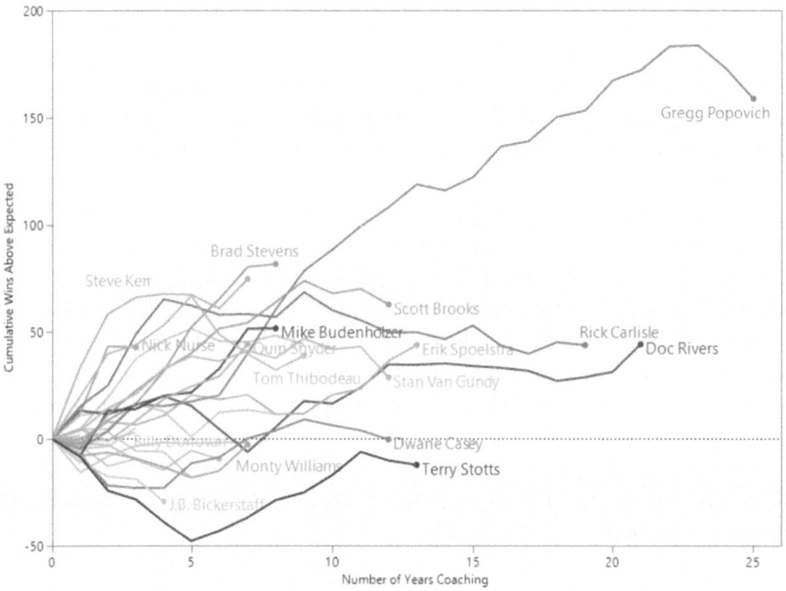

Fig. 5. Cumulative WAE for only the set of active NBA coaches as of the 2020–2021 season.

Erik Spoelstra has been doing very well of late, but actually got off to a slow start despite winning championships with LeBron James, Dwayne Wade, and Chris Bosh in Miami. Although he may have gained more accolades when coaching those three players (and winning titles), his performance is actually more impressive over the last five years of the database. Monty Williams only reversed the direction of his cumulative WAE in the last two seasons of our database, but his cumulative WAE was still below zero after 2020–2021 due to a slow start to his career. In fact, this trend seems evident among a number of younger coaches who experienced slow starts and then an upturn in performance after three to five years of below-average WAE.

Finally, while a number of coaches have accumulated WAE more quickly over the first few years of their careers than Gregg Popovich, it will be interesting to note if any of them can repeat the consistency of excellence that has marked Popovich's career. As of 2021, the league appears to have been packed with good young coaches. Perhaps a few of them will produce Popovich-like numbers over the next 10–20 years.

4 Conclusion

In conclusion, this paper presents a new technique and statistic called *wins above expected*, or WAE, that is useful for evaluating coaching performance. We presented the technique in general, which could be applied to a number of professional sports. Modifications would necessarily need to be made for other events or sports where the players' contributions are estimated in a similar fashion as presented above. For example, in football where players are generally only considered either offensive or defensive players, the minutes played (MP) variable described above is less meaningful and will need to be adjusted to a comparable metric in order to calculate a team's rating. In terms of the current analysis, we presented the WAE in detail for the use case of the NBA showing results for 21 seasons of play. The WAE identifies elite coaching and can provide additional data to voters when considering Coach of the Year Awards in the future. The statistic can also be used by general managers when evaluating coaching performance and making hiring/firing decisions. Accumulating WAE over the course of a coach's career proves to be an effective way to identify truly elite coaches. Gregg Popovich, Steve Kerr, and others are the current gold standard of NBA coaching based on the WAE.

Disclosure of Interests. The authors have no competing interests to declare that are relevant to the content of this article.

References

1. Calculating PER. https://www.basketball-reference.com/about/per.html
2. NBA coach register. https://www.basketball-reference.com/coaches/NBA_stats.html
3. Day, D.: Professionals, Amateurs and Performance: Sports Coaching in England, 1789–1914. Peter Lang (2012)

4. Forman, S.: Baseball-reference.com WAR explained. Baseball-Reference.com. https://www.baseball-reference.com/about/war_explained.shtml
5. Forman, S.: WAR comparison chart: WAR-like stats timeline. Baseball-Reference.com. https://www.baseball-reference.com/about/war_explained_comparison.shtml
6. Fort, R., Lee, Y.H., Berri, D.: Race, technical efficiency, and retention: the case of NBA coaches. Int. J. Sport Finance **3**(2), 84 (2008)
7. Kidane, B.: Who are the best coaches in the NBA entering the 2021–22 season? NBA.com (2021). https://ca.nba.com/news/who-are-the-best-coaches-in-the-nba-entering-the-2021-22-season-ranking/1mng22uytr4k71157lcfpgy05j
8. Nelson, L., Groom, R., Potrac, P.: Research Methods in Sports Coaching. Routledge, London (2014)
9. Ranker NBA: The best NBA coaches right now. Ranker.com (2021). https://www.ranker.com/list/best-current-nba-coaches/ranker-nba
10. Sherman, C.A., Fuller, R., Speed, H.D.: Gender comparisons of preferred coaching behaviors in Australian sports. J. Sport Behav. **23**(4), 389 (2000)
11. Smith, M.: NBAs 10 greatest coaches of all time. Bleacher report (2008). https://bleacherreport.com/articles/78885-nbas-10-greatest-coaches-of-all-time

Querying Football Matches for Event Data: Towards Using Large Language Models

Alexander Schilling, James Anurathan, Johannes Mühlberger, Felix Gerschner, Manfred Rössle, Andreas Theissler, and Marco Klaiber(✉)

Aalen University of Applied Sciences, Beethovenstr. 1, 73430 Aalen, Germany
marco.klaiber@hs-aalen.de

Abstract. Football, being one of the most popular sports in the world, has attracted significant attention from researchers exploring the potential of Artificial Intelligence (AI). In particular, Large Language Models (LLMs), exemplified by digital assistants such as ChatGPT, have proven their capabilities and offer a potentially effective avenue for football research. However, accessibility of football data remains a challenge, as the datasets collected by providers are often inaccessible. This case study presents a proof-of-concept that addresses this challenge by introducing an innovative web scraping approach to extract football event data and making it accessible e.g. for scientific research with LLMs. To this end, the extracted data is structured into coherent sentences for linguistic compatibility. The results show the successful integration of LLMs with football event data, enabling the extraction of information through retrieval-augmented generation. This work makes a first contribution to the field by bridging the gap between football and LLMs, demonstrating the potential for further analysis.

Keywords: Large Language Models · Event Data · Football

1 Introduction

Football (soccer) is considered one of the most popular sports in the world, captivating large numbers of people and experiencing strong and continuous growth in recent years [2,9]. However, like many other sectors, this multimillion-dollar market is undergoing a data-driven transformation [25]. This is due to the fact that both the quantity and quality of data collected have increased rapidly in recent years [13,16]. This availability of data offers opportunities and challenges in creating interfaces between data science and sports science, which is generally seen as a potential game changer in football [16,17]. Nevertheless, the accessibility of football data, explicitly for high-quality event data, is considered a challenge for scientific studies, as those datasets are often inaccessible or only available for high fees from providers [28]. Large and high-quality datasets are

J. S. Dong et al. (Eds.): ISACE 2024, LNCS 14794, pp. 216–227, 2024.
https://doi.org/10.1007/978-3-031-69073-0_19

needed to progress in developing new innovative approaches through Machine Learning (ML) or Artificial Intelligence (AI), which can further support, for example, match understanding [12,14] or scouting [10,15].

Progress in AI has boomed with the emergence of Large Language Models (LLMs), making them potentially attractive for football research [5]. Furthermore, LLMs are becoming increasingly popular due to their potential for data analysis and knowledge extraction [1]. Therefore, the ability of LLMs to improve data availability in football is conceivable, for example, for the preparation and extraction of datasets, as well as their subsequent processing [6]. To obtain as versatile data as possible, we deliberately focus on event data in our study, as these record all events during an entire football match and are considered detailed logs of actions, capturing information such as the number of assists or shots on goal [4,27,28,36]. Due to the rich spatio-temporal information, event data provide the basis for many different studies [18,29,31,33], further emphasizing the relevance of our focus.

Consequently, our case study aims to improve the accessibility of football event data through the integration of LLMs and to demonstrate its potential applications. To this end, we are exploring the possibility of using football websites that provide this information to the public with real-time dissemination of football event data [24]. On this basis, we address the research gap that no current study deals with football event data extraction and mapping for LLM deployments. The growing number of publications in the field of LLMs and the importance of football event data underline the need for this research, by which we want to create the basis for this research direction with our approach.

Therefore, our work offers the following contributions:

1. We present a web scraping approach to extract football event data to create a reliable and efficient method for data access.[1]
2. We prepare football event data for effective use in LLMs by ensuring linguistic compatibility through coherent sentences.
3. Through our proof-of-concept, we provide a framework for the use of event data in football in combination with LLMs to advance scientific research and innovation in football analytics.
4. We offer a first approach in this field of research and highlight open points and further directions.

2 Related Work

Football analysis in combination with LLMs is still a young field of research. Nevertheless, there are individual papers that have taken a similar research direction, which we present below and distinguish from our own research.

To our knowledge, there is currently only one paper that is directly related to our work and combines football analysis with the use of LLMs. Caron and Müller [6] have proposed TacticalGPT, an LLM for predicting tactics and testing the

[1] Code and prompts are available online: https://ml-and-vis.org/football-query/.

ability of LLMs to provide on-demand insights about football. The LLM model can answer textual questions such as *who* and *what*, as well as spatial questions such as *where*. Furthermore, Pappalardo et al. [28] presented another work that also deals with the scarcity of event data in football and presented a publicly accessible data set of spatio-temporal match events. The paper examines various attributes of the dataset and identifies what is responsible for the success or failure of an individual player or team. In other sports, such as basketball, there is also a similar approach, namely the work of Sanguesa et al. [32], where a method was proposed that allows automatic extraction of sensor data and uses it to identify different basketball plays and processes during the game.

The work most similar to our approach was presented by Caron and Müller [6], but in contrast to TacticalGPT we (a) focus specifically on the extraction process of football event data, (b) add more and open-ended questions, especially about game-specific events and information, and (c) aim to provide a first proof of concept as part of our case study. To our knowledge, there is no current study of this kind that combines the extraction of football event data with web scraping and mapping for LLM datasets, in which we demonstrate a first approach.

3 Methodology

3.1 Data Understanding

The data is sourced from the platform *Understat.com*[2], which provides detailed football data for every match in the top European leagues since the 2014/2015 season. In addition to simple match statistics, *Understat* also offers comprehensive and detailed information on individual players and events in games. We use web scraping techniques to extract the essential data from the platform. Therefore, we used various Python libraries to create the web scraper. Our generated data is a result of mapping these features and composing new sentences to comprehend the events of the match.

3.2 Implementing in LLM

We utilize GPT 3.5 through ChatGPT as the LLM in our approach. In addition, LangChain [7] is used, which has emerged as an effective approach in NLP research [26,35], to retrieve information from our data framework using the GPT 3.5 model. Using LangChain as a framework, different technologies can be abstracted, and we are able to link the LLM prompts to each other [19]. This allows us to better utilize question answering and text generation for LLM.

One of the components of LangChain is the "text splitter", which is responsible for breaking down large pieces of text into segments that can be processed by the LLM [30]. The splitting is done by creating chunks smaller than 512 letters. An embedding function was initialized to convert the generated chunk text data into vectors and redirect them to the Facebook AI Similarity Search (FAISS)

[2] https://understat.com/.

[11]. FAISS offers an efficient way to quickly identify data information in large vector datasets that are similar to each other and functions as an in-memory index that does not persist data across sessions [20,34].

In our case, FAISS stores and manages the embedded chunks of our football event data in vector form. The RetrievalQA chain, a component of the LangChain framework, uses the vectorized data stored in FAISS to perform retrieval-augmented generation [19]. When a query is submitted, the RetrievalQA chain retrieves the most relevant data from the vector store and builds a prompt [23]. The LLM then uses this data to generate accurate and contextually relevant responses for the user. The individual process steps are shown in Fig. 1.

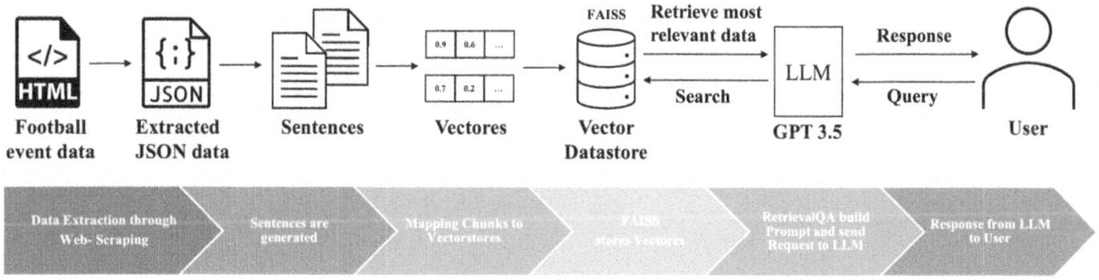

Fig. 1. Overview of the individual steps of our framework.

4 Results

For our use case, we evaluated a match from the German Bundesliga between *VfL Wolfsburg* and *RB Leipzig* (Matchday 12, 2023/11/25). The results of our approach show that the LLM we used has the required understanding and reading capabilities for our data. The use of vectors ensured that the content was understood. It should be noted that each game to be analyzed requires an independent selection via the URL parameter, on which the processes of web scraping and sentence generation are based and performed accordingly.

To evaluate the effectiveness of our approach, the questions were divided into two different difficulty levels: *easy* and *hard*. The classification of the questions was based on the authors' assessment, as well as with regard to the processing and calculation effort within the process. Table 1 shows examples of two questions for the respective categories, as well as the answers and whether they were correct or incorrect. Further results are provided in the Appendix.

When considering the *easy* questions, our approach was able to achieve very good results and provide correct answers in each case. We focus on *easy* questions designed to ask basic information about the game. With regard to the *hard* questions, only partial correct answers could be provided, although more complex values, such as the expected goals (xGoals) value, were still applicable. For this purpose, formulations were deliberately changed by synonyms that nevertheless aim at the same result, such as from *event* to *action* or from *match* to *game*

(Fig. 9 and Fig. 10), whereby our approach had difficulties interpreting those formulations correctly and providing the correct answer. Furthermore, it was not clear which keyword could be better interpreted, which is why explicit questions are necessary to facilitate understanding and obtain correct answers. For this purpose, the question specificity of the questions was tested (Fig. 14 and Fig. 15), whereby the correct answer can be obtained by textual additions within the questions, as otherwise only one team is considered in this case.

Table 1. Exemplary questions and answers; two per level of difficulty

Difficulty	Question	Answer	True/False
Easy	Who scored goals?	Rogerio and Jonas Wind scored goals for Wolfsburg, while Yussuf Poulsen scored a goal for RasenBallsport Leipzig	True
Easy	Which teams are playing?	The teams playing are Wolfsburg and RasenBallsport Leipzig	True
Hard	When was the last event of the game?	The last event of the game was Lois Openda's shot being blocked for RasenBallsport Leipzig in the 78th min	True
Hard	When was the last action in the game?	The last action in the game was Rogerio scoring a goal for Wolfsburg in the 65th min	False

5 Discussion

In the following, we discuss our findings and address open questions that we encountered during our case study.

One challenge of our approach is the generation of the vectors for use in the LLM, which should be taken into account and, in our view, may have led to inaccuracies in the responses. The inadequacy of poorly structured vectors impairs the ability to retrieve and interpret values accurately, which can lead to incorrect LLM results. When looking at the questions "*When was the last action in the game*?" and "*What was the last event in the game?*" this is noticeable, and we suspect that this is due to the LLM not retrieving all values from the vectors or misinterpreting the results. Another misbehaviour was identified in the questions "*Who played the shortest time?*" and "*Who played the shortest time in both teams?*", where the correct answer could only be given with the addition "*in both teams*". The reason for this could be a misunderstanding of the LLM or an incorrect vector retrieval. In contrast to the first misbehaviour, this can be remedied by a more specific question, from which it can be concluded that more specific questions are likely to lead to correct answers.

Another challenge is the selection of the LLM, which in our case was potentially not the optimal solution, as the suitability of a model depends on the task at hand, the type of data and the specific requirements. It is conceivable that a fine-tuned model for football will be used in future work, which meets the specific requirements and has already been implemented with good results in other domains, e.g. [8,37].

It is worth noting that the FAISS retriever may not be suitable for handling large amounts of data, as it removes and discards data once it reaches a predefined limit [21]. This was not an issue in our paper, but it should be considered for future reference and can be addressed using external databases. By doing so, the approach could be made more scalable.

Our approach in the context of football could help provide relevant data for a variety of games and make it accessible. Simple but specific questions could be used to obtain information on any game or players, allowing coaches or scouts, for example, to obtain the desired information without having to laboriously look at every event. Especially in the course of a larger database, it is conceivable that the coaching team will use this approach to prepare for the next opponents, whereby good preparation can potentially increase the chances of winning [3,22]. Accordingly, a kind of "digital football assistant" could be created that can provide intuitive answers. This allows information to be retrieved that is currently implemented with more time-consuming methods, such as finding out who has received the least playing time, which can be implemented more efficiently with our approach.

To conclude, we have identified the following limitations in the course of our research: (1) The use of the OpenAI model, although effective for our case study, could result in prohibitive computational and licensing costs on a larger scale. (2) Compatibility issues arose that prevented the inclusion of a separate database, which would have significantly expanded the model's capabilities. These points should be addressed in future work, which will further expand our approach.

6 Conclusion

In this case study, we propose a first concept for data extraction and mapping of football event data. This involves transforming the extracted data into coherent and interpretable information, making it understandable for LLMs, and creating the possibility of generating and using accessible football event data. Our results indicate a successful incorporation of the data into the LLM, as well as an effective understanding of it. However, there are questions that have led to misleading answers, especially for keyword-sensitive sentences.

As this work is an initial proof of concept, there are some approaches that should be explored in future work, such as the use of a separate database, the application of a fine-tuned LLM as well as other test patterns or the introduction of objective metrics for evaluation. Also conceivable is, for example, the possible use of visual information or the introduction of structured football event data for analysis. Another direction we would like to address in the future is the use of multiple data sources or the consideration of evolving patterns of teams or players over time. Nevertheless, this work shows the potential of LLMs in combination with the complexity of football, with our work forming the basis for future work in this area.

A Appendix

A.1 Overview of the Different Prompts, Their Difficulty and Results

(See Table 2).

Table 2. All RetrievalQA Chain questions with reference to their answer figures

Difficulty	Question	True/False	Answer
Easy	Who scored goals?	True	Figure 2
Easy	Which teams are playing?	True	Figure 3
Easy	Did a player get a red card?	True	Figure 4
Easy	When happened the first goal?	True	Figure 5
Hard	Who has the highest expected goal value?	True	Figure 6
Hard	Who is expected to score the most goals?	True	Figure 7
Hard	What are the informations about Rogerio?	True	Figure 8
Hard	When was the first action happening in the match?	True	Figure 9
Hard	When was the first action happening in the game?	False	Figure 10
Hard	What was the first event happening in the match?	False	Figure 11
Hard	When was the last action in the game?	False	Figure 12
Hard	What was the last event of the game?	True	Figure 13
Hard	Who played the shortest time?	False	Figure 14
Hard	Who played the shortest time in both teams?	True	Figure 15

A.2 Prompts and Answers of the Model

`Q1: Who scored goals?`

```
> Entering new RetrievalQA chain...

> Finished chain.
Rogerio and Jonas Wind scored goals for Wolfsburg, while Yussuf Poulsen scored a goal for RasenBallsport Leipzig.
```

Fig. 2. Question 1 with RetrievalQA chain answer (Difficulty: easy)

`Q2: Which teams are playing?`

```
> Entering new RetrievalQA chain...

> Finished chain.
The teams playing are Wolfsburg and RasenBallsport Leipzig.
```

Fig. 3. Question 2 with RetrievalQA chain answer (Difficulty: easy)

```
Q3: Did a player get a red card?
```

```
> Entering new RetrievalQA chain...

> Finished chain.
Based on the given context, there is no information about any player receiving a red card.
```

Fig. 4. Question 3 with RetrievalQA chain answer (Difficulty: easy)

```
Q4: When happened the first goal?
```

```
> Entering new RetrievalQA chain...

> Finished chain.
The first goal was scored by Jonas Wind in the 8th minute.
```

Fig. 5. Question 4 with RetrievalQA chain answer (Difficulty: easy)

```
Q5: Who has the highest expected goal value?
```

```
> Entering new RetrievalQA chain...

> Finished chain.
Yussuf Poulsen has the highest expected goal value with 1.311048150062561.
```

Fig. 6. Question 5 with RetrievalQA chain answer (Difficulty: hard)

```
Q6: Who is expected to score the most goals?
```

```
> Entering new RetrievalQA chain...

> Finished chain.
Yussuf Poulsen is expected to score the most goals with an expected goals value of 1.311048150062561.
```

Fig. 7. Question 6 with RetrievalQA chain answer (Difficulty: hard)

Q7: What are the informations about Rogerio?

```
> Entering new RetrievalQA chain...

> Finished chain.
```
Rogerio plays for Wolfsburg as a DML. He has scored 1 goal and has not provided any assists.

Fig. 8. Question 7 with RetrievalQA chain answer (Difficulty: hard)

Q8: When was the first action happening in the match?

```
> Entering new RetrievalQA chain...

> Finished chain.
```
The first action in the match occurred in the 5th minute when Mattias Svanberg took a shot on target for Wolfsburg.

Fig. 9. Question 8 with RetrievalQA chain answer (Difficulty: hard)

Q9: When was the first action happening in the game?

```
> Entering new RetrievalQA chain...

> Finished chain.
```
The first action in the game occurred in the 16th minute when Loïs Openda had a shot on target, but it was saved by RasenBallsport Leipzig.

Fig. 10. Question 9 with RetrievalQA chain answer (Difficulty: hard)

Q10: What was the first event happening in the match?

```
> Entering new RetrievalQA chain...

> Finished chain.
```
The first event in the match was Loïs Openda's shot on target in the 16th minute, which was saved by RasenBallsport Leipzig.

Fig. 11. Question 10 with RetrievalQA chain answer (Difficulty: hard)

Q11: When was the last action in the game?

```
> Entering new RetrievalQA chain...

> Finished chain.
```
The last action in the game was Rogerio scoring a goal for Wolfsburg in the 65th minute.

Fig. 12. Question 11 with RetrievalQA chain answer (Difficulty: hard)

Q12: What was the last event of the game?

```
> Entering new RetrievalQA chain...

> Finished chain.
The last event of the game was Loïs Openda's shot being blocked for RasenBallsport Leipzig in the 78th minute.
```

Fig. 13. Question 12 with RetrievalQA chain answer (Difficulty: hard)

Q13: Who played the shortest time?

```
> Entering new RetrievalQA chain...

> Finished chain.
Nicolas Seiwald played the shortest time with 3 minutes.
```

Fig. 14. Question 13 with RetrievalQA chain answer (Difficulty: hard)

Q14: Who played the shortest time in both teams?

```
> Entering new RetrievalQA chain...

> Finished chain.
Tiago Tomás played the shortest time in both teams, with only 2 minutes of playing time.
```

Fig. 15. Question 14 with RetrievalQA chain answer (Difficulty: hard)

References

1. Amer-Yahia, S., et al.: From large language models to databases and back: a discussion on research and education. SIGMOD Rec. **52**(3), 49–56 (2023)
2. Anzer, G., Bauer, P.: Expected passes: determining the difficulty of a pass in football (soccer) using spatio-temporal data. Data Min. Knowl. Disc. **36**(1), 295–317 (2022)
3. Arede, J., Ferreira, A.P., Esteves, P., Gonzalo-Skok, O., Leite, N.: Train smarter, play more: insights about preparation and game participation in youth national team. Res. Q. Exerc. Sport **91**(4), 583–593 (2020)

4. Bauer, P., Anzer, G.: Data-driven detection of counterpressing in professional football. Data Min. Knowl. **35**(5), 2009–2049 (2021)
5. Bonner, E., Lege, R., Frazier, E.: Large language model-based artificial intelligence in the language classroom: practical ideas for teaching. Teach. Engl. Technol. **23**(1), 23–41 (2023)
6. Caron, M., Müller, O.: TacticalGPT: uncovering the potential of LLMs for predicting tactical decisions in professional football. In: StatsBomb Conference 2023, pp. 1–11 (2023)
7. Chase, H.: LangChain (2022). https://github.com/langchain-ai/langchain
8. Cloutier, N.A., Japkowicz, N.: Fine-tuned generative LLM oversampling can improve performance over traditional techniques on multiclass imbalanced text classification. In: 2023 IEEE International Conference on Big Data (BigData), pp. 5181–5186 (2023)
9. Cotta, L.: Using FIFA soccer video game data for soccer analytics. In: Workshop on Large Scale Sports Analytics, pp. 1–4 (2016)
10. Ćwiklinski, B., Giełczyk, A., Choraś, M.: Who will score? A machine learning approach to supporting football team building and transfers. Entropy **23**(1), 1–12 (2021)
11. Douze, M., et al.: The Faiss library, pp. 1–21. arXiv preprint arXiv:2401.08281 (2024)
12. Forcher, L., et al.: How coaches can improve their teams' match performance–the influence of in-game changes of tactical formation in professional soccer. Front. Psychol. **13**, 1–12 (2022)
13. Franks, A., D'Amour, A., Cervone, D., Bornn, L.: Meta-analytics: Tools for understanding the statistical properties of sports metrics. J. Quant. Anal. Sports **12**(4), 151–165 (2016)
14. García-Aliaga, A., Marquina, M., Coterón, J., Rodríguez-González, A., Luengo-Sánchez, S.: In-game behaviour analysis of football players using machine learning techniques based on player statistics. Int. J. Sports Sci. Coach. **16**(1), 148–157 (2021)
15. Ghar, S., Patil, S., Arunachalam, V.: Data Driven football scouting assistance with simulated player performance extrapolation. In: 2021 20th IEEE International Conference on Machine Learning and Applications (ICMLA), pp. 1160–1167 (2021)
16. Goes, F.R., Kempe, M., Meerhoff, L.A., Lemmink, K.A.: Not every pass can be an assist: a data-driven model to measure pass effectiveness in professional soccer matches. Big Data **7**(1), 57–70 (2019)
17. Goes, F., et al.: Unlocking the potential of big data to support tactical performance analysis in professional soccer: a systematic review. Eur. J. Sport Sci. **21**(4), 481–496 (2021)
18. Grassetti, L., Bellio, R., Di Gaspero, L., Fonseca, G., Vidoni, P.: An extended regularized adjusted plus-minus analysis for lineup management in basketball using play-by-play data. IMA J. Manag. Math. **32**(4), 385–409 (2021)
19. Jeong, C.: A study on the implementation of generative AI services using an enterprise data-based LLM application architecture. AAIML **3**(4), 1588–1618 (2023)
20. Johnson, J., Douze, M., Jégou, H.: Billion-scale similarity search with GPUs. IEEE Trans. Big Data **7**(3), 535–547 (2019)
21. Leis, V., Haubenschild, M., Kemper, A., Neumann, T.: LeanStore: in-memory data management beyond main memory. In: 2018 IEEE 34th International Conference on Data Engineering (ICDE), pp. 185–196 (2018)
22. Lepschy, H., Wäsche, H., Woll, A.: Success factors in football: an analysis of the German Bundesliga. Int. J. Perform. Anal. Sport **20**(2), 150–164 (2020)

23. Liu, Q., Geng, X., Huang, H., Qin, T., Lu, J., Jiang, D.: MGRC: an end-to-end multigranularity reading comprehension model for question answering. IEEE Trans. Neural Netw. Learn. Syst. **34**(5), 2594–2605 (2023)
24. Löchtefeld, M., Jäckel, C., Krüger, A.: TwitSoccer: knowledge-based crowd-sourcing of live soccer events. In: Proceedings of the 14th International Conference on MUM, pp. 148–151 (2015)
25. Louzada, F., Maiorano, A.C., Ara, A.: iSports: a web-oriented expert system for talent identification in soccer. Expert Syst. Appl. **44**, 400–412 (2016)
26. Minaee, S., et al.: Large language models: a survey, pp. 1–43. arXiv preprint, arXiv:2402.06196 (2024)
27. Moustakidis, S., Plakias, S., Kokkotis, C., Tsatalas, T., Tsaopoulos, D.: Predicting football team performance with explainable AI: leveraging SHAP to identify key team-level performance metrics. Future Internet **15**(5), 174 (2023)
28. Pappalardo, L., et al.: A public data set of spatio-temporal match events in soccer competitions. Sci. Data **6**(1), 236 (2019)
29. Pappalardo, L., Cintia, P., Ferragina, P., Massucco, E., Pedreschi, D., Giannotti, F.: PlayeRank: data-driven performance evaluation and player ranking in soccer via a machine learning approach. ACM Trans. Intell. Syst. Technol. **10**(5), 1–27 (2019)
30. Potluri, J., Gummadi, H., Bhogi, M., Katta, Y.S., Ramesh, G., Meghana Reddy, T.S.: Unveiling covert conversational agents: enhancing insight, archives, and dialog acts with ChatGPT. In: 7th International Conference on I-SMAC (IoT in Social, Mobile, Analytics and Cloud) (I-SMAC), pp. 766–772 (2023)
31. Rahimian, P., Toka, L.: A data-driven approach to assist offensive and defensive players in optimal decision making. Int. J. Sports Sci. Coach. **19**(1), 245–256 (2023)
32. Sangüesa, A.A., Moeslund, T.B., Bahnsen, C.H., Iglesias, R.B.: Identifying basketball plays from sensor data; towards a low-cost automatic extraction of advanced statistics. In: IEEE International Conference on Data Mining Workshops (ICDMW), pp. 894–901 (2017)
33. Shen, L., Tan, Z., Li, Z., Li, Q., Jiang, G.: Tactics analysis and evaluation of women football team based on convolutional neural network. Sci. Rep. **14**(1), 255 (2024)
34. Subramanya, S.J., Devvrit, F., Kadekodi, R., Krishaswamy, R., Simhadri, H.V.: DiskANN: fast accurate billion-point nearest neighbor search on a single node. In: Advances in Neural Information Processing Systems, pp. 1–11 (2019)
35. Taipalus, T.: Vector database management systems: fundamental concepts, use-cases, and current challenges. Cogn. Syst. Res. **1–13**, 101216 (2024)
36. Vidal-Codina, F., Evans, N., El Fakir, B., Billingham, J.: Automatic event detection in football using tracking data. Sports Eng. **25**(8), 1–15 (2022)
37. Yang, J., et al.: Harnessing the power of LLMs in practice: a survey on ChatGPT and beyond. ACM Trans. Knowl. Discov. Data **18**(6), 1–32 (2024)

An Evaluation of the Determinants of Performance in NCAA Division I Women's Basketball: A Dual-Season Investigation

Samah Senbel[1(✉)], N. Sertac Artan[2], Christopher Taber[1], S. Alexander Long[1], Srishti Sharma[3], Mahmud Kandawala[1], Mehul S. Raval[3], Srikrishnan Divakaran[4], and Tolga Kaya[1]

[1] Sacred Heart University, Fairfield, CT, USA
{senbels,taberc,longs3,kayat}@sacredheart.edu, kandawalam@mail.sacredheart.edu

[2] New York Institute of Technology, New York, USA
nartan@nyit.edu

[3] Ahmedabad University, Ahmedabad, India
{srishti.s1,mehul.raval}@ahduni.edu.in

[4] Krea University, Sricity, Andhra Pradesh, India
srikrishnan.divakaran@krea.edu.in

Abstract. Athletic success depends on several factors, including training, sleep, and mental state. The women's Basketball team at Sacred Heart University has been monitored over two consecutive seasons. The first season 21/22 was relatively unsuccessful, followed by a much-improved performance in the 22/23 season, with a higher win percentage. Six metrics have been measured consistently: Training metrics, Sleep, mental state, game workload, jump analysis, and game performance. We compare those metrics over the two seasons, and our findings show the direct relationship between better training, better sleep, and mental health on the team's performance as a group. We also note the improvement of the common players over the two seasons, even before the games started, and the effect of the new players on their performance.

Keywords: Athlete Performance · Basketball · Game Performance · Sport Analytics

1 Introduction

As in all sports, success in competitive basketball requires the development and execution of a finely honed set of technical and tactical skills coupled with requisite athleticism. Although seemingly categorically distinct, technical ability and physicality are inextricably linked, with deficiencies likely limiting individual and team success [1]. Although recent evidence demonstrates the importance of several qualities of athleticism, such as muscular power, strength, and agility [2, 9], the relative contribution of athleticism and technical ability to successful outcomes at higher levels of competition in women's

J. S. Dong et al. (Eds.): ISACE 2024, LNCS 14794, pp. 228–234, 2024.
https://doi.org/10.1007/978-3-031-69073-0_20

basketball remains unclear [3]. Therefore, the purpose of the current investigation is to evaluate the relative contributions of athleticism and sport-specific skill in the success of an NCAA Division I women's basketball program by examining team performance, year-to-year roster changes, and fluctuations in player athleticism across two seasons of competition.

The Sacred Heart University Women's Basketball team (SHU WBB) competes in the North East Conference (NEC) at the Division I level within the National Collegiate Athletic Association (NCAA). While athlete monitoring for the WBB program has been ongoing for nearly a decade, the last few years included more systematic and multimodal data collection strategies, such as heart rate monitoring, assessment of sleep quality and quantity, and determination of workload parameters, along with traditional surveys and countermovement jump performance monitoring [6, 8, 10]. There was a significant shift from the 21/22 to 22/23 season, where the winning percentage improved from 33% to 75%.

In this paper, we study the performance of SHU WBB in the 21/22 and 22/23 competitive seasons. In the 21/22 season, SHU WBB had 11 returning athletes, while 5 were new to the program. In the 22/23 season, 7 athletes returned, and 6 athletes joined the program. For this analysis, we stratified the players into 4 groups, as shown in Table 1. The groups "Common 21/22" and "Common 22/23" represent the athletes who were on the team in both years; we compared the data for these "common" athletes over two consecutive years. The group "21/22 only" is the 9 athletes who left the team after the 21/22 season, and the group "22/23 only" is the 6 athletes who joined the team in the 22/23 season; this group is slightly taller and much lighter than the other groups.

Table 1. Athlete groups over the two seasons

Group name	Number of Athletes	Average height in meters	Average weight in kilograms	Total minutes played	Average minutes per game
21/22 season only	9	1.7526	74.22	3085	21.87
Common 21/22	7 (5 return)	1.7598	76.79	1965	16.65
Common 22/23	7	1.7598	76.93	2569	16.05
22/23 season only	6	1.7650	70.97	4031	24.88

The 21/22 season was challenging for the team, with a win-loss record of 8–17, compared to a much-improved 19–14 in the 22/23 season. The team's home and away performance improved significantly in the latter season (11–6 and 7–7, respectively) compared to the former (4–8 and 4–9). The team's offensive performance improved, scoring an average of 62.3 points per game in 22/23, compared to 60.5 in 21/22.

2 Methods

22 Division-1 female basketball players agreed to participate in this study (age: 21 ± 3 yrs, height: 174.21 ± 19.27 cm; body mass: 73.98 ± 11.52 kg). Athletes were monitored from August 2021 through March 2023. All subjects read and signed informed consent. This project was approved by the university Institutional Review Board (IRB#170720A).

The data collected included indicators of the internal and external workload: Session RPE, A composite workload score was calculated each week by summing the total work completed in practice, conditioning, strength training, and competitive matches. And the game workload metrics *(Polar Data),* During competitive matches, each athlete was affixed with a heart rate strap and Polar Team Pro unit.

Two indicators of athlete recovery data were collected: **Sleep Data** *(Whoop Data),* all athletes were given Whoop straps and instructed to wear them all time except for practice and competitive matches. Data was collected and analyzed using Whoop's proprietary software. And **Subjective Questionnaire Data** *(SRSS),* Twice per week, athletes were instructed to complete a short recovery and stress questionnaire (SRSS) consisting of four recovery and four stress questions. This survey is valid and reliable for athletes [5]. Our key performance indicator (KPI) is the Vertical Jump Testing, collected at the first practice of the week.

3 Results

We now compare the workload, recovery, and performance indicators for both seasons. Each section covers one of the measurement points defined in the previous section. The R programming language [7] was used to perform data analysis.

3.1 Session RPE

Table 2 shows the average session RPE for both seasons. In the 22/23 season, the sessions were less rigorous, and the weekly Trimp Total was 22% less than the previous season. However, sessions were more regular, with less athletes missing sessions due to COVID or injury. This was reflected in a lower weekly standard deviation (11.7% less) and consequently less monotony (15% less) and considerably lower Strain (39.7% less), which led to a reduced rate of injury and better overall team performance.

Table 2. Average RPE metrics for both seasons

	Weekly Trimp Total	Weekly Standard Deviation	Monotony	Strain
21/22 Season	1918.33	329.77	0.7988	1997.48
22/23 Season	1488.93 (22.4% less)	291.15 (11.7% less)	0.6792 (15% less)	1204.21 (40% less)

3.2 Game Workload Metrics (Polar Data)

Table 3 shows the average values for some of the polar strap fields, and we observe a much better performance. Note that the players who joined in 22/23 had a higher average distance, max speed, and average speed, pulling up the team average for the season. Also, 21/22 was a tough season due to multiple factors: the strength trainer loss at this time, several athletes got sick and injured in December and January, and several games were canceled leading to an irregular game schedule.

Table 3. Average game workload metrics for all groups

	HR min [bpm]	HR avg [bpm]	HR max [bpm]	Total distance [m]	Distance /min [m/min]	Max speed [km/h]
21/22 Season	74.73	133.05	193.21	3385	28.53	23.47
22/23 Season	64.46 (14% less)	131.48 (1% less)	200.9 (4% more)	3638 (7% more)	28.92 (1% more)	23.99 (2% more)

3.3 Whoop Sleep Data

The average Whoop strap measurements are shown in Table 4 for both seasons. We observe more hours of sleep and a higher sleep score in the 22/23 season resulting in a better rested team in the 22/23 season.

Table 4. Average Whoop strap measurements for the four groups

	RHR	HRV	Recovery	Sleep Score	Hours of Sleep	Sleep Need	Sleep Efficiency
21/22 Season	59.57	84.09	59.56	76.44	6.90	8.91	88.92
22/23 Season	57.01 (4% less)	97.94 (16% more)	60.31 (1% more)	80.45 (5% more)	7.14 (14% more)	8.73 (2% less)	89.90 (1% more)

3.4 Subjective Questionnaire Data

Table 5 shows the average answers for both seasons and for each group. It shows a 9.2% improvement in the overall recovery and a 20.8% improvement in overall stress, with the 22/23 only players having the lowest stress and highest recovery perception. The common players also showed an improvement in recovery and stress levels.

Table 5. Average survey answer for both seasons

	PPC	MPC	EB	OR	MS	LA	NES	OS
21/22 Season	3.87	4.19	3.72	3.47	3.37	2.98	3.18	3.36
22/23 Season	4.02 (4% more)	4.17 (0.5% less)	3.91 (5% more)	3.79 **(9% more)**	2.81 (17% less)	2.25 (24% less)	2.27 (29% less)	2.66 **(21% less)**

3.5 Vertical Jump Testing

Table 6 shows the vertical jump measurements for all groups. Note that the 22/23 only group is much lighter and has more peak power, RSI, and jump height than the other groups. Also notable are the common players who had a large increase in jump height from about 10.5 in. to about 12 in. This is a big improvement given that their weight did not change. Their peak power also improved by 6.5% in the 22/23 season, when they had better and more regular strength training sessions.

Table 6. Vertical Jump analysis for all groups

	Body Weight	Peak Power	Peak Power per BM	RSI	Jump Height
21/22 Season	75.5	3414	45.3	0.38	10.64
22/23 Season	75.15 (0.5% less)	3798 (11.2% more)	50.7 (12% more)	0.43 (13% more)	12.55 (18% more)

3.6 Game Performance

In the 21/22 season, the team played 25 games, 8 wins and 17 losses, and in the 22/23 they played 31 games, 18 wins and 13 losses. The 21/22 season had mixed results initially, then a series of losses. The 22/23 seasons had a bad start with 7 consecutive losses, then a series of wins. For each game played, each player had a game score [4], which is calculated based on the player's performance. The game score heavily depends on the position embedded within the tactical framework, which favors players involved in scoring points on offensive drives.

We observe that the game scores in the 21/22 season averaged 4.43 but were 30% higher in the 22/23 season averaging 5.77. The common players had generally low average game scores and did not change much between seasons despite better strength training in 22/23. The players that played in the 21/22 season only consistently had a higher score and were replaced in the 22/23 season with new players with much better game scores right from the beginning. We iterate that the game score heavily depends on the position the player is playing in.

4 Results

In the previous section, we analyzed all the different factors separately. In this section, we will examine their effect on the game score. Figure 1 shows the Game Score per minute (normalized as each player played a different number of minutes, and the game score depends on the minutes played) and the RSI for weeks 8–20 when the games were played. It shows a strong correlation between the RSI and game score. The new players were a big factor in the better results; they had a better game score in general. This is in part due to the position they played in the game. As basketball is a team sport, the improvement in the overall game score is more important than that of individual athletes. So, the better indicator of key internal and external workload in 22/23 contributed to the season's success.

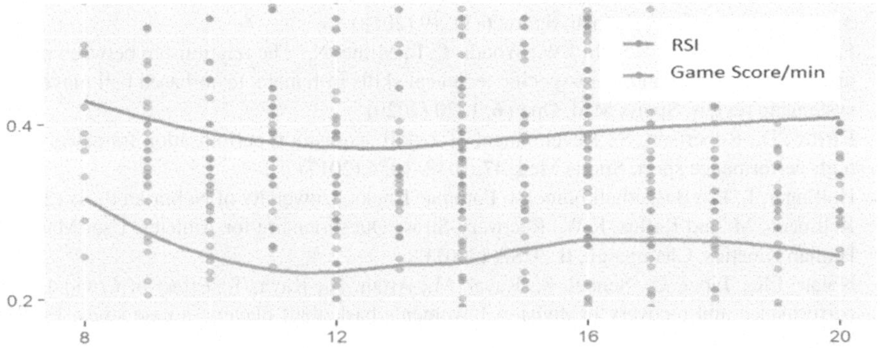

Fig. 1. Correlation between RSI and Game Score/Min.

Overall, performance in basketball can be explained by technical skill, tactical execution, and physicality. In the successful seasons, players had greater technical skill and tactical execution. This was reflected in the greater game score metrics. Underpinning these factors is the overall physical development of the players. Therefore, it is important for basketball players to have the technical abilities on the court and the physical development to carry out the coaches' tactical aspects. To achieve these ends, it is suggested to have a long-term plan in mind that follows the established periodization methods to maximize performance.

5 Conclusion

In this paper we examined various aspects affecting team performance monitored across two consecutive seasons. The 21/22 season was relatively unsuccessful, with several injuries and more losses than wins. In contrast, the 22/23 season saw substantial improvements, with a higher win percentage and about half the team returning players.

Six different athlete metrics were compared: Training scores, game workload, Sleep metrics, mental state, jump analysis, and game scores.

The players trained better in the 22/23 season, with 15% less monotony and 40% less strain. The game metrics were slightly better as well. Also, the sleep scores were about 5% better in the 22/23 season. The SRSS questionnaire showed a 10% increase in overall recovery and 20% less overall stress. Improvement was clear in both the jump analysis and game score due to those factors. We conclude that our analysis shows that all these factors contributed to the success of the team in the 22/23 season. The reactive strength index (RSI) measurement is mirrored in the Game Score/min for the team, and this was a product of better and more consistent training, better sleep, and better mental health.

References

1. Edwards, T., Spiteri, T., Piggott, B., Bonhotal, J., Haff, G.G., Joyce, C.: Monitoring and managing fatigue in basketball. Sports **6**(1), 19 (2018)
2. Farley, J.B., Stein, J., Keogh, J.W., Woods, C.T., Milne, N.: The relationship between physical fitness qualities and sport-specific technical skills in female, team-based ball players: a systematic review. Sports Med. Open **6**, 1–20 (2020)
3. Farrow, D., Robertson, S.: Development of a skill acquisition periodisation framework for high-performance sport. Sports Med. **47**, 1043–1054 (2017)
4. Hollinger, J.: Pro Basketball Forecast. Potomac Books, University of Nebraska Press (2005)
5. Kellmann, M. and Kallus, K.W.: Recovery-Stress Questionnaire for Athletes: User Manual. Human Kinetics, Champaign, IL, USA (2001)
6. Nolan, J.K., Taber, C., Senbel, S., Raval, M., Artan, N., Kaya, T.: Effect of Covid-19 on performance and recovery of division 1 women's basketball players: a case study. Eur. J. Sport. Sci. **3**, 1–8 (2024)
7. R Foundation for Statistical Computing, Version 4.3.1; R Core Team, Vienna, Austria
8. Senbel, S., et al.: Impact of sleep and training on game performance and injury in division-1 women's basketball amidst the pandemic. IEEE Access **10**, 15516–15527 (2022)
9. Spiteri, T., Binetti, M., Scanlan, A.T., Dalbo, V.J., Dolci, F., Specos, C.: Physical determinants of division 1 collegiate basketball, women's national basketball league, and women's national basketball association athletes: with reference to lower-body sidedness. J. Streng. Condit. Res. **33**(1), 159–166 (2019)
10. Taber, C.B., et al.: A holistic approach to performance prediction in collegiate athletics: player, team, and conference perspectives. Sci. Rep. **14**(1), 1162 (2024)

Application and Development of the Expected Goals for Hockey Player Evaluation

Nikolay Shmakov(✉)

Centre for Econometrics and Business Analytics (CEBA), St. Petersburg State University, 7/9 Universitetskaya nab., St. Petersburg 199034, Russia
st095555@student.spbu.ru

Abstract. Hockey clubs are currently subject to strict budgetary and regulatory restrictions, which increase competition and struggle for the best players, according to the ratio between expected salaries and final utility to the team. These restrictions force clubs to evaluate the effectiveness of player contracts and continuously benchmark them with the transfer market to find reinforcements. This article aims to create a framework for evaluating any hockey player in any professional league. The built framework is based on the Expected Goals model (XG). The XG model calculates the probability of each shot being a goal by solving a binary probabilistic classification task. The final rating is calculated using the explainable and auditable Expected Goals on Target model (XGoT), which complements the classical Expected Goals model by adding information about points on the gate plane for the shots on goal. This introduces the realization factor into the model. This article expands the discussion of the XG methodology for evaluating player efficiency and puts forward a new way of player evaluation in ice hockey. The traditional approach of rating creation in hockey has been strengthened by the implementation of the opposition level that balances the game in equal strengths, power play, and penalty kill to assemble an overall rating. The resulting fully interpretable framework facilitates stakeholders to make transfer decisions based on reliable analytics.

Keywords: Transfer Policy · Player Evaluation · Player Efficiency · Expected Goals · Salary Fund

1 Introduction

The salary budgets of hockey clubs in the Kontinental Hockey League (KHL)[1] range between approximately 4 and 9 million euros, accounting for 20–50% of the clubs' annual budgets. Their analysis is significant, both due to regulatory restrictions on amount and the specific nature of player transfers between teams. The measurement of players'

[1] The Kontinental Hockey League (KHL) is an international hockey league, the winner of which receives the title of champion of KHL and the title of champion of Russia in ice hockey. KHL is the biggest hockey league in Europe according the number of participants and average salary budget.

J. S. Dong et al. (Eds.): ISACE 2024, LNCS 14794, pp. 235–248, 2024.
https://doi.org/10.1007/978-3-031-69073-0_21

return on investment (ROI), at both individual and aggregated levels, is one of the most important in evaluating the performance of management teams in hockey by owners and other stakeholders. Given tight financial constraints, ROI is a proxy metric for the club's sports result, which is the main objective for the season. The greater a hockey club manages its budget to attract top players, the better its chances to succeed. The effectiveness of budget execution has a growing impact on the overall sports result, with the influence of the budget factor decreasing, i.e. the difference between the absolute figures of the salary budget between teams.

The reduction of budget factor impact is one of the main goals of the KHL's Board of Directors, which has been implemented since the start of the 2020–21 season. There is a clear trend towards a decline in the difference in salary budgets. This decreases the disparity between clubs with different financial capabilities. The minimum limit of the salary budget (or "Salary Floor") for the 2023–24 season has been set at 4.5 million euros, while the maximum (or "Salary Cap") has remained unchanged for four consecutive seasons at 9 million euros according to KHL's strategy. From the 2024–25 season onwards, the salary cap is becoming "tight", meaning that bonuses exceeding 10% of the total salary amount are considered when calculating the salary cap. The salary floor has also been increased to 450 million or 50% of this cap. The limitation of the salary cap and floor is aimed at strengthening the competitiveness of participating clubs in the tournament and increasing uncertainty in the results of individual games and the entire championship. Controlled uncertainty in individual games and throughout tournament has a positive impact on spectator interest and participation [11].

The ever-tightening budget constraints significantly increase the cost of transfer mistakes of both types: acquiring an unsuitable player, and not acquiring a suitable one. This study and built framework aim to support managers in current transfer operations by providing them an analytical substrate digi targets on the transfer market. A single dashboard provides complex analyses of the players' performances against market benchmarks, shaping the built framework's main strength. Using the dashboard, hockey organizations can make their recruitment process more transparent and analytical. Depending on their chosen strategy, they will be able to either significantly increase the average level of players on a team roster, which will improve their chances of winning championship, boosting television ratings, and securing sponsorship agreements, or they can maintain the current performance level by reducing their payroll costs.

2 Player Evaluation Evolution

The earliest attempt to measure the player value was to compare the results of their attacking and defensive actions, rewarding players for key positive actions – a goal scored against an opposing team, and punishing them for negative actions – a goal for their own team. The "plus-minus" indicator is calculated for each player by taking the difference between the number of goals scored and the number of times the player conceded a goal while the player was on the ice. Plus-minus is easy to calculate and understand, which has made it popular today among managers, coaches, fans, and media [10]. There is a common practice of giving individual bonuses to players who make it into the top of this indicator at the end of a tournament or exceed a certain threshold.

One of the first attempts to adjust plus-minus on partnerships and opposition levels using a regression model has been proposed in [14]. The influence of evaluated hockey player on game events is determined by changing the difference in the probability estimates of scoring and conceding a goal during the next 10 s of play. A linear regression with binary variables is created for each player in the sample. However, the derived indicator does not correlate with classic plus-minus utility ratings, and player ratings remain stable over several seasons, even when the team changes. This indicates the stability of the indicator and eliminates the influence of microenvironmental factors on the final result. A similar adjustment based on logistic regression with regularization proposed in [12]. The introduction of regularization is justified by the fact that players often play with regular partners, which leads to multicollinearity problem when assessing the mutual influence. Regularizing regression coefficients stabilizes player scores. The players with the greatest impact on goals scored are identified, given their team level and partners' influence.

Plus-minus also has the disadvantage of missing the influence of the game's context. This means that the impact of a goal scored depends on the time and the score in the game. This shortcoming has been corrected in the studies [7, 8] where each target action is evaluated in terms of its impact on the outcome – a change in the expected number of points scored in the game. Both players who benefited at key moments in the game, exerting a strong influence on the outcome, and players with high plus-minus numbers were identified. But when considering the influence of the game's context, their importance to the team significantly decreased, indicating a bias in estimating some players' final effectiveness when using classical metrics. Plus-minus is often calculated when the difference in score is less than one in order to filter out goals that have a minimal impact on the game outcome. However, this simplification ignores goal time and deprives the analysis of a significant number of observations that should be considered when calculating players' scores.

The desire to take more game events into account led to the creation of the "Corsi" indicator [4]. Corsi calculates shots towards the goal instead of focusing on relatively rare goals. Each shot is then considered a potential scoring threat, and players are compared based on this difference. Corsi is based on how many shots a player contributes to both teams' total shots when he was on the ice, rather than focusing on the difference in shots. Corsi is calculated by counting all shots towards the goals, including blocked and missed ones, and is scaled to a range from 0 to 100%. The method of counting Corsi without blocked shots is called "Fenwick."

With an increase in the frequency of using such indicators in managerial decision-making, their predictive and representative abilities decreased. Due to the lack of a threshold for classifying the shot danger, players began to take a large number of shots mainly from a long-range, maximizing the value of the estimated indicator without commensurate effect on the total shot danger. A switch was made to summarizing probabilistic estimates of shots being a goal to restore representational strength of indicators based on shots. This assessment is obtained by constructing a classifier that predicts the shot probability of becoming a goal, based on the feature values embedded in the model. Within the sports world, these models are called XG (Expected Goals).

The first attempt to quantify the influence of positional and contextual factors in hockey on the shot danger was made in [9]. Data was collected in real time during the 2002–03 season. For each shot, distance to the net, time before the shot, shot type, and last game action type were determined. The rating is defined as the difference between expected goals scored and conceded, while the player was on the ice. The "plus-minus" indicator has been transformed from the traditional to the expected one. Estimates of the overall shots' probability don't correlate with Corsi. This displays differences in a shot quality between teams. Teams can employ different attack strategies, such as maximizing the risk associated with individual shots or maximizing the total shots' number. Models became more complex due to advanced machine-learning techniques applications and feature space enhancement [15]. XG models are widely used in soccer to evaluate shots and compile player ratings [13]. Analytics in soccer are at a higher analytical maturity level than in hockey. Therefore, many studies aim not only to create deep and accurate models but also to achieve high interpretability and understandability for stakeholders [16–18]. Attempts was made to estimate the total number of expected goals in a game for each team based on the aggregated values of shooting metrics [6]. However, this approach has not been further developed because of the limited use of these indicators for analyzing individual players' game episodes and the lack of intuition behind this method.

The impact of implementing probability indicators on the game is assessed by comparing shot metrics between two different eras. During the era of Corsi teams were maximizing the difference in score by making more shots [5]. For this era, a goal threat means any shot, while during the era of XG teams were maximizing the single-shot danger. It was revealed that the Corsi Era in the NHL had begun in 2015–16 due to significant increase of average number of expected goals per 60 min while maintaining the total number of shots. The main driver of this growth is a decrease in average shot distance to the net. This factor has the greatest impact on shot danger, so players increasingly abandon long-range shots to reduce this distance and increase the potential for danger.

XG-based indicators eliminate the influence of the random component on player ratings and mathematically fairly reward and penalize players for events on the ice. This can be strengthened by adjusting for players on the ice difference between teams and considering microenvironment parameters through classical indicators adaptation. However, the problem of separating and distributing the contributions of ice hockey, i.e. evaluating the value of actions remains unsolved on medium-detailed and affordable hockey data. In studies [1–3] based on deeper data, the value of an action is assessed through deep reinforcement learning to fit the game context. The final metric is a summary of the estimates for the actions taken by the player. According to the studies, this metric remains stable throughout the season and correlates strongly with traditional performance indicators and contract value. The proposed method has a great intuition, and the performance metrics are also high. However, the data used in these studies are highly detailed and costly, which makes it inaccessible to most teams. This makes it impossible to apply this approach to evaluate players in various interesting and competitive hockey leagues, including KHL and many others.

3 Methodology

3.1 Our Approach

In an attempt to evaluate player performance, hockey analytics have moved from plus-minus to Corsi and Fenwick and then to XG. As a result, analytics in hockey came to the following formula for determining players' efficiency:

$$XG(p) = \sum_{i=1}^{n} P(Y = Goal|X^{(i)}) * b(i)_p - \sum_{j=1}^{m} P(Y = Goal|X^{(j)}) * b(j)_p \quad (1)$$

where $b(iorj)_p$ – the tag of player b presence on the ice at the shot time;

$X^{(i\,or\,j)}$ – values of features for the shot;

$\sum_{i=1}^{n} P(Y = \text{гол} \mid X^{(i)})$ – the expected number of goals scored when player b was on the ice on equal strengths;

$\sum_{j=1}^{m} P(Y = \text{гол} | \, X^{(j)})$– the expected number of goals missed when player b was on the ice on equal strengths.

Many other game actions for which we all love hockey have not been considered. Using the actions that directly affect the change in score makes the rating objective, and most importantly – valuable. One should note that formula (1) can be correctly used to evaluate player efficiency only on equal strengths. It is also possible and necessary to remove shootouts and empty-net shots in order to clear the rating and make it more objective. But how to use this formula for assessing players in unequal strengths? There is an approach.

3.2 Building a Rating

Direct application of formula (1) on unequal strengths is incorrect, as the players during the power play has an advantage in creating danger shots and preventing it. Application of formula (1) in equal strengths is possible because the left side is balanced by the right. The attack equalizes the defense under the conditions when equal or almost equal teams play with each other. To correctly calculate the efficiency on the power play (penalty kill), one needs to introduce a balancing part that allows to determine the following: how much more total danger the team created (prevented) on the power play (penalty kill) compared to the average performance level of opposing team. As an average performance level might be taken the total XG divided by total time:

$$XG(team\,on\,PP) = \frac{\sum_{i=1}^{n} P(Y = Goal|X^{(i)}) - \sum_{j=1}^{m} P(Y = Goal|X^{(j)})}{\sum Time\,on\,Power\,Play} \quad (2)$$

In order to use this formula on the penalty kill, one should swap the right and left parts and replace time in denominator. Comparing the quality of game on the power play (penalty kill) with the average quality of game on the penalty kill (power play), which are measured as the average XG difference per unit of time, it is possible to evaluate the player efficiency in unequal strengths:

$$(XG(player\,on\,PP) - XG(team\,on\,PK)) * \sum Player\,time\,on\,PP \quad (3)$$

$$(XG(player\ on\ PK) - XG(team\ on\ PP)) * \sum Player\ time\ on\ PK \quad (4)$$

The resulting values represent the XG amount added or saved considering the player's time spent. Player ratings will be greater than zero if their performance on the power play or penalty kill is better than the average level of the opposing team's performance. The main advantage of this approach is that players who play in different types of strength are compared without discrimination with those who do not have ice time in unequal strengths because this approach focuses on the added XG. Identically, the level of the opposition can be considered when evaluating player performance on equal strengths. One need applies formula (3) to assess the performance in attack and formula (4) for assess the performance in defense. It is important to note that the average performance level of the opposing team is used instead of the entire league because the differences between the teams on unequal strengths are more pronounced than those on equal ones. However, what are the implications of using the average?

The main disadvantage of the average application is the requirement for a larger number of data to make the average unbiased. With an increase in the number of observations, the stability of model outputs also increases. The most obvious way is using the averages based on the entire regular season. But it is odd and counterintuitive that the player efficiency at the end of the season also depends on the quality of the opposing team's play at the season's beginning. And what is to be done at the beginning of the season when the average team's performance is unknown? How to take into account teams' ups and downs during the season? This can be strengthened by predicting the teams' future performances regarding their rosters and the ability of players to influence each other to consider the possible multiple effects of player interaction. We leave this for future research. In built framework we calculate average performance levels in components for each team without estimated game and following ones. For the first 10 games, we use averages from the previous season, gradually reducing their impact through a weighted average.

3.3 Difference Between XG and XGoT Models

One should distinguish models predicting a danger of position and danger of shot. The first group is called Expected Goals models (XG), and the second one is Expected Goals on Target models (XGoT). XGoT model evaluates only the shots on target and includes information received after a shot. It is the endpoint of a shot in the gate plane. The classic XG model calculates the likelihood of a shot without this information. Therefore, XG assesses a shot solely based on its positional attributes, whereas XGoT also takes into account realization characteristics. Positional factors include shot distance, shot angle, type of previous event, etc. It is correct to apply the XG model for assessing the probability of all shots and the XGoT model only for assessing the probability of shots on goal. The sum of predictions of both models should be the same because the number of goals is identical in both cases.

An intriguing question arises regarding boundary factors, such as shot speed and type, which cannot entirely be attributed to position or realization factors. These factors might be attributed both to position factors and realization ones. It is difficult to hit with maximum power when a player is in the slot surrounded by opponents, and a few would think about slapshot being behind the net. It is still an open question how to divide their influence and include it correctly in the models. The answer might be to predict the features values according to position factors and include those predictions in the XG model. The actual values should be attributed to the XGoT model. In this case the output difference for shots on goal between XGoT and XG assesses properly the realization factor. We leave this for future deeper research because we haven't these factors in our feature space.

4 Methods

4.1 Data Setup

We examined 1,154,969 shots from the 2019–2020, 2020–21 and 2021–2022 seasons to build XG and XGoT models. Data was collected in the following leagues: NHL, AHL, Swiss League, SHL, Liiga, DEL, KHL, MHL, VHL, NCAA, WHL, USHL. Different sets of leagues in samples should demonstrate the versatility of created models, as well as the same nature of goal generation, regardless of players' levels and their average age. One of the points that we are trying to prove is that the nature of goals is the same everywhere. In the games reviewed, 1,154,969 shots were taken – an average of 97 per game. The sample was divided into two datasets: the training dataset included 749,402 shots in the 2019/2020 and 2020/2021 seasons, and shots in the 2021/2022 season formed the closed test dataset.

Information extracted was about the shot and the action that preceded it from the play-by-play data. Interestingly, the information about the penultimate action turned out to be insignificant for the model; therefore, only a time window that is equal to one action has a significant impact on shot probability to be a goal. Finally, the following feature space was obtained:

- Shot distance
- Shot angle
- Type of preceded action
- Distance from preceded action to the net
- Angle from preceded action to the net
- Distance between shot and preceded action
- Time between shot and preceded action
- Type of shot
- Goalie visibility
- Difference between strengths during the shot
- League type
- Distance to goalpost (only for the shots on goal)
- Distance to crossbar (only for the shots on goal)

The creation of features began with the polar coordinates of the shooting point. The coordinates relative to the attacking team were marked in the data for each shot. It was decided to abandon binning the hockey rink into a large number of squares in favor of polar coordinates due to their greater interpretability and consistency with hockey logic. Shot distance is the most important feature for determining danger according to the results of previous research [9, 15]. According to data reviewed in work, danger zone (or "slot") accounts for more than 80% of the total number of scoring shots and goal conversion is twice the conversion rate of the entire sample.

Polar coordinates of shots (and also preceded action) were calculated to the nearest corner, as the most dangerous shots are directed in its areas of the net; in addition, it increases the reliability of estimates of shots from sharp and negative angles. The following six values of "Type on preceded action" feature account for 85% values: Pass accurate, Zone entry Successful, Puck battles, Faceoff, Shot on goal, Takeaway. Feature "Time between shot and preceded action" is a proxy feature to display player density near the shooting player: the more time has passed, the fewer and further opponents there are. Feature "Type of shot" comprises the following values: Slapshot, Wrist shot, Backhand shot, Deflection, Rebound shot, and shot from behind the net. The greatest doubts were about the feature "Difference between strengths during the shot" because the danger of a shot must not be determined by score, and a significant impact of its feature will indicate only a psychological aspect in goal scoring.

4.2 Feature Selection

XG and XGoT models are the core of the proposed estimation method. Meaningful part of the work is the selection of features that have a significant impact on the shot probability to be a goal. Therefore, a reliable wrapper method on the basis of bootstrap for feature selection was used. The essence of it is very simple: two datasets with different ranges of features (typically one dataset contains the checked feature, and one does not) are used as the input of any ML models (in our case it is gradient boosting with parameters contributing to the rapid study), we do it 1000 times with different samples from the train dataset, and then we assess statistical significance of a metric increment on validation dataset. The metric of area under the curve (AUC-ROC) was used for assessing the performance of all models in the article. Also pipeline for feature selection was constructed: we have checked the influence of all potential features on XG and XGoT models. If the feature had a statistically significant influence on one model and does not on another, it means that this feature includes information about a probability to be a shot on goal, causing overfitting.

The first stage involves verifying the "shot angle" feature, significance of "Shot distance" was set by default, the p-value of adding was less than 5% for XG and XGoT, therefore we did not remove this feature (Fig. 1):

Features were checked according to the above order and the following remained:

- Shot distance. Significance was set by default. The average AUC-ROC for the XG and XGoT models is 79.3% and 84.5%, respectively based only on this feature
- Shot angle (XG p-value = 1.24e-10, XGoT p-value = 4.90e-11)
- Type of preceded action (XG p-value = 6.88e-88, XGoT p-value = 3.76e-67)
- Distance from preceded action to the net and Angle from preceded action to the net (XG p-value = 0.0004, XGoT p-value = 0.0029)
- Distance between shot and preceded action (XG p-value = 8.41e-40, XGoT p-value = 2.88e-32)

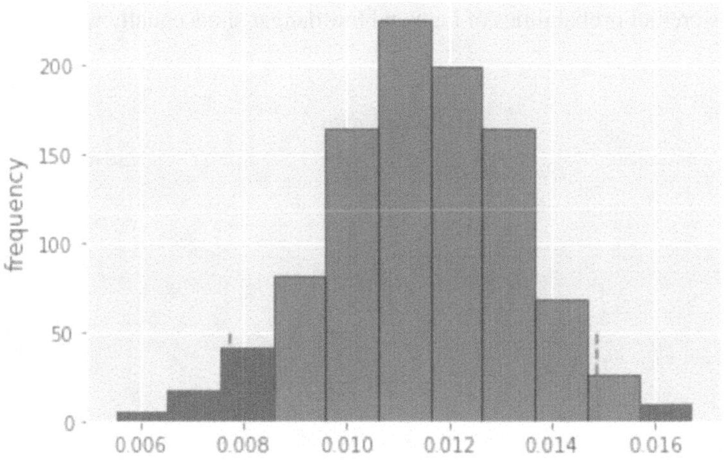

Fig. 1. Histogram of bootstrapped data obtained by checking the statistical significance of the area under the curve increment after adding the feature "Shot angle" to XG model

- Time between shot and preceded action (XG p-value = 8.41e-40, XGoT p-value = 2.88e-32)
- Type of shot (XG p-value = 1.16e-5, XGoT p-value = 7.64e-05)
- Goalie visibility (XG p-value = 0.0492, XGoT p-value = 0.0029)
- Difference between strengths during the shot (XG p-value = 0.2557, XGoT p-value = 0.2219)
- League type (XG p-value = 0.4464, XGoT p-value = 0.7293)
- Distance to goalpost (only for the shots on goal). Significance was set by default.
- Distance to crossbar (only for the shots on goal). Significance was set by default.

This greedy feature selection method demands full understanding of the order in which the features are checked. Separate addition of "Distance from preceded action to the net" and "Angle from preceded action to the net" was insignificant, but the addition of both features on one iteration was significant. As expected, the influence of the feature "Difference between strengths during the shot" was insignificant. In addition, the feature "League type" was also checked, but the statistical difference in score has not been found. This proves that the lows of goal scoring are the same in all professional leagues and don't depend on average players' level and age.

4.3 Building Models

Based on the selected features, XG and XGoT models were created, hyperparameters were selected on the validation dataset by using Hyperopt framework. Both models use deep trees (depth equals eight for both models) and are very regularized (value of L2-regularization coefficient is high for both models). Area under the curve for the XG model on hold-out dataset equals to 91.08% and 93.78% for XGoT, but what is the most important – models are well calibrated and predict unbiased probabilities. The calibration curve is close to bisectrix, and calibration error and Brier score are low, which means that models predict probabilities of high and low danger shots equally well (Figs. 2 and 3).

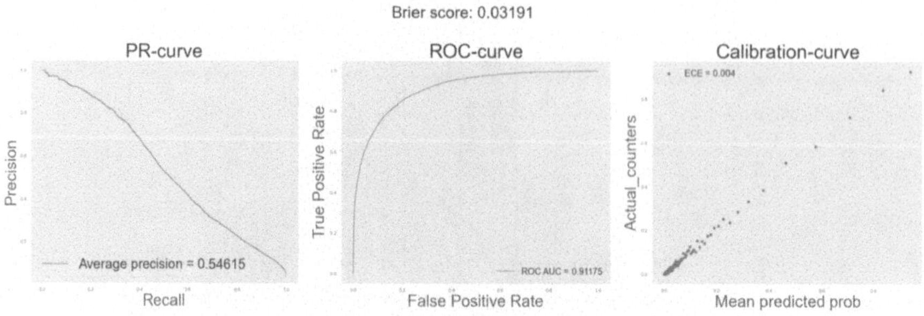

Fig. 2. XG model performance on test dataset

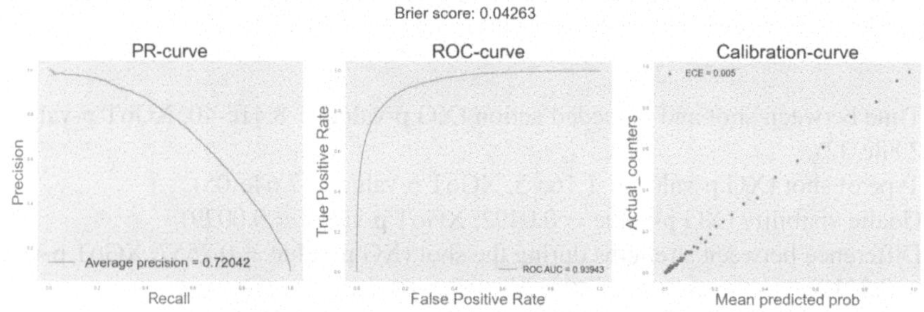

Fig. 3. XGoT model performance on test dataset

Additionally, we tried to predict the difference between the model's predictions in order to make sure that models do not include the probability of being a shot on goal, in this case, it would mean an overfitting. Gradient boosting with default params was built, its aim was to predict the difference by using positional factors available for both models: R2 score equals 3%, that indicates the absence of overfitting.

4.4 Models' Explanation

To interpret the model's results, SHAP values were used. It was essential for us that the orders of feature importance were almost the same in both models, of course not taking into account two resulting features in the XGoT model. In addition, the order and degree of feature influence have to pass the eye test. And created models passed this set of tests. The most influential feature is "Shot distance", "Time between shot and preceded action" is the next in order; the smaller the shot distance is, the greater the impact it has on the models' outputs. The dependence is direct for the "Time between shot and preceded action". It is a curious conclusion that the distance to goalpost is more vital than distance to crossbar. This seems to be a bit of a philosophical question, which is still answered. There is also a big influence of the feature "Type of preceded action" (Figs. 4 and 5).

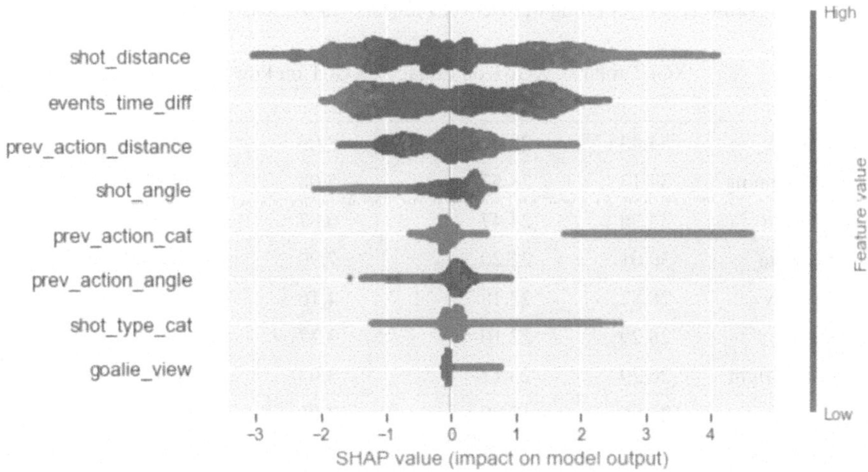

Fig. 4. XG model feature importance

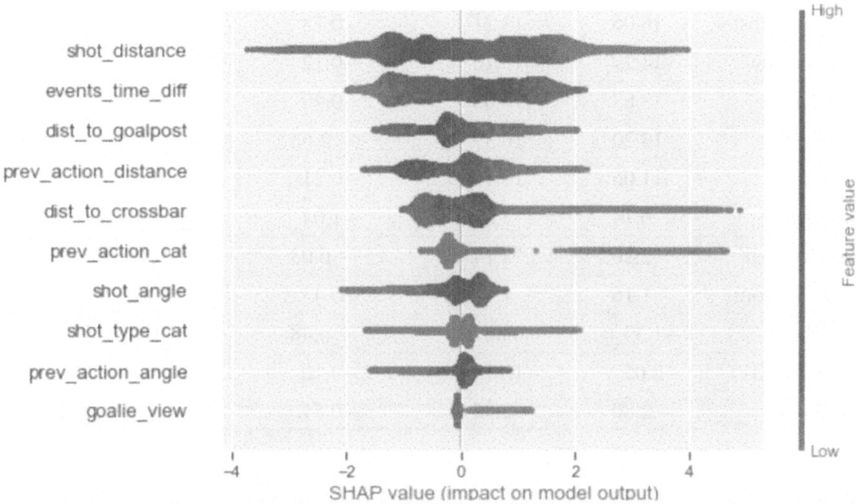

Fig. 5. XGoT model feature importance

5 Application

Player rating is constructed using the XGoT model because it better approximates the process of goal scoring. In the built framework XG-model is used only to find deviations from XGoT to make a feature "realization effect". The model operation demonstration is shown using data extracted from "Denver Pioneers" games in the NCAA league during the 2021–22 season. This subsample was removed from the data used in the models' creation.

Table 1. Player rating of "Denver Pioneers" in the season 2021–22.

Player	XGoT total	XGoT on Equal Strength	XGoT on Power Play	XGoT on Penalty Kill
Bobby Brink	34.43	28.46	8.06	−2.08
Michael Benning	34.13	28.57	5.08	0.48
Carter Mazur	33.38	24.47	6.87	2.04
Carter Savoie	30.01	22.20	7.90	−0.09
Brett Stapley	28.82	22.18	4.16	2.48
Shai Buium	28.29	22.10	3.77	2.42
Cameron Wright	26.29	23.11	3.03	0.14
Sean Behrens	25.86	17.28	7.06	1.53
Massimo Rizzo	24.62	21.27	2.43	0.92
Cole Guttman	21.78	20.31	8.38	−6.92
Antti Tuomisto	21.73	21.45	0.06	0.22
Ryan Barrow	16.80	14.24	1.40	1.15
McKade Webster	16.06	13.21	−0.78	3.63
Kyle Mayhew	14.29	13.10	−0.12	1.31
Justin Lee	13.83	17.06	−0.49	−2.74
Jack Devine	13.20	10.37	2.68	0.15
Reid Irwin	11.06	10.17	−0.21	1.11
Carter King	6.14	3.65	−1.04	3.53
Lane Krenzen	2.20	2.14	− 0.03	0.09
Connor Caponi	1.16	1.13	−0.43	0.46
Owen Ozar	−1.35	−0.86	− 0.48	−0.02
Brett Edwards	−2.05	−1.17	−0.10	−0.77
Jack Works	− 2.80	− 2.32	−0.51	0.03

"XGoT in all components" is the final player ranking, which is a sum of player ranking in equal strengths, power play, and penalty kill. A greater contribution to the overall indicator is made by play in equal strength. This is explained by the distribution of playtime and the generated total danger between game components. Table (1) is a shortened version of the overall dashboard, which indicates players' performance indicators. The extended version also displays individual XG, XGoT, and classic indicators such as plus-minus, Corsi from the danger zone and etc.

6 Discussion

While the built rating approximates the player efficiency well, it is still worth to draw some of the drawbacks. This approach works well at a distance, not only because the average team's level becomes more robust with an increasing number of games played, but also because the total player performance is robust too: deviations are smoothed out over time. The player's score in a game can change a lot due to a single episode, which the player may not have had the opportunity to influence. Therefore, we recommend applying this approach to evaluate player efficiency in a large segment of games. At the same time, when evaluating team efficiency, the period does not matter.

The aspect that can be strengthened is forecasting team's performance depending on the player and their efficiency. Firstly, this will introduce a second level of opposition into the model. Hockey players battle against certain opponents but not against the line of average players, so their efficiency depends on the opponents' level of efficiency. Secondly, it will also help to build the rating at the beginning of the season in such leagues, where the rosters vary significantly not only between seasons but also within one season.

The meaningful aspect that has to be improved is players' comparison in different leagues and forecasting their future performance in another league. High-performance metrics of a player, for example, in the SHL do not reduce uncertainty about his future efficiency in the NHL, since no formula balances players from different leagues.

Efforts should be made to identify positional and shot quality factors. It will shed more light on snipers' efficiency and their quality to find a moment for shooting and realize it. Also, it will reduce entropy in disputes about the realization influence on the player and team's results.

7 Conclusion

While the value of the majority of shots is low, we find that there are game situations when the probability to score is higher than not. Player's performance player is determined mostly by position factors, but leaders in addition can increase a potential danger of their shots.

Whereas the approach for player assessing has some limitations and disadvantages, its main advantage is that it can rate players in any league. It makes possible to scout almost any player. The data obtained can be used as a digital substrate for managerial decisions.

Along the way interpreted XG and XGoT models were built that evolves discussion about the goals' nature. We proved that the goals nature in considered leagues are the same. That's why we offer to apply XG and XGoT in all leagues without any doubt instead of Corsi, Fenwick, and Plus-Minus.

Acknowledgments. The authors acknowledge Saint-Petersburg State University for a research project 103905424.

References

1. Liu, G., Schulte, O.: Deep reinforcement learning in ice hockey for context-aware player evaluation. arXiv preprint arXiv:1805.11088 (2018)
2. Schulte, O., Khademi, M., Gholami, S., Zhao, Z., Javan, M., Desaulniers, P.: A Markov game model for valuing actions, locations, and team performance in ice hockey. Data Min. Knowl. Disc. **31**, 1735–1757 (2017). https://doi.org/10.1007/s10618-017-0496-z
3. Schulte, O., Zhao, Z., Javan, M., Desaulnier, P.: Apples-to-Apples: Clustering and Ranking NHL Players Using Location Information and Scoring Impact. In: 2017 Sloan Sports Analytics Conference (2017)
4. Nandakumar, N., Jensen, S.T.: Historical perspectives and current directions in hockey analytics. Ann. Rev. Stat. Appl. **6**, 19–36 (2019). https://doi.org/10.1146/annurev-statistics-030718-105202
5. Johansson, U., Erik, W., Arsalan, S.: How analytics is changing ice hockey. In: Linköping Hockey Analytics Conference (2022)
6. Macdonald, B.: An expected goals model for evaluating NHL teams and players. In: Proceedings for MIT Sloan Sports Analytics Conference (2012)
7. Lambrix, P., Carlsson, N.: Performance metrics for ice hockey accounting for goal importance. In: Linköping Hockey Analytics Conference, pp. 11–25, September 2022. https://doi.org/10.3384/ecp191003
8. Vik, J., Shih, M.C., Jansher, R., Carlsson, N., Lambrix, P.: Not all goals are equally important-a study for the NHL (Extended). In: Presented at 8th MathSport International, p. 1 (2021)
9. Ryder A.: Shot quality. Work. Pap., Hockey Analytics (2004). http://hockeyanalytics.com/Research_files/Shot_Quality.pdf
10. Vollman, R.: Hockey Abstract Presents... Stat Shot: The Ultimate Guide to Hockey Analyt-ics. ECW Press (2016)
11. Mauboussin, M.J.: The Success Equation: Untangling Skill and Luck in Business, Sports, and Investing. Harvard Business Review Press, Cambridge (2012)
12. Gramacy, R.B., Jensen, S.T., Taddy, M.: Estimating player contribution in hockey with regularized logistic regression. J. Quant. Anal. Sports **9**(1), 97–111 (2013). https://doi.org/10.1515/jqas-2012-0001
13. Rathke, A.: An examination of expected goals and shot efficiency in soccer. J. Hum. Sport Exercise **12**(2), 514–529 (2017)
14. Schuckers, M.E., Lock, D.F., Wells, C., Knickerbocker, C.J., Lock, R.H.: National Hockey League skater ratings based upon all on-ice events: an adjusted minus/plus probability (AMPP) approach. Unpublished manuscript, vol. 59 (2011)
15. Tegen E.: The best predictor for future performance is expected goals (2015). http://11tegen11.net/2015/01/05/the-best-predictor-for-future-performance-is-expected-goals/
16. Cavus, M., Biecek, P.: Explainable expected goal models for performance analysis in football analytics. In: 2022 IEEE 9th International Conference on Data Science and Advanced Analytics (DSAA), pp. 1–9. IEEE, October 2022. https://doi.org/10.1109/DSAA54385.2022.10032440
17. Bransen, L., Davis, J.: Women's football analyzed: Interpretable expected goals models for women. In: Proceedings of the AI for Sports Analytics (AISA) Workshop at IJCAI, vol. 2021, May 2021
18. Van Haaren, J.: Why would i trust your numbers? On the explainability of expected values in soccer (2021). arXiv preprint arXiv:2105.13778

Soccer Strategy Analytics Using Probabilistic Model Checkers

Rajdeep Singh Hundal[1(✉)], Zhaoyu Liu[1], Bimlesh Wadhwa[1], Zhe Hou[2], Kan Jiang[1], and Jin Song Dong[1]

[1] National University of Singapore, Singapore, Singapore
{rajdeep,e0253678}@u.nus.edu, {bimlesh,jiangkan,dongjs}@comp.nus.edu.sg
[2] Griffith University, Brisbane, Australia
z.hou@griffith.edu.au

Abstract. When it comes to predicting the outcome of soccer matches, there are two main techniques that dominate the betting industry: deep learning and machine learning. However, as with many state-of-the-art applications, these methods often exhibit significant drawbacks. Primarily, they act as *black boxes* where the internal operations are not transparent, making it difficult to discern the cause when predictions fail. In this paper, we explore the potential of using probabilistic model checkers as an alternative approach for predicting soccer match outcomes. This technique, while unconventional, offers greater transparency or *white box* visibility into its operations when compared to state-of-the-art methods. The choice of utilizing probabilistic model checkers is often overlooked due to their propensity to induce state explosion in complex models. To address this, we propose specific strategies aimed at minimizing the state space of a soccer match, thereby mitigating the state explosion issue. We assess the effectiveness of the probabilistic model through various metrics and compare its performance against established deep learning and machine learning baselines. To evaluate its real-world applicability, we also simulate betting based on the predictions of the probabilistic model. This paper concludes by addressing the practical challenges involved in implementing such a predictive model.

Keywords: Soccer Strategy Analytics · Probabilistic Model Checkers

1 Introduction

Soccer, with its dynamic and unpredictable nature, is considered one of the most challenging sports to predict. The complexity arises from the interactions of 22 players and a multitude of possible events such as fouls, free kicks, and penalties that can drastically alter a match's trajectory. This unpredictability is exemplified by incidents like refereeing errors or changes in team formation mid-match, which frequently lead to unexpected match outcomes. One such example is the dramatic 2019/20 UEFA Champions League quarterfinal where Bayern Munich defeated Barcelona with a final match score of 8–2 [2].

J. S. Dong et al. (Eds.): ISACE 2024, LNCS 14794, pp. 249–264, 2024.
https://doi.org/10.1007/978-3-031-69073-0_22

The unpredictability of soccer outcomes not only affects the teams involved but also has wider implications, influencing everything from media coverage to fan reactions and betting markets. Despite these challenges, soccer remains the most watched sport globally, with approximately three billion fans [1]. This immense popularity underscores the significant influence of soccer, impacting not only individuals but also nations and businesses worldwide.

Given the complexities involved, state-of-the-art prediction methods like deep learning and machine learning often fall short due to their *black box* nature, where the reasons behind predictions are not transparent, making it difficult to understand or trust the outcomes. This paper explores the use of probabilistic model checkers as an alternative predictive tool, offering greater transparency and the ability to manage complex model states without overwhelming computational resources. These probabilistic models provide a *white box* approach, enhancing the explainability of predictions, which is crucial for acceptance and reliance in real-world applications.

The primary motivation for adopting probabilistic models lies in their explicit nature, where the processes and transitions are clearly defined and understandable, making these models not only easy to debug but also simple to modify. Such features are essential for adapting to the rapidly changing dynamics of a soccer game. This paper introduces new abstraction strategies to mitigate issues like state explosion and utilizes Electronic Art's FIFA player ratings [7] as probabilistic weights, aiming to refine the accuracy and reliability of soccer match predictions. The effectiveness of our model is assessed against conventional deep learning and machine learning benchmarks, and their real-world applicability is demonstrated through the simulation of betting scenarios, offering insights into both the potential and limitations of this approach.

2 Related Work

Dong et al. [4] researched with using Process Analysis Toolkit (PAT) [8–10], a probabilistic model checker, to analyse tennis matches. In particular, the authors predicted the winning probability of the players during a tiebreak set. The authors then generalised their tiebreak model's winning chance into determining which player has the better overall winning chance with the assumption that a player in favour of winning the tiebreak would also be in favour of winning the entire game. Furthermore, the authors represented the playing ground as a grid. With this notion, the authors applied their probabilistic model to an Australian Open match between Roger Federer and Rafael Nadal and successfully predicted the outcome. During evaluation, so as to get a real-world validation of their prediction strategy, the authors also simulated betting on tennis matches that were in 2014 and reported a net profit of 22.35%.

Siddharth et al. [5] on the other hand, researched on using model-driven inputs (i.e., deep learning predictions) as opposed to those that are driven by empirical match data when predicting the best possible actions soccer players should take once in possession of the ball. In particular, the authors made the case that for a complex sport like soccer, a goal is not determined by a single good event (i.e., action) but rather a sequence of good events. Works done by Spearman [6] supports this notion of considering the events that happen before the shot as well. As such, the authors designed a stateful model based on a Markov Decision Process (MDP) to predict the best action a player should take (i.e., predict the successor state) once in possession of the ball (i.e., current state). Similar to the aforementioned research by Dong et al., the authors divided the playing ground into a 38-zoned grid where the size of each zone represents the expected player density. The authors then evaluated their model's accuracy in determining the next action to take by taking the model's predictions and comparing them with real-life match scenarios. The model attained an accuracy of 0.685 in terms of the top 3 predictions.

In this paper, we adopt a different approach from existing literature as we focus on soccer matches instead of tennis and predict the outcome of a match instead of the best possible action. However, we do follow the existing literature on some modeling and evaluation aspects:

1. **Grid playing ground.** Similar to existing literature, we represented the playing ground as a grid since it significantly reduces the model complexity, as opposed to just points in a vector space. However, we did not split the grid according to player density but rather chose to split the grid symmetrically. This was primarily due to the fact that our probabilistic model already considered player density via other means.
2. **Sequence of good events.** The notion of a goal being the result of a sequence of good events rather than a single event by Siddharth et al. seemed to hold truth in most sports, particularly soccer. Thus, in our efforts to accurately predict the outcome of a soccer match, we similarly used a stateful model which also considers the events leading up to a goal.
3. **Historical player dataset.** Some form of historical player data is needed for any model predicting sports match outcomes, as observed in existing literature. Therefore, we used Electronic Art's FIFA player ratings as our historical player dataset. However, we used the player ratings directly as probabilistic weights as opposed to Siddharth et al. which used them as inputs to their deep learning models instead.
4. **Model driven inputs.** The notion of using a learning-based model to process/filter the initial raw data inputs before they get passed through the stateful model by Siddharth et al. is something that we found incredibly useful and also practiced when designing the probabilistic model for soccer. As the raw data is bound to be noisy, there are numerous machine learning techniques (e.g., recursive feature elimination) that can assist in determining the best features to use.
5. **Probability generalisation.** Dong et al. generalised their tiebreak model's winning chance to the overall winning chance with the assumption that if a player is favoured to win the tiebreak, the player would then be in favour to win the entire match. We found this assumption to be quite reasonable as it then eliminates the need of modelling an entire match. Thus, we only

modelled a segment of a soccer game and generalised the winning chance attained to the overall winning chance.

6. **Betting.** To attain a real-world benchmark of their model, Dong et al. simulated betting over a year's worth of tennis matches. We found this to be an accurate way of determining if a model is indeed better than those currently used in the industry. Likewise, we simulated betting over six years worth of English Premier League soccer matches.

3 Probabilistic Model for Soccer

In this section, we first introduce the issue of state explosion in complex stateful models, in the context of a soccer match. After that, we define the three key abstractions any stateful model of a soccer match needs in order to avoid this issue and remove any redundancies to further improve processing speeds. Lastly, we formally define the CSP [8] and PCSP [10] models for soccer using PAT [9], CSP#, and PCSP#.

3.1 State Explosion

State explosion is where the number of states increases exponentially during a program execution, thereby incurring additional computational overhead and processing time. A sport like tennis is less susceptible to state explosion since it only involves two players but for a sport like soccer, one can easily see how the number of states would get out of control, as shown in Fig. 1a. Firstly to simplify things, the pitch can be represented by a $3 \times 7 + 2$ grid with two teams on it, the blue team and the red team. We then define a match's state to be the positions of the players and the ball on the grid. In Fig. 1a, we can see that the player in possession of the ball has many choices to make. The player could shoot, pass, dribble, or get tackled – all of which would result in a different state. Moreover, there are still twenty-one players left and they can move anywhere on the pitch, changing the state of the match at any given instant.

To really get an estimate of how big the state space is, the grid in Fig. 1a following constraints: (1) there can only be one player in a box at any time; (2) the ball must always be with a player. We see that there are $23! \approx 2.59 \times$ 1022 possible states (i.e., permutations without replacement) for the just player positions alone. Coupling this with the twenty two possible ball positions for each permutation we arrive at a grand total of $23! \times 22$ states. It is simply infeasible to deal with a model of such magnitude. Thus, in order to efficiently model soccer matches in a stateful manner, the complexity of the problem has to be reduced even further with abstractions.

3.2 Abstractions

We have in fact been using an abstracted model all this while. Representing the pitch as a $3{\times}7{+}2$ grid is actually one form of abstraction as it puts a constraint on

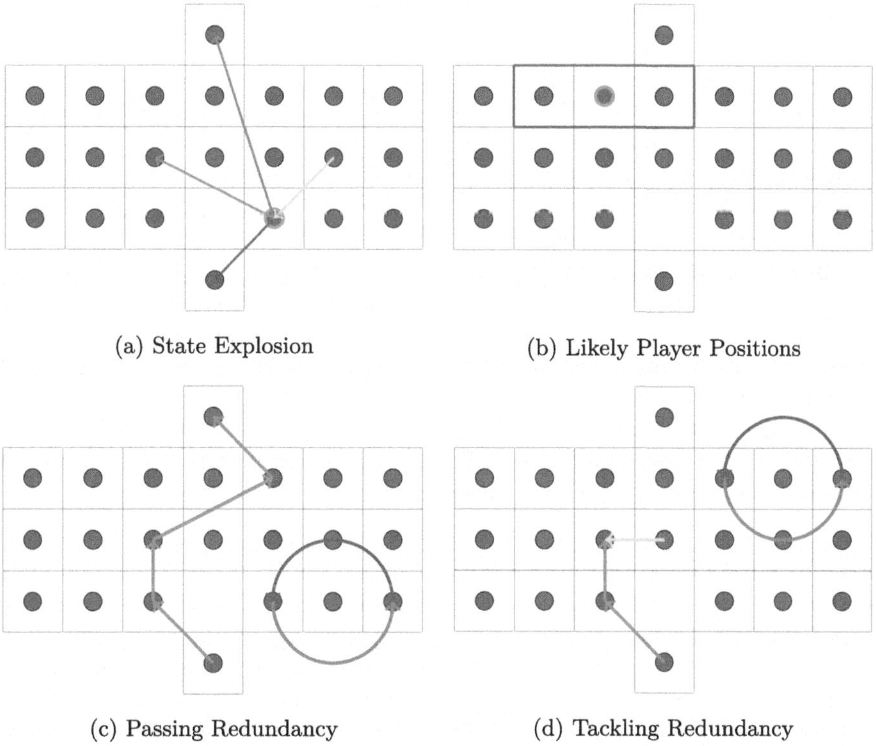

Fig. 1. (a) State explosion example where a green circle around a player represents that the player currently is in possession of the ball, a cyan arrow represents a shot, a magenta arrow represents a pass, a brown arrow represents dribbling, and a yellow arrow represents getting tackled. (b) A left forward (i.e., the player with the green circle) is most likely to be in the positions indicated by the magenta box than any other position. (c) The magenta and cyan arrows represent players passing side-ways to each other i.e., a redundant infinite loop. The brown arrows represent an example where players are only allowed to pass forward, removing the redundancy. (d) The magenta and cyan arrows represent players tackling each other, another redundant infinite loop. The brown and yellow arrows represent an example where the state trace stops once a player gets tackled, removing the redundancy. (Color figure online)

the possible positions which players can be at. The number of possible states and redundancies can however be further reduced with three additional abstraction techniques.

Fixed Positions Only. One of the ways to effectively reduce the state space is to simply disallow players from moving. Doing this would bring the total number of states down to just 1×22. The effects of such an abstraction is twofold:

1. **Increased accuracy.** At first glance, cutting down the states by such an amount might seem like a con rather than a pro due to the amount of information that is just being frivolously discarded. However when it comes to soccer, most of the time the teams follow a formation which their managers instruct them to play in. Take a left forward for example. Very rarely will a left forward be found behind the midfielders or on the right side of the pitch, as seen in Fig. 1b. The exact same reasoning can be applied to all the other positions as well. In hindsight, the information loss by fixing the positions of players is not as huge as it seems as players mostly stick to their position in the formation (or relatively near to their position) throughout the match anyways. In fact, a model keeping to formation is bound to be more accurate than a model which allows players to instantly be anywhere on the pitch at any point of time.
2. **No more state explosion.** With the number of states brought down to a mere 1×22 states, a model modelling this number of states would no doubt be free from any sort of state explosion.

Pass Forward Only. Having 1×22 instead of $23! \times 22$ states would definitely speed up the processing time of the soccer model in question, but it can be even faster if existing redundancies in the model are removed. In Fig. 1c, it is observed that passing sideways (or backwards) inadvertently creates infinite loops, which are of no use as they provide no further information, given that the match is not progressing. By adopting a pass forward only strategy, as shown in Fig. 1c, players are restricted to passing only to teammates ahead, thereby eliminating redundant loops and reducing the number of state transitions, further speeding up the processing time.

Score Only. Having removed loops between players of the same team, consideration of loops between players of opposing teams shows that two players tackling each other, as depicted in Fig. 1d, also causes a redundant loop. To address this, we can terminate the state trace once a player is tackled. Further refining this approach, we halt the traces where a player loses the ball to the opposing team, thereby eliminating the loop where the ball is indefinitely transferred between the two teams. This results in two types of traces, those that were stopped (i.e., player loses ball to opposing team) and those that were not (i.e., team retains the ball). Intuitively, traces that were not stopped generally lead to a team scoring, while stopped traces result in a failure to score, hence the name score only. This now builds the foundation for a CSP soccer model where, for some known initial state:

$$\begin{aligned} \text{chanceScore} &= \frac{\Sigma \text{tracesNotStopped}}{\Sigma \text{traces}}, \\ \text{chanceNotScore} &= 1 - \text{chanceScore} \end{aligned} \tag{1}$$

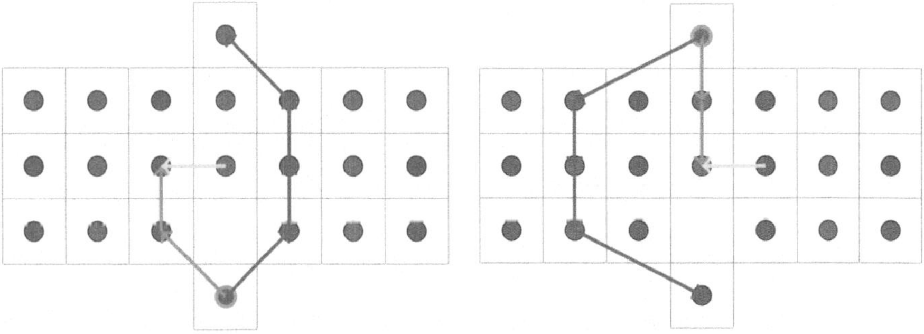

(a) Blue Team Model (b) Red Team Model

Fig. 2. For both models, there are two types of traces present. The first type is represented by the brown and yellow arrows which signify the respective team losing the ball to the opposing team (i.e., not scoring). The second type is represented by the magenta arrows which signify the respective team scoring. The green circle signifies the start of both trace types (i.e., the goalkeeper). (Color figure online)

3.3 CSP Soccer Model

Equation 1 defines the scope of what a CSP soccer prediction model should generally output, i.e., the chance of scoring. However, to make this practically useful, Eq. 1 can be further simplified:

$$\begin{aligned} \text{chanceScoreBlue} &= \frac{\Sigma\text{tracesNotStoppedBlue}}{\Sigma\text{tracesBlue}}, \\ \text{chanceScoreRed} &= \frac{\Sigma\text{tracesNotStoppedRed}}{\Sigma\text{tracesRed}} \end{aligned} \tag{2}$$

This allows for a direct comparison between the scoring chances of both teams. The challenge, however, is how a model checker can differentiate between the blue team's traces and the red team's traces to achieve the output specified in Eq. 2. A straightforward solution to this issue is to maintain two separate models, one for each team, as illustrated in Fig. 2, facilitating clear differentiation and individual analysis of each team's scoring potential. In Fig. 2a, the ball begins with the blue team's goalkeeper, representing the initial state. As there are only two types of tracesthose that are stopped (i.e., when a player loses the ball to the opposing team) and those that are not stopped (i.e., when the team retains the ball and scores)it follows that all state traces in Fig. 2a pertain to ΣtracesBlue, where the blue team attacks and the red team defends. Similarily, all state traces in Fig. 2b pertains to ΣtracesRed. This structure allows for a straightforward analysis of each team's offensive and defensive dynamics based on the type of traces observed.

CSP# Semantics. Having established the necessity for two models in CSP#, we now delve into the modeling specifics, using the blue team as an example. Given that in CSP#, ProcessA = ProcessB [ ] ProcessC means that either ProcessB or ProcessC may execute once ProcessA is called, each player can be modelled as a process. Modelling each player in the blue team and the red team's goal keeper as processes, we have:

$$\begin{aligned} \text{KepBlue} &= K_1, \\ \text{DefBlue} &= D_1 \; [\,] \; D_2 \; [\,] \; \cdots \; [\,] \; D_i, \\ \text{MidBlue} &= M_1 \; [\,] \; M_2 \; [\,] \; \cdots \; [\,] \; M_j, \\ \text{ForBlue} &= F_1 \; [\,] \; F_2 \; [\,] \; \cdots \; [\,] \; F_k, \\ \text{KepRed} &= K_2 \end{aligned} \tag{3}$$

where $i + j + k = 10$, reflecting the eleven players on the blue team. Building on the fact that in CSP#, a process at its core engages in events which can in turn be followed up by another process i.e., ProcessA = eventA → ProcessB, each player process engages in an event before passing control to the next player process:

$$\begin{aligned} K_1 &= \text{event}K_1 \rightarrow \text{DefBlue}, \\ D_l &= \text{event}D_l \rightarrow \text{MidBlue}, \\ M_m &= \text{event}M_m \rightarrow \text{ForBlue}, \\ F_n &= \text{event}F_n \rightarrow \text{KepRed}, \\ K_2 &= \text{event}K_2 \rightarrow \text{Skip} \end{aligned} \tag{4}$$

where $1 \leq l \leq i$, $1 \leq m \leq j$, and $1 \leq n \leq k$. These constraints are designed to enforce the *pass forward only* abstraction. For example, starting the match with the process KepBlue leads to the following trace pattern:

$$\text{event}K_1 \rightarrow \text{event}D_l \rightarrow \text{event}M_m \rightarrow \text{event}F_n \rightarrow \text{event}K_2 \rightarrow \text{Skip} \tag{5}$$

with Skip gracefully terminating the current process. Lastly, we enhance the model to include multiple events for each player:

$$\begin{aligned} K_1 &= (\text{event}_1 K_1 \rightarrow \text{DefBlue}) \; [\,] \; \cdots \; [\,] \; (\text{event}_o K_1 \rightarrow \text{DefBlue}), \\ D_l &= (\text{event}_1 D_l \rightarrow \text{MidBlue}) \; [\,] \; \cdots \; [\,] \; (\text{event}_p D_l \rightarrow \text{MidBlue}), \\ M_m &= (\text{event}_1 M_m \rightarrow \text{ForBlue}) \; [\,] \; \cdots \; [\,] \; (\text{event}_q M_m \rightarrow \text{ForBlue}), \\ F_n &= (\text{event}_1 F_n \rightarrow \text{KepRed}) \; [\,] \; \cdots \; [\,] \; (\text{event}_r F_n \rightarrow \text{KepRed}), \\ K_2 &= (\text{event}_1 K_2 \rightarrow \text{Skip}) \; [\,] \; \cdots \; [\,] \; (\text{event}_s K_2 \rightarrow \text{Skip}) \end{aligned} \tag{6}$$

where the blue team's goal keeper, defenders, midfielders, forwards, and red team's goal keeper has o, p, q, r, and s events respectively. Furthermore, by specifying these events to be non-movement based events like short and long passes, the *fixed positions only* abstraction can be implicitly enforced.

3.4 PCSP Soccer Model

Having defined the CSP soccer model, it might initially seem complete. However, the model presents a fundamental flawit assumes that events within a match occur non-deterministically. According to Eq. 6, the selection of events is modeled without determinism. Yet, in realistic soccer gameplay, players are more likely to engage in actions they are proficient in rather than those they are less skilled at. For instance, defenders are generally more inclined to pass than shoot. This discrepancy between model and reality can be addressed by transitioning from a CSP to a PCSP (Probabilistic CSP) model, which incorporates the likelihood of players performing actions based on their skills and typical behaviors, thereby refining the model to better mirror actual soccer dynamics.

PCSP# Semantics. By integrating probabilistic weights to Eq. 6, we shift from non-deterministic to probabilistic event handling in the model. For brevity, only the blue team's goal keeper's events are depicted, but this approach is applicable across all player processes:

$$K_1 = \begin{cases} (\text{event}_1 K_1 \rightarrow \text{DefBlue}) & \text{weight}_1 K_1 \\ (\text{event}_2 K_1 \rightarrow \text{DefBlue}) & \text{weight}_2 K_1 \\ \vdots & \\ (\text{event}_o K_1 \rightarrow \text{DefBlue}) & \text{weight}_o K_1 \end{cases} \tag{7}$$

This enhancement facilitates the application of the *score only* abstraction, distinguishing events as either successful (not losing the ball to the opposing team) or unsuccessful (losing the ball, leading to the immediate termination of the trace) with their respective probabilistic weights:

$$K_1 = \begin{cases} (\text{successful}_1 K_1 \rightarrow \text{DefBlue}) & \text{weight}_1 K_1 \\ (\text{successful}_2 K_1 \rightarrow \text{DefBlue}) & \text{weight}_2 K_1 \\ \vdots & \\ (\text{unsuccessful}_o K_1 \rightarrow \text{Skip}) & \text{weight}_o K_1 \end{cases} \tag{8}$$

The format in Eq. 8, when applied to all player processes in Eq. 3, explicitly models the scoring probability for the blue team as outlined in Eq. 2 chanceScoreBlue can be attained by finding the probability that process KepBlue reaches the end without any stoppages in PAT. Replicating these steps for the red team completes the model, enabling similar calculations for their scoring chances as well. This comprehensive modeling provides a robust framework for predicting outcomes based on team behaviors and game dynamics.

3.5 Probability Generalisation

With the calculated probabilities of scoring during an attack for both the blue and red teams, we employ probability generalization to infer that the team with a higher likelihood of scoring during an attack is also more likely to win the match. The rationale for this generalization is twofold:

1. **Reduced model complexity.** This simplification allows the model to represent only a part of the entire 90-min soccer match, further aiding in the reduction of the state space and averting state explosion alongside other abstractions already applied.
2. **Speed.** The diminished state space considerably accelerates PAT's evaluation process. For example, evaluating a whole season's worth of matches (380 matches with 2 models each totaling 760 models) takes PAT merely 6 min. This translates to approximately 5 s per model or 10 s per match, demonstrating the efficiency of the applied abstractions.

3.6 Events and Probabilistic Weights

To determine the events and their respective weights we utilized data from Electronic Art's FIFA franchise. The FIFA franchise is an online soccer video game which provides ratings (on a scale of 1–100) for approximately 35 events, for every soccer player. Using statistical methods such as Correlation Heat Maps, Select-K-Best, and Recursive Feature Elimination, we narrowed down these events to 11 events as depicted in Table 1. Using intuition, we further assigned these 11 events to each of the five different process types. For example, goal keeping events are only applicable to goal keepers, shooting events are not applicable to defenders since they rarely shoot etc. The event ratings are directly used as the probabilistic weights in PAT for the player processes. In the context of a defender player process, but also applicable to other process types as well, Eq. 8 now becomes:

$$D_l = \begin{cases} (\text{shortPassing} \rightarrow \text{MidBlue}) & \text{weight}_{shp}D_l \\ (\text{longPassing} \rightarrow \text{MidBlue}) & \text{weight}_{lop}D_l \\ (\text{intercepted} \rightarrow \text{Skip}) & \text{weight}_{int}D_l \\ (\text{standingTackled} \rightarrow \text{Skip}) & \text{weight}_{stt}D_l \\ (\text{slidingTackled} \rightarrow \text{Skip}) & \text{weight}_{slt}D_l \end{cases} \tag{9}$$

where $\text{weight}_{shp}D_l$ and $\text{weight}_{lop}D_l$ are taken from defender D_l's FIFA event ratings. In contrast, $\text{weight}_{int}D_l$, $\text{weight}_{stt}D_l$, and $\text{weight}_{slt}D_l$ are aggregated from the red team's forward's FIFA event ratings. In other words, the unsuccessful event weights for a player from the attacking team are taken from the defending team's players that are positioned near the attacking team player. This was implemented as the probability of failure should come from the defending team's ability to defend instead of the attacking team.

3.7 Formation Remapping and Differentiating Passing Events

With a fixed grid configuration of $3 \times 7 + 2$, some team formations like 3–5–1–1 cannot be directly fitted onto the grid. Thus, we remapped formations which

Table 1. Selected events for the five different process types.

Event	Event Type	K_1	D_l	M_m	F_n	K_2
Finishing	Successful				✓	
Heading Accuracy	Successful				✓	
Short Passing	Successful		✓	✓		
Volleys	Successful				✓	
Long Passing	Successful		✓	✓		
Long Shots	Successful			✓	✓	
Interceptions	Unsuccessful		✓	✓	✓	
Standing Tackle	Unsuccessful		✓	✓	✓	
Sliding Tackle	Unsuccessful		✓	✓	✓	
Goal Keeper Handling	Unsuccessful					✓
Goal Keeper Kicking	Successful	✓				

Table 2. The coordinates of the player passing the ball with respect to the $3 \times 7 + 2$ grid is (i, j) and depending on what type of passing happens, only certain players will be eligible to receive the ball.

Event	Eligible Players
Short Passing	$(i-2, j+1)$, $(i-1, j+1)$, $\cdots$,$(i+2, j+1)$
Long Passing	$(i-6, j+1)$, $(i-5, j+1)$, $\cdots$, $(i-3, j+1)$
	$(i+3, j+1)$, $(i+4, j+1)$, $\cdots$, $(i+6, j+1)$

could not fitted into something similar that could. For example, 3–5–1–1 was remapped to 3–6–1. There was also a need to differentiate between short passes and long passes. As depicted in Fig. 3a, the current model architecture inherently allows player processes to execute a short pass and long pass to players of similar distances away. Thus, we used a player eligibility matrix, shown in Table 2, to effectively differentiate the two passing events via distance as demonstrated in Fig. 3b. Process guards were used to enforce this notion of eligibility, transforming Eq. 3 to:

$$\begin{aligned}
\text{KepBlue} &= [\text{guard}K_1]K_1, \\
\text{DefBlue} &= [\text{guard}D_1]D_1 \ [\,] \ [\text{guard}D_2]D_2 \ [\,] \ \cdots \ [\,] \ [\text{guard}D_i]D_i, \\
\text{MidBlue} &= [\text{guard}M_1]M_1 \ [\,] \ [\text{guard}M_2]M_2 \ [\,] \ \cdots \ [\,] \ [\text{guard}M_j]M_j, \\
\text{ForBlue} &= [\text{guard}F_1]F_1 \ [\,] \ [\text{guard}F_2]F_2 \ [\,] \ \cdots \ [\,] \ [\text{guard}F_k]F_k, \\
\text{KepRed} &= [\text{guard}K_2]K_2
\end{aligned} \tag{10}$$

where player processes are blocked from being executed by their respective guards if they are ineligible to receive the ball.

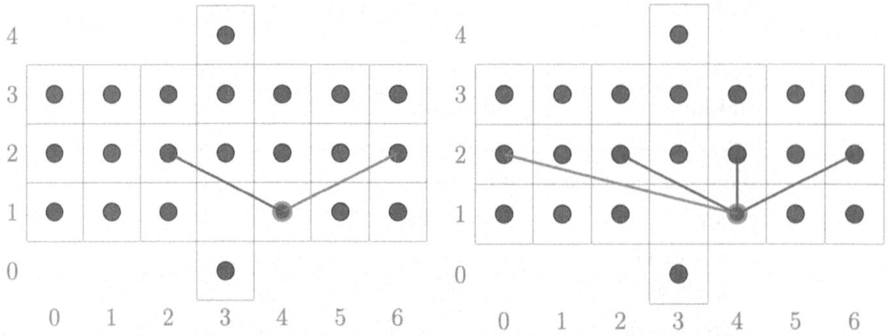

(a) Without Eligibility Matrix (b) With Eligibility Matrix

Fig. 3. (a) Here the blue team's defender has the ball (green circle) at box coordinates (4, 1). Furthermore, the magenta arrow depicts a short pass to a midfielder at (2, 2) while the cyan arrow depicts a long pass to another midfielder at (6, 2). (b) Based off Table 2, the players now eligible to receive a short pass from (4, 1) are (2, 2), (4, 2), and (6, 2). Likewise, the only player eligible to receive a long pass from (4, 1) is (0, 2). (Color figure online)

4 Results

In this section we discuss the experimental setting which includes the data sets, baselines, and metrics used to evaluate the proposed PCSP model. Secondly, we present and discuss the evaluation results.

4.1 Experimental Setting

The PCSP model uses two distinct types of input, leading to the use of two different datasets for evaluation:

1. **Match Dataset.** Sourced through web crawling, this dataset provides essential information from the past six seasons of the English Premier League (EPL), from 2015/16 to 2020/21. It includes team names, players, formations, and match outcomes, with formations being the official ones submitted to the EPL by team managers before the match.
2. **Ratings Dataset.** Acquired from online repositories like Kaggle, this dataset includes FIFA game events and player ratings across six editions, from FIFA 16 to FIFA 21. The FIFA series names its editions with respect to the forthcoming season, so FIFA 16 ratings are used for the 2015/16 season, FIFA 17 for 2016/17 etc.

Furthermore, two different split variations were used on the data sets:

1. **No Split.** This is used to determine the PCSP model's raw prediction accuracy. Since stateful models do not require training, there is no need to divide the dataset into training and testing subsets.

2. **Random Split.** Due to learning-based algorithms inherent need for distinct training and testing subsets, the dataset is randomly split in an 80:20 ratio (i.e., 80% for training and 20% for testing). For a fair comparison, the PCSP model for this setting is only assessed using the test set.

As with any classification problem, there needs to be some form metric so as to gauge the quality of the results. As such, two metrics were used in addition to accuracy:

1. **F1 Score.** Combining precision and recall into a single value, the F1 Score (F1) is a widely used metric when evaluating classifiers. As there are multiple F1 variations, Macro F1 was used where all classes are treated equally so as to maintain fairness.
2. **Mean Absolute Error.** By assigning weights to the prediction outcome, Mean Absolute Error (MAE) can also be used to evaluate the classifiers with respect to the EPL table. For example, in the EPL table a win is considered as three points, a draw is considered as one point and a loss is considered as zero points. So if the actual outcome was a win but a draw was predicted, the error with respect to the EPL table would be $3 - 1 = 2$.

In order to benchmark the PCSP model, there needs to be baselines. The state-of-the-art applications used for prediction in most betting organisations is undoubtedly deep learning and machine learning. Thus, these two applications were configured and then used as baselines for the PCSP model. Moreover so as to maintain fairness, these baselines only took in as input the exact same features used in the PCSP model. For the deep learning baseline, a fully connected three layer classifier was configured with the Adam optimizer and properly regularised to reduce over fitting (i.e., complexity reduction, input normalization, and early stopping). For the machine learning baseline, we used K-Nearest-Neighbour (KNN), Support Vector Machine (SVM), and Silas [3].

Lastly, since this is a multi-class classification problem with three possible categories (i.e., draw, home win, or away win), unlike the learning-based baselines where the number of categories for classification can be explicitly configured, the PCSP model requires some additional post-processing. Since for every match there are two PCSP models, one where the home team attacks and another where the away team attacks, PAT evaluates these models and outputs the attacking team's scoring chance for each model. Moreover, as the scoring chance is in the format of $[min, max]$, the mean was used as the overall scoring chance of the attacking team. For example, if the home team was attacking, their scoring chance would be $c_{home} = (min_{home} + max_{home})/2$. The scoring chance is then generalised to be the overall winning chance. The match outcome was subsequently classified as such:

$$\text{Prediction} = \begin{cases} \text{Draw} & \text{if } |c_{\text{home}} - c_{\text{away}}| < \text{threshold} \\ \text{Home Win} & \text{if } c_{\text{home}} > c_{\text{away}} \\ \text{Away Win} & \text{if } c_{\text{away}} > c_{\text{home}} \end{cases} \tag{11}$$

Table 3. This table depicts the no-split multi-class classification results for the PCSP model with varying threshold values. OAccuracy refers to the overall accuracy while HAccuracy, AAccuracy, and DAccuracy refers to accuracy for the individual classes, that is, home win, away win, and draw respectively.

Threshold	OAccuracy	HAccuracy	AAccuracy	DAccuracy	F1 Score	MAE Score
0.0001	0.493	0.626	0.666	0.004	0.373	1.164
0.0005	0.489	0.617	0.652	0.026	0.384	1.160
0.0010	0.486	0.610	0.637	0.043	0.390	1.155
0.0050	0.459	0.521	0.556	0.209	0.422	1.141
0.0100	0.432	0.425	0.471	0.390	0.425	1.110
0.0500	0.244	0.036	0.021	0.944	0.160	1.207
0.1000	0.232	0.006	0.003	0.974	0.131	1.221

Table 4. This table depicts the random split multi-class classification results for the PCSP model as well as the baselines. Furthermore, DL+PCSP and KNN+PCSP refers to models where the predictions from the PCSP model were included as features into the respective learning-based models to determine if they could benefit from the PCSP model's predictions.

Model	OAccuracy	HAccuracy	AAccuracy	DAccuracy	F1 Score	MAE Score
PCSP	0.432	0.423	0.454	**0.425**	**0.423**	1.167
DL	0.524	0.760	0.549	0.004	0.379	1.112
KNN	0.432	0.664	0.331	0.075	0.339	1.298
SILAS	0.548	0.809	0.531	0.028	0.413	1.018
DL+PCSP	0.524	0.757	0.558	0.000	0.381	1.110
KNN+PCSP	0.450	0.659	0.362	0.123	0.372	1.213

4.2 Evaluation Results and Discussions

Table 3 summarises the raw accuracy of the PCSP model for the no-split variation. It can be seen that with low threshold values, the overall accuracy increases but at the expense of the draw accuracy. Thus, a threshold value of 0.0100 was found to be optimal as it has the best balance between all of the accuracy metrics and the best F1 and MAE scores. Although the overall accuracy of 0.432 might seem subpar, the PCSP model is inherently better than randomly guessing as that would only lead to an accuracy of 0.333. This inherently shows that **there is some value to be gained** by using FIFA player ratings as probabilistic approximations with appropriate abstractions in a stateful model.

Table 4 summarises the multi-class classification results for the PCSP model as well as the baselines when evaluated on the random split data set. It can be seen that in terms of overall accuracy, DL and SILAS outperforms PCSP while KNN matches PCSP. However, when it comes to predicting draws, PCSP outperforms all of the learning-based models by a significant margin. Moreover, PCSP has the best F1 scoremost likely due to its ability to accurately classify draws

Table 5. Here, the 1×2 net profit/loss when betting \$100 per match is shown for six betting companies. B365, BW, IN, PS, VCB and WH refers to Bet365, Bet&Win, Interwetten, Pinnacle Sports, VC Bet, and William Hill respectively.

Season	Matches	B365	BW	IN	PS	VCB	WH
2015/16	380	-2553	-3507	-4027	-2325	-2620	-3625
2016/17	380	-321	-1228	-1116	-211	-240	-943
2017/18	380	430	-488	-1174	814	356	-947
2018/19	380	-1496	-2255	-2178	-1389	-1649	-2347
2019/20	380	2506	2481	2346	3231	2837	2423
2020/21	184	428	450	340	909	413	406
Total	2084	-1006	-4547	-5809	1029	-903	-5033

and thus, achieve a good balance between HAccuracy, AAccuracy, and DAccuracy. Furthermore, although DL+PCSP achieved the same overall accuracy as DL (which could be attributed to the fact that deep learning heavily relies on large data sets), it is observed that KNN+PCSP achieved better overall accuracy, draw accuracy, F1, and MAE scores then KNN. Thus, this shows that **the value gained from probabilistic models can then be transferred** to these learning-based models as well. Lastly, in order to attain a real world benchmark of the PCSP model, we simulated betting as shown in Table 5. It was observed that the PCSP model was only **effective in the two most recent EPL seasons**, resulting in a profit across all six betting companies used in 2019/20 and 2020/21. The reason for this could be attributed to technological advancements where FIFA player ratings are more accurate in the recent seasons.

5 Conclusion

In conclusion, the feasibility of a probabilistic model for soccer has been established, facilitated by strategic abstractions to curb state explosion. The probabilistic model's effectiveness was gauged against learning-based baselines, and while it did not top the charts in overall prediction accuracy, it excelled particularly in predicting draws which demonstrated the value of using probabilistic models. Furthermore, this value was then showed to be transferable to learning-based models as well. Real-world applicability was also tested through simulated betting using the probabilistic model's predictions, with profitable outcomes in recent seasons due to more accurate FIFA player ratings. Thus, we recommend for future research in this domain to explore more on player rating adjustments for more accurate probabilistic weights.

Declarations

Disclosure of Interests. The authors have no competing interests to declare that are relevant to the content of this article.

References

1. Most popular sport by country 2024. https://worldpopulationreview.com/country-rankings/most-popular-sport-by-country. Accessed 20 May 2024
2. FC Barcelona 28 FC Bayern Munich. http://en.wikipedia.org/w/index.php?title=FC%20Barcelona%202%E2%80%938%20FC%20Bayern%20Munich&oldid=1223325536 (2024). Accessed 20 May 2024
3. Bride, H., et al.: Silas: a high-performance machine learning foundation for logical reasoning and verification. Expert Syst. Appl. **176**, 114806 (2021)
4. Dong, J.S., Shi, L., Jiang, K., Sun, J., et al.: Sports strategy analytics using probabilistic reasoning. In: 2015 20th International Conference on Engineering of Complex Computer Systems (ICECCS), pp. 182–185. IEEE (2015)
5. Siddharth, S., Saurav, S., Kan, J., Bimlesh, W., Song, D.J.: Model driven inputs to aid athlete's decision making. In: 2020 27th Asia-Pacific Software Engineering Conference (APSEC), pp. 485–489. IEEE (2020)
6. Spearman, W.: Beyond expected goals. In: Proceedings of the 12th MIT Sloan Sports Analytics Conference, pp. 1–17 (2018)
7. Sports, E.A.: Ea sports fifa. [PC] (2015-2023). https://www.ea.com/games/fifa/fifa-23
8. Sun, J., Liu, Y., Dong, J.S., Chen, C.: Integrating specification and programs for system modeling and verification. In: 2009 Third IEEE International Symposium on Theoretical Aspects of Software Engineering, pp. 127–135. IEEE (2009)
9. Sun, J., Liu, Y., Dong, J.S., Pang, J.: PAT: towards flexible verification under fairness. In: Bouajjani, A., Maler, O. (eds.) CAV 2009. LNCS, vol. 5643, pp. 709–714. Springer, Heidelberg (2009). https://doi.org/10.1007/978-3-642-02658-4_59
10. Sun, J., Song, S., Liu, Y.: Model checking hierarchical probabilistic systems. In: Dong, J.S., Zhu, H. (eds.) ICFEM 2010. LNCS, vol. 6447, pp. 388–403. Springer, Heidelberg (2010). https://doi.org/10.1007/978-3-642-16901-4_26

Predicting Real-Time Exercise Exertion with Deep Learning: Insights from Wearable Device Data

Aref Smiley(✉) and Joseph Finkelstein

Department of Biomedical Informatics, University of Utah, Salt Lake City, UT, USA
aref.smiley@utah.edu

Abstract. This research utilized physiological signals gathered from wearable devices to forecast levels of physical exertion during exercise using deep learning methods for classification and regression. The study involved ten healthy participants who engaged in cycling exercises lasting 16 min. Data such as ECG, heart rate, oxygen levels, and pedal speed (RPM) were monitored across varying intensities throughout each session. Additionally, participants self-reported their exertion levels at one-minute intervals. These sessions were segmented into eight parts of two minutes each, during which averages of heart rate, RPM, oxygen saturation, and reported exertion levels were calculated for model training. Furthermore, we extracted heart rate variability (HRV) as additional predictive indicators. Employing several feature selection techniques, we identified the most impactful predictors for model training. Our models demonstrated significant accuracy and precision, with training accuracies and F1 scores peaking at 98.2% and 98%, and testing performances achieving a top accuracy and F1 score of 80%.

Keywords: Wearable Technology · Exercise Exertion Prediction · Deep Learning Models

1 Introduction

Regular physical activity is essential for healthy aging, as it helps prevent or slow the progression of various chronic diseases [1, 2]. The American Heart Association and the American College of Sports Medicine recommend that older adults engage in moderate-intensity exercise for at least 30 min, five days a week [3]. An increasing number of older adults and individuals with chronic health conditions participate in unsupervised rehabilitative home-based exercise programs. Such programs often demand physical exertion, which healthcare professionals usually monitor. Continuous monitoring is necessary to mitigate health risks associated with excessive exercise exertion, especially for seniors and individuals with cardiovascular conditions. Currently, exercise exertion levels are assessed in healthcare settings using the Borg Rating of Perceived Exertion (RPE) scale, where patients rate their exertion during exercise [4]. This method, however, has its challenges, particularly during unsupervised sessions. Individuals with limited health literacy might struggle without the guidance of a professional, and engaging in exercise

J. S. Dong et al. (Eds.): ISACE 2024, LNCS 14794, pp. 265–277, 2024.
https://doi.org/10.1007/978-3-031-69073-0_23

can hinder their ability to check the scale consistently. This necessitates the development of an automated system to measure exercise exertion levels in real time using physiological data.

Physical exertion during exercise is closely associated with the activity of the sympathetic nervous system (SNS), a key component of the autonomic nervous system (ANS) [5]. Heart rate variability (HRV), a primary indicator of ANS regulation, plays a crucial role in monitoring physical exertion [6]. By analyzing HRV, we can gain valuable insights into the state of the ANS and consequently understand the levels of exertion experienced during physical activities and rest periods. However, individual differences in HRV responses present a challenge, sparking debate over the best metrics and thresholds for real-time evaluation of exertion levels [7–13].

This exploratory research was designed to create and assess deep learning models, both regression and classification types, for automatically predicting real-time levels of exercise exertion. Through the use of wearable technology, we harvested real-time physiological data and rotational speed measurements (RPMs) from exercise sessions conducted on the interactive bicycle iBikE. These data served as the foundation for training our models, allowing us to accurately examine their ability to forecast exercise exertion.

2 Methods

2.1 System and Data Acquisition

A group of ten healthy adults, ranging in age from 21 to 61 years and comprising 60% females, engaged in a sixteen-minute cycling activity using the innovative iBikE technology [14]. Participants followed a uniform protocol for each session, starting with two minutes of low intensity pedaling without resistance. This was followed by a medium resistance phase lasting four minutes, culminating in a high-intensity session of ten minutes under maximum resistance. The design of the iBikE allowed for on-the-fly adjustments to resistance without disrupting the exercise flow. Participants were encouraged to pedal at their fastest possible rate for the intensive final stretch under the highest resistance setting. This standardized approach ensured consistency across all sessions. Revolutions per minute (RPM) data were collected in real-time using a custom-developed application for the iBikE, which was identified for later use as a predictive factor in our analysis models. Moreover, each minute of the workout, participants were asked to report their perceived exertion level using the revised 1–10 Borg Scale of Perceived Exertion [4], resulting in sixteen exertion ratings per session for each participant.

Throughout the 16-min cycling exercises, participants wore two wearable sensors to gather real-time physiological data, serving as primary predictive variables for our deep-learning analyses. The Actiheart 5, a discreet chest-mounted device integrating a single-lead ECG and activity tracking, was employed for ECG data collection [15]. Renowned for its versatility in research, Actiheart 5 captures ECG waveforms at a fidelity of up to 1024 Hz. This ECG data facilitated the analysis of heart rate variability (HRV) across both time and frequency spectrums, allowing for the extraction of predictive metrics as outlined in Table 2. In addition, oxygen saturation levels and pulse rates were monitored using the WristOx2® pulse oximeter, Model 3150 [16], contributing further predictive inputs to the study (Table 1).

Table 1. Revised 1–10 Borg scale of perceived exertion [4].

10	Maximal (Like my hardest race)
9	Really, Really, Hard
8	Really Hard
7	
6	Hard
5	Challenging
4	Moderate
3	Easy
2	Really Easy
1	Rest

2.2 Analysis

The analysis of collected data involved dividing each 16-min cycling session into eight separate 2-min intervals, ensuring there was no overlap between them. The first interval began at the start of the session and lasted until the 120-s mark, with the following interval starting at 121 s (2:01) and ending at 240 s (4:00), and this pattern continued until all eight 2-min segments were defined. For each segment, we computed the averages for pulse rate, oxygen saturation, self-reported ratings of perceived exertion (RPE), and revolutions per minute (RPM). Consequently, this process yielded eight composite values for each participant's session, each value representing the summarized data from one of the 2-min intervals.

The Kubios HRV software, well-known for its scientific analysis capabilities, evaluated the ECG signals captured during each 2-min window across both time and frequency domains. Table 2 presents the comprehensive HRV features derived using the Kubios HRV software. This software outputs the analysis in a MATLAB® MAT file format, encompassing raw ECG data and RR intervals, along with all results and parameters from the analysis.

Regression and classification analyses were conducted on the identified predictive features. For regression analysis, we utilized the average ratings of perceived exertion (RPE) from each 2-min window. In contrast, for classification analysis, we categorized the sets of predictive features from each 2-min window into two classes based on exertion levels: high exertion, where the average 2-min window RPEs exceeded 3.5, and low exertion, where they were below 3.5.

In order to enhance the predictive capability of the deep learning models, the Rating of Perceived Exertion (RPE) from each 2-min window during the 16-min cycling

Table 2. HRV Parameters Extracted Using the Kubios HRV Software, Adapted from the Kubios HRV User Guide [17].

Parameter (Predictors)	Units	Description
Overview		
Stress index	-	Square root of Baevsky's stress index
PNS index	-	Parasympathetic nervous system activity compared to normal resting values
SNS index	-	Sympathetic nervous system activity compared to normal resting values
HR zones*	[%]	Time spent in Maximum, Hard, Moderate, Light, Very light, and Inactive HR zones
PNS zones*	[%]	Time spent in Very high, High, Normal, Low and Very Low PNS index levels
SNS zones**	[%]	Time spent in Very high, High, Normal, Low and Very low SNS index levels
Energy exp.*	[kcal/min]	Activity related energy expenditure (EE) estimated using Keytel's model
TRIMP*	[TRIMP/min]	Training impulse (TRIMP) according to Banister's exponetial model
Time-Domain		
$\overline{\text{RR}}$	[ms]	The mean of RR intervals
STD RR (SDNN)	[ms]	Standard deviation of RR intervals
$\overline{\text{HR}}$	[1/min]	The mean heart rate
STD HR	[1/min]	Standard deviation of instantaneous heart rate values
Min & Max HR	[1/min]	Minimum and maximum HR computed using N beat moving average (default value: $N = 5$)
RMSSD	[ms]	Square root of the mean squared differences between successive RR intervals
NNxx	[beats]	Number of successive RR interval pairs that differ more than xx ms (default value: xx= 50)
pNNxx	[%]	NNxx divided by the total number of RR intervals
HRV triangular index	-	The integral of the RR interval histogram divided by the height of the histogram
TINN	[ms]	Baseline width of the RR interval histogram
DC, AC**	[ms]	HR deceleration capacity (DC) and acceleration capacity (AC)
SDANN	[ms]	Standard deviation of the averages of RR intervals in 5-min segments
SDNNI	[ms]	Mean of the standard deviations of RR intervals in 5-min segments
Frequency-Domain		
Spectrum		Welch's (or Lomb-Scargle*) periodogram and AR spectrum estimates
Peak frequency	[Hz]	VLF, LF, and HF band peak frequencies
Absolute power	[ms^2]	Absolute powers of VLF, LF, and HF bands
Absolute power	[log]	Natural logarithm transformed values of absolute powers of VLF, LF, and HF bands
Relative power	[%]	Relative powers of VLF, LF, and HF bands VLF [%] = VLF [ms^2]/total power [ms^2] × 100% LF [%] = LF [ms^2]/total power [ms^2] × 100% HF [%] = HF [ms^2]/total power [ms^2] × 100%
Normalized power	[n.u.]	Powers of LF and HF bands in normalised units LF [n.u.] = LF [ms^2]/(total power [ms^2] − VLF [ms^2]) HF [n.u.] = HF [ms^2]/(total power [ms^2] − VLF [ms^2])
LF/HF	-	Ratio between LF and HF band powers
RESP**	[Hz]	Respiration rate (derived from ECG and RR data)
Nonlinear		
SD1	[ms]	In Poincaré plot, the standard deviation perpendicular to the line-of-identity
SD2	[ms]	In Poincaré plot, the standard deviation along the line-of-identity
SD2/SD1	-	Ratio between SD2 and SD1
ApEn	-	Approximate entropy
SampEn	-	Sample entropy
DFA, α_1	-	In detrended fluctuation analysis, short term fluctuation slope
DFA, α_2	-	In detrended fluctuation analysis, long term fluctuation slope
D_2**	-	Correlation dimension
RPA**:		Recurrence plot analysis:
Lmean	[beats]	Mean line length
Lmax	[beats]	Maximum line length
REC	[%]	Recurrence rate
DET	[%]	Determinism
ShanEn		Shannon entropy
MSE**	-	Multiscale entropy for scale factor values $\tau = 1, 2, \ldots, 20$
Time-Varying**		
Overview parameters: Stress index, PNS index, SNS index, EE, TRIMP and RESP		
Time-domain parameters: $\overline{\text{RR}}$, SDNN, $\overline{\text{HR}}$, STD HR, Min HR, Max HR, RMSSD, NNxx, pNNxx, HRV tri ind., TINN		
Frequency-domain parameters: Time-varying spectrum (Spectrogram); VLF, LF and HF peak frequencies; VLF, LF and HF powers in ms^2, log and %; LF and HF powers in n.u.; LF/HF ratio		
Nonlinear parameters: SD1, SD2, SD2/SD1, ApEn, SampEn, DFA α_1 and α_2		

sessions was aligned with the predictive features from the preceding 2-min window. Consequently, this setup allowed the classification and regression algorithms to use these features for forecasting the RPE of the subsequent 2-min window. However, the final 2-min window of each session was excluded from this predictive model due to the absence of a subsequent RPE to predict. This approach led to the incorporation of only the initial seven 2-min windows from each 16-min session into each predictive parameter.

Due to the similarities between the HR data taken from the pulse oximeter and the Actiheart chest-worn sensor, we discarded the data from the pulse oximeter in the final dataset. However, using the pulse oximeter is much easier for data acquisition than the chest-worn sensor. In addition, the RPM and the mean HR values of all 2-min windows were normalized with the first 2-min window mean value. Therefore, we set the value of the first window to 100 and modified the rest of the window RPM means accordingly.

3 Results

3.1 Regression Analysis

In the regression analysis phase, the initial step involved identifying the most effective predictive features through the application of three feature selection algorithms: the F-test, RReliefF, and minimum redundancy maximum relevance (mRMR). The highest-ranking features identified by these methods were subsequently employed to develop and evaluate both Long Short-Term Memory (LSTM) and Gated Recurrent Unit (GRU) deep learning models. The execution of these algorithms and the subsequent modeling processes were conducted using MATLAB, version R2023a.

Feature Selection for Regression Analysis. The dataset, encompassing data from all exercise sessions along with predictive features, served as the input for the algorithms. Figure 1A illustrates the outcomes of the feature selection via the F-test algorithm. This algorithm, identified as fsrftest() in MATLAB, is tailored for regression analyses involving both categorical and continuous data types. It assesses the significance of each predictor individually through an F-test and assigns ranks based on the p-values from the F-test statistics. The top five features that scored highest according to the F-test were selected for developing and evaluating the LSTM and GRU models. These leading features included: 1) "RPM": Revolutions per minute (sourced from iBikE); 2) "mean_HRn": The normalized average heart rate; 3) "RMSSD": The root mean square of successive RR interval differences; 4) "Poincare_SD 1": The standard deviation perpendicular to the line-of-identity on a Poincaré plot; 5) "max_HR": The maximum heart rate, calculated using a 5-beat moving average.

Figure 1B presents the selection results from the RReliefF algorithm. This algorithm, relieff(), also in MATLAB, caters to both regression and classification issues, handling categorical and continuous data types. The top five predictors identified by the RReliefF regression algorithm, selected for the LSTM and GRU models training and testing, were: 1) "RPM": Rotations per minute, from iBikE; 2) "mean_HRn": The normalized mean heart rate; 3) "HF_peak2": The high-frequency peak (Hz), estimated using Welch's periodogram; 4) "EDR": The respiration rate (Hz); 5) "PAI": Pulse Amplitude Index, measured in each exercise session with a Nonin pulse oximeter.

Figure 2 displays the selections made by the mRMR (minimum Redundancy Maximum Relevance) algorithm for feature selection. This algorithm, implemented as fsrmrmr() in MATLAB, is designed for regression analyses incorporating both categorical and continuous features. Features with higher scores in the mRMR analysis are deemed more reliable for selection. For the training and testing of the LSTM and GRU models, the five features with the highest mRMR scores were selected. These include: 1)

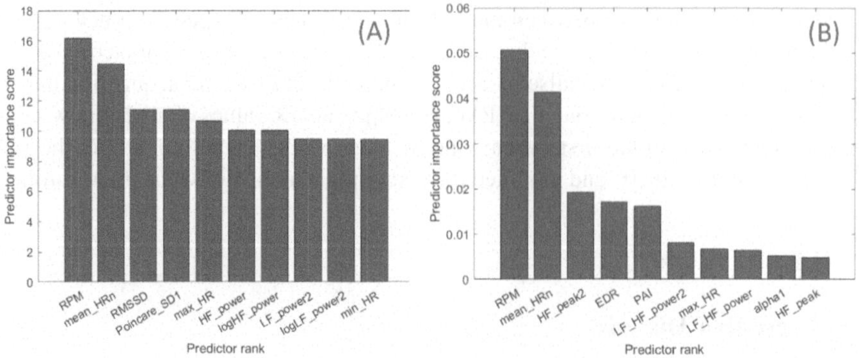

Fig. 1. A) Outcomes from the feature selection via the F-test algorithm. B) Outcomes from the RReliefF feature selection algorithm tailored for regression analysis.

"mean_HRn": Normalized heart rate values recorded during each exercise session; 2) "ApEn": Approximate Entropy; 3) "LF_power_prc": The percentage of low-frequency power, calculated using Welch's periodogram method; 4) "PAI": Pulse Amplitude Index, measured in every exercise session with a Nonin pulse oximeter; 5) "REC": The rate of recurrence.

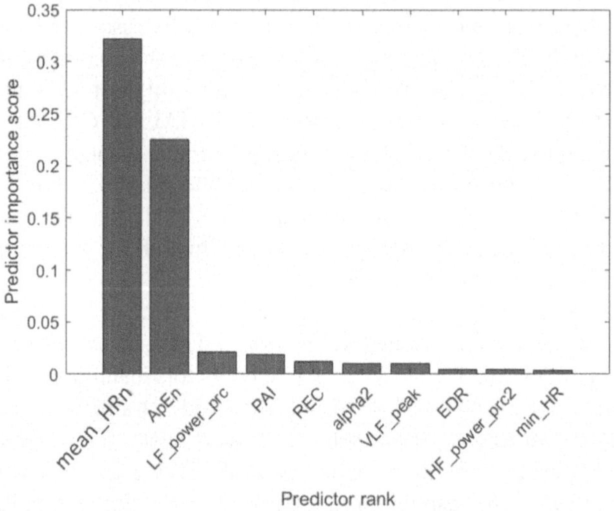

Fig. 2. Results of the mRMR algorithm's feature selection for regression analysis.

LSTM Regression Model. The Long Short-Term Memory (LSTM) model, a type of Recurrent Neural Network (RNN), is a powerful tool in deep learning for handling sequential data. Unlike traditional neural networks, an LSTM node processes inputs and produces outputs, which are then combined with subsequent inputs for future computations. What sets LSTM apart is its unique ability to maintain an internal state, allowing it to effectively manage long sequences of data. This is a significant advantage over standard RNNs, which tend to focus on more recent information [18]. This characteristic of LSTM makes it particularly effective for forecasting in domains such as time series analysis, financial and economic forecasting, including the volatility of the S&P 500, demonstrating its significant utility in predicting complex patterns over extended periods [19–21].

The LSTM network's structure, developed in MATLAB, consists of a four-layer architecture. It begins with a "sequence input layer" designed to handle five inputs corresponding to the top features identified by each feature selection method. Following this, the "LSTM layer" comes next, featuring 40 hidden units configured to output only the final element of the sequence. The determination of the number of hidden units was through a process of trial and error. The architecture is completed with a fully connected layer with a single output, indicating its focus on regression tasks, and a "regression layer" to finalize the model's predictions. The Adam optimization algorithm was chosen as the solver for the training configuration, with the training process set to run for a maximum of 250 epochs. Settings for the "Gradient Threshold" and "Initial Learn Rate" were fine-tuned to 0.1 and 0.01, respectively, and were determined through trial and error to optimize the network's performance on regression tasks.

Three LSTM regression models were trained utilizing 80% of the dataset, with the remaining 20% reserved for testing, based on the features selected by the F-test, RReliefF, and mRMR algorithms. Figure 3 illustrates the performance of these models in predicting the test dataset. To assess the accuracy of each model, we computed the Mean Squared Error (MSE), which measures the average of the squares of the errors or deviations—that is, the difference between the estimator and what is estimated. The MSEs for the models, corresponding to the feature selection algorithms of F-test, RReliefF, and mRMR, were 1.26, 2.31, and 0.65, respectively. These values indicate the predictive accuracy of the models, with lower MSE values representing more accurate predictions. The mRMR-based model demonstrated the highest accuracy, evidenced by its lowest MSE value.

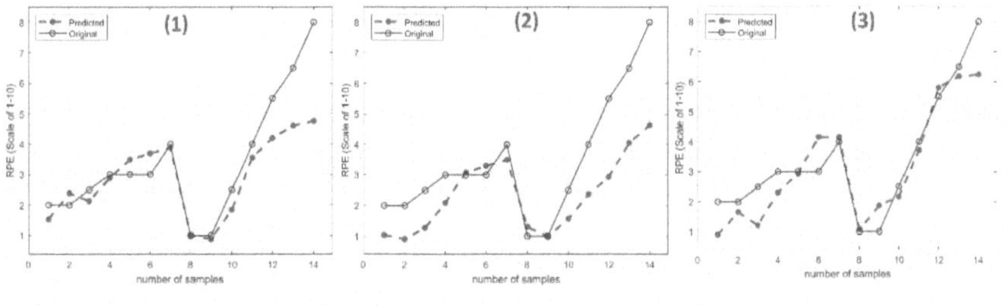

Fig. 3. Results of the LSTM regression analysis conducted on the best selected features derived from the (1) F-test, (2) RReliefF, and (3) mRMR algorithms.

GRU Regression Model. The Gated Recurrent Unit (GRU) model, an RNN variant, is adept at learning temporal dependencies within time series and sequential data. It was crafted like the LSTM model, with the primary modification substituting the LSTM layer with a GRU layer. This change was made while keeping the training parameters consistent across models. Utilizing the features identified through the F-test, RReliefF, and mRMR algorithms, three distinct GRU regression models were developed, trained on 80% of the dataset, and evaluated on the remaining 20%. The performances of these models on the test dataset are showcased in Fig. 4. The MSE values, indicative of the model's prediction accuracy, were recorded as 1.72, 1.64, and 1.38 for the models based on the best-selected features from the F-test, RReliefF, and mRMR algorithms, respectively. These MSE values reflect the models' effectiveness in accurately predicting the test data, with lower values denoting higher accuracy.

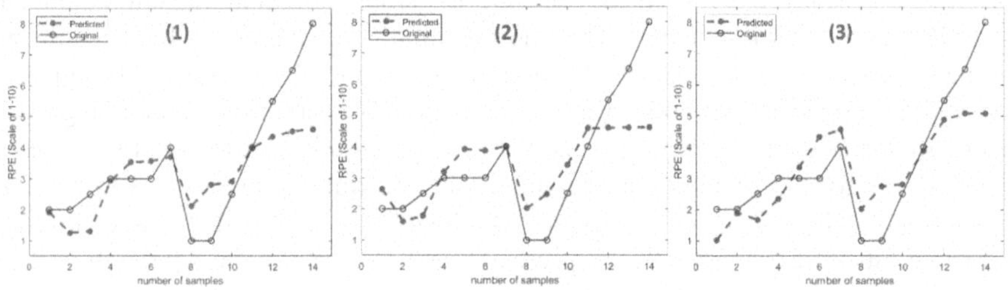

Fig. 4. Results of the GRU regression analysis implemented on the best selected features resulted from (1) F-test, (2) RReliefF, and (3) mRMR algorithms.

3.2 Classification Analysis

For the classification analysis, the initial step involved identifying the most predictive features using four distinct feature selection algorithms: univariate feature ranking, the ReliefF algorithm, neighborhood component analysis (NCA), and mRMR method. The features that ranked highest across these methods were subsequently utilized to train and evaluate LSTM and GRU models for classification purposes. These procedures, including the application of the feature selection algorithms and the training and testing of the models, were conducted within MATLAB, version R2023a.

Feature Selection for Classification Analysis. The dataset, comprising data from all exercise sessions and predictive features, was used as input for the models. Figure 5A illustrates the results from the univariate feature ranking algorithm (fscchi2()) in MATLAB, tailored for classification tasks involving categorical and continuous features. This method evaluates the independence of each predictive feature from a response variable through chi-square tests, ranking the features based on the chi-square test statistics' p-values. The five highest-scoring predictors identified by this algorithm were selected for the LSTM and GRU model training and testing phases. The chosen top features include: 1) "RPM": Rotations per minute (sourced from iBikE); 2) "mean_HRn": Normalized mean heart rate; 3) "VLF_power": Very low-frequency power, determined using Welch's periodogram; 4) "logVLF_power": Logarithm of very low-frequency power, also using Welch's periodogram; 5) "D2": Correlation dimension, a measure from nonlinear analysis.

Figure 5B shows the results of the feature selection using the ReliefF algorithm (relieff() function in MATLAB). The five highest-scoring predictors identified by the ReliefF method were selected for the training and testing phases of both the LSTM and GRU models. The selected top features include: 1) "RPM": Rotations per minute (obtained from iBikE); 2) "mean_HRn": Normalized mean heart rate; 3) "VLF_power_prc": The percentage of very low-frequency power, calculated using Welch's periodogram; 4) "max_HR": The maximum heart rate, determined using a 5 beat moving average; 5) "min_HR": The minimum heart rate, also calculated using a 5 beat moving average.

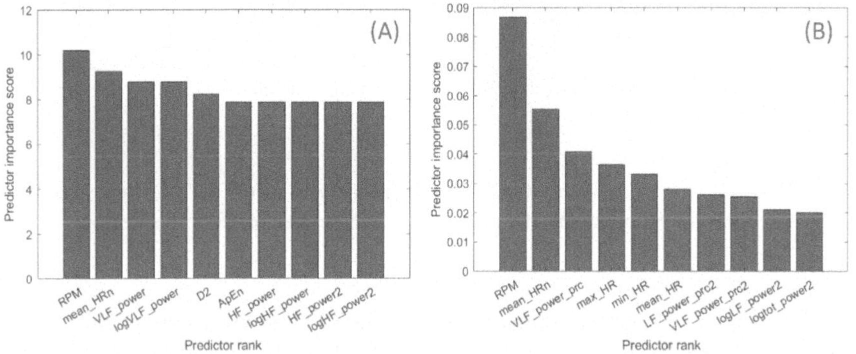

Fig. 5. A) Results from the univariate feature ranking algorithm applied for classification purposes. B) Results from the feature selection process using the ReliefF algorithm for classification.

Figure 6A displays the findings from the neighborhood component analysis (NCA) algorithm feature selection, implemented as fscnca() in MATLAB, which is particularly suited for datasets with continuous features. This algorithm assigns weights to features through a diagonal adaptation of the NCA, focusing on optimizing the selection for predictive performance. The top five predictors, identified based on their performance in the univariate feature ranking algorithm, were utilized to train and evaluate the LSTM and GRU models. The prioritized features for this phase were: 1) "RPM": Rotations per minute, acquired from iBikE; 2) "tot_power2": The total spectral power, derived from the autoregressive (AR) spectrum; 3) "mean_HRn": The normalized mean heart rate; 4) "max_HR": The maximum heart rate, calculated using a 5 beat moving average; 5) "mean_HRn": Normalized mean heart rate, noted twice, suggesting its significant predictive value.

Figure 6B illustrates the results from the mRMR algorithm's feature selection, as executed in MATLAB (fscmrmr()), for classification tasks incorporating both categorical and continuous data types. Higher scores in the mRMR analysis suggest a greater confidence in feature selection. The five features that received the highest scores were selected for the training and evaluation of the LSTM and GRU classification models. The top-selected features include: 1) "VLF_power2": The percentage of very low-frequency power, determined using the AR spectrum estimate method; 2) "HF_power_prc": The percentage of high-frequency power, calculated with Welch's periodogram estimation method; 3) "RPM": Rotations per minute, obtained from iBikE; 4) "mean_HR": Average heart rate; 5) "VLF_peak2": Peak frequency in the very low-frequency band, estimated using the AR spectrum method.

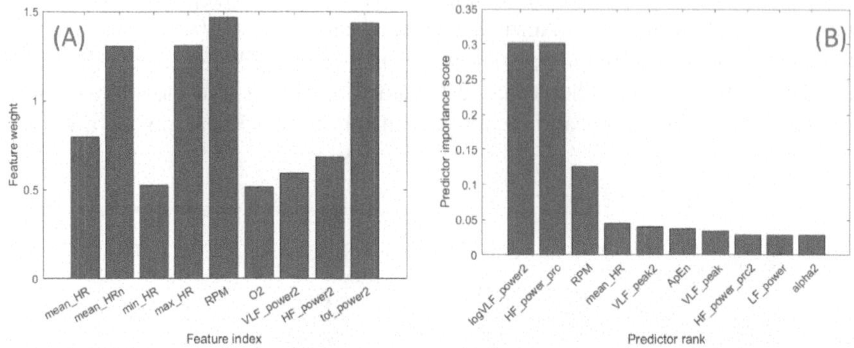

Fig. 6. A) Results of the neighborhood component analysis algorithm's feature selection for classification. B) Results of the mRMR algorithm's feature selection for classification.

LSTM and GRU Classification Models. The LSTM and GRU classification models were constructed in MATLAB, featuring a specifically tailored network architecture for analyzing sequences with one-dimensional inputs. The initial layer termed the "sequence input layer," was configured to be 1 in size, catering to the dimensional nature of our input data. Following this, the architecture diverged based on the model type: the LSTM model incorporated an "LSTM layer," whereas the GRU model employed a "GRU Layer." Both of these layers were equipped with 40 hidden units and designed to output the final element of the input sequence.

To facilitate the classification into two distinct categories—high exertion versus low exertion—a "fully connected layer" with a size of 2 was introduced. This layer was succeeded by a "softmax layer," which normalizes the output to a probability distribution over the predicted output classes, and a "classification layer" that interprets these probabilities into class labels.

The models' training was optimized using the Adam solver, with training parameters including a maximum of 70 epochs and a "Mini Batch Size" of 20, which indicates the number of training examples considered simultaneously during the optimization process. These parameters were finely tuned through a methodical process of trial and error to achieve optimal performance.

Tables 3 and 4 detail the effectiveness and performance of these LSTM and GRU models in classification tasks and present a comprehensive summary of the training and testing results.

Table 3. Training results of LSTM and GRU models using optimally selected features from various feature selection algorithms.

Model	Accuracy (%), Feature Selection Methods				F1 Score (%), Feature Selection Methods			
	Univariate	ReliefF	NCA	mRMR	Univariate	ReliefF	NCA	mRMR
LSTM	82.1	83.9	96.4	85.7	0.85	0.85	0.96	0.87
GRU	85.7	85.7	98.2	87.5	0.88	0.86	0.98	0.88

Table 4. Testing results of LSTM and GRU models using optimally selected features from various feature selection algorithms.

Model	Accuracy (%), Feature Selection Methods				F1 Score (%), Feature Selection Methods			
	Univariate	ReliefF	NCA	mRMR	Univariate	ReliefF	NCA	mRMR
LSTM	71.4	78.6	78.6	78.6	0.71	0.8	0.8	0.8
GRU	64.2	78.6	78.6	78.6	0.61	0.8	0.8	0.8

The features derived from the neighborhood component analysis yielded the highest levels of accuracy and F1 score when used to train both the LSTM and GRU models. Regarding the testing phase, aside from the features obtained through the univariate feature selection algorithm, the features identified by the remaining algorithms all demonstrated identical testing accuracy and F1 scores, at 78.6% and 0.8, respectively.

4 Discussion

Our pilot study's findings indicate that RPM data gathered from the iBikE and physiological data from wearable devices can be leveraged to predict exertion levels by developing real-time, automated prediction algorithms. Analysis of Heart Rate Variability (HRV) in both time and frequency domains revealed that certain HRV metrics indicate varying levels of exercise exertion. A unique aspect of our approach is that we do not directly use RPMs and HRV measurements as straightforward predictors of exertion levels. This is the first study to utilize data from wearable devices as input for deep-learning models to predict exertion levels during continuous cycling exercises. Borg's Rating of Perceived Exertion serves as the benchmark. By employing GRU and LSTM models, we identified specific patterns in RPM and HRV responses to varying exertion levels. We conducted regression and classification analyses to estimate the Rate of Perceived Exertion (RPE). Feature extraction was performed using 2-min windows, a methodology from prior research indicating that averaging data over brief intervals can facilitate signal smoothing and artifact reduction [22, 23]. Moreover, a minimum of 2-min RR intervals is necessary to obtain meaningful HRV metrics in the frequency domain. In total, seventy features were extracted, predominantly from HRV analysis in time and frequency domains, alongside RPM data from iBikE. A major limitation of this study was the relatively small size of the dataset used for feature extraction. Future work will aim to significantly expand the dataset to encompass a broader and more diverse cohort of participants.

We utilized various algorithms to identify the top five predictive features for feature selection in our regression and classification models. Except for the mRMR algorithm in regression analysis, normalized RPM and the normalized mean HR were consistently identified as top predictive features across both model types. The mRMR algorithm singled out normalized HR values and Approximate Entropy from HRV analysis as key predictors for regression, while it identified specific frequency domain features from HRV analysis as critical for classification.

Data collection during cycling sessions came from two sources: a pulse oximeter and the chest-worn Actiheart monitor. Due to the overlap in the data they provided, we opted to use one and exclude the other from our final dataset. While the Actiheart offers higher accuracy and comprehensive ECG data, the pulse oximeter is more user-friendly due to its simplicity and resistance to motion artifacts.

The recurrent neural network models were constructed using LSTM and GRU layers. Despite the GRU model's simplicity and fewer parameters, both models demonstrated the potential for predicting exertion levels effectively. However, further research is necessary before this predictive method can be clinically recommended. Future work will involve extensive testing across diverse patient groups with varying chronic conditions and conducting randomized clinical trials to evaluate the impact of this approach on patient safety, exercise adherence, and overall health outcomes.

References

1. Physical activity and health: a report of the surgeon general [Internet]. Cdc.gov. (cited 2023 Sep 6). https://www.cdc.gov/nccdphp/sgr/index.htm
2. Ashe, M.C., Miller, W.C., Eng, J.J., Noreau, L.: Older adults, chronic disease and leisure-time physical activity. Gerontology **55**(1), 64–72 (2009)
3. Nelson, M.E., Rejeski, W.J., Blair, S.N., Duncan, P.W., Judge, J.O., King, A.C., et al.: Physical activity and public health in older adults: recommendation from the American college of sports medicine and the American heart association. Med. Sci. Sports Exerc. **39**(8), 1435–1445 (2007)
4. Borg, G.A.: Psychophysical bases of perceived exertion. Med. Sci Sports Exerc. **14**(5), 377–381 (1982)
5. Avrutsky, M.J.A., Katkovsky, D.G., Guseinov, T.J.U., Musichin, L.V., Finkelstein, I.E.: Application of intravenous low-intensity laser irradiation as part of anesthetic care during invasive surgery. J. Clin. Laser Med. Surg. **10**(4), 291–295 (1992)
6. Freeman, J.V., Dewey, F.E., Hadley, D.M., Myers, J., Froelicher, V.F.: Autonomic nervous system interaction with the cardiovascular system during exercise. Prog. Cardiovasc. Dis. **48**(5), 342–362 (2006)
7. Hossen, A., Al-Wadahi, F., Jervase, J.A.: Classification of modulation signals using statistical signal characterization and artificial neural networks. Eng. Appl. Artif. Intell. **20**(4), 463–472 (2007)
8. Tanantong, T., Nantajeewarawat, E., Thiemjarus, S.: Toward continuous ambulatory monitoring using a wearable and wireless ECG- recording system: a study on the effects of signal quality on arrhythmia detection. Biomed. Mater. Eng. **24**(1), 391–404 (2014)

9. Li, J., Zhou, H., Zuo, D., Hou, K.-M., De Vaulx, C.: Ubiquitous health monitoring and real-time cardiac arrhythmias detection: a case study. Biomed. Mater. Eng. **24**(1), 1027–1033 (2014)
10. Kadhiresan, K., Carlson, G.: The role of implantable sensors for management of heart failure. Stud. Health Technol. Inf. **108**, 219–227 (2004)
11. Hossen, A., Jaju, D., Al-Ghunaimi, B., Al-Faqeer, B., Al-Yahyai, T., Hassan, M.O., et al.: Classification of sleep apnea using wavelet-based spectral analysis of heart rate variability. Technol. Health Care **21**(4), 291–303 (2013)
12. Jeong, I.C., Finkelstein, J.: Comparative utility of time and frequency HRV domains for automated classification of exercise exertion levels. In: 2015 IEEE International Conference on Bioinformatics and Biomedicine (BIBM), pp. 983–989. IEEE (2015)
13. Finkelstein, J., Jeong, I.C.: Using heart rate variability for automated identification of exercise exertion levels. Stud. Health Technol. Inform. **208**, 137–141 (2015)
14. Smiley, A., Tsai, T.-Y., Cui, W., Parvanova, I., Lyu, J., Zakashansky, E., et al.: Telemonitoring of home-based biking exercise: Assessment of wireless interfaces. JMIR Biomed Eng. **7**(2), e41782 (2022)
15. Actiheart-5 [Internet]. camntech. [cited 2023 Sep 6]
16. WristOx2® model 3150 with USB [Internet]. Nonin. Nonin Medical Inc; 2018 (cited 2023 Sep 6). https://www.nonin.com/products/3150-usb/
17. Heart rate variability software - Kubios HRV [Internet]. Kubios. 2020 (cited 2023 Sep 6). https://www.kubios.com/
18. Hung, C.-L.: Deep learning in biomedical informatics. In: Zheng, Y., Wu, Z., (ed). Intelligent Nanotechnology, pp. 307–329. Elsevier. (2023)
19. Chowdhury, S.R., Khare, Y., Mazumdar, S.: Classification of diseases from CT images using LSTM-based CNN. In: Polat, K., Öztürk, S. (eds.) Diagnostic Biomedical Signal and Image Processing Applications with Deep Learning Methods, pp. 235–249. Elsevier, San Diego, CA (2023)
20. Schmidhuber, J.: Deep learning in neural networks: an overview. Neural Netw. **61**, 85–117 (2015)
21. Huck, N.: Pairs selection and outranking: an application to the S&P 100 index. Eur. J. Oper. Res. **196**(2), 819–825 (2009)
22. Finkelstein, J., Wood, J.: Predicting asthma exacerbations using artificial intelligence. Stud. Health Technol. Inform. **190**, 56–58 (2013)
23. Finkelstein, J., Jeong, I.C.: Using CART for advanced prediction of asthma attacks based on telemonitoring data. In: 2016 IEEE 7th Annual Ubiquitous Computing, Electronics & Mobile Communication Conference (UEMCON), pp. 1–5. IEEE (2016)

Age of Peak Performance Among Soccer Players in Sweden

Rasmus Säfvenberg[1], Anders Nordgaard[1], Ola Lidmark Eriksson[2], Niklas Carlsson[1], and Patrick Lambrix[1](✉)

[1] Linköping University, Linköping, Sweden
patrick.lambrix@liu.se
[2] Football Analytics Sweden AB, Stockholm, Sweden

Abstract. Performance and age have an intertwined relationship in soccer. However, despite the sport's popularity and the great value of insight into this topic to decision-making personnel, this is a fairly unexplored topic, particularly for lower-ranked leagues. In this paper, we use a novel performance metric to investigate the peak age among soccer players in Sweden for goalkeepers, defenders, midfielders, and forwards. Each playing position is analyzed separately using univariate and bivariate methods and is also modeled by a hierarchical Bayesian model with player-specific age trajectories.

The results indicate an average overall peak age between 25 and 27. Forwards typically peak at 25, while defenders and midfielders reach their peak performance between the ages of 25 and 27. For goalkeepers, the peak generally occurs by age 27. The performance decline post-peak is the steepest among forwards and midfielders. Defenders and goalkeepers see a long-lasting and slow decline.

1 Introduction

In the global industry that soccer has become, it is important for teams to acquire the right players for the right position and for the right price. Much research in soccer analytics has recently been performed to define performance metrics to value a player's performance. Some examples are VAEP (Valuing Actions by Estimating Probabilities) [7], expected threat [22], action-value functions [18], plus-minus [15], and expected passes [2].

Studies have shown, however, that performance varies as a function of age and this relationship can be captured by an aging curve which tends to be inverted-U shaped with a peak, as well as possibly varying levels of slopes before and after the peak [3]. Insight into the aging curves and expected performance trajectories is, therefore, of interest for player acquisition [10], the development and improvement of training regimes and management of the squad [14].

Investigating the relationship between performance metrics and age has been performed in different sports such as tennis [16], baseball [4], basketball [26], and ice hockey [5]. Sports with a high emphasis on agility, power, and strength, tend

J. S. Dong et al. (Eds.): ISACE 2024, LNCS 14794, pp. 278–290, 2024.
https://doi.org/10.1007/978-3-031-69073-0_24

to have athletes that peak in their early or mid-20s while finesse and endurance-based sports generally perform optimally in their late-20s.

Studies analyzing the age-performance relationship in soccer have utilized different metrics, methods and data for their analyses.

In [8], the relationship between age and performance for field players from the highest tiers in England, Germany, Italy, and Spain during five consecutive seasons, starting from 2010–2011, was investigated. As performance metric, the performance ratings from WhoScored.com were used. Two polynomial regression models with either population-level ("fixed") or group-level ("random") effects were developed. The peak age occurred between ages 25 and 27. Forwards peaked the earliest, followed by midfielders and defenders.

In [14], players in the UEFA Champions League during 1992–1993 to 2017–2018 and how their market valuation related to age, were analyzed. The variables used in the study were number of seasons in the club, number of Champions Leagues won, and team performance. For data analysis, one-way ANOVA and a linear regression were used. Their findings revealed peak market value in the 26–30 age group, with center backs and goalkeepers peaking later than attacking players.

The same authors investigated physical and technical performance among Bundesliga players during the 2012–2013 to 2014–2015 seasons [21]. The variables used in the study were total distance covered, number of fast runs, number of sprints, and percentage of successful passes. They observed that players aged 30 or older exhibited significantly reduced physical performance across all positions except wide midfielders, yet ability to make successful passes increased with age.

In another study, [19] used the nomination for individual awards such as the Ballon d'Or, as a proxy of performance. Data regarding 685 retired players from 1956 to 2019 was used. Using this proxy, the overall peak age ranges from 27 to 28, showing variations across positions, with forwards peaking earlier (26) and goalkeepers reaching their peak later (31).

As existing work in soccer on the age of peak performance of players has focused on top leagues in Europe, it is not clear whether these results can be used for lower tier leagues. Lower tier leagues may not be seen as the final destination for many players and thus the makeup of the teams in the lower leagues tends to consist of younger players aiming for top leagues, players for which the lower tier league is their highest achievable level, and end-of-career players that have played in top leagues earlier. As an example, we use the top Swedish league, Allsvenskan, which in November 2023 ranked 23rd among European leagues according to [25]. In Swedish soccer and similar nations, a notable trend involves players migrating to higher-ranked foreign leagues. For example, reports indicate that many Swedish players relocate abroad before turning 23 [9].

This paper estimates at which age male soccer players in Sweden perform optimally, and explores if findings from top-tier leagues align with a lower-tier league. We note, however, that previous approaches have used different metrics of performance, which do not fit a lower-tier league or for which data is not available. For instance, the features used in [21] are nowadays part of modern metrics. Further, there are no player ratings from WhoScored.com (as used by

Table 1. Attributes in the SPADL data representation.

Attribute	Description
Match id	Unique id of the match
Action id	Unique id of the action within the match
Period id	The id of the period/half
Seconds	Time of the action
Player id	The id of the player performing the action
Team id	The team id of the player
X start	X coordinate at the start of the action
Y start	Y coordinate at the start of the action
X end	X coordinate at the end of the action
Y end	Y coordinate at the end of the action
Action	The action being performed by the player
Result	The result of the action
Body part	The part of the body used to perform the action

[8]) for Swedish leagues, few teams from the Swedish leagues play in the UEFA Champions League (as used in [14]), and players in the Swedish leagues would not receive individual awards such as the Ballon d'Or (as used in [19]). Therefore, we needed to use a metric that can be measured using the available data. As more and more game data is available nowadays, we decided to use event data and use modern performance metrics. The data we use for the analysis covers event data from the three highest Swedish leagues and is described in Sect. 2. We quantify player performance by constructing a novel metric that combines modern metrics and employing Bayesian hierarchical modeling for estimation (Sect. 3). For each position (goalkeepers, defenders, midfielders, and forwards) a separate estimation is performed. We present results in Sect. 4, a discussion in Sect. 5, and our conclusions in Sect. 6.

2 Data

In this paper, two datasets were used. The first and main dataset contains event data for the three highest leagues in the Swedish male soccer hierarchy between seasons 2015 and 2021, 2016 and 2021, as well as 2020 and 2021 for the first (Allsvenskan), second (Superettan), and third (Ettan Södra and Ettan Norra) highest levels, respectively. This data was provided by Football Analytics Sweden AB. The other dataset contains information about age and playing position and was gathered from Transfermarkt.com. In the data, there were unique identifiers for each game and event. The game-level data contained information regarding home and away teams, final score, and date, while the event-level data contained information about the event type, the player(s) and their teams involved in the event, as well as the result, body part, time, start- and end-coordinates of each event (Tables 1 and 2).

Table 2. Action types in the SPADL representation. Adapted from [7].

Action type	Description	Result
Bad touch	Player makes a bad touch and loses the ball	Fail, Own goal[a]
Clearance	Player clearance	Success
Cross	Cross into the box	Success[b], Fail, Offside
Crossed corner	Corner crossed into the box	Success[b], Fail
Crossed free kick	Free kick crossed into the penalty box	Success[b], Fail, Offside
Dribble	Player dribbles at least 3 m with the ball	Success
Foul	Foul	Fail, Red card, Yellow card
Free kick shot	Direct free kick on goal	Success[c], Fail
Goal kick	Goal kick	Success
Goalkeeper claim	Keeper catches a cross	Success[d], Fail
Goalkeeper pick-up	Keeper picks up the ball	Success
Goalkeeper punch	Keeper punches the ball clear	Success
Goalkeeper save	Keeper saves a shot on goal	Success
Interception	Interception of the ball	Success[e], Fail
Pass	Normal pass in open play	Success[b], Fail, Offside
Penalty shot	Penalty shot	Success[c], Fail
Short corner	Short corner	Success[b], Fail
Short free kick	Short free kick	Success[b], Fail, Offside
Shot	Shot attempt not from penalty or free kick	Success[c], Fail
Tackle	Tackle on the ball	Success[e], Fail
Take-on	Attempt to dribble past opponent	Success[f], Fail
Throw-in	Throw-in	Success[b], Fail

[a]Was originally the result of a shot but now is the result of a bad touch. [b]Reaches teammate. [c]Goal. [d]Does not drop the ball. [e]Regains possession. [f]Keeps possession.

3 Method

The method consisted of three major steps: (1) data preprocessing, (2) computing a performance metric, and (3) estimating the peak age of performance.

3.1 Data Preprocessing

As a first step, we transformed the data from its original long format representation (where information about an event could be distributed in different rows) to its representation in the Soccer Player Action Description Language (SPADL, [7]). Events not present in the SPADL representation were excluded. Based on the coordinates we added information about throw-ins and short corners. In addition, for the earliest seasons, the data did not record explicit events for corners and free kicks. Corner kicks were added based on the coordinates of the shot and free kicks based on the fact that they are preceded by a foul. Further, we needed to deal with some inconsistencies regarding minutes played as well as matching player names from the different data sources.

The players were divided into 4 distinct groups according to position: forwards (strikers, wingers), midfielders (wide, defensive, central, attacking midfielders), defenders (left, right, center backs), and goalkeepers. We removed players with less than 450 min played in a season (equivalent to 5 full games) to filter out players having extreme performances per minute while rarely playing. The filtering led to 308 observations (out of originally 535) for 101 goalkeepers, 1422 (originally 2089) for 422 defenders, 1328 (originally 2170) for 419 midfielders, and 974 (originally 1596) for 317 forwards.

The age of the players was recorded as a continuous variable and computed once per season with the date of measurement on June 1th each calendar year, as this date approximately aligns with the beginning of the summer intermission in Swedish soccer. Figure 1 shows the distribution of age per group.

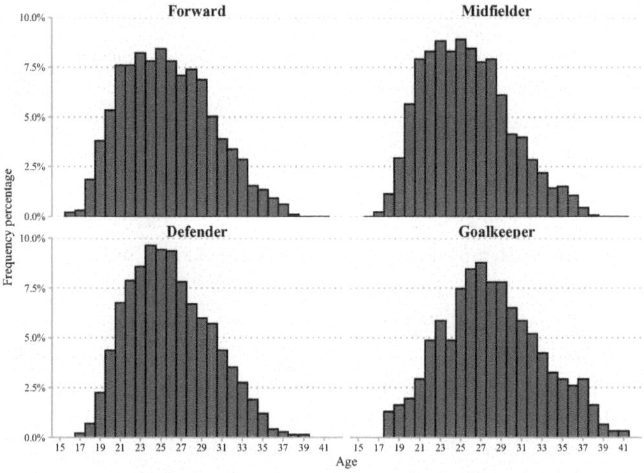

Fig. 1. Distribution of age by position.

3.2 Performance Metric

In contrast to previous methods where a proxy or a few specific variables were used, we decided to define a performance metric based on several state-of-the-art and currently popular metrics.

The first component in our metric is based on the VAEP (Valuing Actions by Estimating Probabilities) framework [7] which aims to estimate offensive and defensive values of events to determine the impact on scoring or conceding a goal within the next 10 events. VAEP values are computed in two stages: one for the offensive aspect where the outcome is a Bernoulli random variable with a value of 1 if the team scores within the next 10 events and 0 otherwise, and another for the defensive aspect where another Bernoulli distributed random variable is the outcome if a team concedes within the next 10 events (1) or not (0). The VAEP value is then the difference between offensive and negative defensive value. Since it is framed as a binary classification task, the choice of classification method is up to the user, and in this case, the choice is an eXtreme Gradient Boosting (XGBoost) model. As the VAEP framework estimates two separate probabilities, each aspect can be used as a metric. Furthermore, the offensive value in VAEP tends to be dominated by goal-scoring as they often receive probabilities close to 1 while the other probabilities lie closer to 0. Thus, it may be desirable to split the offensive value into two sub-components: shot offensive value and non-shot offensive value, since the components have different importance for different positions.

Another metric that has attained high popularity is xT (Expected Threat, method originally proposed by S Rudd, reproposed and coined by K Singh) [22], which is used to evaluate how a choice of pass impacts the team's probability of scoring. This is computed using Markov chains where the pitch is represented by a grid of 12×8 zones, where each zone is assigned a value based on how probable a goal is from the zone. The xT in a zone depends on the probability of scoring from that zone by a shot as well as on the xT of other zones to which the ball can be moved. In general, the most threatening areas on the pitch are within the penalty box of the opposing team. The threat of an action is defined as the difference in xT between the start zone and the end zone of the action.

As goalkeepers have a unique role in the game, we add a unique component to the performance evaluation. One suggested metric for this is that of post-shot expected goals (PSxG) [13], which evaluates how probable a goal is from a shot on target. The estimation of this value is done by utilizing information regarding, e.g., shot location, angle, direction, and goalkeeper position. Further, we also consider the difference between post-shot expected goals (PSxG) and actual goals allowed (GA), i.e., PSxG - GA. A positive value indicates that a goalkeeper saved more shots than expected.

After computing these metrics for each event in all games the values were then summed per player and season. The season-level values for each metric were then divided by the total minutes played during the season to adjust for players playing a different number of minutes during a season and then multiplied by 90 (length of a soccer game). We chose season-summarized statistics as individual games have larger variability than a full season. After computing the minute-adjusted metrics each respective metric was standardized to have mean zero and unit variance. Furthermore, players who had participated in only one season were removed as their peak age would be the age at that particular season.

Using the above metrics, we define a performance metric for goalkeepers y_{GK} and one for field players y_F as follows:

$$y_{GK} = \text{PSxG-GA} + \text{Non-shot offensive value} + \text{Defensive value} + \text{xT}, \qquad (1)$$

$$y_F = \text{Shot offensive value} + \text{Non-shot offensive value} + \text{Defensive value} + \text{xT}. \quad (2)$$

For goalkeepers we do not use the shot offensive value as they rarely shoot the ball toward the other team's goal. For field players we do not use PSxG-GA.

3.3 Estimation

In this step we investigate the relationship between performance and age. As the ages of players were unevenly distributed, with fewer young and old players, we utilized a model with partial pooling, which uses shrinkage to combine information from both rare and common ages for a more informative estimation. We developed a mixed model consisting of performance as the outcome with a thin-plate smoothing spline as well as player-level intercepts and slopes. This choice of spline was based on its computational efficiency, the circumvention of the knot placement issues that tend to arise when fitting splines, and does not impact the inference and diagnostics of models [27]. The impetus behind the inclusion of player-level intercepts and slopes was that players are not expected to share the same peak or aging trajectory. Therefore, we allow for each player an intercept that adjusts the aging curve vertically and a slope that rotates and stretches the curve to match the trajectory [23]. More specifically, a hierarchical Bayesian model was implemented and is fit for each position p with sample size n_p as in Fig. 2, where s is a smoothing spline and (τ_μ, τ_σ) are the standard deviations of μ and σ, respectively, that model the variability and smoothness of the respective term. The half-Cauchy distribution corresponds to the right half of a symmetrical Cauchy distribution, while LKJcorr is the log-likelihood that, in this case, serves as a uniformly distributed prior (with default parameter value $\eta = 1$) for the correlation matrix $\mathbf{R}$ [17]. The priors for the intercepts α, both population and player-level, as well as the player-level slope β were set as generic weakly informative prior as described in [12]. Similarly, the priors for (τ_μ, τ_σ) were also set as weakly informative based on [11]. Finally, the priors for the player-level standard deviations $(\nu_{\alpha_\mu}, \nu_{\beta_\mu})$ were set to reflect the prior belief that, due to the data structure, with few observations per player and a larger set of players, a high standard deviation is less likely, and thus more centered near the lower limit of zero. The models were estimated using four Markov chains, each with 20 000 Hamiltonian Monte Carlo iterations and adapt delta of 0.99 from the brms package [6].

4 Results

With the model structure previously defined, we obtain both a population-level smooth spline for age as well as player-level intercept and slope that can then be used to estimate the peak age. Specifically, each player has an age where their performance is at its maximum given by the season in which they participated. Before showcasing the results of the model, we should also shed some light on the quality of the model. In particular, we can investigate the posterior predictive distribution of each model and verify if draws from the distribution align with the original data. This is visualized in Fig. 3 where 100 such draws from each model are compared to the data. From the respective distributions, we can see that each model captures the general structure of the original data, although some deviations can be observed. The draws for midfielders and defenders are most similar to the original data, while the data for forward and goalkeepers

$$
\begin{aligned}
y_i &\sim \text{Normal}(\mu_i, \sigma_i), \quad i = 1, \ldots, n_p \\
\mu_i &= \alpha_{\mu,\text{player}[i]} + \beta_{\mu,\text{player}[i]} + s(\text{Age}_i, \tau_\mu) \\
\sigma_i &= \alpha_\sigma + s(\text{Age}_i, \tau_\sigma) \\
\begin{bmatrix} \alpha_{\mu,\text{player}} \\ \beta_{\mu,\text{player}} \end{bmatrix} &\sim \text{MVNormal}\left(\begin{bmatrix} \alpha_\mu \\ \beta_\mu \end{bmatrix}, \boldsymbol{\Sigma}_\mu \right) \\
\boldsymbol{\Sigma}_\mu &= \begin{bmatrix} \nu_{\alpha_\mu} & 0 \\ 0 & \nu_{\beta_\mu} \end{bmatrix} \mathbf{R}_\mu \begin{bmatrix} \nu_{\alpha_\mu} & 0 \\ 0 & \nu_{\beta_\mu} \end{bmatrix} \\
(\alpha_\mu, \alpha_\sigma, \beta_\mu) &\sim \text{Normal}(0, 1) \\
(\tau_\mu, \tau_\sigma) &\sim \text{HalfCauchy}(0, 1) \\
\nu_{\alpha_\mu} &\sim \text{HalfCauchy}(0, 0.5) \\
\nu_{\beta_\mu} &\sim \text{HalfCauchy}(0, 0.1) \\
\mathbf{R}_\mu &\sim \text{LKJcorr}(1)
\end{aligned}
$$

Fig. 2. Model.

is somewhat lower than the simulations suggest. Some bends in the curvature can also be noted for goalkeepers for the higher positive values. In general, these findings indicate that the models capture the overall performance pattern present in the data for each position group.

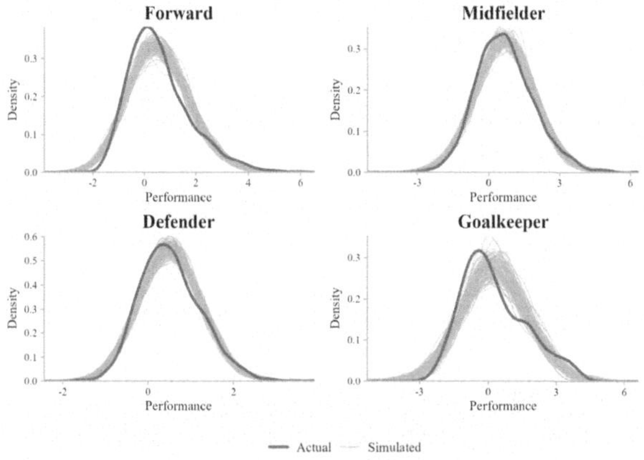

Fig. 3. Comparison of 100 simulated draws from the posterior predictive distribution and the performance for each position.

The conditional effects for each position can be seen in Fig. 4 while the summary statistics of the player-level fits are described in Table 3. From the figure, it can be discerned that the aging curve varies by position, with forwards having the sharpest decline post-peak while defenders have the slowest decline. Among forwards, the peak was found around age 25 which is preceded by a steeper

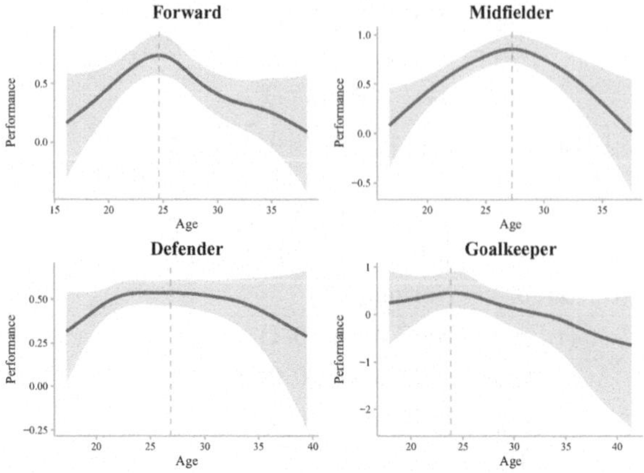

Fig. 4. Conditional effects of age by position. The vertical lines indicate the age of peak performance.

increase toward the peak and then followed by a sharp decrease in performance after the apex. In addition, the post-peak slope decreases after age 30, although this is coupled with an increasing standard error. Midfielders and defenders attain a later peak than forwards, between 26 and 28 years of age. The aging curve of midfielders exhibits a shape akin to a second-degree polynomial, where the slope before and after the maximum is similar. For defenders, the aging curve remains largely constant for many years, with a near-horizontal slope starting at age 23 and ending at age 30. Moreover, the performance curve for defenders has the lowest range, although the standard error is higher. Goalkeepers achieved the earliest peak, by age 24 according to the smoothing splines, which is then followed by a fairly constant decrease.

Table 3. Summary statistics of peak age from the hierarchical model.

	Percentile			Mean	Std. Dev.
	25th	50th	75th		
Forwards	23.0	24.6	27.2	25.1	3.25
Midfielders	22.9	25.8	27.4	25.4	3.15
Defenders	23.1	24.7	27.8	25.6	3.43
Goalkeepers	23.9	25.6	29.1	26.6	3.95

When considering the summary statistics, it can be noted that the mean age of peak performance was between 25.1 and 25.6 for field players and 26.6 for goalkeepers. The quantiles also range from approximately 23 to 28 for field players while goalkeepers are approximately between 24 and 29. Moreover, the standard deviation obtained is somewhat high relative to the mean, mainly due to the players available in the data having a large dispersion between the youngest and oldest players for each position as well as few observations per player. Moreover, since each player is given an individual maximum point and there are players in the data with only a few seasons, the age at which they peak may not be their actual peak as it may lay outside the range of the recorded data. For instance, the data contains players for which the observations cover ages 16–18 or 35–40. Consequently, the peak age for these players may be far after or before their actual peak, which in turn increases the standard deviation seen in Table 3.

5 Discussion

The results of this paper indicate that professional soccer players in Sweden peak between the ages of 24 and 27, which also varies by playing position. Interestingly, although different performance metrics were used and, as explained in the introduction, the situation for top leagues and lower-tier leagues differs, the peak ages seem to be similar for the Swedish league and the results reported for top leagues in previous work.

We note that the results stand in agreement with the general physical and skill-based profile of athletes. Soccer is a mixed-skill sport with high requirements on both physical and physiological abilities. With the high endurance expected of soccer players, where field players on average run 10–12 kilometers and goalkeepers 4 km, at an intensity near the anaerobic threshold of 80–90% of maximal heart rate [24], a tendency towards higher peak age may be expected. However, as performance in soccer also relies on aspects such as high-intensity running, jumping, and tackling, this should in turn lead to a lower peak age, as reported in sports such as track and field as well as swimming [8]. Moreover, the apparent differences between positions also highlight different expectations and emphases. In particular, forwards had a rapid decline post-peak while defenders and goalkeepers had a lesser decline. This can be explained by the higher number of high-intensity sprints and duels forwards engage in compared to, e.g., defenders [21]. Similarly, the length of near-peak performance of defenders also highlights a possible shift in playing style where more emphasis is placed on anticipation, positioning, and decision-making, which are all gained through experience rather than physical ability. The leverage of experience is what can enable a player to maintain high performance after their peak. However, there is a trade-off between gained experience and a decline in physiological capacity that typically results in a dominance of physiology rather than experience. This is particularly evident among forwards. Perhaps somewhat peculiar was that the peak age among goalkeepers occurred by age 25 according to the conditional age effect, though the mean peak age was also found at 26.6. As [20] notes, goalkeepers are the position with the lowest physiological expectations and risk of injury, which tends to lead to longer playing careers and can thus lead to longer periods of near-peak performance. However, this was not the case for our performance metric.

There are some limitations for this study. First, as a team sport, it is difficult to fully isolate and evaluate players without team and teammate quality impacting the results. Next, the data does not consist of information about full careers for the players. Instead, some players only have a few, e.g., one or two seasons where data is recorded, potentially giving a false representation of their actual peak. Specifically, as some players only have data for low (below 20) or high ages (above 35), the variance of the results will subsequently be inflated with each player being given a peak age. This also ties in with the stature of the leagues investigated, since the Swedish soccer leagues belong to the lower tier, the best players tend to be sold to clubs in higher-ranked leagues, leading to potential bias. Similarly, older players playing in higher-ranked leagues may choose to move to a lower-ranked league in the final year(s) of their careers, which also may skew the results. This may in turn also impact the modeling capability, as it will not be able to fully recover each player's aging trajectory due to a lack of data. Lastly, the positional grouping used here may not fully represent the intricacies within a team as the same position in one team can have vastly different roles and expectations in another team. For instance, a wing-back for a worse team may be expected to mainly contribute defensively while for a top team, the expectations may be more shifted toward offensive contribution.

6 Conclusion

This paper presents a study on age of peak performance for players in the top three Swedish leagues where performance is measured based on state-of-the-art metrics. As previous work dealt with top leagues, the Swedish leagues were chosen as representatives of a lower-tier league that has different prerequisites, in terms of large player turnover and different transfer patterns, than the top leagues. The results suggest that soccer players in these leagues attain peak performance between the ages of 25 and 27. For the given playing positions, forwards had the earliest peak at age 25, followed by midfielders and defenders. Goalkeepers had the highest average peak age.

Future work may take into account a more fine-grained classification of the players based on player roles. However, finding the right number of roles (e.g., [1] proposes 21 roles) and still retaining enough data per role may be a challenge. Another interesting problem is to try to relate performances in different leagues which would allow us to use data from different leagues in the computation of peak performances. Also, the use of other performance metrics for lower-tier leagues is an avenue for further work, as well as applying our metric to top leagues.

References

1. Aalbers, B., Van Haaren, J.: Distinguishing between roles of football players in play-by-play match event data. In: Brefeld, U., Davis, J., Van Haaren, J., Zimmermann, A. (eds.) MLSA 2018. LNCS (LNAI), vol. 11330, pp. 31–41. Springer, Cham (2019). https://doi.org/10.1007/978-3-030-17274-9_3
2. Anzer, G., Bauer, P.: Expected passes. Data Min. Knowl. Disc. **36**(1), 295–317 (2022). https://doi.org/10.1007/S10618-021-00810-3

3. Berthelot, G., et al.: The age-performance relationship in the general population and strategies to delay age related decline in performance. Arch. Public Health **77**, 51 (2019). https://doi.org/10.1186/s13690-019-0375-8
4. Bradbury, J.C.: Peak athletic performance and ageing: evidence from baseball. J. Sports Sci. **27**(6), 599–610 (2009). https://doi.org/10.1080/02640410802691348
5. Brander, J.A., Egan, E.J., Yeung, L.: Estimating the effects of age on NHL player performance. J. Quant. Anal. Sports **10**(2), 241–259 (2014). https://doi.org/10.1515/jqas-2013-0085
6. Bürkner, P.C.: brms: an R package for Bayesian multilevel models using Stan. J. Stat. Softw. **80**, 1–28 (2017). https://doi.org/10.18637/jss.v080.i01
7. Decroos, T., Bransen, L., Van Haaren, J., Davis, J.: Actions speak louder than goals: valuing player actions in soccer. In: 25th ACM SIGKDD International Conference on Knowledge Discovery & Data Mining, pp. 1851–1861 (2019). https://doi.org/10.1145/3292500.3330758
8. Dendir, S.: When do soccer players peak? A note. J. Sports Anal. **2**(2), 89–105 (2016). https://doi.org/10.3233/JSA-160021
9. Eliasson, A.: The European football market, globalization and mobility among players. Soccer Soc. **10**(3–4), 386–397 (2009). https://doi.org/10.1080/14660970902771449
10. Frick, B.: Performance, salaries, and contract length: empirical evidence from German soccer. Int. J. Sport Financ. **6**(2), 87–118 (2011)
11. Gelman, A.: Prior distributions for variance parameters in hierarchical models (comment on article by Browne and Draper). Bayesian Anal. **1**(3), 515–534 (2006). https://doi.org/10.1214/06-BA117A
12. Gelman, A., et al.: Bayesian workflow. arXiv:2011.01808 (2020)
13. Goodman, M.: A new way to measure keepers' shot stopping: post-shot expected goals (2018). https://statsbomb.com/articles/soccer/a-new-way-to-measure-keepers-shot-stopping-post-shot-expected-goals/
14. Kalén, A., Rey, E., Sal de Rellán-Guerra, A., Lago-Peñas, C.: Are soccer players older now than before? Aging trends and market value in the last three decades of the UEFA champions league. Front. Psychol. **10**, 76 (2019). https://doi.org/10.3389/fpsyg.2019.00076
15. Kharrat, T., McHale, I.G., Peña, J.L.: Plus–minus player ratings for soccer. Eur. J. Oper. Res. **283**(2), 726–736 (2020). https://doi.org/10.1016/j.ejor.2019.11.026
16. Kovalchik, S.A.: The older they rise the younger they fall: age and performance trends in men's professional tennis from 1991 to 2012. J. Quant. Anal. Sports **10**(2), 99–107 (2014). https://doi.org/10.1515/jqas-2013-0091
17. Lewandowski, D., Kurowicka, D., Joe, H.: Generating random correlation matrices based on vines and extended onion method. J. Multivar. Anal. **100**(9), 1989–2001 (2009). https://doi.org/10.1016/j.jmva.2009.04.008
18. Liu, G., Luo, Y., Schulte, O., Kharrat, T.: Deep soccer analytics: learning an action-value function for evaluating soccer players. Data Min. Knowl. Disc. **34**(5), 1531–1559 (2020). https://doi.org/10.1007/S10618-020-00705-9
19. Oterhals, G., Lorås, H., Pedersen, A.V.: Age at nomination among soccer players nominated for major international individual awards: a better proxy for the age of peak individual soccer performance? Front. Psychol. **12**(661523) (2021). https://doi.org/10.3389/fpsyg.2021.661523
20. Perez-Arroniz, M., Calleja-González, J., Zabala-Lili, J., Zubillaga, A.: The soccer goalkeeper profile: bibliographic review. Phys. Sportsmedicine 1–10 (2022). https://doi.org/10.1080/00913847.2022.2040889

21. Sal de Rellán-Guerra, A., Rey, E., Kalén, A., Lago-Peñas, C.: Age-related physical and technical match performance changes in elite soccer players. Scand. J. Med. Sci. Sports **29**(9), 1421–1427 (2019). https://doi.org/10.1111/sms.13463
22. Singh, K.: Introducing expected threat (XT) (2019). https://karun.in/blog/expected-threat.html. Accessed 3 Feb 2022
23. Sóskuthy, M.: Generalised additive mixed models for dynamic analysis in linguistics: a practical introduction. arXiv:1703.05339 (2017)
24. Stølen, T., Chamari, K., Castagna, C., Wisløff, U.: Physiology of soccer. Sports Med. **35**(6), 501–536 (2005). https://doi.org/10.2165/00007256-200535060-00004
25. UEFA.com: Country coefficients (2023). https://www.uefa.com/nationalassociations/uefarankings/country/#/yr/2024
26. Vaci, N., Cocić, D., Gula, B., Bilalić, M.: Large data and Bayesian modeling - aging curves of NBA players. Behav. Res. Methods **51**(4), 1544–1564 (2019). https://doi.org/10.3758/s13428-018-1183-8
27. Wood, S.N.: Thin plate regression splines. J. R. Stat. Soc.: Ser. B (Stat. Methodol.) **65**(1), 95–114 (2003). https://doi.org/10.1111/1467-9868.00374

Structure From Motion and Its Application in Augmented Reality and Sports Optical Tracking

Masoumeh Izadi(✉) and Ehsan Goodarzi

Television Content Analysis, 1 Changi S Ln, 01, Singapore 486070, Singapore
{masoumeh.izadi,ehsan.goodarzi}@tvconal.com
http://www.tvconal.com

Abstract. The growing use of Augmented Reality (AR) and Virtual Reality (VR) in sports is due to the overall enhancements these visualization techniques provide. These technologies have the potential to enhance athlete performance, optimize training outcomes, and improve the overall quality and fairness of sports competitions. While AR and VR technologies have made significant strides in enhancing various aspects of sports, there are still several gaps and challenges that need to be addressed to fully realize their potential in the sports industry. Some of the notable gaps include motion tracking accuracy. Achieving high-precision motion tracking in three-dimensional (3D) environments, especially during fast-paced sports activities, can be challenging. Ensuring accurate tracking of athlete movements, gestures, and interactions is crucial for providing fair judging, and immersive and responsive experiences. In this paper, we address the improvements in the underlying algorithms that are responsible for the accurate 3D reconstruction of objects using Structure from Motion (SfM). To demonstrate the practical applications and implications of this technology in real-world sporting scenarios, we present a case study focused on ball tracking in cricket and show how these techniques can improve tracking accuracy for better match adjudication.

Keywords: 3D reconstruction · Structure from motion · Bundle adjustment · Cricket · Virtual reality

1 Introduction

Advancements in sensor technology, computer vision algorithms, and data processing techniques have enabled the accurate reconstruction of sports moments in three dimensions [1]. The 3D reconstruction technology has revolutionized the analysis and understanding of sports performance, providing detailed insights into athlete movements and interactions. They enable broadcasters to deliver immersive, interactive, and personalized viewing experiences that transcend traditional 2D broadcasts, enhancing viewer engagement and enjoyment of the sporting event. Enhanced visualization for judges with views of significant game

J. S. Dong et al. (Eds.): ISACE 2024, LNCS 14794, pp. 291–301, 2024.
https://doi.org/10.1007/978-3-031-69073-0_25

events from multiple angles and perspectives is another crucial role of these sports technologies. For example, judges in gymnastics or figure skating competitions can see real-time scores, performance metrics, or instant replays overlaid onto the live video feed, facilitating more informed and objective scoring decisions. The enhanced visualization by AR and VR can also improve coaching and athlete training by providing a more comprehensive understanding of performance. Tracking the movements and positions of athletes in 3D space, coaches and sports scientists can analyze biomechanical parameters, kinematics, and other performance measures to identify areas for improvement and optimize training regimens with quantitative feedback. For example, athletes in track and field events can receive instant feedback on their running technique, stride length, or jump trajectory through AR overlays displayed in their field of view.

As AR and VR technologies become more prevalent in sports, addressing associated challenges and concerns becomes more critical. Establishing clear guidelines and regulations to safeguard data privacy and data accuracy while maximizing the benefits of AR and VR technologies in sports is an ongoing challenge. Integrating real-time data feeds and analytics seamlessly into AR and VR environments remains another challenge. While there are solutions for displaying real-time statistics and information overlays, ensuring accuracy, reliability, and synchronization with live sports events requires robust data processing and communication protocols. Addressing these challenges requires interdisciplinary collaboration among technology developers, sports organizations, athletes, broadcasters, and other stakeholders.

In this paper, we focus on accuracy concerns in 3D reconstruction of game events. In particular, we use Structure from Motion (SfM) to address the challenge of localizing objects while tracking in real-world dimensions. SfM is a technique used in computer vision and photogrammetry to reconstruct three-dimensional structures from a sequence of two-dimensional images. This very well formulates the problem of viewing a moving object from different cameras in a sports match to reconstruct the exact location of the object at any point in time and its distance or position from other important locations or objects in the game.

While SfM is primarily used for 3D reconstruction, it can indirectly aid in stabilizing multiple camera calibration as well. SfM relies on identifying and tracking features across multiple images to estimate camera poses and reconstruct 3D structures. By accurately tracking these features, SfM helps in understanding the relative motion between cameras, which is essential for camera calibration ensuring consistency and coherence across multiple views in a multi-camera broadcast. We selected a case study in cricket, where the 3D location of a ball poses important decisions in the game regarding identifying illegal actions, assigning penalties, and even player dismissals. Generally, in a televised cricket match, there are multiple cameras around the pitch that contribute not only to capturing the bowling and batting events but also to help the umpires make decisions about whether or not the action taken by the bowler and the batsman in every ball delivery complied with the rules of the game according to the International Cricket Council, ICCs protocols.

The present study proposes the use of SfM and its sub-module mechanisms such as bundle adjustment to improve the localization accuracy of the moving ball in a small window of time after it is released from the bowler's hand and before it is hit by the batsman's body or the bat. We show how the proposed method can reduce the error in tracking the ball in a multi-camera broadcast setup where many cameras around the pitch capture the ball's motion inside the pitch.

2 Background

In this section, we explain the principles of the SfM framework. Figure 1 shows the SfM problem setup.

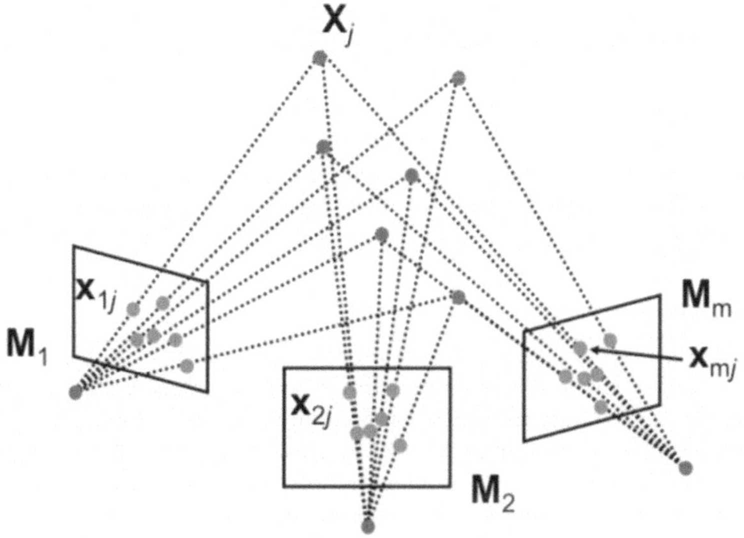

Fig. 1. The setup in SfM [2]

Suppose we have m cameras with camera transformations M_i encoding both the intrinsic and extrinsic parameters for the cameras. Let X_j be one of the n 3D points in the scene. Each 3D point may be visible in multiple cameras at the location x_{ij}, which is the projection of X_j to the image of the camera i using the projective transformation Mi. Structure from motion aims to recover both the structure of the scene (the n 3D points X_j) and the motion of the cameras (the m projection matrices M_i) from all the observations x_i.

SfM algorithms often assume the pinhole camera model (Fig. 2) as the underlying projection model for capturing images. This model describes how points in

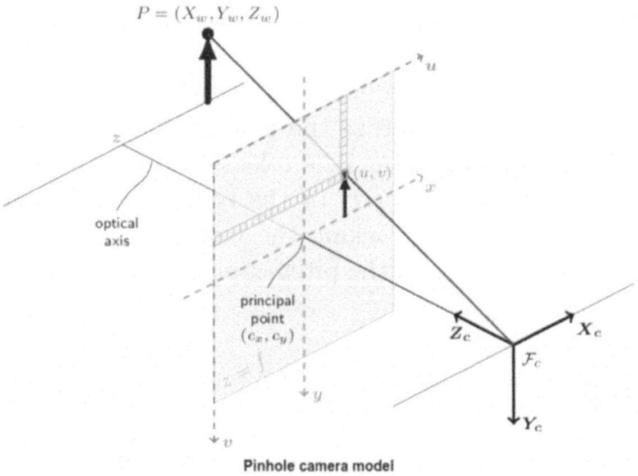

Fig. 2. The pinhole camera model [3]

the 3D world project onto the image plane of the camera, forming the basis for triangulating 3D points from corresponding 2D image points. Camera calibration needs to be performed to ensure accurate mapping between the 3D world and the 2D image plane, enabling precise alignment of virtual objects in the AR/VR environment. Imprecise camera calibration and quantization errors in estimating discrete temporal offsets result in significant errors in the reconstruction of moving points [4].

2.1 Triangulation

In the SfM context, triangulation is the process of estimating the 3D coordinates of a point in space by intersecting rays from multiple cameras that observe the same point in 2D images. Triangulation is a fundamental step in reconstructing the 3D structure of a scene from a set of images. Mathematically, triangulation involves solving the intersection problem between rays emanating from different camera centers (also known as camera poses) and passing through corresponding image points. Given the calibrated intrinsic parameters of each camera and the extrinsic parameters (position and orientation) of the cameras relative to each other, triangulation computes the 3D coordinates of a point by finding the intersection of these rays in 3D space. The projection equations map a 3D point (X, Y, Z) in camera coordinates to its corresponding image point (u, v) using the camera's intrinsic parameters (i.e. focal length, principal point, and lens distortion) and the camera's extrinsic parameters (position and orientation).

$$(u, v, 1) = K[R \;\; t][X, Y, Z, 1] \tag{1}$$

where (u, v) are the coordinates of the image point K is the camera's intrinsic matrix, R is the rotation matrix representing the camera's orientation, and t is the translation vector representing the camera's position. In practice lenses usually have some distortion, mostly radial distortion, and slight tangential distortion. Given corresponding image points $(u1, v1)$ and $(u2, v2)$ observed by two cameras with known poses, the 3D coordinates (X, Y, Z) of the point can be computed by solving the intersection of the rays emanating from the camera centers (C1 and C2) and passing through the image points: $P = (X, Y, Z)P = C1 + \lambda1 \cdot r1 = C2 + \lambda2 \cdot r2$ where: C1 and C2 are the camera centers, r1 and r2 are the normalized ray directions corresponding to the image points, $\lambda1$ and $\lambda2$ are scalar parameters representing the distances along the rays. The 3D coordinates (X, Y, Z) can be computed as the intersection point of the two rays.

2.2 Bundle Adjustment

Optimization models are used in SfM algorithms to estimate camera poses and 3D structures from a set of 2D images. One of the key optimization techniques used in SfM is bundle adjustment, which is a nonlinear least squares optimization problem [5]. Bundle adjustment aims to minimize the reprojection error between observed feature points in the images and their corresponding 3D points, while simultaneously refining the parameters of the camera poses and 3D structure. The objective function for bundle adjustment typically involves minimizing the sum of squared reprojection errors across all images:

$$E = \sum_{i=1}^{N} \sum_{j=1}^{M_i} ||P_{ij} - \pi_i P(j)||^2 \tag{2}$$

where N is the number of images, M_i is the number of feature points in the ith image, Pij is the observed 2D position of the jth feature point in the ith image, Pj is the corresponding 3D position of the jth feature point in the frame, π_i is the projection function that projects 3D points into the image plane of the ith camera. Bundle adjustment jointly optimizes camera intrinsics and extrinsic (position and orientation) and 3D point triangulation to reconstruct a static scene. In the next section, we explain the special application in our case study that allows certain assumptions and simplifications of the SfM, and the underlying bundle adjustment for ball tracking in cricket.

3 Methods

We assume M cameras observe N 3D points over time. The relation between the 3D point $X^n(t)$ and its 2D projection $x_m^n(f)$ on camera m at frame f is given by:

$$[x_m^n(f), 1] \equiv K_m(f)[R_m(f), T_m(f)][X^n(t), 1] \tag{3}$$

where $K_m(f)$ is the intrinsic camera matrix, $R_m(f)$ and $T_m(f)$ are the relative camera rotation and translation, respectively. This transformation can be denoted as $x_m^n(f) = P_m(f, X^n(t))$ where P is a 3×4 Projection matrix consisting of two parts - the intrinsic matrix (K) that contains the intrinsic parameters and the extrinsic matrix ($[R|t)]$) that is a combination of 3×3 rotation matrix R and a 3×1 translation t vector.

$$P = K * [R|t] \tag{4}$$

The time corresponding to frame f is related to the continuous global time t linearly: $f = \alpha_m t + \beta_m$, where α_m and β_m are the camera frame rate and time offset. For a static 3D point, $X^n(t)$ is a constant.

The intrinsic matrix K is upper triangular, as follows

$$K = \begin{bmatrix} f_x & \gamma & c_x \\ 0 & f_y & c_y \\ 0 & 0 & 1 \end{bmatrix} \tag{5}$$

where f_x, f_y are the x and y focal lengths; c_x, c_y are the x and y coordinates of the optical center in the image plane; gamma is the skew between the axes.

Before utilizing SfM for AR/VR applications, the cameras used for capturing the event need to be calibrated. Our objective is reconstructing 3D trajectories of a moving ball, while the ball is seen from multiple stationary cameras. Naturally, moving points that are often closer to the cameras provide tighter constraints for precise camera calibration. In the vast majority of dynamic scenes captured by multiple independent video cameras, no two cameras see the 3D point at the same instant of time. This fact trivially invalidates the triangulation constraint. In this application, we recover stable camera poses, then we defer the requirement for temporally consistent points across the scene and reconstruct only a set of points per timestep. These points will eventually present the real coordinates of the ball along a trajectory. The next step is pose estimation. The positions and orientation at different time instances or frames in a video sequence are recovered. The pinhole camera model is used to relate the 3D scene points to their corresponding 2D image points, enabling the estimation of camera poses based on the observed image projections.

Since we have a set of stationary cameras and a set of reference points that are known (Fig. 3), our setup slightly differs from the traditional bundle adjustment in that it uses unknown reference points. Due to the visibility of these points from multiple views and the standard measures amongst different stadiums, we can use this special case to refine the camera parameters and 3D structure estimates by minimizing the reprojection error between observed feature points and their corresponding 3D points. During this customized bundle adjustment, the relative positions and orientations of cameras are optimized to ensure consistency across multiple views.

3.1 Fine Tuning the Trajectory

In the realm of 3D reconstruction of the cricket ball, precision is paramount. Not only must the ball be captured within the field of view of at least two cameras, but it also demands precise detection by machine learning models.

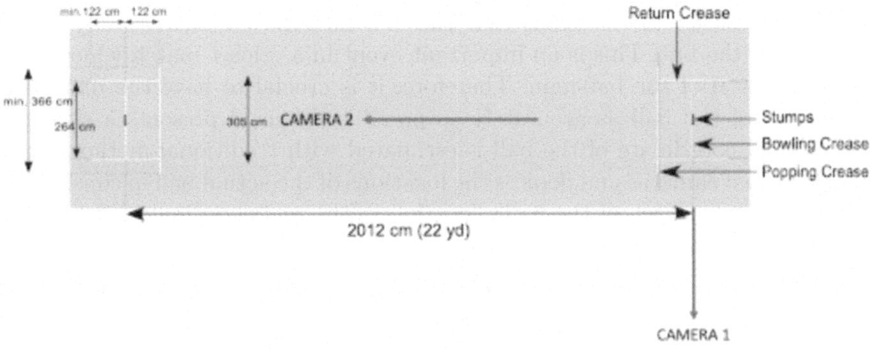

Fig. 3. The scene of a cricket pitch in the view of two cameras

However, various complexities can arise, potentially complicating the trajectory reconstruction process.

One such complexity stems from the presence of false positives within the ball detection model. These erroneous detections, along with miss detections of the ball's center, can introduce discrepancies in the reconstructed trajectory. To address this challenge, statistical methods such as mean square error (MSE) analysis prove invaluable.

Through MSE analysis, detections significantly deviating from the mean are identified as potential false positives and subsequently removed from the dataset. This iterative process of false positive removal continues until a satisfactory balance between sensitivity and specificity is achieved, bolstering the reliability of the reconstructed trajectory.

Moreover, in cases where the center of the ball is misdetected, the application of curve fitting serves as an effective strategy for noise removal. By fitting a curve to the data, erroneous fluctuations can be smoothed out, enhancing the accuracy of the reconstructed trajectory.

In essence, by meticulously addressing false positives and miss detections through statistical analysis and curve fitting, the accuracy and reliability of cricket ball 3D reconstruction are significantly bolstered, paving the way for enhanced insights into the dynamics of the game.

4 Experiments

In our experiments, we used two orthogonal cameras at a time to see the ball flight from the bowling moment to the batting action. These cameras in the broadcast terms are called runout and lbw, as they are located respectively in the side views (left and right of the bowler and left and right of the batsman), and front or back view (both ends of the pitch). In this setup, our objective is to get the real-world coordinates of the ball at each frame of the video over its trajectory inside the pitch. This is to confirm whether or not the bounce position of the ball and the impact point of the ball with the bat or body are following the rules of cricket in the event that the ball hits the batsman's body before contact with the bat. This is an important event in a cricket match which leads to the dismissal of the batsman. Therefore, it is crucial to have the real-world coordinates of the ball as accurately as possible. Figure 4 presents a situation when the 3D coordinate of the ball is estimated with traditional methods from two orthogonal cameras and depicts the locations of the actual ball in consecutive frames. The inaccuracy of the ball's location in the real coordinates can lead to incorrect decisions with heavy consequences.

Fig. 4. Projected 3D balls on the estimated trajectory versus the actual ball locations with poor calibration accuracy.

We performed camera calibration using OpenCV to find the intrinsic parameters of the seven cameras around the pitch. Each camera that is capturing the side-view and front-view needs to be calibrated in isolation, because the focal length, distortion coefficient, and other parameters vary from camera to camera, even if they are from the same brand or the same model. We used a standard checkerboard for calibration and from each camera took at least 20 images. The images are at different angles and distances because the calibration code needs various points with different perspectives.

The pixel coordinates (u, v) of each 3D point are determined in OpenCV for each image. Then using the 3D points, the pixel coordinates (u, v), and distortion coefficients from intrinsic value, we minimize reprojection error for all cameras to optimize extrinsic camera features as well as focal length by the customized bundle adjustment method (Fig. 5).

Table 1 presents the error in each camera location concerning pixel value after a bundle adjustment. The approximate pixel value is 7mm in the real world for the used camera views and that is negligible with the current standard in practice for the decision review system and umpire assistance. We used distances in

Table 1. Reprojection results on static 3D points on the pitch.

Point Location	Runout (pixel)	LBW (pixel)	Error Runout	Error LBW
BowlingCrease right	[1665, 802]	[1314, 617]	0.22	0.2
BowlinCrease left	[1658, 752]	[626, 624]	0.13	0.21
PoppingCrease left	[1303, 746]	[624, 654]	0.45	0.43
PoppingCrease right	[1297, 795]	[1323, 646]	0.1	0.09
Wicket Center top	[1662, 776]	[967, 620]	0.36	0.26
WicketCente bottom	[1661, 567]	[964, 437]	1.06	1.46
ProtectedArea left	[867, 736]	[563, 693]	0.46	0.42
ProtectedArea right	[846, 791]	[1384, 684]	0.7	0.63

Fig. 5. Accurate reprojection of ball location with bundle adjustment in multiple cameras.

Fig. 6. Virtual ball trajectory with a 360-degree visualization of a player dismissal.

the real world such as the ball diameter and the thickness of the lines marking a popping crease and a bowling crease and other similar measures as ground truth to see the error of the reprojection. In almost all our experiments with bundle adjustment, the error is bounded by 3.3 mm, which is expected based on the pixel error reported in the recovery of reference points in Table 1. The results make this reprojection in 3D suitable for VR visualization of the trajectories and accurate ball tracking in three dimensions (Fig. 6) that enhance the decision-making process in cricket by providing umpires with additional information to review contentious decisions and ensure fair play. By leveraging advanced computer vision and tracking technologies, decision-review systems contribute to the integrity and transparency of the game.

5 Conclusions and Future Work

This paper proposed the use of SfM in accurately tracking objects in sports optical tracking and visualization of those objects in a 3D space from the viewpoint of multiple cameras. The practical use case for this application for match adjudication and umpire assistance in cricket was presented. We used a customized bundle adjustment technique as an optimization problem to reduce the reprojection error in real coordinates. The triangulation constraint in bundle adjustment however is invalid for moving points captured in multiple unsynchronized videos. Typically, this happens when the camera moves or shakes. Such cases happen in practice as the cameras are not stable at all times. We plan to use nonlinear optimization algorithms [6–8] to solve the bundle adjustment problem in such cases. In addition to bundle adjustment, other optimization models and techniques may be used in SfM algorithms depending on the specific implementation and requirements of the application. These may include techniques for global optimization, and regularization to improve the accuracy and robustness of the reconstructed 3D models [9]. We intend to apply this research extension in cricket VR systems in future work. This approach is applicable to other sports as well. More detailed experiments with other sports and in other scenarios are planned in future works. Additionally, we will incorporate Kalman filter approaches to effectively remove noise from the ball detection process, further enhancing the precision and reliability of our 3D reconstruction system.

References

1. Crosilla, F., Beinat, A., Fusiello, A., Maset, E., Visintini, D.: Advanced Procrustes Analysis Models in Photogrammetric Computer Vision. Springer, Cham (2019)
2. OpenCV documentation. https://www.docs.opencv.org/3.4/d9/d0c/group-calib3d.html. Accessed 05 Feb 2024
3. Avidan, S., Shashua, A.: Trajectory triangulation: 3D reconstruction of moving points from a monocular image sequence. PAMI (2000)
4. Van Riel, S.: Exploring the use of 3D GIS as an analytical tool in archaeological excavation practice (2016)

5. Schönberger, J.L., Frahm, J.M.: Structure-from-motion revisited. In: Proceedings of the IEEE Conference on Computer Vision and Pattern Recognition, Las Vegas, NV, USA, 27–30 June (2016)
6. Fülöp-Balogh, B.-E., Tursman, E., Tompkin, J., Digne, J., Bonneel, N.: Dynamic scene novel view synthesis via deferred spatio-temporal consistency. Comput. Graph. **107**, 220 (2022)
7. Vijayanarasimhan, S., Ricco, S., Schmid, C., Sukthankar, R., Fragkiadaki, K.: SfM-Net: Learning of Structure and Motion from Video (2017)
8. He, X., et al.: Detector-Free Structure from Motion (2023)
9. Vo, M., Narasimhan, S.G.: Spatiotemporal bundle adjustment for dynamic 3D reconstruction. In: CVPR (2016)

Effects of KF94 Face Mask on Cardiopulmonary Function and Subjective Sensation During Graded Exercise: A Comparison of KF94 2D and 3D Face Masks

Sungheum Um[1] and Robert Seungbok Lee[2,3](✉)

[1] Fortium Research Institute of Sports Science, Korea University, Seoul, Republic of Korea
[2] Yonsei Enabling Science and Technology Research Clinic (YESTEC), Yonsei University, Seoul, Republic of Korea
supermandrlee@gmail.com
[3] Korea Sports and Olympic Council Wheelchair Rugby Association, Seoul, Republic of Korea

Abstract. This study aimed to compare the effects of wearing KF94 2D and 3D face masks on cardiopulmonary function and subjective sensations during graded exercise in adult males. This crossover study categorized 12 adult males into a group wearing a 2D face mask (experimental group) initially and the same group wearing a 3D face mask (control group) following a washout period. The application of KF94 masks was of two brands—ibanari(2D) and Good Vibes(3D)—approved by the Food and Drug Administration of Sb Global Healthcare Co., Ltd. Li et al.'s questionnaire (2015) was used to observe changes in cardiorespiratory function (SBP, DBP, Rf, VT, VE, VO2, FiO2) of study participants who underwent a graded exercise test. The subjective discomfort from wearing a face mask during exercise was assessed. There was no significant difference in Rf, VT, VE, VO2, FiO2, and exercise end time when the 2D and 3D masks were worn during cardiorespiratory function and maximal exercise ($p > .05$), but when the 2D mask was worn, VO2 value was high ($p < .05$). However, from VO2 to the 6th point, 2D was significantly higher than 3D group ($p < 0.05$). Subjective sensation immediately after maximal exercise was higher in respiratory resistance immediately after exercise in the 2D (6.29 ± 2.4 points) than in the 3D group (4.16 ± 3.0 points) ($p < 0.05$). We concluded that the design type features of the 2D and 3D face masks are not significantly affected by filtration efficacy and breathability during maximum exercise in the otherwise healthy adult male participants.

Keywords: 2D face mask · 3D face mask · cardiopulmonary function · subjective sensation · graded exercise

1 Introduction

The recent pandemic was an unprecedented occurrence that impacted scores of lives and the well-being and health of many people around the globe. As of January 17, 2023, a total of 668,282,808 cases of the Coronavirus Disease-19 (COVID-19) have been confirmed

S. Um and R. S. Lee have contributed equally to the work.

J. S. Dong et al. (Eds.): ISACE 2024, LNCS 14794, pp. 302–312, 2024.
https://doi.org/10.1007/978-3-031-69073-0_26

in 229 countries, resulting in 6,730,814 deaths [1]. In South Korea, following the report of its first case on January 17, 2020, the Center for Disease Control and Prevention (2023) confirmed a total of 29,861,234 cases in the nation with 33,014 fatalities [1, 2]. Public health experts continually emphasized the highly contagious features of the disease via direct (e.g., droplets released from aerosolized particles through sneezing, coughing, or talking) and indirect (e.g., contact with infected individuals or contaminated surfaces) modes of transmission [3]. Due to the rapid spread of COVID-19, the applications of personal protective equipment (e.g., masks and other protective wearable coverings) became critical. Moreover, the proactivity of putting on self-protective measures was strongly emphasized globally to avoid the contraction and spread of the potentially lethal infection [4].

The application of face masks in the context of the COVID-19 pandemic has been approved by the WHO (2020) after policymakers implemented and enforced the practice as the law in most countries [4]. This legislative mandate stemmed from the initial evidence that face masks alone reduced transmission of the virus among healthcare workers [5]. Health officials at the Korea Center for Disease Control and Prevention (2020) strongly urged the public to always wear face masks to reduce the probability of transmission and spread [2]. Accordingly, the practice has become routine for all to wear either a KF80, KF90, or KF94 type mask. The masks were approved by the National Institute for Occupational Safety and Health to protect humans from smog and yellow dust composed of ultrafine particles (particulate matter with a diameter of less than 2.5μm) based on published research evidence by Song et al. (2020) [6].

Face masks are useful in that they can be worn during daily life or leisure activities. Shurlock et al. (2021) suggested that using a face mask while exercising is recommended amid the pandemic [7]. However, wearing masks can diminish the passage of air via the associated anatomy which can impact the body's physiological response to exercise and may also interfere with exercise performance [7]. Furthermore, it was reported that hypoxemia could pose a potential threat to the health of individuals [7]. Thus, concerns surmounted regarding the negative aspects of using face masks under the setting of the COVID-19 pandemic. These included increased respiratory work, changes in respiratory gas exchange associated with the rebreathing of exhaled CO2, and reduced ventilation during exercise performance [8].

The potentially negative aspects may lead to reduced physical activity especially while wearing masks may be required under the circumstances. Studies have also reported the importance of fitness and exercise amid the public health crisis since decreased physical activity can pose serious consequences in cardiopulmonary, metabolic, and psychological aspects of an individual [9]. The habitual lack of exercise increases the risk of developing cardiovascular disease and diabetes while enhancing clinical complications in individuals infected with COVID-19 [10]. Therefore, it is essential to minimize the risk of viral transmission by determining whether wearing a face mask during exercise has significant physiological effects that may affect exercise performance.

In addition to the inherent filtration capabilities of the fabric material, the effectiveness of a face mask also depends on facial compatibility, user compliance, and correct application practices. Compliant users will also discover that wearing a face mask presents an obstacle to basic daily life activities such as limitations to speech, auditory acuity, sense of smell, and even fogging of glasses. The challenges to manufacturing a user-friendly mask that adequately blocks the passage of air at the mask interface of the nose, cheeks, and chin areas cannot also be discounted. Konda et al. (2020) suggested that the gap between the mask and the skin area due to improper wearing can reduce the achievable filtration efficiency by up to 60% [11]. This aspect is especially challenging given the variations in the human anatomy of facial features whereby exhaled air leaks out through masks around the protruding areas of the face [12]. Therefore, increasing emphasis is placed on the development of customized face masks suitable for individuals with varying features of facial anatomy. To this end, the design features such as metal strips at the nose border, tissue adhesive at the edges of the mask, and bands or reinforcements at the chin area have been incorporated into commercial masks.

Morishima et al. (2015) attempted to optimize mask pattern development for various facial features and shapes by innovatively performing geometric analysis of 2D patterns based on 3D coordinates [13]. Recently, Korea University's Sports Science Research Institute (Fortium) conducted tests with ergonomically designed 2D and 3D printed mannequins to develop the optimal mask patterns suitable for facial movements while speaking. Among several models of the "Ibanari" mask series, the KF94 2D mask was aerodynamically designed (Fortium, Ltd. Co, Korea) to adjust the top panel portion of the mask that enables reduced fogging when wearing glasses by directing airflow away from the eyes. Darby et al. (2021) found that most leaks from medical facial masks occurred around the eyes and cheeks [14]. Regarding the 3D masks, Verberne et al., (2020) reported that the most common leakage areas were the nose, cheeks, mouth, and chin [15]. Appropriate exercise is an effective way to prevent disease and promote a favorable prognosis. However, the effects of 2D and 3D face masks on cardiopulmonary function and subjective sensation during exercise remain unclear.

Recent studies have demonstrated the development of 2D, and 3D customized face masks based on polyamide composites to address these underlying challenges [16–18]. However, no studies have been conducted regarding athletic performance and subjective sense of discomfort from wearing these innovative masks during exercise activities. This study compared and reviewed the effects on cardiopulmonary function and subjective sensations caused by wearing KF94 2D and 3D face masks during incremental load exercise in a cohort of otherwise healthy adult men.

2 Methods

2.1 Participants

The study subjects were 12 adult males (22.7 $\pm$ 2.6 years old) students at 'K' and 'G' Universities all of whom were engaged in daily exercise habits. In this crossover study, the group wearing a 2D face mask was categorized into the experimental group and the group wearing a 3D face mask as a control group, whereby measurements were collected after a washout period of 7 days. Only participants who volunteered to fully participate in the study were evaluated after being informed of the study's purposes and procedures. We obtained written consent for all participants. During the subject selection process, those with diseases that significantly limited physical activity, such as any musculoskeletal or

Table 1. Basic clinical characteristics.

Table 1. Clinical Characteristics (n=12)

Variables	Mean±SD
Age (years)	22.7±2.6
Height (cm)	175.5±5.5
Weight (kg)	71.5±8.0
Body mass index (kg/m2)	23.1±1.6
Skeletal muscle mass (kg)	33.7±3.4
Body fat mass (kg)	11.8±3.0
Body fat percentage (%)	16.4±2.9
Resting heart rate (beats/min)	70.6±10.3
Resting systolic blood pressure (mmHg)	120.8±6.3
Resting diastolic blood pressure (mmHg)	72.0±4.7

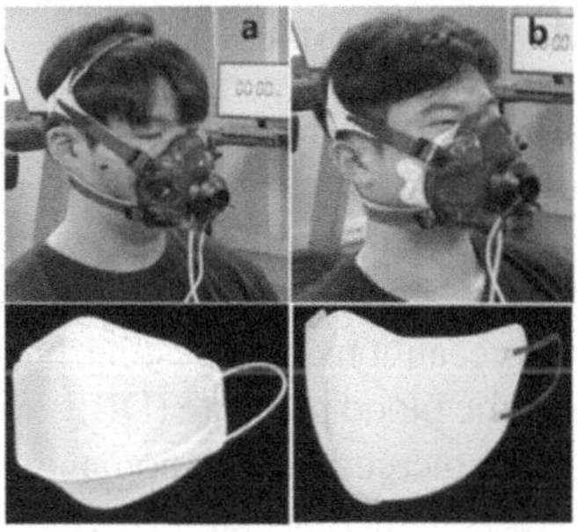

Fig. 1. 2D and 3D masks.

cardiovascular diseases, were excluded. The basic clinical characteristics of the study participants are shown in Table 1.

2.2 Body Composition

Body composition was evaluated using a bioelectrical impedance analysis device (Inbody 720; Rep. of Korea) to measure height, weight, body fat mass, fat-free mass, and body fat percentage.

2.3 Face Masks

All participants used two types of face masks, "ibanari" (2D) and "Good Vibes" (3D), approved by the Food and Drug Administration from SB Global Healthcare Co., Ltd. (Fig. 1). The ibanari 2D face mask with a triple-layer structure (tertiary filtration) (size: 134 ± 10 mm wide Good Vibes 3D face mask with elastic ear straps: polyurethane 160 mm) and quadruple structure (4th filtration; size: width 207.8 ± 10 mm × 162 ± 10 mm; filter: non-woven polypropylene outer; lining: non-woven fabric; nose piece: polypropylene coated wire; elastic ear strap: polyurethane 160 mm) is manufactured for the purpose of protecting the respiratory tract from magnetic harmful substances such as yellow dust and fine dust and infectious agents. The two types of masks used in this study are the 2D and 3D types of KF94 grade. These have an average thickness of 0.4 μm, 94% collection efficiency, facial intake resistance of less than 70Pa, and a leakage rate of less than 11%. These are certified products with strict standards and are frequently used domestically in South Korea.

2.4 Exercise Stress Test

Participants were instructed to abstain from the consumption of caffeine, alcohol, tobacco, and high-intensity exercise 24 h prior to measurements for data acquisition. After a restful night of sleep participants arrived at the laboratory; actual measurements were preceded by a 30 min rest period after receiving preliminary instructions in safety and precautions. For resting blood pressure (BP), systolic blood pressure (SBP) and diastolic blood pressure (DBP) were measured on the left upper arm in a sitting position using a mercury sphygmomanometer (Germany). Measurements were recorded in millimeters of mercury (mmHg) units. BP during exercise was measured and recorded every 2 min using the standing mercury sphygmomanometer. All experiments were conducted in an artificial chamber room at 'K' University maintained at ambient temperature with a humidity of 24 °C and 50% relative humidity. Before wearing the KF94 2D and 3D face masks, a facial mask valve was manually shut to block airflow; a proper mask fit was ensured by subjective exhalation with maximum force to identify any air leaks. The fit was subsequently checked for leakage (e.g., lifting the mask from the face or by subjective whistling). The respiratory measurement parameters were observed throughout testing. Subjective sensations were measured using a questionnaire on a treadmill (STEX 8100TD; Rep. of Korea) before incremental load exercise and immediately after maximal exercise. The exercise stress test was conducted in a stepwise manner: warm-up for two minutes at 4.2 km/h on a 5% incline treadmill, using an automatic respiratory gas analyzer (Ultima CPX; USA) for measurements, while gradually increasing the speed by 0.3 km/h every minute to completion after a total of 12 min of exercise. A multi-stage incremental loading method was used in which only the slope was increased by 2% [19]. During this portion of the experiment, changes in heart rate (HR) and subjective exercise intensity—ratings of perceived exertion (RPE)—were continually monitored to rule out any physiological and psychological abnormalities. During exercise BP, HR, respiratory rate (Rf), tidal volume (VT), ventilation per minute (VE), oxygen intake (VO2), inspired oxygen concentration (FiO2), and RPE were recorded every 2 min. The criteria for determining VO2max is based on whether three or more of the following conditions have been met: 1) when VO2 does not increase despite increased exercise intensity, 2) when 90% or more of HRmax (220-age) is achieved, and 3) respiratory exchange ratio (RER) exceeds 1.15, 4) RPE is 18 or greater, and 5) participant expresses the intention to stop [20]. All experimental procedures were conducted at the same time. Double blinding was maintained by random group assignments to both arms (experimental vs. controls) in a cross-over design, including a one-week washout period.

2.5 Subjective Sensation

The sensation of wearing the face mask—'comfort level'—during exercise was quantified (Li et al., 2015) by surveying 10 areas: 1) humidity, 2) heat, 3) breathing resistance, 4) itchiness, 5) stuffiness, 6) saltiness, 7) feeling unwell, 8) odor, 9) fatigue, and 10) overall discomfort [16]. Participants were asked to rate any perceived levels of 'discomfort' 10 min after each exercise stress test using a visual analog scale (VAS) from 0 to 10 (0 = not at all; 5 = moderate or "mild"; 10 = strong). RPE (Borg, 1973) was used to allow participants to subjectively understand their exercise intensity levels [21].

2.6 Data Analysis

All data processing was completed using the SPSS 23.0 statistical program. Measurement results of each data item were expressed as mean ± standard deviation. An independent t-test was conducted to analyze the mean difference in dependent variables between the two groups (2D mask vs. 3D mask) with statistical significance levels set at $\alpha = 0.05$.

3 Results

The comparisons in the temporal changes in average cardiorespiratory function (SBP, DBP, HR, Rf, VT, VE, VO2, FiO2) when wearing 2D and 3D masks are shown in Fig. 2. The change pattern was similar, reaching the highest point when all was out.

From VO2 to the 6th point, 2D was significantly higher than when wearing a 3D mask ($p < 0.05$), and there was a tendency for it to be higher in all sections. After wearing 2D and 3D masks, there was no difference in all variables (Rf, VT, VE, VO2, FiO2, exercise end time) of cardiopulmonary function during maximal exercise ($p >$ .05) (Table 2).

Table 2. Comparing masks by cardiopulmonary function.

Table 2. Comparison of cardiopulmonary function immediately after maximal exercise by wearing KF94 2D and 3D face masks.

Variables	2D Mask	3D Mask	P
Rf (l/min)	32.2±6.1	41.5±7.2	.43
VT (l)	2.20±0.4	2.20±0.5	.88
VE (l/min)	83.9±8.8	89.6±14.2	.26
VO2 (l/min)	2.92±0.3	2.74±0.4	.59
FiO2 (%)	20.7±0.1	20.7±0.1	.87
Exercise duration (min)	16.7±1.7	16.5±1.9	.86

Rf: Respiratory frequency(rate); VT: tidal volume; VE: minute ventilation; VO2: oxygen intake; FiO2: inspired oxygen concentration;

*$p < 0.05$; SBP: systolic blood pressure; DBP: diastolic blood pressure; HR: heart rate; Rf: respiratory frequency; VT: tidal volume; VE: minute ventilation; VO2: oxygen. intake; FiO2: inspired oxygen concentration.

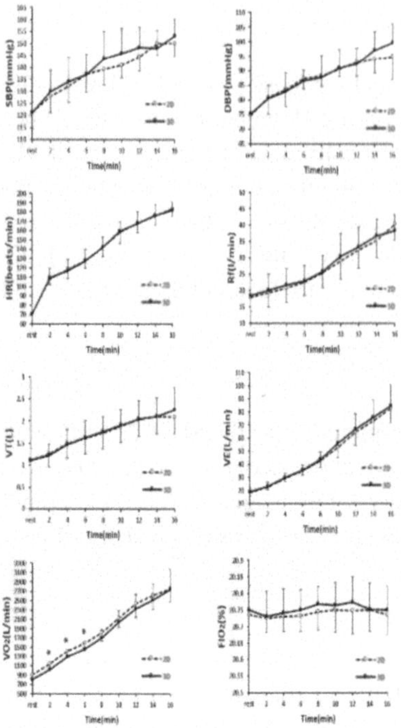

Fig. 2. Comparison of KF94 2D and 3D face masks by changes in cardiopulmonary function during incremental load exercise.

No statistical difference was observed in subjective sensation and RPE at rest (Table 3). However, respiratory resistance immediately after exercise was higher when wearing a 2D (6.29 ± 2.4 points) mask compared to a 3D (4.16 ± 3.0 points) mask ($p < 0.05$).

4 Discussion

The use of face masks in public has been on the rise for medical and health reasons since the unprecedented pandemic but there are no clear guidelines for their application while engaging in exercise. Fikenzer et al. (2020) reported that the N95 2D mask had a significant effect on subjective discomfort, RPE, and cardiopulmonary function during incremental load exercise whereby VO2max was shown to be reduced by 13% [17]. Shaw et al. (2020) found that, in young healthy adults, wearing a face mask during strenuous exercise performance was not associated with increased delivery of O2 supply to blood and muscle cells or athletic performance [18]. These studies were based on a comparison of maximum exercise capacity. Our study comparatively examined the effects on cardiorespiratory function and subjective sensation from wearing KF94 2D and 3D face masks during incremental load exercise.

The temporal change pattern of cardiorespiratory function (SBP, DBP, HR, Rf, VT, VE, VO2, FiO2) was similar until the ‘all out’ interval. VO2 was significantly higher in

Table 3. Comparison of KF94 2D and 3D masks

Table 3. KF94 2D and 3D face masks compared by subjective sensation and RPE at rest and immediately after maximal exercise.

	2D Mask	3DMask	*P*
At rest			
Humidity	0.13±0.3	0.66±1.3	.18
Heat	0.22±0.4	0.58±1.0	.26
Breathing resistance	1.31±1.1	0.62±0.9	.11
Itchiness	0.08±0.3	0.00±0.0	.33
Stuffiness	0.68±1.7	1.04±2.1	.65
Salty taste	0.18±0.6	0.41±1.4	.61
Unsuitable feeling	0.40±0.6	0.25±0.9	.61
Malodorous	0.72±1.2	0.75±1.6	.97
Fatigue	3.72±3.2	3.00±2.7	.96
Overall discomfort	0.68±0.8	0.83±1.0	.69
RPE	18.9±2.8	18.1±1.2	.51
Immediately after maximal exercise			
Humidity	4.81±2.3	4.25±2.1	.53
Heat	5.18±2.6	4.54±2.0	.50
Breathing resistance	6.29±2.4	4.16±3.0	**.04***
Itchiness	1.00±1.9	1.00±1.8	1.0
Stuffiness	2.81±3.2	1.83±2.9	.44
Salty taste	0.63±1.1	0.75±1.8	.85
Unsuitable feeling	2.13±2.5	2.00±2.6	.90
Malodorous	0.81±1.4	1.16±2.3	.66
Fatigue	3.72±3.2	3.00±2.7	.55
Overall discomfort	4.45±2.4	3.91±2.2	.58
RPE	18.9±2.8	18.1±1.2	.93

*$p<.05$; RPE: Subjective exercise intensity

the 2D group compared to the 3D group up to the '6 min' point ($p < 0.05$). Leite do Prado et al. (2022) conducted an exercise stress test on long-distance athletes while wearing a 3D face mask which showed a low ventilatory response (Rf/VT ratio) [22]. That is, for a given ventilatory demand, VT increased more rapidly than the respiratory rate. Of note, athletes showed an increase in RPE with reported breathing difficulty while wearing the 3D face mask.

However, the results of this study show that exercise capacity, as measured by maximal capacity (VO2max), is not affected by wearing a 2D or 3D face mask. These results suggest that healthy people can use the face mask during strenuous exercise with minimal impact on blood and muscle oxygenation. This simply means you can wear a mask, and according to Jang et al. (2020), it is favorable since respiratory droplets accumulate from increased breathing during strenuous exercise in crowded, enclosed exercise facilities [23]. According to this study's results, both 2D and 3D face masks affect blood flow and exercise performance. Thus, wearing masks during exercise does negatively impact underlying cardiopulmonary function.

The type of face mask did not affect FiO2 during exercise, and the results were consistent with a previous study comparing surgical masks and N95 filtering face masks [5]. Moreover, Leung et al. (2020) reported that wearing a 2D face mask during incremental load exercise had a minimal and statistically inconsistent effect on oxygen saturation among healthy subjects [24]. This suggests that face masks do not significantly affect alveolar ventilation or gas exchange (Wong et al., 2020) [25].

Therefore, in healthy and active people, wearing a 2D or 3D face mask during vigorous exercise is believed to have minimal effects on arterial or muscle O2 levels and no effect on maximal exercise performance [26].

Exercising while wearing a face mask is subjectively perceived as uncomfortable, which has a negative impact on exercise tolerance. Factors related to difficulty breathing, heat stress, humidity, pressure, and general discomfort are common complaints that affect perceived exercise during physical fitness activity while wearing a mask. The most important factor that determines the comfort of wearing a mask is breathing resistance, which consists of expiratory and inspiratory resistance. Generally, the inspiratory resistance is greater than the expiratory resistance [27]. A mask with high filtration efficiency and low intake resistance is ideal, but theoretically, filtration efficiency is inversely proportional to the intake resistance of the mask. Masks with a high level of filtration efficiency enhance CO2 accumulation indoors [28]. Moreover, exercising while wearing a mask induces a hypoxic environment (hypercapnic hypoxia), which promotes the inappropriate gas exchange of O2 and CO2 across the respiratory system, resulting in a state of acidemia [29, 30]. Therefore, choosing the appropriate mask is essential and seen as a balancing act between protection, breathability, and comfort.

In this study, respiratory resistance was significantly higher in the 2D mask group (6.29 ± 2.4 points) then in the 3D mask group (4.16 ± 3.0 points), which made it difficult to test sufficient O2 levels until the '6th-minute' point of exercise. However, there was no difference in humidity, heat, itchiness, stuffiness, saltiness, feeling unwell, smell, fatigue, and overall discomfort which can be interpreted as having similar perceptions of subjective sensation between the groups.

4.1 Limitations

The study involved adult college-age and healthy males in their 20s, thus limiting the generalizability of findings to a broader population, which could have included females and individuals of varying ages. Furthermore, a considerably larger sample population and broader variation could enhance the statistical reliability and robustness of results. The trial setting may not have fully represented real-world performance conditions. Replicating the study under different environmental settings or during various physical activities could yield a more comprehensive understanding of the mask effects. Studying the effects of prolonged exercise duration while wearing different types of masks—KF94 and KF80—could have provided a more enhanced understanding of their impact on cardiorespiratory function thereby broadening the applicability of findings to other types of masks commonly used in other parts of the globe.

5 Conclusion

There were no differences observed in cardiorespiratory function (Rf, VT, VE, O2, FiO2) after incremental load exercise performance while wearing a 2D triple-layer structure (third filtration) mask or a 3D quadruple-layer (fourth filtration) mask. Subjective sensations assessed by breathing resistance showed a higher level of comfort while wearing a 2D mask than the 3D mask.

Acknowledgment. We would like to thank the volunteer study participants for their valuable contribution to this work.

Disclosures Interest. The authors declare no conflict of interest.

References

1. Korea Centers for Disease Control and Prevention. Coronavirus infection-19. Press release, Ministry of Health, and Welfare (2023)
2. Korea Centers for Disease Control and Prevention. Coronavirus infection-19. Press release, Ministry of Health, and Welfare (2020)
3. Ningthoujam, R.: COVID 19 can spread through breathing, talking, study estimates. Curr. Med. Res. Pract. **10**, 132–133 (2020)
4. World Health Organization: Advice on the use of masks in the context of COVID-19: interim guidance. Geneva, Switzerland: World Health Organization (2020), updated 2020 Jun 5; accessed 2020 Jul 23. Available from: https://apps.who.int/iris/bitstream/handle/10665/332293/WHO-2019-nCov-IPC_Masks-2020.4-eng.pdf?sequence=1&isAllowed=y. View Full Reference List
5. Chu, D.K., Akl, E.A., Duda, S., Solo, K., Yaacoub, S., Schünemann, H.J.: Physical distancing, face masks, and eye protection to prevent person-to person transmission of SARS-CoV-2 and COVID-19: a systematic review and meta-analysis. Lancet **395**(10242), 1973–1987 (2020)
6. Song, J.Y., Yun, J.G., Noh, J.Y., Cheong, H.J., Kim, W.J.: Covid-19 in South Korea-challenges of subclinical manifestations. N. Engl. J. Med. **382**, 1858–1859 (2020)
7. Shurlock, J., Muniz-Pardos, B., Tucker, R., et al.: Recommendations for face coverings while exercising during the COVID-19 pandemic. Sports Med. **7**, p19 (2021)
8. Hopkins, S.R., et al.: Face masks and the cardiorespiratory response to physical activity in health and disease. Ann. Am. Thorac. Soc. **18**, 399–407 (2021)
9. Pieh, C., Budimir, S., Probst, T.: The effect of age, gender, income, work, and physical activity on mental health during coronavirus disease (COVID-19) lockdown in Austria. J. Psychosom. Res. **136**, 110186 (2020). https://doi.org/10.1016/j.jpsychores.2020.110186
10. Nishiga, M., Wang, D.W., Han, Y., Lewis, D.B., Wu, J.C.: COVID-19 and cardiovascular disease: from basic mechanisms to clinical perspectives. Nat. Rev. Cardiol. **17**(9), 543–558 (2020)
11. Konda, A., Prakash, A., Moss, G.A., Schmoldt, M., Grant, G.D., Guha, S.: Aerosol filtration efficiency of common fabrics used in respiratory cloth masks. ACS Nano **14**, 6339–6347 (2020)
12. Pippin, D.J., Verderame, R.A., Weber, K.K.: Efficacy of face masks in preventing inhalation of airborne contaminants. J. Oral Maxillofac. Surg. **45**, 319–323 (1987)

13. Morishima, M., Shimizu, Y., Fujiyama, T., Mitsuno, T.: Analysis of the fitting of patterns of hygiene masks for the closed mouth. Text. Res. J. **85**, 828–837 (2015)
14. Darby, S., et al.: COVID-19: Mask efficacy is dependent on both fabric and fit. Future J. Microbiol. **16**, 5–11 (2021)
15. Verberne, J.W., Worsley, P.R., Bader, D.L.: A 3D registration methodology to evaluate the goodness of fit at the individual-respiratory mask interface. Comput. Methods Biomech. Biomed. Engin. **26**, 1–12 (2020)
16. Li, X., et al.: Electreted polyetherimide-silica fibrous membranes for enhanced filtration of fine particles. Int. Sci. **439**, 12–20 (2015)
17. Sven Fikenzer, T., Uhe, D.L., Rudolph, U., Falz, R., Busse, M., Hepp, P., Laufs, U.: Effects of surgical and FFP2/N95 face masks on cardiopulmonary exercise capacity. Clin. Res. Cardiol. (2020). https://doi.org/10.1007/s00392-020-01704-y
18. Shaw, K., Butcher, S., Ko, J., Zello, G.A., Chilibeck, P.D.: Wearing of cloth or disposable surgical face masks has no effect on vigorous exercise performance in healthy individuals. Int. J. Environ. Res. Public Health **17**(21), 8110 (2020)
19. Nho, H., Tanaka, K., Kim, H.S., Watanabe, Y., Hiyama, T.: Exercise training in female patients with a family history of hypertension. Eur. J. Appl. Physiol. **78**, 1–6 (1998)
20. Evans, H.J.L., Ferrar, K.E., Smith, A.E., Parfitt, G., Eston, P.G.: A systematic review of methods to predict maximal oxygen uptake from submaximal, open circuit spirometry in healthy adults. J. Sci. Med. Sport **18**, 183–188 (2015)
21. Borg, G.: Perceived exertion: a note on (history) and methods. Med. Sci. Sports Exerc. **5**, 90–93 (1973)
22. Leite do Prado, D.M., Silvino, V.O., Motta-Santos, Daisy, Pereira dos Santos, M.A.: The effect of the protective face mask on cardiorespiratory response during aerobic exercise. Clin. Exper. Pharmacol. Physiol. 49: 453–461 (2022)
23. Jang, S., Han, S.H., Rhee, J.Y.: Cluster of coronavirus disease associated with fitness dance classes, South Korea. Emerg. Infect. Dis. **26**, 1917–1920 (2020)
24. Leung, N.H., et al.: Respiratory virus shedding in exhaled breath and efficacy of face masks. Nat. Med. **26**(5), 676–680 (2020)
25. Wong, Y.Y., et al.: Impact of the COVID-19 pandemic on sports and exercise. Asia-Pacific J. Sports Med. Arthros. Rehab. Technol. **22**, 39–44 (2020)
26. Epstein, D., et al.: Return to training in the COVID-19 era: the physiological effects of face masks during exercise. Scand. J. Med. Sci. Sports **31**(1), 70–75 (2020)
27. Choi, S., Park, R., Hur, N., Kim, W.: Evaluation of wearing comfort of dust masks. PLOS ONE **15**, e0237848 (2020)
28. van Rensburg, J., Pillay, L., Hendricks, S., Hamuy Blanco, J.A.: Year of the face mask: do's and don'ts during exercise. South African J. Sports Med. **32**, 1–2 (2020)
29. Roberge, R.J., Coca, A., Williams, W.J., Powellm, J.B., Palmierom, A.J.: Physiological impact of the N95 filtering facepiece respirator on health care workers. Respir. Care **55**(5), 569–577 (2010)
30. Spurling, K.J., Moonsie, I.K., Perks, J.L.: Hypercapnic respiratory acidosis during an in-flight oxygen assessment. Aerosp. Med. Human Perfor. **87**(2), 144–147 (2016)
31. Staymates, M.: Flow visualization of an N95 respirator with and without an exhalation valve using Schlieren imaging and light scattering. Phys. Fluids **32**(11), 111703 (2020)

Learning Predictive Models for Match Outcomes in US Sports, and Using Them to Bet

Albrecht Zimmermann(✉)

Normandie Univ, UNICAEN, ENSICAEN, CNRS, GREYC, 14000 Caen, France
albrecht.zimmermann@unicaen.fr

Abstract. Evaluating the accuracies of models for match outcome predictions is nice and well but in the end the real proof is in the money to be made by betting. To evaluate the question whether the models developed by us could be used easily to make money via sports betting, we evaluate three cases: NCAAB post-season, NBA season, and NFL season, and find that it is possible yet not without its pitfalls. In particular, we illustrate that high accuracy does not automatically equal high payout, by looking at the type of match-ups that are predicted correctly by different models. We then put our results to practical use by betting on matches, and find that some observed pitfalls are harder to avoid than others.

1 Introduction

Using advanced sports analytics statistics and Machine Learning (or well-crafted mathematical) models, we can predict match outcomes for a variety of sports – achieving predictive accuracies that are better than chance, a home-field advantage rule-of-thumb, or majority instincts. While this is an interesting (and in our opinion worthwhile) academic exercise, however, the question whether such work is actually useful becomes difficult to avoid. Or, to paraphrase a practitioner of sports betting: "You should compare yourself to betting agencies and see whether you can make money!".

In this work, we intend to do exactly this: using the example of three US sports attracting large betting volumes:

– the main post-season tournament of university (NCAA) basketball – $ 9.2 billion bet ($ 262 million legally),
– both regular and post-season of the National Basketball Association (NBA),
– regular and post-season of the National Football League (NFL) – Super Bowl alone $ 4.1 billion bet ($ 132 million legally),

we show not only predictive accuracies but also accumulated sports betting outcomes had we used their predictions to consistently place bets in 2015/2016.

We find rather varying outcomes, and, in particular, that very similar accuracies can lead to strongly diverging monetary payoffs. To explore this phenomenon

J. S. Dong et al. (Eds.): ISACE 2024, LNCS 14794, pp. 313–327, 2024.
https://doi.org/10.1007/978-3-031-69073-0_27

further, we relate this to the way sports betting is handicapped. Finally, we go one step further and employed the derived betting strategy on the NFL and NBA for the 2016/2017 season, as well as the NFL for 2017/2018.

In the following section, we discuss sports betting, and in particular how money-lines should be interpreted and are calibrated. We then discuss our experimental set-up before discussing hypothetical betting outcomes for the 2015/2016 NCAAB post-season, NBA season, and NFL season, respectively, followed by actual betting outcomes for the 2016/2017, and 2017/2018 seasons.

2 Basics of Team Sports Betting

To understand the following discussions, it is necessary to understand money-lines offered by operators of sports betting services (*sports books*), and to have some insight into how those money lines are derived. US sports books offer two ways of betting on match outcomes:

1. *Over-under*, where bettors attempt to correctly foresee the difference between points scored.
2. *Money-line* betting, where bettors attempt to correctly divine the eventual winner of a match.

Given that we have had weak results with trying to predict match scores in the past[1], we ignore the first setting for now, and focus on the second one, which allows us to relate binary predictions to monetary values. Money-lines offered by a sports book for a particular match look as in Table 1.

Table 1. NBA money-line examples

Match-up	Favorite (FAV)	Underdog (DOG)	FAV-Line	DOG-Line
Detroit Pistons at Atlanta Hawks	ATL	DET	300	240
Utah Jazz at Detroit Pistons	DET	UTH	110	−110

For each match, a probable winner (the Favorite) is identified, making the other team the probable loser (Underdog). The associated lines indicate the possible pay-out:

- The **FAV-Line** shows how much money one would **have to bet** to *win* $100,
- the **DOG-Line** how much money one would *win* if one **were to bet** $100.

To make those two settings comparable, we can reformulate the FAV-Line since betting \$ 100 would net the bettor \$ 10000/FAV-Line. For the first example given in Table 1, Atlanta was considered the favorite, so betting $100 on them and winning would have paid out $33.33. Detroit was expected to lose but if one had bet on them and they had defied predictions, one would have won $240.

Sports books do their best to calibrate those lines, trying to balance two attractions for bettors:

[1] Not yet published.

1. Betting on the favorite is less risky ⇒ has a higher **chance** to pay out.
2. Betting on the underdog and winning will lead to a higher **absolute** pay-out.

Ideally, a match's handicap attracts bettors in such way that the wins that the sports book needs to pay out are offset by the losses of those who bet on the other team (minus some profit for the sports book itself). This can be most clearly seen in the second example in Table 1, a so-called **Pick'em**. This is a match where the sports book operators do not have enough information to reliably predict one team as winning so betting on either one gives the same pay-off: $ 10000/110 = 90.90. Given a large enough number of bettors, one would expect that roughly half bets on either team and since the sports book pays out $91 for every $100 bet, it would stand to make a profit of 9%.

3 Simulation Set-Up

Since we are going to use the same general set-up in the succeeding sections, we describe it here.

For each predictive setting, we have collected the money lines for all matches from http://www.vegasinsider.com/. The site lists the money-lines offered by the major sports books operating out of Las Vegas, Nevada, which occasionally differ slightly from each other. Additionally, money-lines vary with time, either due to the influx of new information (injuries, player arrests, coaches' announcements), or in reaction to bettors' behavior: too much interest in one team will lead to adjustment in favor of the other one. To avoid undue optimism when evaluating our predictors, we selected the most conservative line for our prediction. If a match is, for instance, listed (1) with FAV-Line=175, DOG-Line=155, and (2) with FAV-Line=165, DOG-Line=145, we will choose

- (1) if our model predicts the favorite to win, since this will pay out **less**, and
- (2) if our model predicts an upset, since we would only get $145 instead of $155.

We use our models' predictions to select on which team to place the bet, and assume that we bet $100 on **every match**[2] in the time period. Correctly predicting a win by the favorite increases the model's winnings by $(10000/FAV-Line)$\$, correctly predicting an underdog's win by DOG-Line$, and correctly predicting the winner of a Pick'em by 90.90$. Incorrectly predicting a match outcome decreases winnings by $100. For the sake of convenience, we predict matches, and tally up winnings, per day.

The preceding paragraph illustrates an important dynamic – incorrectly predicting is always bad but not all correct predictions are equal:

- Correctly predicting **underdog** wins is the most attractive option and depending on the money-line can balance out several incorrect predictions.
- Correctly predicting **Pick'ems** still gives a relatively high pay-out.
- Correctly predicting **favorite** wins, on the other hand, needs to happen at a high rate to make up for incorrect predictions.

[2] No matter the odds.

4 2015/2016 NCAAB Predictions (and Simulated Bets)

In our first setting, we consider the NCAAB post-season tournament, also referred to as "March Madness", for the interest and amount of sports betting it generates. This is the smallest of the settings we discuss since the tournament involved only 67 matches.

For US basketball, we base our choices on the evaluation of representations and classifiers reported in [13]. Based on the results reported therein, we use the *Adjusted Efficiencies* pioneered by Ken Pomeroy [9], combined into a weighted average over the season, to encode teams, as well as season-level statistics such as the

- win percentage
- margin of victory – how many more points the team scores in wins than its opponent
- point differential – how many more (or less) points the team scores than its opponent on average

We evaluate three classifiers: *Naïve Bayes* (NB), *Multi-layer Perceptron* (ANN), and a simplified version of Ken Pomeroy's predictor based on the Pythagorean Expectation (KP). We referred to this classifier as "simplified" since we did not estimate the involved coefficients ourselves but based them on the discussions found on his blog. NB and ANN are used in their Weka [6] implementations, with default parameters, except that for NB *Kernel estimator* is set to *true*.

Before discussing the performance of our models, we need to establish the baseline. This means basing ourselves on the money-lines offered by sports books by assuming that we always follow the lead of the money-line. Concretely, if the team designated as favorite wins, we count this as a correct prediction for a **hypothetical "Vegas" model**, if the underdog wins, an incorrect one, with winnings accrued as described above. The main problem for this baseline is posed by Pick'ems: since the money lines give no indication but we would have to make a prediction, this amounts to flipping a coin for each Pick'em. In the best case, we, as a bettor, get each of those coin flips right, in the worst case, every single one wrong. Since the difference between getting a Pick'em right and wrong amounts to \$190.90 per match (the lost gain + the \$100 bet), this leads to a large difference over the course of a season. Since we would assume to get half the coin flips right, we report this as **expected** accuracy/pay-out in Table 2.

Table 2. Predictive accuracies/betting pay-outs for "Vegas" for the NCAAB post-season

w/o Pick'ems		w/ Pick'ems (5)					
Accuracy	Pay-out	Best Acc.	Pay-out	Exp. Acc	Pay-out	Worst Acc.	Pay-out
0.7419	30.26	0.7611	484.76	0.7313	7.51	0.6865	−469.73

We can see that always picking favorites would have gotten about 3/4 of the matches right, and paid out approximately $30. Flipping coins on the Pick'ems can lead to winnings of almost $500 but also to losses of the same magnitude. Especially for so few (five) Pick'ems, this is a very real risk.

Table 3. Predictive accuracies and betting pay-outs for three predictive models (left), Correct predictions by money-line characterization (right) for the NCAAB.

Classifier	NB	ANN	KP
Accuracy	0.6865	0.6417	0.7014
Pay-out	293.52	-605.92	-231.34

Classifier	Favs	Dogs	Pick'ems (of 5)
NB	39	5	2 (0.4)
ANN	38	2	3 (0.6)
KP	43	0	4 (0.8)

Results for the predictive models are shown on the left-hand side of Table 3. Two things are immediately noticeable: 1) the relative high predictive accuracies – the KP model performs almost as well as the expected "Vegas" result, and 2) that high accuracy do not translate into a high pay-out. Indeed, while Naïve Bayes performs 1.5% points worse than KP, it shows solid gains (better than using moneylines to bet only on favorites), while KP loses money.

We find some explanation for this phenomenon by looking at the right-hand side of Table 3. NB predicts 5 upsets correctly, and even though KP predicts favorite wins and close Pick'ems better, this makes all the financial difference.

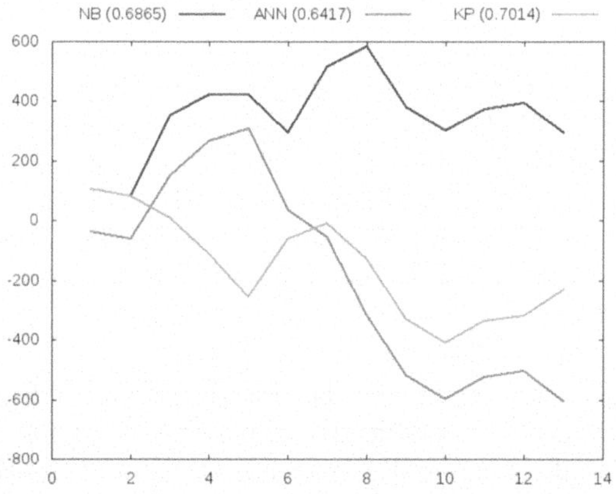

Fig. 1. Classifier winnings over the course of the post-season, NCAAB

The winnings curve for the different classifiers are shown in Fig. 1 and shows that the winning behavior is rather erratic. Especially the ANN, which at some point posts winnings similar to the final outcome for NB, drops off into steep loss. But even the NB *could* have returned twice of the final pay-out, a peak that is flanked by losses, however.

5 2015/2016 NBA Predictions (and Simulated Bets)

Our second setting concerns the NBA. We predicted matches for the 2016 regular and post-season. Based on the results in [13], we use NB, ANN, *Random Forest* (RF),[3] as well as the simplified Ken Pomeroy model (KP). Teams were represented by the same statistics as for the NCAAB predictions. We did not predict the first two days of play since at that time a predictor would not have statistics for all teams. As in the preceding section, we establish the baseline, shown in Table 4, both for the regular season, and regular and post-season combined.

Table 4. Predictive accuracies and betting pay-outs for "Vegas" for the NBA

Regular season							
w/o Pick'ems		w/ Pick'ems (109)					
Accuracy	Pay-out	Best Acc.	Pay-out	Exp. Acc	Pay-out	Worst Acc.	Pay-out
0.7096	−1502,00	0.7356	8407.09	0,6904	−1983,14	0.6461	−12402
Regular + post-season							
w/o Pick'ems		w/ Pick'ems (115)					
Accuracy	Pay-out	Best Acc.	Pay-out	Exp. Acc	Pay-out	Worst Acc.	Pay-out
0.7121	−2374.16	0.7375	9125.84	0.6937	−1857.3	0.6492	−12828.81

Following the money line over the course of the entire season, while ignoring the Pick'ems, would lead to a very respectable accuracy but also significant monetary loss. At ~1200 matches, the loss per match is only about \$1 yet over the course of the season this accrues. Correctly predicting half the Pick'ems does of course not improve this by much, even though accuracy would stay high.

Figure 2 plots the development of the different classifiers' winnings over the course of the season, the legend is annotated with predictive accuracies. None of them show a net positive payout, and with the exception of the KP model, they all drop rather low. Notably, they all recover to a certain degree after the mid-point of the season, however, so that one could win money if one could determine *when to start betting*.

The details of the winning curves, showing the difference between the trough and the best result, and its magnitude, can be found in Fig. 3. For the ANN and KP, the best result is in the post-season, for NB and the RF in the regular season, even though NB and KP have the same regular season accuracy. Table 5 shows why: while KP strongly outperforms NB when predicting favorites (as for the NCAAB), it underperforms when it comes to Pick'ems. Pick'ems are clearly the most difficult matches to predict, and with KP combining three estimated influences – adjusted efficiencies, the coefficient in the Pythagorean Expectation, and the home-court adjustment – small errors can spiral. The trough-peak difference aligns with the amount of underdog/pick'em predictions.

[3] Which we omitted for the NCAAB, as its accuracy is too weak.

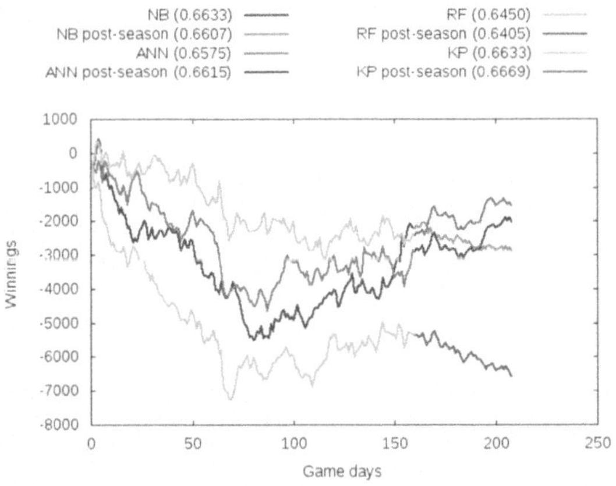

Fig. 2. Classifier winnings over the course of the season, NBA

Those curves also show something else: If one could start betting at the right time, ~day 75 for NB, or 90 for the ANN, one could in theory win quite a bit of money.

Table 5. Correct predictions by money-line characterization for the NBA

Classifier	Regular season			Post-season		
	Favs	Dogs	Pick'ems (109)	Favs	Dogs	Pick'ems (6)
NB	691	57	48 (0.44)	49	5	1 (0.16)
ANN	707	60	22 (0.20)	57	6	0
RF	685	61	28 (0.26)	47	4	0
KP	725	59	12 (0.11)	58	5	0

6 2015/2016 NFL Predictions (and Simulated Bets)

The 2015/2016 season marked our first attempt at NFL predictions. As for basketball, the main question to answer concerns team representations. In basketball matches, individual events are *possessions* that lead to either points, or a number of possibly possession-changing events[4]. In American Football, on the other hand, individual events are *Downs*[5] and their outcome is mainly measured in *yards gained* (or lost). While the discrete outcomes in basketball can be read off the final box score, the fluctuation of yards in football is less well captured.

[4] Fouls, turnovers, missed shots.

[5] A team has 4 downs to advance 10 yards, after which they get a new set of downs.

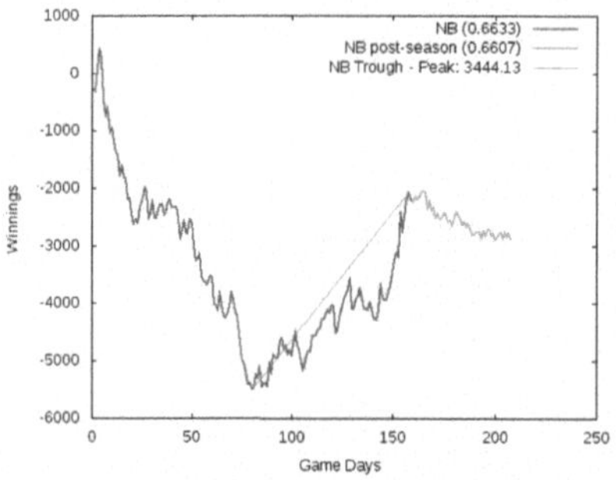

(a) Trough to peak winnings for the NBA season, NB

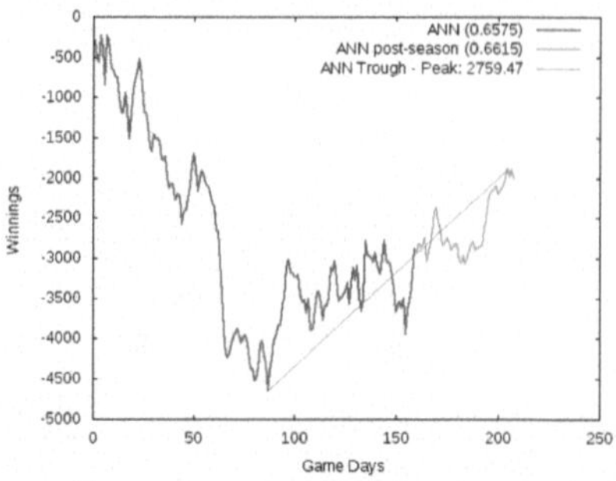

(b) Trough to peak winnings, ANN

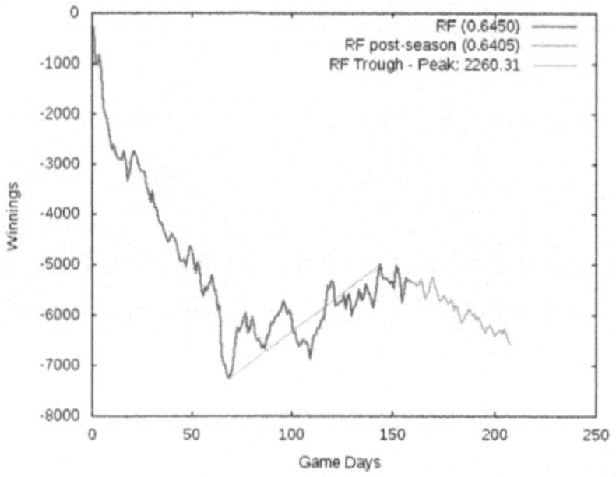

(c) Trough to peak winnings, RF

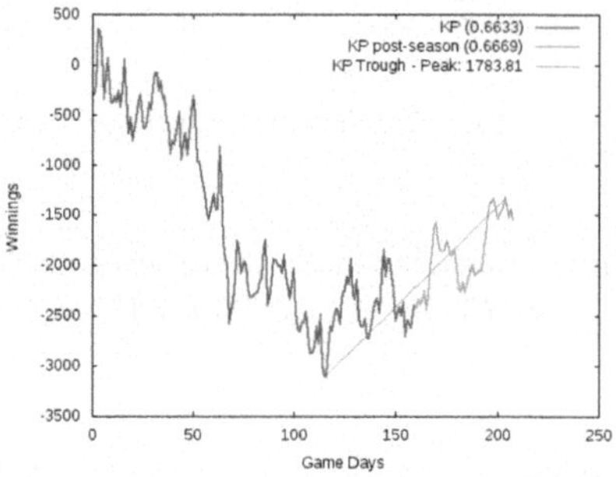

(d) Trough to peak winnings, KP

Fig. 3. Trough to peak winnings for the NBA season, different predictive models

To address this, Football Outsiders have proposed *Defense-adjusted Value Over Average* and *Defense-adjusted Yards Above Replacement* [5], both of which consider the outcome of each down in relation to the league-wide average against a particular *defensive alignment.* Since this requires access to and work with play-by-play statistics, we forwent this approach and instead evaluated several other statistics over past seasons:

- Basic Averages – all the statistics available from a typical box score at [1] under "team stats", normalized for 65 possessions, and averaged in a weighted manner (recent games have more weight), both offensively (scored/gained/committed) and defensively (allowed/caused). This follows similar reasoning as possession-based normalizing and averaging in basketball.
- Opp. Averages – same as above but for the opponents that have been played so far. This is intended to help gauge the competition.
- Adjusted Averages – certain offensive and defensive statistics adjusted by mirror statistics of the respective opponents. That is basically the same idea as Ken Pomeroy's adjusted efficiencies [9]. We calculated those statistics in the same manner as in our work on basketball [13].
- SRS – the "simple rating system" information (SRS, SoS) as described at [10], with the difference that the averaging is weighted, i.e. not divided by number of matches.

The first surprise was that the feature selection techniques contained in the Weka package did not seem to work at all: no consistent set of features could be found across seasons (apart from *rushing yards allowed*), and the set of features was often very small. To address this, we chose to simply evaluate all presentations for several predictors – ANN, NB, RF – for seasons 2009–2014 (Table 6).

Table 6. Evaluation of several team representations for NFL prediction

	Encoding	2009	2010	2011	2012	2013	2014
ANN	Adjusted Avg	0.5863	**0.5663**	0.5863	0.5783	0.5422	0.5703
	Adjusted+SRS	0.5542	0.5462	0.6024	0.5743	0.5663	**0.6546**
	Basic Avg+Opp. Avg	**0.6104**	0.5341	**0.6145**	0.5823	0.5261	0.5984
	Basic+SRS+Opp.	0.5904	0.5261	0.5823	**0.6225**	0.5622	0.6386
	Basic+SRS	0.5663	0.5181	0.5622	0.5663	**0.5904**	0.5904
	Basic Avg	0.5542	0.5020	0.5502	**0.6225**	0.5703	0.5783
	All of the above	0.5863	0.5462	0.6024	0.5904	0.5743	0.6345
NB	Adjusted Avg	0.6305	0.6024	0.6145	0.6265	0.5582	0.3815
	Adjusted+SRS	0.6426	0.6024	0.6305	0.6345	0.5582	0.4016
	Basic Avg+Opp. Avg	0.5863	0.5542	0.6667	0.6064	0.5984	0.6104
	Basic+SRS+Opp.	0.6024	0.5422	0.6627	0.6064	0.5944	**0.6305**
	Basic+SRS	0.6466	**0.6064**	0.6787	0.6024	0.6185	**0.6305**
	Basic Avg	**0.6586**	0.6024	**0.6867**	0.6104	**0.6305**	0.6265
	All of the above	0.5944	0.5622	0.6787	**0.6386**	0.5703	0.4779
RF	Adjusted Avg	0.6064	0.5181	0.6185	0.5622	0.5703	0.6104
	Adjusted+SRS	0.6024	0.5261	0.6345	**0.6064**	0.5542	0.5823
	Basic Avg+Opp. Avg	**0.6305**	0.5422	0.6024	0.5863	0.5582	0.6305
	Basic+SRS+Opp.	0.5502	0.5261	0.6064	0.5462	**0.5904**	0.5984
	Basic+SRS	0.6064	**0.5823**	0.5542	0.5904	0.5622	0.6185
	Basic Avg	0.6145	0.5261	0.6064	0.6024	0.5663	**0.6546**
	All of the above	0.6265	0.5382	**0.6466**	0.5301	0.5301	0.6064

There is no clear trend but it did often seem like a good idea to involve the basic averages. We initially settled on Basic Averages for NB, Basic+Opp. Averages for ANN, and since RF did not present any trend at all, we tried RF with Adjusted Averages. After additional evaluation during the 2015/2016 season, we found better performances by using Basic+Opp. for NB, and Adjusted for ANN and RF.

We also evaluated the SRS. We did not predict the first week's matches since for those matches, since we do not have statistics for the teams at that time. Again, we need to establish the baseline (see Table 7).

The baseline again shows consistent behavior: the accuracy is relatively high but if one follows money-line predictions one loses – not much per individual game but quite a bit in the aggregate.

Table 7. Predictive accuracies and betting pay-outs for "Vegas" for the NFL (2015/2016 season)

Regular season							
w/o Pick'ems (28)		w/ Pick'ems					
Accuracy	Pay-out	Best Acc.	Pay-out	Exp. Acc	Pay-out	Worst Acc.	Pay-out
0.6367	−1443.45	0.6791	1102.49	0.6208	−1570.11	0.6375	−4242.71
Regular + post-season							
w/o Pick'ems		w/ Pick'ems (29)					
Accuracy	Pay-out	Best Acc.	Pay-out	Exp. Acc	Pay-out	Worst Acc.	Pay-out
0.6441	−1215.69	0.6852	1420.68	0.6294	−1251.92	0.5697	−4115.42

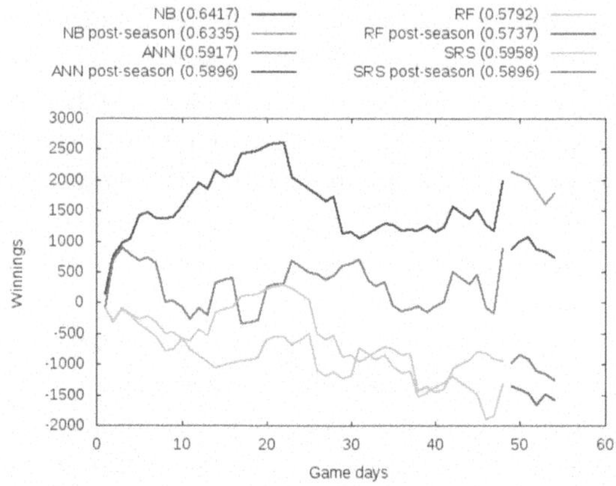

Fig. 4. Classifier winnings over the course of the season, NFL

The results of the predictors, shown in Fig. 4, are very interesting. The first thing to notice is that NB, using rather straight-forward statistics, achieves comparative accuracy to "Vegas" and a much better pay-out. In fact, its pay-out is better than that for the best-case "Vegas"-scenario in the regular season. Even the ANN, with much lower accuracy, achieves a good pay-out. Additionally, we again see the influence of which picks to predict correctly at play: even though ANN and SRS have very similar accuracies, betting according to SRS would be a clear loss, and the difference can be explained by the fact that the ANN trades off accuracy on favorites against accuracy on underdogs (Table 8).

A final monetary realization is that each predictor reaches a high point that comes before the end of the season. In fact, following NB all to the end of the regular season would mean forfeiting more than \$ 600, with losses for all models in the post-season. While for NBA predictions it seems to be important to know when to get *in*, for the NFL is important to know when to get *out* – a decision that might be slightly easier to make.

Table 8. Correct predictions by money-line characterization for the NFL

Classifier	Regular season			Post-season		
	Favs	Dogs	Pick'ems (28)	Favs	Dogs	Pick'ems (1)
NB	115	25	14 (0.5)	4	1	0
ANN	98	29	15 (0.54)	5	0	1 (1.0)
RF	107	16	16 (0.57)	4	1	0
SRS	111	18	14 (0.5)	4	0	1 (1.0)

7 Use Cases – Actual Betting

7.1 2016/2017 Seasons

Based on our simulated results, we employed the following betting strategy:

- For the NFL, we began betting with the first match of the second week. Its peak was reached on 05/11/2015, so we would stop after the first week in November 2016, or if we were at risk of losing more than €1500 (€100 · 15 matches per week).
- For the NBA, we began betting with the last day of matches before the All-Star break (16/02/2017), with the intention to continue until the end of the regular season.

Given the results of our simulation, and particular its performance regarding underdog and Pick'em-wins, we used Naïve Bayes predictions. We placed our bets on the website 1xbet.com. Because there were restrictions in place regarding the transfer of funds online, we only bet €50 on each match on the second Sunday of the NFL season (18/09/2016) – our second day of betting – and €100 on all matches before and after.

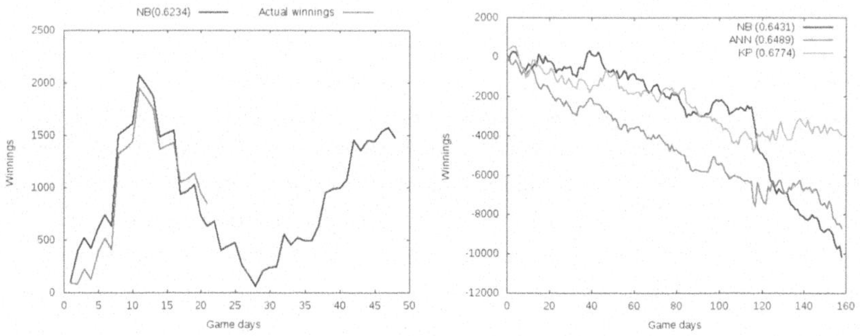

Fig. 5. Betting outcomes for the 2016/2017 season, NFL (left), and NBA (right)

The left-hand side of Fig. 5 shows the outcomes for 2016/2017, with the curve labeled "NB" indicating the winnings according to Vegas moneylines[6], and the curve labeled "Actual Winnings" the payout from 1xbet.com. The peak that we had observed in 2015/2016 appears again but unfortunately **much earlier** (09/10/2016). Had we stopped at that moment, we would have won about €2000. Instead, we continued until 31/10/2016, eventually winning ≈€850, from an initial investment of €1200.[7] A notable development is that the actual winnings at some point increased over those according to the Vegas moneylines. It is our understanding that online sports books eventually individualize odds to discourage too-successful bettors from certain bets but since we bet indiscriminately, this had no effect on our behavior. At the peak, we had bet on sixty matches, and NB had an accuracy of 68.33%, and had correctly predicted **seventeen** underdog wins! When we stopped, the accuracy had dropped to 59.78%, with only two more correctly predicted underdog wins. However, as the figure shows, there was a second (smaller) peak towards the end of the season. Over the course of the entire season, NB with averages + opponent averages achieved an accuracy of 0.6234, and had predicted twenty-seven underdog wins, or almost a quarter of all correct predictions.

This partial success is however tempered by our experience with NBA betting. The right-hand side of Fig. 5 tracks the performance of our betting strategy (NB) as quantified by Vegas money lines. Not only did we not experience a climb out of the trough but the classifier quickly lost money. We stopped the experiment after only nine days of betting, after having lost the entire winnings of the NFL experiment. Apart from the fact that all classifiers continuously lost money, the NB fell off a cliff after 3/4 of the season. Notably, the other classifiers would not have really improved the outcome.

7.2 2017/2018 NFL Season

The 2016 season's NBA results discouraged us but encouraged by the results of the 2015/2016 simulation, and 2016/2017 betting results, we also bet during the 2017/2018 season on the NFL.

As Fig. 6 shows, this has not been rewarded. All classifiers (including the NB(Avg+OAvg) which we used for betting) lost heavily early on. This has a very concrete effect on the bets: losing 600 € in the first week means that one cannot continue with the 100 € per match strategy, unless one adds significant additional funds. Instead, we either split remaining money among all matches or focused on high-yield bets. As a result, our actual winnings fall back behind the simulated results. As the plot also shows, it is not clear which classifier and which representation to choose.

[6] We show this for comparison's sakes since 1xbet.com's moneylines were slightly different.

[7] We withdrew ≈€2050 from the website.

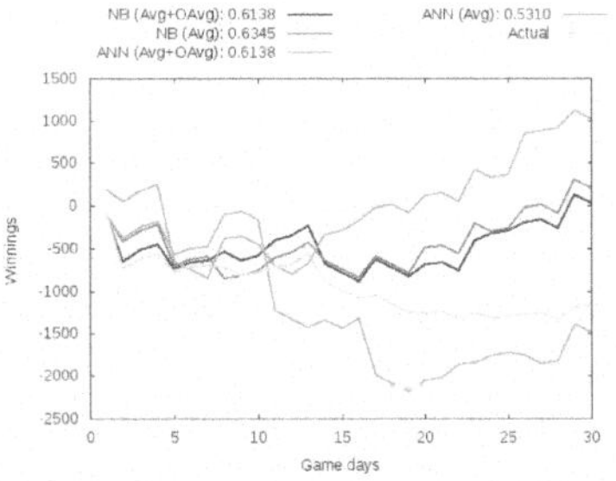

Fig. 6. Winnings for the 2017/2018 NFL season

8 Related Work

The majority of work on sports betting is concerned with the question of how to exploit the difference between implied win probabilities and those predicted by different models, a question that we do not touch upon. They also notably usually *do not* actually wager any money using the proposed strategies.

Constantinou [2] exploits a Bayesian network model in simulating betting on the English Premier League. They exploit the difference between predicted probabilities and implied probabilities according to betting odds, and report both of their simulated betting strategies showing significant betting gains.

Langseth [7] also exploit the difference between predicted and implied probabilities in simulating betting on soccer. Evaluating a number of different betting strategies, and remarkably enough, they report that almost all combinations of predictive models and betting strategies would win money (in excess of 10% of the wagered amount). Looking at details, however, they find that a large part of the winnings are due to two underdog wins, and that stopping early would have improved pay-outs.

Pfitzner *et al.* [8] consider NFL football, using regression to predict over-under results. They formulate a kind of adjusted performance statistics, and evaluate different betting strategies. They state that betting strategies must have a win rate of at least 52.4% to beat the built-in sport book profit margin. Notably, betting the same amount on all matches leads to a win rate of 55%, and is therefore viable, in their simulation.

Pessemier *et al.* [3], contrary to our approach, exploits the confidence of model predictions to evaluate a number of different betting strategies, one of which consists of always betting on underdogs at home. The simulate the results of their approach on a number of different European soccer leagues, and find that different leagues might require different strategies. They find that betting the same amount on every match has the highest possible pay-off.

9 Conclusion and Outlook

The answer we intended to explore in this paper was whether it is possible to use match outcome predictions for US sports for betting. Given the evidence presented, the answer has to be "Maybe". We explored three settings, the NCAAB playoffs, NBA, and NFL regular and postseasons. In each case, we built a model using a set of statistics that is relatively easy to acquire (downloadable from publicly accessible websites), and to process. Once a model has been established, it can be used to place bets in a straight-forward manner by betting an equal amount on each match.

We used our models to simulate betting for the 2015/2016 season, and found that having an over-all positive return is possible using the Naïve Bayes classifier. However, the NCAAB post-season contains few matches, leading to rather volatile pay-out. In the NBA, one can win but only after figuring out when to start betting. In the NFL results, finally, straight-forward use could indeed lead to a decent pay-off (admittedly, not attractive to professional gamblers), especially if one stops early enough.

We have also illustrated one of the aspects that make a predictive model more or less well-suited for sports betting, by considering what kind of matches models predict well. In particular, a model that is not very strong in correctly predicting favorites but performs well for Pick'ems, or even better, matches won by underdogs, would be a particular attractive tool, even if its straight-up accuracy is not impressive.

Based on the conclusions from our simulations, we put our work into practice, betting on the 2016/2017 NFL season (stopping early), and NBA season (beginning at roughly the mid-point of the season). We found that the peak in NFL betting does not directly transfer from season to season but that the general behavior – an early peak with a good payoff, followed by a decline in winnings – could in fact be exploited. For the NBA, our simulation results did not transfer, leading to a quick loss of the NFL gains. The 2017/2018 NFL season, finally, showed that significant losses are possible. The main reason for this is chance: a surprising amount of professional US sports matches are decided by chance. Past work has tried to characterize that phenomenon based on particular distributions or upsets by underdogs [4]. Yet underdogs are in the eye of the beholder, and a recent work instead clustered teams and evaluated relative win probabilities [14]. They found that **half** of all match outcomes in college basketball are due to chance and given the relatively low scores in the NFL, it is to be expected that chance plays an even larger role there.

We intend to explore the question of why models perform well or not further by relating models' performance to evaluations based on lift-charts and ROC-like discussions. The final goal would of course be to shift the training of predictive models: away from maximizing predictive accuracy and towards maximizing payouts, which means predicting border-line cases correctly instead of easy ones. A different direction consists of proposing which matches (not) to bet on and/or how much to bet, as has been done in [7,11] for soccer, or in [12] for American Football. Possible approaches include leveraging game theoretic approaches or reinforcement learning.[8] It should be noted, however, that such strategies would make our betting choices susceptible to the adjusted odds mentioned in Sect. 7.

References

1. Pro-football reference. http://www.pro-football-reference.com
2. Constantinou, A.C.: Bayesian networks for prediction, risk assessment and decision making in an inefficient association football gambling market. Ph.D. thesis, Queen Mary, University of London (2013)
3. De Pessemier, T., De Deyn, B., Vanhecke, K., Martens, L.: Recommendations for sports games to bet on. In: Second Workshop on Recommendation in Complex Scenarios (ComplexRec 2018), in conjunction with the 12th ACM Conference on Recommender Systems (RecSys 2018), pp. 8–12 (2018)
4. Ben-Naim, E., Vazquez, F., Redner, S.: Parity and predictability of competitions. J. Quant. Anal. Sports **2**(4) (2006)
5. Football Outsiders: Methods to our madness. http://www.footballoutsiders.com/info/methods
6. Frank, E., Witten, I.H.: Data Mining: Practical Machine Learning Tools and Techniques with Java Implementations. Morgan Kaufmann (1999)
7. Langseth, H.: Beating the bookie: a look at statistical models for prediction of football matches. In: Jaeger, M., Nielsen, T.D., Viappiani, P. (eds.) Twelfth Scandinavian Conference on Artificial Intelligence, SCAI 2013, Aalborg, Denmark, 20–22 November 2013. Frontiers in Artificial Intelligence and Applications, vol. 257, pp. 165–174. IOS Press (2013). https://doi.org/10.3233/978-1-61499-330-8-165
8. Pfitzner, C., Lang, S., Rishel, T.: Factors affecting scoring in NFL games and beating the over/under line. Sport J. (2014)
9. Pomeroy, K.: Advanced analysis of college basketball. http://kenpom.com
10. Pro-Football-Reference.com: A very simply rating system. http://www.pro-football-reference.com/blog/?p=37
11. Snyder, J.A.L.: What actually wins soccer matches: prediction of the 2011–2012 premier league for fun and profit. Master's thesis (2013)
12. Warner, J.: Predicting margin of victory in NFL games: machine learning vs. the Las Vegas line. Technical report (2010)
13. Zimmermann, A.: Basketball predictions in the NCAAB and NBA: similarities and differences. Stat. Anal. Data Min. **9**(5), 350–364 (2016)
14. Zimmermann, A.: Chance and the predictive limit in basketball (both college and professional). In: Bifet, A., Lorena, A.C., Ribeiro, R.P., Gama, J., Abreu, P.H. (eds.) DS 2023. LNCS, vol. 14276, pp. 599–613. Springer, Cham (2023). https://doi.org/10.1007/978-3-031-45275-8_40

[8] We thank prior reviewers for this suggestion.

Author Index

J. S. Dong et al. (Eds.): ISACE 2024, LNCS 14794, pp. 329–330, 2024.
https://doi.org/10.1007/978-3-031-69073-0

The manufacturer's authorised representative in the EU is Springer Nature Customer Service Centre GmbH, Europaplatz 3, 69115 Heidelberg, Germany. If you have any concerns regarding our products, please contact ProductSafety@springernature.com

Printed and bound by CPI Group (UK) Ltd, Croydon, CR0 4YY
01/10/2026
02225908-0011